Defending the Citadel:
Confronting Corporate Management and
Corruption in an Illinois Community College

A Personal Narrative
by
Wayne Lanter

Twiss Hill Press
Freeburg, Illinois

Twiss Hill Press
P. O. Box 122
Freeburg, Illinois 62243

Second Printing

ISBN 13: 978-0-9838412-0-3
ISBN 10: 0-9838412-0-9
LCCN: 2011918013

Acknowledgements:
I wish to thank Donna Biffar, Leslie Lanter, Nathan Lanter and Leo Welch for their reading time, counsel and good advice in preparing the manuscript. I also want to thank the *Belleville News Democrat*, the *Belleville Journal*, *The St. Louis Globe Democrat* and the *St. Louis Post Dispatch* for permission to quote from their pages. I am especially grateful to Lavette Grovesteen the first Board of Trustees Secretary for her diligence in keeping thorough minutes of board proceedings during Belleville Area College's-Southwestern Illinois College's first years. I am indebted to former Belleville Area College librarians Bea Fries, Jan Kramer and Bobby Peduzzi, and part-time librarian Lois Ridenour, for collecting and archiving information on the 1980 faculty strike, as I am to other faculty who have passed on to me memories and stories about their experiences at the college. And special thanks to Jordan E. Kurland, former Associate Editor of *Academe* and longtime member of the AAUP Committee A on Academic Freedom and Tenure, for his support and help.

This book is dedicated to

Donald Libby
Roger Christeck
and
Leo Welch

Defending the Citadel:

Confronting Corporate Management and Corruption in an Illinois Community College

A Personal Narrative

Contents

In the Beginning

Rex Carr and the AAUP

The April 1974 Election

Teaching: Politics and Advocacy

Academic Cleansing

A Regime of Punishments and Rewards

Strike!

The Academic Factory

1992 Negotiations

In Closing

Photo Credits

Figure #1
Page: 141
Caption: BJC AAUP 1966
Photographer: NA
Source: *Dutchman*
Date: circa 1967

Figure #2
Page: 141
Caption: BJC Faculty Senate 1967
Photographer: NA
Source: *Dutchman*
Date: circa 1968

Figure #3
Page: 142
1Caption: BAC Faulty Cafeteria Sit-in
Photographer: Ethel Channon
Source: *Belleville Journal*
Date: October 22, 1980

Figure #4
Page: 142
Caption: Sheehy and Libby at Faculty Sit-in
Photographer: Bob Moore
Source: *St. Louis Globe Democrat*
Date: October 22, 1980

Figure #5
Page: 143
Caption: Ken Pinzke—the Lone Striker
Photographer: Bill DeMestri
Source: *Belleville News Democrat*
Date: November 4, 1980

Figure #6
Page: 143
Caption: Faculty Strike Rally
Photographer: Mark Wakeford
Source: *Belleville News Democrat*
Date: November 17, 1980

Figure #7
Page: 144
Caption: Ad for Teachers to Replace Strikers
Photographer: NA
Source: *St. Louis Globe Democrat*
Date: November 11, 1980

Figure #8
Page: 145
Caption: Josephine Jones, et al.
Photographer: Mark Wakeford
Source: *Belleville News Democrat*
Date: November 16, 1980

Figure #9
Page: 145
Caption: Sit-down
Photographer: Clarence Chaput
Source: *Belleville News Democrat*
Date: November 19, 1980

Figure #10
Page: 146
Caption: Libby Being Arrested
Photographer: Clarence Chaput
Source: *Belleville News Democrat*
Date: November 19, 1980

Figure #11
Page: 147
Caption: Striker on Their Way to Jail
Photographer: Clarence Chaput
Source: *Belleville News Democrat*
Date: November 19, 1980

Figure #12
Page: 147
Caption: BAC Board Meeting
Photographer: Mark Wakeford
Source: *Belleville News Democrat*
Date: November 19, 1980

Figure #13
Page: 148
Caption: BAC Board Meeting
Photographer: Rick Stankoven
Source: *St. Louis Globe Democrat*
Date: November 19, 1980

Figure #14
Page: 148
Caption: Libby and AAUP President Cochran
Photographer: Rick Stankoven
Source: *St. Louis Globe Democrat*
Date: November 4, 1980

Figure #15
Page: 149
Caption: Don Libby
Photographer: Leslie Lanter
Source: NA
Date: circa 1980

Defending the Citadel:

A Personal Narrative

Once you permit those who are convinced of their own superior rightness to censor and silence and suppress those who hold contrary opinions, just at that moment the citadel has been surrendered.

—Archibald MacLeish

There is no justification for any gamble with human lives; even less when the culture, the prestige, the welfare of an entire people are at stake, and through them the welfare of the whole civilized world.

—Kurt von Schuschnigg

And of the Trojans some
Believed him, others for a wily knave
Held him, of whose mind was Laocoon.
Wisely he spake: "A deadly fraud is this,"
He said, "devised by the Achaean chiefs!"
And cried to all straightway to burn the Horse,
And know if aught within its timbers lurked.

—Quintus

I have judged it proper to give an account of the actual events founded not on what was told by the first informant I met, nor of my own opinion. I have described some events at which I was present myself, and what I have heard from other people I have checked in every case as thoroughly as I possibly could. I shall be satisfied if my work is judged useful by those who want a clear picture of what happened, and what is likely, given the human situation, to reoccur in a similar or comparable form in the future.

—Thucydides

Introduction

In 1851 Edward Lasell, a chemistry professor from Williams College, founded the first junior college in the United States, the private Auburndale Female Seminary in Newton, Massachusetts. On leave and teaching at Mount Holyoke Female Seminary in South Hadley, Massachusetts that year, in establishing Auburndale, Lasell hoped to provide a beginning or two-year more-scientific higher education experience for young women. He hoped to attract students not only from the Newton area, but also from wherever interested female students might apply.

Fifty years later, in 1901, William Rainy Harper, President of the University of Chicago, and J. Stanley Brown, Superintendent of Joliet Township High School in Joliet, Illinois, created the first American public junior college, Joliet Junior College. But unlike the private Auburndale Seminary, Harper and Brown described their new college as "an experimental postgraduate high school program (co-ed) to be academically parallel to the first two years of four-year colleges for students who wished to continue studies beyond high school but also wanted to remain in the Joliet community."

In addition to providing college instruction for a local community, the Harper-Brown idea hoped to move lower-division (freshman and sophomore) undergraduate instruction away from the research universities, to allow them to concentrate on upper-division (juniors and seniors), graduate study and research.

In the decades following the Auburndale experiment (later named Lasell) the number of private junior colleges in the United States increased steadily. Although, in the twenty years after World War II, many closed their doors or morphed into four-year institutions, in 1940 there were 325. By 1966 the number of private two-year postsecondary schools had dwindled to 272. Today there are several hundred more, around 415, though they tend to be small (less than 600 students), religious, and expensive.

Following the Joliet experiment, through the first half of the twentieth century, as with the private junior colleges, the number of American public two-year colleges also increased. By 1930 there were 160 public junior colleges in twenty-four states. California had thirty-two, Iowa twenty-seven, and Texas twenty-one. Illinois had only five. By 1946 the number had grown to 328, and as of 2009 there were some 1,150 public junior or community colleges in the United States.

Although Illinois had only five junior colleges in 1930, in 1931, responding to a growing interest in junior colleges, both nationally and in Illinois, the Illinois General Assembly adopted legislation permitting the Board of Education of Chicago to establish a second junior college. Six years later, in 1937, the Illinois Assembly passed the Illinois Junior College Act, making it possible for Illinois high school boards of education to set up junior colleges ". . . by resolution in districts with a population between 25,000 and 250,000 or establishment of junior colleges in smaller district by referendum."

Six years later the Illinois Assembly adopted legislation permitting high school districts, by referenda, to set separate tax rates for both education and building funds for junior college operations. However, legislation providing state funding for junior colleges in Illinois was not passed until 1955.

In 1961 the Illinois Assembly created the Illinois Board of Higher Education, and the 1964 higher education master plan led to the Junior College Act of 1965, creating an independent Class I Junior College system throughout Illinois, by which all Illinois public high schools were assigned to a junior college district.

* * * * *

At the onset public junior colleges in the United States seemed generally intent upon following the Harper-Brown plan to offer students a local venue for instruction parallel with the first two years of college instruction. At a meeting of the American Association of Junior Colleges (formed in St. Louis in 1920) in 1922, public community colleges were described as ". . . institutions offering two years of instruction of strictly collegiate grade." However, in spite of the description, at other times it seems the new schools were not entirely clear about how to provide "strictly collegiate grade instruction." This was, no doubt, due to the junior college lineage, having been formed from the bottom up, as an extension of secondary schools or secondary school progeny, and as Cohen and Brawer note in *The American Community College* (2007), having ". . . no traditions to defend, no alumni to question their role, no autonomous professional staff to be moved aside, no statement of philosophy . . . ." As John H. Frye notes in *The Vision of the Public Junior College, 1900-40: Professional Goals and Popular Aspirations* (1992), "The onset of the junior college was accompanied by no clear mission, set of criteria, nor theoretical framework. One is hard pressed to establish an unambiguous purpose for the first public junior college at Joliet, Illinois or elsewhere."

Thus, it was, while shrouded in the rhetorical claim that junior colleges were collegiate, they were not often guided by the standards and practices of the postsecondary education academy. Lacking a mission or direction, public junior colleges floundered academically. As extensions of high schools, they continued to stir traditional academic disciplines and vocational (community) programs in the same pot. Instead of providing rigorous instruction and a competent conduit through which better academic performers would pass on to universities, heavily influenced by their high school-community roots, junior colleges slipped mostly to training students for the community work force.

The community college practice of negating or ignoring academic standards upon which Western higher education is founded was pervasive. Jencks and Riesman in *The Academic Revolution* (2002), labeled American junior colleges "anti-university." They point out that even by the barest of collegiate standards, instruction and evidence of student mastery of subject matter for a postsecondary associate of science degree, say, in chemistry, English, or mathematics, should require more academic rigor than an associate's certificate in pipe fitting or air-conditioner repair. To contend that it need not, or to ignore that it does, for whatever reasons, remains even today at the heart of the American community college dilemma.

Also, implicit in junior college development was the myopic comercial vision in which American postsecondary educational institutions, through the twentieth century and into the twenty-first century, came to be regarded as economically self-sustaining, product-producing institutions to be modeled on profit-driven corporations. Beneath the weight of the industrial revolution run amuck, there was, in the early twentieth century, a corresponding shift in the American public's attitude about its relationship to the nation's political-social fabric. Until the late nineteenth century Americans favored the belief (among educational philosophers as well as the populace generally) that one's life was best spent in the citizenship of service as embodied in the founding of the nation a bit over a hundred years before. However, following the emergence of the post-Civil War industrial robber barons, the American individuals' allegiances shifted from the ideal of good citizenship to avarice and groveling for money—and eventually to evangelizing greed. This, among other things, enjoined a related shift in and reassignment of the mission of American higher education from educating citizens to providing those who showed up in the classroom a means (instruction) of how best to go about making money. Students became consumers and instruction became more and more akin to a sales pitch for Sears, Montgomery Ward, or JC Penney, imbued with the sophistry of providing whatever happened to be in demand or desired by the customer. College degrees were no longer seen as proof of an education in the rigors of scholarship and good citizenship, but as a ticket to the employment lottery for those hoping to get a hand in the illusory pot-of-honey in the corporate beehive.

While the shift from educating citizens to training consumers featured higher educational institutions as a training ground for future moneymakers, it also promoted the same institutions as businesses to be operated on a money-saving and then money-making agenda. As early as the 1920s, social critics Thorstein Veblen and Upton Sinclair, among others, decried the subjugation of American colleges and universities, in purpose and practice, to business models and to an industrial corporate ideal.

Webster's Third New International Dictionary defines a corporation as "(1) a body of persons associated for some purpose (as standardizing conditions) (2) a group of merchants or traders united in an association." Clearly this is a problematic definition of what a college or university should be, but at the same time what many American postsecondary institutions have become.

Of course, retooling higher education to a corporate mold required a different type of administrative personnel. The traditional practice of moving seasoned professors into the administrative ranks to oversee and guide higher education institutions was abandoned. Now business managers, or I should say managers with business agendas, were hired to establish curriculum and, invariably, to impose corporate values on the schools. Business managers, as part of the growing university-college industry, were brought in to shadow their Wall Street counterparts, too often promoting impervious, self-aggrandizing corporate attitudes and practices. Community colleges, lacking an historical higher education faculty, were particularly vulnerable to this scheme.

As a small, though not insignificant, example of the corporate money-making malaise that has infected postsecondary educational institutions, the kind of thing one can find any day at nearly any college or university in the United States, a Southwestern Illinois College (SWIC) newsletter from the school's president, *CHAT: The Official Employee Newsletter for SWIC,* asks, "Did you know a two-year associate's degree is worth $500,000 more than a high school diploma alone?" The article notes that the best paying jobs require some college and ends with "Bottom-line: institutions like SWIC make dollars and economic sense for the students and the communities they serve; they offer equal-footing educational opportunities for everyone; and when their students succeed the nation thrives."

The blurb was probably not written by the college president at that time, but more than likely picked up or purchased from a national online marketing agency. This is, as I have said, a small example, but one replicated daily by public relations and marketing offices of colleges and universities around the country.

* * * * *

Anyone who consults the literature on American college and university growth and trends knows there is nothing new in what I say here about the problems plaguing current American postsecondary educational institutions. Among the comments and blogs that break out almost daily on websites such as *The Chronicle of Higher Education* (and in a large degree reflect both the sense and nonsense of the academy) are festering reports and complaints about university and college faculty and administrative appointment and hiring irregularities, the thieving of intellectual property rights (IPR), the denial of academic freedom, research malpractice, collusion (conflicts of interest) of professors and administrators with connections to the corporate world, student discipline (seeing students as "customers" who "know what they want to learn"), and the general assault on the professorate by business managers who infest and infect college and university administrations—in other words, corporate activity as usual.

This book, then, is about a school—a community college in Illinois, Belleville Area College (BAC) now Southwestern Illinois College (SWIC) —my experiences, as well as the experiences of other professors there from 1967 until 1995. Its purpose is two-fold.

First, I have set out an historical narrative of some of the more problematic practices pursued by the school's board of trustees, its administration, and faculty members the administration recruited to support these practices.

Second, I have related, within a personal narrative, the response of a majority of the BAC faculty to these practices, a response among other things, in 1967 that activated for the first time an American Association of University Professors (AAUP) chapter as a collective bargaining unit, led to a three week faculty strike in 1980, created the first joint American Association of University Professors-American Federation of Teachers (AFT) local union amalgamation in the country, transferred faculty governance from a traditional Faculty Senate to a collectively bargained contract—at BAC-SWIC, the *Memorandum of Understanding*—and led to the unionization of the entire school.

Additionally, from 1967 to 1995, the BAC faculty entered into the *Memorandum of Understanding,* the AAUP "1940 Statement of Principles on Academic Freedom and Tenure," a contractual control of IPR (the first ever included in a faculty contract by any college or university in the United States) and helped see through the Illinois General Assembly the 1980 Community College Teacher Tenure law and the Illinois Educational Employees Collective Bargaining Act in 1984.

Again, the conflicts these issues generated are endemic and, for well over a hundred years now, have been ongoing in postsecondary educational institutions across the nation. What I report here is a small account of that past, a part of the saga of what the Belleville Area College faculty did to cut into the corporate agenda and to maintain quality higher-education instruction at one community college in Illinois.

Preface

One of the more poignant scenes in mid-twentieth century cinema, if you teach or have ever had the inclination to teach, appears near the beginning of Robert Bolt's social-realist film, *A Man for All Seasons*. The scene is set in the morning outside Thomas More's manor at Chelsea and features a brief exchange between More, a member of the King's Council and soon-to-be Chancellor of England, and Richard Rich, a recent university graduate. Later, Rich will perjure himself to see More beheaded, but in this scene, he is petitioning More for a position at court. More has already asked others if they would recommend Rich, and they have said, "No." However, More has told Rich that he has a position for him.

"You said there was a post?"

"Yes," More says, "I'll offer you a post, with a house, a servant and 12 pounds a year."

"What post?"

"At the new school."

"A teacher!" Rich says with incredulity.

"Why not be a teacher?" More says. "You'd be a fine teacher, perhaps a great one."

"If I was, who would know it?" Rich queries.

"You!" More tells him. "Your pupils. Your friends. God. Not a bad public, that."

By the time I was eight or nine I had already decided I wanted to be a teacher, so these lines hold a special significance for me. Of course, in those neophyte days, I had no idea what I might teach. But I suspected in the coming years, if I set myself to it, I might learn something that would be of value for others to know, and the impulse, the compulsion, you might say, that goes with any art was there. There were those, however, my parents and others, who disparaged the idea, and thought I'd be wasting my time, and I suppose my life. After all, teachers were not very well paid and were viewed by Americans as fussy, insignificant people, say, like the 1950's TV Wally Peepers or Miss Brooks of the *Our Miss Brooks* show. When teaching was mentioned, most thought of the K-12 system, where still today 85-percent of the teachers are female, underpaid and believed to be people who simply cannot find other more lucrative employment. Today newspapers often run stories decrying the unfit teachers in the American education system, as if that, indeed, is all American education is about.

The resistance to education in the United States has been documented often enough. And while there have been novels featuring faculty members or professors as protagonists and significant moral centers: John Williams' *Stoner*; Evan Hunter's *Blackboard Jungle*; Bellow's *Herzog*; my own *The Final Days* to name a few—and a scattering of movies such as: *Up the Down Staircase*; *The Dead Poets' Society*; *Stand and Deliver*; and *The*

History Boys, American literature and pop culture do not often embraced teachers as important people.

Professors were derided as absentminded or eggheads. Sometimes professor-teachers were targets of derision and violence, reminiscent of the deranged student in Vienna in 1936 who killed analytic philosopher Moritz Schlick. Not infrequently in the United States student disappointment and rage and madness have exploded and ended with teachers dying in the physics department at the University of Iowa, in the halls of Columbine High School, and of course at Virginia Tech where Professor Liviu Librescu blocked the classroom door while encouraging his students to escape a killer, literally defending the citadel, and then died along with three other faculty members.

In 1977, a Harris Poll showed that only 29-percent of Americans surveyed gave teachers a very prestigious rating. About the same time, a visiting sociology instructor from England, Keith Justice, polled his BAC classes and found that, of ten occupations listed, his students ranked teaching tenth. And although attitudes about teachers have changed a bit over the years, teachers still do not command a great deal of respect or admiration. A recent national poll in the United States showed teachers running a distant fifth behind number one—firefighters, and number two—anti-terrorists, whatever that is.

On the other hand, we have all profited from classroom instruction provided by people who, in some small way, and in some ways not so small, encouraged us to consciousness and contemplation, people listed in the sourcebooks of our personalities, people whose names we continue to recite throughout our lives as a tribute to who we are.

When asked what the Jesuits taught him James Joyce is reported to have replied, "They taught me to order and to judge." And, as Lawrence Ferlinghetti writes, ". . . without mistaking/anything/for what it may not be." That is what teachers do—they teach us to order and to judge, to logically or analogically understand, to catch life in Jacob Bronowski's "butterfly net of our senses," and as far as is humanly possible to understand what a thing is and to assign it a value as best befits the human condition.

My proclivity for teaching, though it may have been seriously influenced by any number of early environmental and/or hereditary psychological twists, was over the years focused into sharper relief by a pantheon of superb teachers. These people provided not only instruction in the disciplines they professed: history, language, law, literature, mathematics, philosophy, psychology, and the sciences—but also offered a variety of instructional methods and techniques from which an observant, aspiring teacher might readily choose and later appropriate for his purposes.

I did not then, nor do I now, see teaching in and of itself as a profession. Vocation is a matter of profession, although I do not imagine that it need be attached to financial profit. Boethius reminds us that the value of what someone does can best be judged by the compensation he receives for his efforts. And those rewarded with money, to his mind, are not doing much. Being in line for an inheritance or winning the lottery hardly classify as worthy vocations.

Teaching, at best, is always an avocation. It is not enough to simply go into a classroom as a teacher. Teaching is an activity people in a profession sometimes undertake in addition to, or as a part of, their vocation. Medical doctors and lawyers teach, chemists teach, as do mathematicians and biologists. Novelists, poets, playwrights, and journalists all teach. Sometimes, even politicians teach.

As a teacher, one enters the classroom as a member of a larger profession—a gathering of scholars of common rights and interests—with the knowledge and/or skills, the état métier of an educated group or profession. A true teacher is not one sent to a classroom simply to present and dispense whatever he is assigned for that day. That reduces the teacher to a salesman endeavoring to sell for profit whatever happens to be in the area. As the AFT has pointed out "good teaching always draws on new scholarship," and I might add, on scholarship specifically and generally, but always the scholarship of individual disciplines. In truth, teaching is an art—and good teachers are good artists. But like art, only a limited number in the human community, regardless of breeding or education, can do it well. It's something like hitting a baseball or performing as an air-traffic controller. Some few can do it and do it well. Most can't do it at all. The skills required for good teaching can be encouraged or developed in those who have the talent, but it cannot be taught to those who do not.

In the end teaching is an art closely tied to a discipline, an art by which professionals elucidate or profess their discipline. Anatole France noted, "The whole art of teaching is only the art of awakening the curiosity of the young minds for the purpose of satisfying it afterwards." But it is most certainly an art.

As I said, we can all list teachers who have taken us in and guided us to enquiry and explication, sometimes gently and with compassion, and sometimes with a not-so-gentle voice, depending on their passions. And so we should list them, naming them as a child names those who have fed and clothed it. As William Butler Yeats says, we should ". . . write it out in verse."

My personal list of professionals I came across in the classroom includes philosophers: Vernon Burke, Thomas Langan, Joseph McAllen, SJ, William Wade, SJ, and Missouri Supreme Court justice Joseph J. Simeone (from St. Louis University Law School); poets: James Hearst, Richard Hugo, and John Knoepfle; novelists: Vance Bourjaily, Mary Carter, Robert Coover, William Price Fox, John Frederick, and Bienvenido Santos; professor of social work at the University of Illinois, Chicago: Ord Matek; as well as Kurt von Schuschnigg, a former Chancellor of Austria; and my high school coach Austin Mulkey, who taught Latin and English. I should add to this list the principal at Freeburg High School my freshman year, E. R. Perry.

Of course, there were others who were not philosophers, poets, novelists, chancellors, coaches, or principals. As a high school sophomore, I came under tutelage of biologist Harold St. Aubin and a woman we knew as Mrs. Palmer, though she was no longer married and showed up for class most Monday mornings seriously hungover, much to the chagrin of no one. Madame Palmer had a passionate and contagious love for literature—that was her profession.

Since written literature is an essential ingredient of our culture it is necessary that we have experts to instruct us in how to approach and understand written texts—especially literary texts. This is what Madame Palmer did for us. It was her passion for poetry and drama that sparked my interest in literature and finally to write poetry and fiction. Her love of Tennyson, Lord Byron, and the Shelleys pervaded the classroom like the buffeting fragrance of bread baking. She could have opened an office on Main Street and hung out a shingle. Lover of Literature: Interpretive Hours 12 a.m.-12 p.m., Inquire Within.

At St. Louis University I studied with Mesdames Sullivan and Murray, two exuberant, vivacious literary women who, likewise, had been smacked with an enthusiasm and love for literature and writing, and who were not at all hesitant about sharing it with their introduction to literature students.

Still, for years, I suppressed the inclination to teach. Shortly after high school I determined to become a writer, although I spent two years in engineering school, three years playing minor league baseball, two years in law school, did a hitch in the Marine Corps, and worked in Chicago with the Jewish Children's Bureau's residential therapy program for adolescent boys with affective disorders—pretty much the kinds of things young writers do, looking at the world to see what they might write about.

During this time, however, as a hedge against the likelihood that I might eventually end up behind the desk in a classroom, I did complete a B.S. in English and Philosophy at Saint Louis University. Then, in the fall of 1967, having exhausted other possibilities, I took a job in the English department at Evanston High School in Evanston, Illinois.

When I joined the faculty, Evanston was the premiere ranked public high school in the nation. I was one of the few people on the faculty who did not have a master's or doctorate, and so decided after that first year, that to continue teaching I would need an advanced degree.

In the spring of 1968 I was accepted in the Graduate Program in Creative Writing at the University of Iowa and in the Graduate Program for Creative Writing at San Francisco State. When both schools offered me a slot, although San Francisco State sweetened the acceptance with a substantial stipend, I chose Iowa.

Beginning in 1966 I had been involved in open housing, civil rights, and anti-war demonstrations and marches with Martin Luther King, Jr. in

Chicago, and in some of the more troublesome open housing marches in Evanston, as well as in the aftermath of the Chicago riots that followed the assassination of Dr. King in the spring of 1968. At the time I prepared to attend graduate school, San Francisco State was going through a great deal of political turmoil. After Chicago I wanted a quiet place, a place to sit and think and write, so I chose the cornfields of Iowa, the future of W. P. Kinsella and *Shoeless Joe*. Moreover, a friend of mine, Truman Metzel, the proprietor of the Great Expectations bookstore under the Foster Street El, a few blocks from Northwestern University, who supplied many of the university faculty with books and who served for several years as president of the university philosophy club, advised that I might consider taking a degree from a school with a sound and substantial academic reputation. Without any pejorative for San Francisco State, after all I am a Mid-westerner, I chose Iowa. The Iowa Graduate Program in Creative Writing is the oldest in the country, established in 1936.

In the fall of 1968 I ended up at Iowa, though ironically, with the Kent State shootings in May 1970, Iowa City and the university became a radicalized hotbed of turmoil and mayhem. And as a member of a voluntary ad hoc graduate student group attempting to provide a physical buffer between the police and the rioting students, once again I ended up in the soup.

At Iowa, in addition to working on an MFA, I served as poetry editor for a university magazine, *The Iowa State Liquor Store*, a rather dubiously entitled publication named by workshop student-would-be-author and journalist George E. Kimball III (December 20, 1943-July 6, 2011), who later worked for the *Boston Herald*.

I also taught in the workshop as a Writing Fellow, and in the summer of 1969, conducted fiction and poetry writing seminars with Iowa poet James Hearst for the Aspen School of Contemporary Art in Aspen, Colorado.

In June 1970, after completing the Iowa program, I set out to locate a college faculty position. Reflecting the reticence and skepticism of the early '70s, the postsecondary education job market had retreated and dried up. Early on there were offers from high schools and from several corporations to edit in-house newsletters or bulletins. I chose to pass on these. In spite of a prolonged and determined search, I was unable to find a college spot. Finally, after working with a highway bridge crew in Iowa City for several months, I hired on at the River King Coal Mine in Freeburg, Illinois.

My dad and brother-in-law worked at River King, and I had wanted to return to Southern Illinois, so it was a natural enough thing to do. And though working at the mine provided me with ample time for writing, as well as an adequate salary, I wanted to get back to the classroom. Since I was living in Freeburg, BAC seemed a logical place to look. In the fall of 1971, I submitted an application and was assigned an English101 Rhetoric and Composition class. Then, during the fall of 1972 I became a fulltime writing instructor at the college. I did this with a great deal of enthusiasm, in spite of the advice proffered by one of my mentors at the University of Iowa, Filipino writer Bienvenido Santos. Shortly before I left Iowa Ben inquired about what I might do in the near and not-too-distant future. When I replied that in addition to writing, I hoped to teach writing, he warned me to "... not take a job in a university or college. There is nothing going on there that a writer can use. Nothing," he said, "nothing there to write about."

Even though I would have preferred a university environment, BAC had a number of things to recommend it. For one, it was in Southern Illinois. For another, although the college had existed since 1946, it had been recently (1966) certified as a Class I Junior College. In 1972 the faculty and staff were putting the finishing touches on a new campus, and the school was in the process of becoming a full-fledged postsecondary educational institution. Here was a chance to get in very nearly on the ground floor, so I accepted the appointment and ended doing what I had always intended to do but had furtively avoided. Now I could not only work at writing, but I could also teach writing. It was good to get paid for doing what I intended to do anyway—and maybe my friend Ben Santos was mistaken. So, at long last I could say with Robert Frost. "But yield who will to their separation/My object in life is to unite/My vocation and avocation/As my two eyes make one in sight."

Defending the Citadel

In the Beginning

> Laws for the liberal education of youth are
> so extremely wise and useful that to a
> humane and generous mind, no expense
> for this purpose would be thought extra-
> vagant.
>
> —John Adams

Belleville Junior College, Belleville, Illinois

Southwestern Illinois College (SWIC), formerly Belleville Area College (BAC) in Belleville, Illinois, opened its doors in the fall of 1946 as Belleville Township Junior College (BTJC), administered by Belleville High School District 201. The junior college was created under the 1937 Illinois Junior College Act that provided for the establishment of a junior college through board resolution by any secondary board of education in districts with a population between 25,000 and 250,000.

There appears to have been both economic and political reasons for establishing BTJC in 1946. The Great Depression that engulfed the United States in the '30s had ended with WWII, and by then the war, too, was over and the allied victory in the war portended a greater optimism and pros- perity for the country. Additionally, there seems to have been, at least in part, a patriotic interest in serving the large numbers of returning veterans registering in colleges and universities across the country. The first issue of the BTJC catalogue, *Announcements,* states, "It is believed that the opening of BTJC is particularly timely because of the present overcrowded condition of four-year colleges and universities."

However, beyond the patriotic helping veterans to a cheaper first two years of college, the high school district board and administration seems also to have had an eye on the revenue soldiers-become-students would provide to the high school-junior college district under the Servicemen's Readjustment Act (the G.I. Bill of Rights) signed into law by President Franklin D. Roosevelt in 1944. The BTJC *Announcements* contends that "The new junior college will be particularly beneficial to veterans who are residents of Belleville in that they may take the first two years of college or university courses at home at little expense, and save their educational benefits under the G. I. Bill for the more expensive part of their education which must be completed at the university." Several weeks before classes began the *Belleville News Democrat (BND)* reports that Belleville High School Superintendent Dr. Hal O. Hall ". . . announced the school's junior college which begins September 16, has an enrollment of 137 students of which 55 are non-residents and must pay a $100 per semester tuition fee," and that the "State Department of Education has certified the junior college as eligible for the training of war veterans and that it would be able to file a claim against the Veterans' Administration for such training."

If, in establishing the college, the high school board intended to serve veterans, at least in the first year, District 201 was not prepared to appoint additional faculty or offer anything more than the bare necessities. According to the *BND*, "There is no intent of the Township High School Board of Education to offer night classes in its junior college which opens next Monday, Mr. Hal O. Hall, superintendent, said today in reply to a group of WWII veterans who have asked for night classes.

"'We have an enrollment of 152 at present,' said Dr. Hall, 'of which 92 are veterans planning a four-year college course. The present enrollment will utilize the present faculty to the limit, and a few members will carry an overload.'

"'Because of this condition the only junior college classes which can be offered in the evening will be those which are transferred from the day school to relieve congestion. Announcement of the transfers will be made next week.'"

The 1946 BTJC *Announcements* listed thirty faculty selected from the high school to handle the junior colleges' classes. The range of academic expertise of the listed teachers included such diverse subjects as accounting, art, engineering drawing, English, chemistry, German, hygiene for women (and men), Latin, mathematics, shorthand, typing, and zoology. The *Announcements* notes further that ". . . junior college instruction will be offered in . . . pre-commerce, pre-legal, pre-engineering, pre-medicine, pre-dentistry, pre-teaching, liberal arts, commerce, accounting, and secretarial curricula," or pretty much the same curriculum as the high school. The listing was, however, careful to note, to legitimize college teaching qualifications, that all of the teachers assigned to the new college held a master's degree.

* * * * *

For the next twenty years the college remained attached to the Belleville High School District 201, sharing the high school facilities and teachers, during which time enrollment continued to grow, though somewhat spasmodically. In the middle '50s, as the nation and the BTJC area prospered and more and more prospective students went away to college or found employment immediately after high school, enrollment sagged to less than 100 students a semester. However, slowly and steadily, in the early '60s enrollment again increased–so by 1965 BTJC had an enrollment of 206 students.

Then, in October of 1966 in accordance with the Illinois Junior College Act of 1965 a general referendum was scheduled for voters of eastern St. Clair County, Illinois. The plebiscite included Illinois school districts of Belleville, Freeburg, Lebanon, Marissa, Mascoutah, New Athens, and

O'Fallon, to establish BTJC as a Class I Junior College.

A major talking point for a college district independent of high school District 201 suggested that freeing the college from the high school district would result in a tax savings, pour monies from grants and entitlements into the new school's coffers, and bring state and federal dollars into the local economy. Shortly before the referendum the *BND* reported that "under the junior college act, districts can obtain 50% grants for education and 75% grants for buildings from the state. The law was adopted last year and already some 20 areas in the state have created districts." The *BND* pointed out that founding a Class I Junior College in Belleville would mirror the establishment of colleges in Centralia and Rend Lake, Illinois.

Still, as upbeat and encouraging as the campaign was, not everything about the 1966 referendum was positive. In a leadup to the vote, in a provincial, racist editorial on October 28, 1966, I suspect reflecting the attitude of the larger voting public of Southwestern Illinois, the *BND* endorsed the referendum and warned voters that only at their peril should they reject the founding of the new college. The peril? Well, the predominantly black population of East St. Louis, the editorial contended, lurked in the weeds waiting to be assigned to a district with Belleville that could, because of East St. Louis' larger population, turn the people of Belleville into slaves. The editorial rationale went like this:

> Although the new law [in Illinois] has been in effect only a little over a year, already 20 communities have created new junior college districts.
>
> In the event that after a reasonable interlude local initiative is found to be lacking in certain areas, the state can be counted on to step in to accomplish the task in its own way. Probably it will force mergers to create junior college districts in much the same way it eliminated all non-high school districts ten years ago.
>
> To illustrate, if by the time District 201 were still bumbling along as an unaffiliated 'loner,' the state could decree our marriage with, say, East St. Louis. From the Illinois Board of Higher Education meeting room in Chicago, this might seem a logical move.
>
> But a shotgun marriage would be a calamity, nonetheless. For here, up close, it is easy to see that no two near neighbors could be less alike. There is absolutely no community of interest among Belleville and East St. Louis.
>
> The needs of each district are not at all parallel; in fact, they are 180-degree opposites. Most urgent need of East St. Louis is for a huge remedial program in basics, whereas our District 201 people have long since mastered the fundamentals and are

ready for more serious, more productive fare.

But, based on East St. Louis' preponderant population and assessed valuation, Belleville wouldn't have a chance. So, in the end we would wind up stuck in a hopeless partnership, a voiceless slave but obligated no less to help support a junior college establishment that would be virtually worthless to our people.

Believe us when we say that this hazard of inaction now on the junior college question is very great. We simply cannot afford to take the stupid risk of community subjugation in a foreseeably abortive union. Nor need we do so.

At any rate, the referendum was scheduled for Saturday, October 29, 1966. The day before the vote the *BND* carried headlines, "20,000 Expected to Vote on Junior College Issue Saturday." The lead article claims:

> A record vote for a school election in St. Clair County and possibly Southern Illinois is likely in tomorrow's referendum on the proposed establishment of a Class I junior college district to take in seven high school districts in the eastern portion of St. Clair County.
>
> County Superintendent of Schools Clarence D. Blair, who called the election, estimated 20,000 votes would be cast making it by far the biggest school election in his 28-year career as head of the county's schools.

Despite Blair's optimism, just a little over half that number showed up at the 46 polling places. Even with a minimum of pre-election opposition to the plan, only 11,874 voters cast ballots; 9,779 votes for the new junior college district and 2,095 against.

* * * * *

Once the votes were counted and the new junior college district authorized, as he was required to do, Blair scheduled an election to provide a seven-member board of trustees for the college. In a matter of days, the District 522 election was announced and set for early Decemer. Within the next weeks forty-three candidates filed for the seven seats, an altogether exceptional number considering that eight years later, in 1974, only four candidates would file for two board seats. To aid voters in the December 1966 election, the *BND* and other newspapers in Junior College District 522 carried a picture of each candidate and a brief list of social and business organizations to which he or she belonged, followed by a statement postulating his or her personal qualifications for a board position.

The A-to-Z of their stated affiliations, or in this instance the A-to-W, ran from the Air Force Reserve and American Legion to West Side Optimist Club by way of organizations such as Century Brass Works, River Bluffs' Council Girl Scouts, and Walnut Hill Cemetery Future Care Fund.

Even with significant advertising and campaigning by the candidates during the two months between the referendum and the board election, by December of 1966, enthusiasm for the new district, as marked by voter turnout, had dwindled significantly. Now, only 8,300 voters showed up at the polls—though the Christmas season may have had something to do with that.

In the December election, District 522 voters chose: J. Paul Bedel, CPA; Richard W. Hilgard, manager of Ideal Stencil and Machine Company; Joseph P. Keck, Jr., owner of a Tom Boy Market; Friederich E. Lutz, president of Century Brass Works; Fred R. Schroder, superintendent of Peabody Midwest Coal Mine; Patricia Schroeder, a former school teacher; and Orison R. Seibert, a farmer and auctioneer, as the first Board of Trustees of Belleville Junior College (BJC).

American Association of University Professors

During the following months the board advertised for a president for the new college and received forty-six applications for the position. In the spring of 1967, under the direction of Lowell Fischer, coordinator of school and college relations at the University of Illinois and state chairman of North Central Association of Colleges and Secondary Schools, the BTJC Board of Trustees selected H. (Hugo) J. Haberaecker, the superintendent at Belleville High School District 201, as the college's first president.

Hugo J. Haberaecker was a native of South Dakota with a degree in Education Administration from Wartburg College, a small religious liberal arts school in Waverly, Iowa. Before arriving at Belleville District 201 he had served as a secondary school administrator at Goose Lake, Iowa; Kewanee, Illinois; Butler, Missouri; and Beardstown, Illinois. From 1942-45 he served in the Army Air Corps, was commissioned a bomber pilot, and reached the rank of colonel. He was awarded an Air Medal three times, a Distinguished Flying Cross twice, five battle stars, a Bronze Star, and a Presidential Unit Citation.

But even beneath the bright light of Haberaecker's military ribbons and stars, it appears that in the board's first choice for the junior college's primary administrator, its provincial squint limited its ability to see beyond the shadow of the watertower or in this case, beyond the local high school principal's office. It is hard to imagine that, even with his military record, Haberaecker was the best educationally or experientially qualified of the forty-six candidates under review for the college presidency, many from outside the Belleville area who were already serving or had served as college administrators.

However it was, Haberaecker was in—and when he arrived at the new college in 1967, he did what corporate chief executives frequently do when they change venues: he brought his coterie with him—administrators and faculty who had served in the 201 District, either in the high school, in the junior college or in both, as well as others he had befriended from the high schools of the newly created college District 522.

Although the people Haberaecker brought in, administrators and faculty, came exclusively from secondary school rosters, when the faculty, the board, and the Haberaecker administration set up the new BTJC in 1967, they appeared to have had something of a collegiate model in mind. They established a Faculty Senate, a Student Senate, and by 1968 divided faculty members (as they were appointed) into academic departments.

The teachers at District 201 had belonged to the AFT, Local 434, since 1935. And though I am not certain how many of them were in the union in 1965, when the Illinois Junior College Act became law in 1966, at least fifteen of the District 201 faculty handling the BTJC classes thought of themselves enough as college professors to have formed an AAUP chapter. This chapter was brought to the new college in 1967, by a 32-4-2 vote over the National Education Association (NEA) and AFT.

Immediately the new AAUP chapter set up a committee to serve as a liaison between the faculty and the board. This committee quickly morphed into a salary committee to represent the faculty. And within the first months of 1968 the new college board sanctioned the AAUP Salary Committee as a board appendage, giving it official status as an advisory bargaining agent. Members of the first committee were: William Saunders (English); Neale Fadden (Mathematics); Roger Crane (English); Jan Milligan (English); D. C. Edwards (Chemistry); and A. J. Woods (Counseling).

It is of interest that, although the board seemed amenable enough to the Salary Committee innovation, it was not so easily convinced that the faculty should have a senate, and only when AAUP General Secretary Bertram Davis visited the campus to speak with the trustees did the board agree to sanction the senate and give the senate the power to adjudicate academic freedom and tenure as set out in the AAUP's "1940 Statement on the Principles of Academic Freedom and Tenure."

At that time, all of the members of BTJC District 522 AAUP chapter committees, as well as the Faculty Senate, were recommended to the board by Haberaecker and certified by a board vote—as were the three professors chosen for the Coordinating Council of the College Council. It was this certification that tied the AAUP chapter and the Faculty Senate to the board in a symbiosis similar to that of most other teachers' organizations of the time, such as the original NEA which was, until the late twentieth century, an administrative-approved association or a company union. In this, the BTJC faculty committees' ties with the board fell within the general rubric of shared governance, though the committee, nonetheless, remained not independent of the board, but subservient to it.

The concept and, I dare say, the prospective of a professors' committee advising the board on salary issues appears to have been brought over from AFT Local 434 at BTHS where the teachers annually consulted with the board on salary matters. The traditional college practice for salary discussions was for department chairs to submit budgets to their deans, who would then consult with the president, who in turn would approach the governing board with a total budget to include recommended pay raises or other remunerations for professors. So the BTJC-AAUP arrangement was, if not new, at least unusual at the college level.

The AAUP journal, *Academe,* recalls in "75 Years: A Retrospective on the Occasion of The Seventy-fifth Annual Meeting" that:

> Although the faculty did not believe the AFT had enough experience handling community colleges in higher educa-tion, no collective bargaining agency existed that did. Only the AAUP exclusively spoke for higher education, but the AAUP had not yet embraced the idea of collective bargaining. Nevertheless, the Belleville faculty, most of whom already belonged to the AAUP chapter on campus [29 out of 47 faculty belonged to the AAUP], believed it was their only recourse. So by a nearly unanimous vote, the Belleville faculty gave the AAUP its first collective bargaining chapter. And the national office knew nothing about it.
>
> "I remember saying I was not sure the AAUP would approve of us," recalls Genevieve Snider, a mathematics professor and first president of the BAC-AAUP chapter. It was a radical move. In 1967, the AAUP was embroiled in arguments regarding the merits and dangers of taking up the collective bargaining mantle, and a special committee had just published a proposed statement of faculty representation that was the subject of much debate.
>
> To Belleville faculty, however, their vote seemed quite reasonable. "We were anxious to be as college-like as we could," Snider recalls. "The AFT would just put us back in the high school bracket. The AAUP was the only way we could go." And the Belleville faculty didn't perceive their action as the groundbreaking event it turned out to be; they had assumed that at least a handful of similar AAUP units existed around the country.
>
> The Belleville chapter knew it would have to inform the national office sooner or later. Snider, who had already planned to attend the AAUP's Annual Meeting in Cleveland that

year, volunteered to inform the national staff while there. She had not counted on one development, however. Israel Kugler of the AFT made a very strong speech at the meeting calling on the AAUP to join forces with the AFT, a proposal, says Snider, in which "the AAUP was not interested, to put it mildly. I decided this was no time or place to tell them we had voted for them as our bargaining unit."

Soon after her return to Belleville, Snider and Jan Milligan, then chapter president, decided they would have to break the news by phone. Snider placed a call to Robert Van Waes in the AAUP's Washington office and asked, very matter-of-factly, if he realized Belleville had voted the AAUP as their bargaining unit.

"Mr. Van Waes retorted by asking me a jillion questions," recalls Snider. "I was so surprised. I thought it was kind of routine. I didn't realize it wasn't." Then, Snider says the story goes, Van Waes put down the phone to tell the other people in the office. The response:

"They did *what?!*"

But the chapter's collective bargaining status was kept quiet to the AAUP national membership until Rutgers University was certified as an AAUP collective bargaining chapter in 1970; a formal announcement was finally made at the 1970 Annual Meeting in Los Angeles. "By that time, two or three other chapters had joined up, and it was beginning to show," says Snider (*Academe*, May-June 1989).

Even where there was tolerance or support for Belleville's activity, many in the national AAUP hierarchy were alarmed that the BAC chapter had not consulted with the national AAUP beforehand. There was serious concern that the arrangement might stain the elite AAUP ivory-tower white-collar prestige with a working-class blue tint. But I might add there was also a serious, near fatal failure to recognize that colleges and universities across the country were no longer the sole province of the faculty but had already been turned into management institutions with clear divisions between the faculty on one hand and boards and their administrations on the other.

It is not entirely clear why the BAC-AAUP did not notify the national AAUP beforehand of the impending arrangement with the BAC board— unless it was not pending. Perhaps the BTJC chapter didn't know the board would sanction it as an advisory bargaining agent for the faculty or didn't fully realize what it was getting into or what board approval of their committee meant until it happened.

And although there was AAUP opposition to the BTJC chapter's newly found activities, the AAUP president at the time, Clark Byse, was not one to object. He chose to characterize the innovative transgression as an attempt by the BTJC chapter to separate itself from the high school and join the postsecondary education assemblage and assumed it would continue to negotiate informally with the board.

* * * * *

The AAUP traces its origins to the early 1900s and the firing of economist-sociologist Edward Ross at Stanford University because Mrs. Leland Stanford, co-grantor of the university, disapproved of Ross' views on the gold standard, as well as those he held about immigrant labor and railroad monopolies, of which she was a substantial financial recipient. Ross was accused of scholarly incompetence and summarily fired, though seven of his colleagues, including philosopher Arthur O. Lovejoy, resigned from Stanford in protest of the firing.

Ross' persecution in 1901 was one of the more blatant, though far from the last, of many just such historical injustices, not unlike that suffered by Socrates or even Galileo, who was forced to inquire of his Vatican inquisitors what opinion it might be proper to hold and rewarded for his scientific integrity with house arrest. Consider, too, philosopher Bertrand Russell whose appointment to the philosophy department at City College of New York was revoked in 1940 because a woman, Jean Kay, claimed Russell would corrupt her daughter's morals, though the girl was not a student at the college and had never met Russell. In the Kay suit a New York court upheld the college's decision, a finding that has gone down as one of the more notorious violations of American judicial due process (Kay v. Board of Higher Ed. of City of New York, 18 N.Y.S.2d 821 [1940]).

The Ross incident at Stanford, followed by a rash of similar incidents in American universities in the early 1900s, encouraged Lovejoy in 1913, by then a Johns Hopkins faculty member, to convene a meeting of scholars, a society of professors, in January of that year in New York City. Two years later the society formed the Association of University Professors and elected John Dewey, the education philosopher, as president. In "The Critical State of Shared Governance" (2001), Joan Wallach Scott writes that "Almost immediately, the AAUP launched a series of investigations into violations of academic freedom, the freedom enjoyed by those with disciplinary cre-dentials grounded in their scholarly expertise to express their ideas, however critical; to call established beliefs into question; and to open new areas of scholarly inquiry, even if doing so meant challenging what was taken to be received wisdom or common sense."

In the beginning the AAUP restricted its membership to faculty, by invitation only, as a somewhat sacred society of the privileged–not unlike medieval guilds. The view of scholars and guild members as special persons has informed European universities for centuries. There is a story that Leo Szilard, the nuclear physicist-biologist, after he received a doctorate in physics from the University of Berlin, thought he might pursue another doctorate in economics. He applied to the university and, after being fobbed off for several months by university officials, ended discussing the matter with the university provost. Szilard asked why he had not been admitted to the program or at least been denied entry. Succinctly, but with apologies, the provost is reported to have confessed to Szilard that in bestowing a doctorate in physics on him (Szilard), the university had certified that to their best judgment he was an outstanding scholar of admirable character, a man of exceptional intelligence, honor and integrity. And in the provost's words, "Having done that once, Mr. Szilard, I do not see how we can do it again."

It seems, as well, to have been the AAUP's attitude that not for a mere compilation or accumulation of theories and/or data, but for character, intelligence, and talent that scholars were to be recognized and degrees bestowed.

In "Educationists and the Tradition of Learning," from *The Barbarian Within* (1962) Walter Ong writes that ". . . the Medieval University was a group of teachers' guilds—or, at Bologna and Salamanca, an association of students hiring their own teachers and preparing themselves to enter the guilds to which the teachers belonged whom they hired!"

For the guilds, knowledge was a precious commodity. When someone left a guild with the knowledge, skills, and expertise the guild had provided, it was not uncommon for the guild, in a rather effective though vicious way of protecting IPR, to send out an assassin to track down and, before he could disseminate the information or instruct others in the skills the guild had provided, to kill the defector.

But this is where the guild and AAUP comparison ends. Though the AAUP thought of scholars as artisans, it also saw them as individuals, a good bit different from guild members. Furthermore, the AAUP was not an activist or protectionist institution, but more an idealistic, philosophical association to give voice to intellectual tolerance and integrity. It was not the dismissal of individual professors the AAUP originally hoped to prohibit, but that the removal of scholars, when it is done, be done for proper reasons.

From its inception the AAUP advocated and advertised the highest of academic-ivory-tower principles. Organizational hearings were held, and position papers were developed and published. But beyond verbal sanctions and reprimands, the AAUP failed to develop any real power. Over the years, though a handful of individual members would become activists, when practical push came to shove, the AAUP did not push back. It complained and "censured" in a sort of shame-on-you condescension—then went on about its business. Occasionally, it contacted politicians to advise them of the academy's views—according to the AAUP.

My first run-in with the AAUP's passive-aggressive attitudes and practices came several years after I arrived at BAC, when a colleague, a long time AAUP supporter, told me about an AAUP faculty at an Illinois college who protested a series of administrative abuses by not wearing mortarboards and tassels to graduation. I asked why the teachers had done that, and he replied, "Well, what else are you to do?"

In the beginning the AAUP was somewhat analogous to the American Medical Association (AMA) and the American Bar Association (ABA). If the professors "are the university," and scholars loosely assembled, each a well-schooled fiefdom, independent as many doctors and lawyers are today, the AAUP would not have needed to be more than a national watchdog with a political voice to influence the ethics of the membership. However, the AAUP is nothing at all like the AMA or the ABA.

Over the years, the AMA and ABA have organized their members into powerful political units while the AAUP progressed as an insular top-heavy administrative organization. Then, too, the AMA and ABA saw themselves as powerless and, therefore, needing to invest in politics and government. For their part, the AAUP believed that professors, through faculty governance, had power and to a large extent controlled the higher educational process and therefore controlled their individual colleges and universities. The belief was that as long as scholars who had come up through the ranks belonging to the AAUP populated college and university administrative offices, the AAUP would have a good bit of political clout. But as post-secondary educational institutions became the property of elected or appointed boards and imported corporate managers, and the dollars of student matriculation and product sales rather than research and learning became the primary focus of institutions of higher education, the AAUP found itself with no real power to protect or influence the scholar-teachers' professional welfare. The professors "as the university" belief seems to have dominated the early AAUP, even though by the time the AAUP was founded, faculty governance at American colleges and universities was already coming undone.

Moreover, the AMA and ABA had the advantage of recruiting prospective doctors and lawyers from the professional schools. By simply canvassing the highly academically selective rosters of schools of medicine and law one has at hand a list of candidates most likely to take up an AMA and ABA membership. The vast majority of those completing medical school will become practicing physicians who will be interested in the AMA. The vast majority of those completing law school will become practicing attorneys who can be served by the ABA. On the other hand, the vast majority of those receiving graduate degrees in history, psychology, philosophy, sociology, literature, mathematics, chemistry or physics, to mention only a few of the academic disciplines, are quite unlikely to become college or university professors, and so have little interest in the AAUP. Even as members of a group who saw themselves as an educated elite, college and university professors are academically heterogeneous and individual, and therefore not easily organized. More than that, guilds were, as the AMA and ABA are, mostly economic trade organizations, which the AAUP clearly is not.

In the end, the AAUP did not have the money to develop the political clout to take on the massive government run and subsidized public education corporations that pass as universities and colleges. And because of its lack of political clout, the AAUP acquiesced (in its unwillingness to actively confront college or university administrations) to the robber baron assumptions of the American nineteenth century that those who control the purse strings have the right to appoint or disappoint.

Then in the spring of 1967 the AAUP found itself moving in a new direction, nudged away from its traditional passivity by a small activist bubble on its outer fringe. On May 17, 1967 BTJC (the college would not be named Belleville Area College until August of 1968) Genevieve Snider placed a phone call to the national AAUP office to announce that the BTJC AAUP Salary Committee had become a bargaining agent for the faculty.

When Genevieve Snider died, Hans P. Johnson wrote in "President of first AAUP collective bargaining chapter dies," (*Academe,* July-August 2000) of her historic call to the AAUP offices that day.

> Her campus colleagues remember her as an astute leader, a skilled professor of mathematics, and a steadfast presence on the picket line. But in AAUP lore, Genevieve Snider of Belleville Area College in Illinois may best be remembered as the woman who made a fateful phone call.
>
> In 1967 Snider found herself in the awkward role of informing the Association's national office that the local AAUP chapter had become the collective bargaining agent for faculty at her campus. Then a four-year member of the Association and president of the local chapter, Snider anticipated that the news of the landslide vote would engender some scowls. She did not expect to be told that she was, in the less-than-elated assessment of national officers, a pioneer. On the occasion of Snider's death on March 31 (2000) at age 84, colleagues recalled her years of leadership, which included organizing what unwittingly became the first AAUP collective bargaining chapter.
>
> "This was before we had any set policies on unionization," recalls Bertram Davis, who was the (national) AAUP's general secretary in 1967. 'My attitude was that we should let the chapter do it, but at the time there were strong opinions on both sides.' The vote by Snider and her colleagues came up years before the Association formally entered the world of faculty unions with its

Statement on Collective Bargaining in 1973. "In some ways," says Davis, "the Belleville chapter's headlong decision made it easier for us to make that transition because it was a fait accompli."

AAUP president at the time, Clark Byse, wrote, "Thus, did collective bargaining come to the AAUP in Belleville, Illinois, without the knowledge, encouragement or consent of the General Secretary or the officers or Council of the AAUP. Indeed, had a request been made to the General Secretary, I know not what the answer would have been." Byse later said, "I cannot say I am displeased with the development."

However, sanguine as these remembrances are, the national unionization of the AAUP did not come easily. Even after 1967, the AAUP's "1973 Statement on Collective Bargaining," and increasing numbers of AAUP chapters following BTJC's pioneering move to establish individual chapters as collective bargaining units, the national AAUP continued to lurk and sulk furtively at the edges of the union campsite.

It's not that the AAUP's principles were not well thought out. They were and are—sometimes, beautifully and accurately so. And many of the rules derived from AAUP principles are substantive. But ideas alone do not bring change, and position papers require more than an authority, no matter how revered and esteemed, sitting in a cluttered office somewhere claiming, that's the way it is supposed to be.

In 1967, the AAUP was turned, if ever so slightly, toward the union movement, and eventually, following the establishment of the first AAUP-AFT local union, Local 4183 at BAC in 1982, because so many AAUP chapters followed the BAC example and took up collective bargaining, in 2007 the National Labor Relations Board (NLRB) notified the AAUP that it was required to register as a union.

Interestingly, the NLRB edict came at a time when increasing numbers of voices inside the AAUP were questioning the ethics of a vocally principled professorate sidestepping activism, in a reworking of "Do as I say, but don't expect me to do anything."

Haves and Have-nots

Although the original BTJC faculty used its AAUP chapter for bargaining, and it could be argued that the Salary Committee was a remnant of BTHS Local 434 bargaining unit brought to the college by the AAUP faculty who were also AFT members, in other matters the college and its faculty took on a decidedly more secondary school visage. Haberaecker said in 1969, ". . . the college began operation under the policies of 'higher education.' Before that it was governed by the policies of the Common School Code as applied to high schools. When it became a Class I College it had two choices—either to 'throw away' everything of the past and set up new rules under higher education, or to gradually move from a secondary school operation to a higher education operation." He said he believed the "faculty would be much happier with the system of gradual change."

Happier with the secondary model, I might add, as was Mr. Haberaecker, since the new BTJC board had no experience with educational institutions, and Haberaecker had none with institutions of higher education.

As Haberaecker said, he and the board found it easier, more convenient, to align themselves with practices and procedures already in place, though distinctly secondary. But it is precisely at this juncture the board and its administration turned away from its obligation to create a college. This split—on one hand of referring to itself as a college, and in some ways behaving like a college, while on the other hand emulating secondary school practices and procedures—would be a defining practice at BTJC-BAC.

* * * * *

Though Haberaecker claimed to have had the high school model in mind for the faculty, clearly, he still thought of himself as something more than a high school principal. One of the more amusing anecdotes involving his assessment of his position as a college president came from the first board meeting. During the meeting Haberaecker was seated next to Norman Nold, the newly appointed board attorney, who a few years before had come out of the St. Clair County State's Attorney's Office. Sometime before the meeting began, Haberaecker leaned over and said to Nold, "Welcome to the big time." Without even looking at Haberaecker, Nold nodded and replied, "If you want to talk about the 'big time,' H. J., keep in mind that last year I paid more in income tax than you made."

I'm not sure what Haberaecker meant by "the big time," though it seems obvious what Nold was thinking.

* * * * *

The newly elected (1967) BAC board members were, as noted previously, men and women closely related to business who thought of themselves as community leaders. Quite expectedly the statements the candidates gave the newspaper prior to the election were laced with an authoritative pretense of their qualifications to serve on a board of an institution of higher education.

It is not uncommon for politicians to estimate their personal merit or value or abilities in terms of the money they have made or inherited, and to carry these attitudes into elected office. At the heart of the American system, democracy has come to mean the right to make a corporate profit—and citizenship has come to mean the pursuit of dollars and to consume. So, even though they are enfranchised by a democratic electorate, boards of education often view institutions they are elected to serve as private ventures that should be self-sustaining or making money—or at least should operate on the smallest expenditure of money possible, with an intention of showing a profit next year.

Otherwise, boards of education are necessarily hierarchical and feudal—and dictatorial—and school board members with business backgrounds are wont to view teachers, including college faculty, not as the educational officers they are, say, as lawyers are officers of the court, but as clerks, hired hands, or factory workers—to be treated summarily as businesses most often treat their workers. Over the years these kinds of board attitudes, and the practices the attitudes inform, have become the bane of public education in the United States.

* * * * *

In keeping with the times and the American capitalist ideology, the newly elected 1967 BAC board, without other traditions to guide it, quickly adopted the mantra of business, a policy described by the AFT in "Governance of Higher Education (2002)," by which "shared governance in college and universities would eventually be under attack by (1) outsourcing of instruction (2) redirecting teaching to part-time and temporary instructors, particularly (but not limited to) learning technology (3) re-orienting curriculum to business oriented coursework."

I do not want to underestimate the difficulty of setting up a new college and its faculty contract, especially by people who have no practical experience with operating a college. Not only is it difficult to anticipate what might best serve the faculty's academic mission, and then the students' educational pursuits, since the raison d'être of a school is to bring faculty and students together, but once the academic and educational missions are identified, it is many times difficult to get an agreement within the administration and board on what needs to be done to honor that mission, and how to do it.

Moreover, there are always faculty members who have little interest in the faculty's academic mission and attempt to derail or at least sidetrack programs for their personal benefit—not to mention administration or board members who believe they must control the faculty to insure the faculty remains subservient.

In keeping with the business mantra, from 1967 until the early '90s, the BAC board and administration adhered tenaciously to the fiction of faculty as hired-help. In communication with the faculty, within the faculty contract, as well as in general terms of daily commerce, the administration demanded that faculty members not refer to or reference themselves as professors. The faculty members were addressed always as instructors or teachers, but not professors.

By the middle of the twentieth century in American grade and high school systems nationwide, the appellation "teacher" had come to mean a subservient and necessarily obeisant individual contracted for whatever purposes an administration deemed necessary, which too often had little or nothing to do with teaching. At BAC "teacher" and "instructor" designations were applied by the board and administration to enforce the board's contention that faculty members were day-laborers, and that the class-rooms and the labs were factory assembly lines attended by these day-laborers. It was well understood that the term "professor" would have given teachers, instructors, an advanced psychological-social-educational pres-tige, as well as a dollar and cents claim, that the board did not want to recognize.

These attempts to demean and dislocate the faculty were, however, not isolated to BAC, later SWIC, or community colleges in general. Even in more prestigious four-year higher education institutions, in keeping with the college or university as corporation, boards and administrations, intending to rid the schools of anti-corporation values-based instruction have taken to denigrating and maligning faculty and purging the schools where they can of those who do not buckle under.

Joan Wallach Scott, Harold F. Linder Professor of Social Science at the Institute for Advanced Study, tells us in "The Critical State of Shared Governance," the AAUP's first annual Neil Rappaport Lecture (2001) that

> . . . with what has come to be called the corporate model of university administration, a model that treats educational institutions as businesses and applies managerial techniques geared to profit making, to institutions whose mission is the provision of service, and a special kind of service at that . . . governing boards of colleges and universities mean to encroach on long standing faculty prerogatives. At the University of Minnesota, the regents called for a revision of the tenure code with no consultation with professors until faculty protests (and an intense unionization drive) forced it. At the University of Iowa, the board began to restructure courses and teaching loads without faculty participation. At James Madison University, a new member of the board, a follower of the Christian Coalition, announced his intention to go through the catalog course by course and weed out all the courses that "have no place on our campus."

* * * * *

If in some ways the BTJC high school-college split was advantageous, in others it was unfortunate. The university practice, since universities are by nature Medieval institutions, is to have "masters" or "doctors" arranged in a general academic pyramid of professor, associate professor, assistant professor, lecturer, and instructor, squinting into the rising sun of their individual interests, sometimes collecting reasonable salaries, while farming out less interesting work to "apprentice" grad students who teach a class or two and are paid substantially less for their labors. One's position in the pyramid determines salary and perks and power. Secondary schools, however, tend to be more egalitarian, both in pay and working conditions, staffing their needs mostly with fulltime faculty.

Although at the time the big push in the junior college movement in the United States and in Illinois had only just begun, the BTJC administration in 1967 probably looked around to see what other junior colleges were doing. And though the Haberaecker administration followed the secondary school practice of filling all daytime (7:30 a.m.-4:30 p.m.) academic assignments with fulltime faculty, BTJC evening classes were outsourced individually and paid for on a reduced formula, by the hour, with the part-time faculty who served without a collective-contract designated as employees-at-will or factory workers. At the same time fulltime faculty overloads, extra classes, work that in the unionized industrial world is salaried at time-and-a-half or double-time pay, was to be compensated on a seriously reduced pay-scale. In 1967 the BTJC-AAUP agreed by contract to both arrangements.

In addition to outsourcing evening classes, the BTJC-AAUP also agreed to reduced pay or "science-lab equations" for fulltime faculty. In universities, especially in the lab sciences, professors give lectures and grad students handle labs. Jonathan Sterne writes in *Bad Subjects* (Issue #29, November 1996), "Strike! The labor theory of graduate school" that "At the University of Illinois, graduate employees teach more than 40% of all lower division undergraduate courses and run the majority of research laboratories on campus." In high schools the same instructor usually handles both the classroom and the lab, if there is a lab.

At BTJC in 1967 the board and the faculty agreed to the fiction that lab instruction is somehow different from classroom instruction, and lab instructors are somehow not the same as instructors who give lectures, even if they are the same persons. This redefined professors in labs as a kind of custodial personnel who, since they are not lecturing, should be paid less for the education and expertise they bring to the lab. For assignment and pay purposes, BTJC lab hours in the physical sciences, as well as in nursing, were equated at less than one hour of lecture.

And although the public four-year college teaching load is usually no more than twelve hours a week, the 1967 BTJC faculty and board installed a secondary school load of five classes, a fifteen-hour instructtional week, plus ten office hours, along with whatever committee hours and student counseling were necessary.

More than likely, the 1967 BTJC-AAUP concession on lab equations was to avoid the high school practice of employing enough fulltime teachers to cover all instructional hours (for which the board did not want to pay) while handling labs without grad students. But the fact remains that paying fulltime faculty less for lab instruction reduced compensation for academic expertise, and further added to defining salaried faculty as factory workers.

Other schools handled the problem differently, and with better results. In 1966, when the Cook County College Teachers Union (CCCTU), Local 1600, AFT-IFT was formed, moving the college faculty away from the high school union that had served it until then, one of the first items negotiated eliminated the science-lab formula and contracted lab instruction at 1:1—as it was with lectures.

* * * * *

By the middle '60s an American high school diploma was no longer enough to advance one's future—and postsecondary education and training and their formal printed documents as proof thereof were more and more becoming necessities for financial upward mobility. College certificates and/or diplomas came to be seen as a property right, a *need,* without which one could not live a good life.

In Americana-think, democracy has come to mean that everyone is a winner and winners all deserve the same privileges—not merely the opportunity for an education, but the education itself, whether one is willing to work for it or not. This, of course, invokes the academic quality-quantity conundrum. In the continuing corporatization of institutions of postsecondary education, operated by administrators who are more than willing to satisfy their customers with a new, though significantly watered-down product, the dichotomy is seldom openly or honestly broached. As a result, instead of "college educated" referring to one proficient at intellectual and/or academic tasks and ultimately a master's or doctorate through diligent and prolonged study, a college education has become a piece of paper (diploma or degree or certificate) granted to whomever might show up, pay the requisite fee, and, for a short time, tolerate some small instruction, especially if it is mundane and innocuous.

* * * * *

Literacy, and how best to bring students to it, has plagued the American education system from the beginning. American K-12 schools and public universities and colleges have not been very enthusiastic about teaching writing, about bringing students in from the dim recesses of the unschooled to the bright halls of the well-phrased and literate, though not necessarily literary.

Traditionally, public college and university English departments have split the instruction of writing and literature–both by assignment and staffing. Lower division students (freshmen and sophomores) are instructed by grad students in the practicality of mechanics and grammar. Upper division students (juniors and seniors) are taught by professors and are expected to be a good bit more academic and literary, although few of them will ever write about literature or write anything literary. Robert Scholes writes in *The Rise and Fall of English* (1999), that "teachers of literature [are] the priests and theologians of English, while teachers of composition [are] the nuns, barred from the priesthood, doing the shitwork of the field."

Moreover, at the time BTJC established an independent district and set up shop as a Class I junior college, beginning in the mid-60s and accelerating throughout the '70s, the United States experienced a substantial decline in literacy. Cohen and Brawer in *The American Community College* (2002) state that illiteracy was exacerbated when:

> ... numerous events came together: the coming of age of the first generation reared on television, a breakdown in respect for authority and the professions, a pervasive attitude that the written word is not as important as it once was, the imposition of various other-than-academic expectations on the public schools, the increasing numbers of students whose native language is other than English, and a decline in academic requirements and expectations at all levels of schooling.

In 1967 the BAC board and its administration, as well as the faculty, seem not to have been at all clear about any of this. The civil rights demonstrations and marches, the Vietnam War unrest, and the corporate attack on postsecondary education at the time all seriously clouded the educational-social landscape. Equally, there was a great deal of student-as-victim nonsense afoot in educational institutions generally. If professors demanded that they learn, students howled that they were being browbeaten and victimized by unreasonable old white men. If they were given the grade they wanted without any demands and matriculated only to find that they did not have the academic skills to move on to the next level, they howled that they had been victimized. All of this came from students' newly claimed privilege demanding that they had a right to decide what they would learn and "a right to their own language." And, of course, what many wanted was to avoid reading and writing and "to learn" without becoming literate.

* * * * *

Still, at BAC in 1967, one of the exceptions to the basic five-class faculty teaching load negotiated by the AAUP Salary Committee was the English department's paper-weighted classes. In an attempt to address the problem of handling college writing instruction without graduate students to do the work, writing classes were equated at 1.3.

The arithmetic in writing classes is simple. Even with only four classes at twenty-five students, there are 100 students and ten papers of four pages each or four thousand pages of script per class to read and mark each semester. This should be the minimum number of pages of writing per college freshman per semester that needs to be scored and evaluated. Again, universities deal these classes off to graduate students who usually teach no more than one or, at the most, two classes. Private colleges usually do not have writing courses per se but include writing in the curriculum generally with instructors or professors teaching only two or three classes—and many times with small classes.

This meant that because of the writing paper-load, equating writing classes with the 1.3 formula, BAC English teachers were contracted to teach only four three-hour classes a semester. Also, again, because of the amount of work required to get a student through a semester of ten to twelve four-page papers, the contract limited the number of students assigned to regular writing classes to twenty-five, and to remedial writing classes to twenty.

It might be worth noting here that the contract stipulations equating lab hours as less than "one instructional hour" and limiting lab enrollment to "the number of stations available," did not address the problem of lab instructors' paper-load, which often exceeds 100 pages per student of lab manuals each semester, that must be read and scored.

Otherwise, BTJC did not require "writing across the curriculum" and, as far as I know, the administration did little to encourage it. It is not a money-making item—although channeling huge numbers of students into non-transferable remedial courses was and is. As in most community colleges, assigning papers in classes, other than Rhetoric and Composition 101 and 102, has been left to the discretion of the individual instructor. And as it stands, most junior college instructors outside of English departments do not require much written work from their students. Very few classes have essay or written exams. Most teachers use multiple-choice or true-false tests that can be quickly hand marked or scored with electronic devices. This leaves the Rhetoric and Composition 101 and 102 teachers alone to provide a writing-instruction blanket for the school.

Despite the need for writing instruction at the heart of the college educational process, many of the BTJC non-AAUP faculty saw the reduced load the AAUP Salary Committee had negotiated for writing class teachers as preferential treatment, especially since three of the five members of the original AAUP Salary Committee were from the English department. Those teaching classes that required neither lab reports nor extensive writing were some of the more vocal critics of the writing-teaching formula—

though not of the lab formulas. One day, when I reminded a complaining colleague why English writing instructors were teaching four classes instead of five, he stated, "That's their problem. It goes with the territory, and they knew that when they became English teachers. I shouldn't be penalized for it." When I asked how he was being penalized by someone else receiving reasonable compensation for what he/she was doing, he turned and walked away.

It seems obvious that early BTJC faculty contracts were robbing Peter to pay Paul with a reduced payrate for science-lab instruction to offset the cost of a reduced schedule of classes for writing instructors.

* * * * *

In 1967 the BTJC fulltime faculty used the AAUP chapter to develop the *Faculty Personnel Procedures* which contained a basic outline for faculty relations with the board. The document the Salary Committee, led by Jan Milligan, who had been on the Belleville High School salary committees, signed off on included a tiered salary scale based on longevity and degrees held. This was more akin to high school compensation categories and practices than to those generally used in colleges and universities.

Within the rubrics of the tiered pay-scale faculty coming in from the high school, with their years of experience, and as friends of the administration, were placed well up the compensation ladder. This, of course, fueled administrative salaries, since administrators (the elite power brokers) were assigning salaries and were not about to pay themselves less than the teachers. Additionally, the tiered scale gave administrators the possibility of saving money for themselves and their friends on the faculty by paying newly appointed teachers absurdly anemic salaries—salaries that advanced only marginally from year to year and by which the late arrivals could and would be exploited for years to come.

To add to the compensation inequities in the original tiered scale, in the 1969 negotiations the board offered a yearly salary increment that advanced the pay of those at the bottom of the scale only by half of what those at the top received. This was, to say the least, problematic and caused a great deal of discord among the faculty. Additionally, pay for teaching extra (overload) classes was not a fixed or flat rate, but derived from a formula based on the graduate steps of the tiered pay scale. Simply put, those at the top received more.

During my first year at BAC (1972-73) there were only a handful of English classes taught in the summer. Jan Milligan had the department chair, and though most of the English faculty did not want to work during the summer, what few classes there were she divvied up among herself and her friends—the senior members of the department. The irony of this is that the first BAC faculty contract with the board in 1968-69 contained a clause stating that ". . . preference for summer classes to be given to junior members of the department."

A year earlier I had worked at the River King Mine in Freeburg. The practice in mines unionized by the United Mine Workers was to assign extra work through a "turn-sheet." The following fall I raised a stink about the summer assignments and ended up on a committee (stacked) with English faculty members Gerald Taylor and Darrel Kohlmiller to set up a schema for assigning summer school classes. I pointed out that because of the tiered salary schedule and overload formula, sometimes on a single class on the same subject, senior members were compensated two or three times greater than a junior member. Equity alone would require that summer teaching not be assigned by class, but by the remuneration each teacher would receive for whatever summer assignments he or she might be given. Assigning summer classes on a class count basis to the senior members of the department only exacerbated the already absurd salary disparity. The idea of equity was not popular with the older faculty, however, and my suggestion did not receive much of a hearing, though the following summer we did end up with a turn-sheet for summer school assignments.

* * * * *

From 1968 until 1977 the BAC faculty worked under a series of one-year contracts. Mostly these agreements advanced salaries on the tiered scale by percentage, so each year junior faculty (at the bottom of the scale) received a smaller raise than did the senior faculty. On the degree-completed side of the equation in the BAC *Memorandum of Understanding*, from 1968 to 1999, the low end of the pay cale, the bottom entry, "Below Master" increased from 6,400 to 34,381 dollars or 27,981 dollars. On the high end, "PhD," the top advanced from 13,600 to 65,543 dollars or 51,943 dollars. Again, I have not seen research to suggest senior, more experienced faculty are better at instruction or that their students advance academically beyond those instructed by junior, less experienced faculty.

Moreover, longevity pay opened faculty compensation to criticism from those sponsoring the myths of privatization and merit pay. Granted, some teachers are more effective at classroom instruction than others. And, granted, some teachers are better at teaching some subjects than they might be at teaching others. But, as Cohen and Brawer relate in *The American Community College* (2004), "Teaching as a profession has not developed to the point at which proper conduct in the instructional process can be defined and enforced in the face of individual deviation." It is never clear who is to deserve and receive merit pay and why. A classroom filled with As is far less likely to be a portrait of a good teacher than a classroom filled with Ds and Fs is to be a portrait of a bad one.

Common sense would dictate that if everyone is doing the same job, then everyone should receive the same pay. If they are not doing the same job, then one should delineate clearly what it is and in what ways they differ and for what, exactly, they are to be paid.

Beyond the longevity problems with the pay-scale, the practice at BAC of picking and choosing for placement of incoming teachers on a tiered salary schedule caused even more animosity and division among the faculty. Too often, after securing a teaching position at BAC, a teacher would discover that another teacher appointed the same year, a teacher, let's say, with less experience and a questionable degree, but a friend of the administrators in charge of faculty selection, had been placed several notches higher on the salary scale. This inequitable practice resulted in at least one lawsuit—and probably should have produced more than that.

At the outset the AAUP Salary Committee might have negotiated the same wage for all faculty members, using a dollar paid for an instructional hour provided, instead of tying the pay-scale to years on the job or advanced degrees, without attempting to determine which degree or which teacher is more valuable. Future negotiations could then have advanced wages, using either a percentage or a given dollar amount, since they would have been the same, and new appointees could have been brought in at the same pay as those already there.

During the '70s, '80s, and '90s at the negotiating table, I always tried to encourage across-the-board raises, by which everyone would receive the same dollar increase in each year of the new contract. Since most of those I was dealing with were faculty elder statesmen, as well as friends of the administration, I did not often get any support for this position.

On the other side of the coin, although it hasn't yet happened, it is probably only a matter of time until, following a negotiated percentage raise on a tiered compensation scale, someone at the bottom of the scale who received less money will take a union to court for violating its duty to fair representation.

* * * * *

Quite admirably, in August of 1968, the same month the school officially became BAC, the board included in the contract what is probably the most valuable section of any college faculty contract "The Right to Academic Freedom." A committee of the Faculty Senate, the administration, staff, and the board agreed on a tenure and academic freedom policy that replicated the AAUP's "1940 Statement of Principles on Academic Freedom and Tenure."

In 1968 the tenure and academic freedom documents were only indirectly alluded to in the *Faculty Personnel Procedures* (which would become the *Memorandum of Understanding*). The AAUP "1940 Statement of Principles" was incorporated into board policy and was monitored by the

Faculty Senate Committee on Tenure, Retirement, and Academic Freedom, which by way of the Faculty Senate, was functioning as a board committee. In 1980, when board policy had to be brought in line with the new Illinois Community College Tenured Teacher Act, the board dropped the AAUP "1940 Statement" which included academic freedom. Later, in 1992, the union encouraged it back into the Board Policy Manual and then negotiated it into the *Memorandum of Understanding.*

In 1968, beyond the grand general tenets, as with salary, what was negotiated into the *Memorandum* was so heavily weighted in favor of the administration and senior faculty who were friendly with the administration, that the contract had the flavor of a company-union document. This was true even before the board and administration started pushing "productivity" and "team concept" to further impair faculty working conditions and salary.

A good example of senior faculty members' collusion with their friends in the administration appeared in contract stipulations, which also severely limited faculty governance, giving the administration the right of approval for faculty selections of academic department heads. This was entered in the contract to protect the older faculty who showed up year after year as department heads. If for some reason a department decided on a new candidate, it gave the administration veto power on the candidate. Imagine, for a moment, that for whatever reason, department XXX chose Madame New over Madame Elder, Madame Elder's friends in the administration could simple deny Madame New's appointment and hold out for Madame Elder. Without the support of a union or stringent contract stipulation, with the Elder half of the faculty and administration on one side and the New contingent, more than likely some of them non-tenured, on the other side, the case would be decided before it began.

Of course, this would come back to haunt us in 1980 when the Wissore administration chose to replace the older faculty with its own, newer friends, and refused to seat any department head that it did not agree with, regardless, and claimed that it was well within the contract, which it was.

A rather poignant example of the have and have-not riff from the early '70s demonstrating how thoroughly the faculty was divided involved one of the more obstreperous haves, Roger Crane, of the English department, who was in trouble much of the time with everyone outside his coterie.

I was never sure, and to this day do not know, how Crane ended up in the English department. Rumor had it he had been a psychology teacher assigned to social sciences and caused enough trouble there that he was set free in the hall for whomever would take him. Apparently, Jan Milligan, one of Crane's friends and a perennial chair of the English department those years, added him to the department roster.

At any rate, he was there in 1971. And, though I was never the target of Crane's attacks, so oppressive and disruptive was his habit of using department meetings to malign and verbally abuse those he did not like, that a year or so after joining the department I sent a memo to the chair informing her that until she got Crane under control, I would no longer attend department meetings.

During the spring of 1971, in a brouhaha worthy of a soap opera, Crane got in a seamy little chest-thumping-shouting match with the Student Senate and Student Senate President Mark Kroenig over what Crane deemed to be Kroenig's misdeeds for objecting to Crane's sleight-of-hand with several hundred dollars collected from a student theatrical production financed by the Student Senate.

It seems the Student Senate had put up 200 dollars to fund a BAC theatrical production to be given at BAC, one performance, one night on one stage. After the initial performance, as faculty sponsor for the event, Crane took the show on the road to four or five local K-12 schools, charging them fifty dollars a performance, which Kroenig and the Student Senate claimed Crane had pocketed. They objected and demanded their money back. Eventually Crane filed a grievance with the Faculty Senate asking it to censure Kroenig.

The content and texture of the disagreement was mostly petty and meaningless. What is meaningful and more interesting, is that when the matter came to a vote, the lines of demarcation among the faculty were clearly drawn. The censure motion was made to the Faculty Senate, May 21, 1971, and by roll call vote, the haves, William Saunders, D. C. Edwards, Jan Milligan, Gene Masek (English), and Elizabeth Oelrich (Business), voted for censure. Charles Pruitt (Mathematics) voted "Present." The have-nots —Vito Benivegna (Spanish), Bobby Poe (Psychology), Richard Melinder (Biology), and Jack Haskell (History)—voted against censure. Except for Oelrich, those voting for censure and/or as "Present" on that 1971 occasion would, nine years later in 1980, honor the faculty strike, and those voting against censure, plus Oelrich who was about to retire, did not. By then Crane had died.

This adversarial grouping of have and have-not, and the influence the haves had on the BAC Board of Trustees in forming the *Memorandum of Understanding,* even beyond lab and writing class equations and the tiered pay scale, made it a lopsided and difficult instrument to defend. Much later (1992), during the Joe Cipfl administration, the union would set out to clean up, much to the faculty's advantage, what Cipfl called a "preposterous, ill-composed document." The downside of it all is that during the first years, the *Memorandum,* which should have united and protected the faculty, did neither.

* * * * *

In some ways these internecine struggles were understandable, especially in a recently established college that had evolved from a high school. Secondary school settings often nurture an informal faculty-administrator intimacy of favor and privilege. Case in point, in the fall of 1946 the Superintendent of District 201, to which BJC was attached, appointed a committee of three administrators, three federation (AFT Local 424) faculty, one non-federation faculty and one faculty member to represent the teachers who had less than two years-experience (presumably non-tenured teachers), to discuss and propose faculty salaries for the following year. Although this kind of committee formation seems also to have been common in other secondary schools at the time, I have not often heard of a college administration appointing a committee composed of three administrators and five faculty members, even if it is only for discussion—unless the faculty members are thought of by the administration as administration-friendly.

The *BND* recounts that in 1946, the college's first year, "BTHS-JC [Belleville Township High School-Junior College] Teachers Ask Closer Ties with Board." The article states that "Local 434 of the AFT, which claims to represent a majority of the teachers at Belleville Township High School's two campuses and the BJC, last night asked the board of education for 'closer relations' with the faculty, particularly at the time when the contract expires.

"The teachers did not request formal recognition of the local as the sole bargaining agency."

Clearly the teachers did not see themselves as separate from the administration—nor did they want the administration and the board, which the teachers thought of as "friendly," to regard them that way.

Twenty years after BJC's founding, in its first year of operation as a Class I Junior College (1967), the BJC board also seemed more benevolent and congenial than confrontational. Shortly after taking office the board recognized the AAUP Salary Committee and agreed to procedures for the instructional part of the school based on AAUP guidelines, neither of which it had to do. It seems obvious that the board did not think of the AAUP as an adversary or as a unit that could or would oppose the board, but as a committee over which it had dominion.

Faculty Senate

In the model proposed by the AAUP, used to set up shop at BJC in 1967, no one item appeared more central to faculty interests than shared governance—and the enabling faculty body at the center of shared governance in the AAUP model is the Faculty Senate. Though the board recognized the AAUP Salary Committee as the official committee with which to discuss and establish faculty salaries, there was a host of working conditions, such as grievances, department and division assignments, and curriculum that fell beyond the scope of the Salary Committee. Previously these matters had been worked out by the faculty with the District 201 high school board in discussion and by mutual agreement, and usually with a measure of goodwill—while accommodating State laws and regulations that were, over the years, slowly falling into place.

Within the first six months of 1967, the BJC Faculty Senate was designated and sanctioned by the board as a faculty-populated board committee to represent the faculty's piece of the shared-governance pie and to advise the BJC administration and board. As a matter of regular business, in October of 1967, by a rollcall vote, the board unanimously ratified the members and officers of a Faculty Senate that had been elected by the faculty.

The Faculty Senate, those first years, established and harbored fifteen committees. These included: Administrative Council; Admissions, Records, Grading and Graduation Standards; College Development; Committee on Committees; Courtesy; Curriculum and Instruction; Extra Curricular Reimbursement; Handbook; Legislation; Nominations and Elections; and Tenure, Retirement and Academic Freedom, as well as Curriculum and Instruction subcommittees on Philosophy; Function and Objectives; Procedures for Changing, Revising and Developing Curriculum; College Catalogue; and Instructor and/or Course Rating.

To get an idea of faculty involvement in problem solving one has only to look at the board faculty-grievance procedure. As stated in the 1967 *Faculty Personnel Procedures,* a grievance was first to be sent to the department head, and if not resolved there, on to the Faculty Senate, to the College President, back to the Faculty Senate, and only then, if not resolved, to the Board of Trustees.

Early on, Faculty Senate minutes contained numerous references to administrative and board compliance and munificence. On January 5, 1968 at a Faculty Senate meeting, President Haberaecker announced "The architect will be present to hear faculty suggestions (for the new building) on Wednesday, January 10, 1968, from 9 a.m. to 12 p.m." Five months later, May 14, 1968, with a good bit of congeniality "The Senate expressed its gratitude for the work done by the Salary Committee, Mr. Haberaecker, Mr. Stumph, Mrs. Milligan, and the board, in the recent salary negotiations."

As noted earlier, during the early BAC years the AAUP Chapter and the Faculty Senate had quasi-interlocking directorates. The same names appeared year after year, alternately at the helm of one or of the other organization. The AAUP represented the faculty in establishing salaries, but because it was house bound, and Illinois did not yet have a collective bargaining law for educational employees, the BAC-AAUP, like the Faculty Senate, was in reality little more than a debating society, a miniature House of Lords, in friendly and close touch with the administration, otherwise noisy, but still, in whatever influence it might bring to bear, dependent on the benevolence of the board.

From 1967 to 1969, at least from the board's point of view, there was very little board-administration-faculty disagreement, and therefore no reason to be recalcitrant, belligerent, or oppressive. It is also easy to imagine that the administration saw the AAUP faculty as a small clique of people who could con the remainder of a docile bunch of teachers into whatever they (either the administration and/or the AAUP) wanted and could then easily be bought off with a hand full of dollars and a few personal perks—giving over the governance of the college to the board and administration.

However, the growing voc-ed program agendas had not yet developed, and no one had gotten around to discussing how limited educational monies would be prioritized, allocated, and dispersed. In other words, the board-faculty intimacy at that time was still filial and paternal.

* * * * *

As sanguine as it may have been in the beginning, the BAC faculty-board honeymoon was short-lived. In the summer of 1969 a skirmish broke out over salary plans for the coming year. By then the administration was up and running full-tilt, scrambling and falling over itself to set up vocational programs.

The idea of "community" in the community-college concept has gone a good bit beyond the historical sense of "town and gown," whereby colleges and universities attempt to keep relations at least congenial with the populace of the towns they inhabit. So pervasive was this that the Illinois General Assembly changed the term "junior college" to "community college" by statute, though one college (Joliet Junior College) in the Illinois system, for historical reasons, has retained the term "junior" in its name. But because of the focus on the community side of the ledger, community colleges came sometimes to look more like YMCAs than colleges. And then again, sometimes they look more like employment agencies than YMCAs.

During the 1966 campaign to establish the college, there had been community steering committees that literally guided the ratification of the formation of District 522. Aware of the role the community had in establishing the school, the first board set up numerous citizens' committees to give advice on new programs, as well as on other issues. Of course, each group had its pet pig. And unfortunately, by 1969, the board was reacting more to what the Chamber of Commerce wanted in the way of vocational programs than it was to good educational sense. In other words, it was politics as usual. The board, composed mostly of businessmen, was familiar with what the junior college business community wanted, or at least what it thought the community needed, that is, trained workers. Additionally, citizens' committees provided the board the readily available public relations conduit of what the board is doing for the community—so much so that town and gown became TOWN and gown.

And while the voc-ed or career programs were advantageous for some students, and certainly for some of the area's businesses, in their scramble to solicit and appease the local Chamber of Commerce, the board, and the administration lost track of the baccalaureate faculty.

Of course, the majority of fulltime faculty in 1969 was in the baccalaureate division and wanted to set educational standards and to run its part of the scholastic operation in an educationally viable way. In history and practice the baccalaureate classes and credits that would transfer to four-year institutions was well established, so the board had little to say about that part of the equation. But as the board and administration focused more and more on turning the school into an employment agency to supply local businesses with secretaries, food management personnel, and welding and air-conditioning specialists, they soon came to see the baccalaureate (mathematics, science, and the arts and humanities) faculties' attempts at governance as a nuisance. The 1967 school yearbook, under the heading "This year, history is made as JC goes Class I" announced that:

> In accordance with the laws accompanying a Class I status, plans were begun to increase the technological program to encompass a minimum of 15-percent of the curriculum. In consultation with local Chambers of Commerce and manufacturing concerns, courses will be designed to meet the needs of the industrial community and prepare students to assume positions in the Metro-East area.

That was in the beginning. But by 1969, what began for the board as a minor irritation with the baccalaureate faculty (just for being there) became, in the board's view, a direct affront to its privilege and power. In the years to come the board's irritation with the baccalaureate faculty, and the Faculty Senate with its idea of shared governance, would harden into stiff opposition to shared governance and advance hand-in-hand with the ongoing corporatization of the college.

Of course, beyond governance there was the question of money. The funds to set up voc-ed programs, some that were questionable, such as horseshoeing and flight attendant training, had to come from somewhere —which usually meant from the education fund out of which the faculty was paid. The obsession with new voc-ed programs came under a Haberaecker rubric that occupational programs were mandated by the state, which was true to a point, but not to the point he and the board attempted to justify.

So voracious was the board's appetite for occupational programs that as late as 1979 transfer faculty were speculating that the baccalaureate division would be shut down—even though at the time the American economy was shifting from hard industries of mines, farms, factories, and assembly lines to the service industries—though not to any specific service. Americans were becoming the paper-pushers of the world. More and more students, especially voc-ed students, needed to be educated for a working life or service career of reading, writing, and thinking, rather than for a single trade or occupation. During the late '60s and the '70s the emphasis on occupational programs at BAC was so intense that students commonly referred to the school as Save Mart Tech.

Then, too, those years the Illinois Community College Board (ICCB) offered higher credit hour remuneration for voc-ed courses than it did for baccalaureate courses. There were already rumblings from the larger four-year state schools that they no longer wanted to attend to baccalaureate program freshman and sophomores but wanted to push them off on to the community colleges.

In 1969 the BAC board, in its revenue-expense formula, was interested in more than just a higher credit hour reimbursement. It also expected the faculty to forgo pay increases.

The concept of 2500 Carlyle Road, Belleville, Illinois, BAC, as a college, was further complicated and demeaned by the inability of the citizens (and their board representatives) to understand what colleges have been, historically. There are various reasons for this misunderstanding. Unlike most colleges and universities, community colleges are generally backyard institutions (like the district high schools), financed in large part by real estate taxes (like the district high schools), and operated by local names and faces elected to the board (like the district high schools). Professors were thought of as high school teachers and expected, as high school teachers are, to subsidize schools by accepting inadequate salaries—schools the electorate willingly authorizes but has not yet been willing to fund.

To meet the college's fulltime faculty needs, still adhering to the secondary school practice of filling positions with fulltime faculty, teachers were appointed at BAC each of the first few years, culminating in the fall of 1972. I say, "To meet the college's fulltime faculty needs." By 1972 the appointment of new or replacement fulltime faculty came, for the most part, to a halt. In 1972 I became the twenty-first member of the English-Philosophy Department at a time when BAC had only four thousand students. And, although enrollment would grow to sixteen thousand plus a few years down the road, I remained, until 1986, the junior member of the English-Philosophy Department. By then the department had shrunk to twelve fulltime members. Meanwhile, the administration ballooned, and the ranks of part-timer teachers continued to swell.

Rex Carr and the AAUP

> Unions have done more for humanity than
> any other organization of men that ever
> existed. They have done more for decency,
> for honesty, for education, for the better-
> ment of the race, for the developing of
> character in men, than any other associ-
> ation of men.
>
> —Clarence Darrow

The Faculty as a Distinct Unit

In January of 1969 the Board Finance Committee, represented by Vice President for Instruction Henry Milander and Dean of Business Services Wayne Stumph, and the AAUP Salary Committee, chaired by D. C. Edwards, entered into discussion about faculty salaries for the coming year. Stumph and Milander showed up claiming that expected revenues would be restricted that year and what money there was had to go into voc-ed pro- grams—a financial scenario that would allow for only minimal faculty raises.

I am not certain who examined the Finance Committee's claims. It was probably D. C. Edwards. Anyway, the Salary Committee disagreed with the Stumph-Milander financial forecast. The discussions continued for several months, and by May the disagreement between the two committees had reached impasse. To circumvent or override the discussions, Haberaecker gave the board a President's Recommendation for faculty salaries and for the *Faculty Personnel Procedures* for 1969-70.

According to board minutes (I quote extensively from the admirably detailed minutes kept and prepared by Board Secretary Lavette Groves- teen), following Haberaecker's presentation:

> Dr. D. C. Edwards, Chairman of the A.A.U.P. Salary Com-
> mittee, asked to speak. He said that the A.A.U.P. Committee
> has met with administrative personnel (Dr. Milander and Mr.
> Stumph) regarding a new salary schedule and faculty Per-
> sonnel Procedures, but the proposal presented cannot be
> considered a joint proposal since there is still disagreement
> on some matters. Since the Committee has not met with the
> Board, it feels that no negotiation has really taken place. The
> Committee feels that the Board should not act on the proposal
> until it has met with the A.A.U.P. Committee. The Committee,
> he said, is ready to discuss differences at whatever time is
> convenient.
>
> Chairman Lutz stated that the Board is anxious to get this
> matter settled, as it has had two men (Dr. Milander and Mr.

Stumph) meeting with the A.A.U.P. Committee since January. He suggested beginning the negotiations at this time, in this public meeting.

Mr. Hilgard moved, seconded by Mrs. Schroeder, to offer to the faculty the proposed salary schedule and Faculty Personnel Procedures for the 1969-70 fiscal year as described in the President's recommendation.

There was considerable discussion among the Board Members as to the wisdom of granting the proposed salary increases at the possible expense of the educational programs—particularly the occupational programs. Mr. Seibert began this discussion. Mrs. Schroeder agreed that the programs should not be curtailed. Besides curtailing the educational programs, other alternatives were mentioned by Mr. Bedel—increasing tuition or borrowing money, calling for a referendum, but he felt that these were not suitable answers to the problem.

Dr. Edwards then stated that the proposal had been presented to the faculty and they had rejected it.

Chairman Lutz called for a vote on the motion to offer the proposal [the President's Recommendation] to the faculty and it carried by . . . a unanimous vote on roll call.

Twelve days later, May 26, 1969, the board convened a Special Meeting ". . . for the purpose of publicly negotiating the Faculty Personnel Procedures for 1969-70." The AAUP Salary Committee, a duly appointed board committee, had met with another board committee, but not with the board itself, and the board and Haberaecker's failure to consult with the Salary Committee indicates that more than likely neither he nor the board understood board protocol or that both were remiss in ignoring board policy.

It also seems strange that the board would accept the Haberaecker proposal by a unanimous vote, then turn around and schedule a special meeting twelve days later to publicly negotiate what they had already accepted—unless their acceptance by vote meant only that board agreed to review what Haberaecker had presented, but had not yet decided to apply the President's Recommendation to faculty salaries. The budget for the President's Recommendation Haberaecker gave to the board included a 125-percent increase in administrative costs for the coming year.

When it became clear that the board would persist in its omission or nonfeasance, sometime before May 26 meeting, the AAUP Salary Committee (no doubt certified by the AAUP Executive Committee) took a most unusual, though thoroughly reasonable step, and retained East St. Louis attorney Rex Carr. At the May 26, 1969 Special Board Meeting Carr took over for the faculty.

That a Board of Trustees' committee would hire its own attorney was extraordinary. At that moment the Salary Committee became possibly the first duly appointed and sanctioned board of education committee in the history of American education to retain an attorney to represent it to the board that sanctioned it and to which it reported. This was truly turning water into wine. But it was at that juncture that the advisory Salary Committee mutated into a bargaining agent.

As the first order of business at the May 26, 1969 meeting, Board minutes report that

> Chairman Lutz addressed Dr. D. C. Edwards, Chairman of the Faculty Salary Committee. He said that at the last meeting the Board had asked the Faculty Salary committee to present their proposal in writing, and he was now inquiring if the Committee had anything to present at this time.
>
> Dr. Edwards introduced Dr. Alfred Sumberg, member of the national staff of the American Association of university Professors, and Mr. Rex Carr who has been employed as attorney for the faculty.
>
> Immediately Mr. Carr stated that he would respond to Mr. Lutz's remarks to Dr. Edwards since he is the faculty's attorney. He then announced that the present seating arrangement was not suitable for negotiating.

*****

Rex Carr graduated from the University of Illinois Law School in 1949. He served as editor of the law review and as class president. After graduation he returned to his hometown, East St. Louis, and prior to representing the BAC-AAUP, led a series of teachers' strikes in East St. Louis, for IFT Teachers Local 765, guiding it finally to a contract in 1968.

In the years following his stint as legal counsel to teachers' unions, as one of the more prominent trial attorneys in the United States, Carr would win eighteen injury-suit verdicts of at least one million dollars each. On three occasions his courtroom successes led to a listing in *The Guinness Book of World Records*. His first *Guinness* inclusion came in 1975 when he won a record 7.5 million-dollar verdict for a teenager injured in a swimming accident. Again, in 1981, *Guinness* listed Carr as the attorney of record for a 9 million-dollar verdict in the libel trial of *Green v Alton Telegraph*. Carr also conducted the longest trial on record—three years, eight months and seventeen days—ending in 1988 against Monsanto in which he won 16 million-dollars for 65 clients.

At the May twenty-sixth meeting, Carr did not ask the board for a negotiations meeting, but rather followed up on Lutz's suggestion to ". . . beginning negotiations at this time, in this public meeting." In "beginning negotiations at this time, in this public meeting," it is not clear what Lutz meant by "negotiations." Certainly, it didn't mean negotiations in the sense used in traditional labor relations or coincide with what Carr had in mind. Board minutes relate that almost as a reflex action, moments after Lutz' suggestion, the board again moved "to offer to the faculty the proposed salary schedule and Faculty Personnel Procedures for 1969-70 as described in the President's Recommendation."

There's good reason to believe that the paternalistic board's idea of "publicly negotiating" meant that within the Public Comments segment of the board meeting, Carr would be permitted to say what he had to say and the board would then say "Yes" or "No," and that would be that. When it wasn't, when Carr demanded that they set rules for negotiations and that the board respond in a manner more appropriate to negotiations, the board, to its last member, was incredulous, and then insulted.

Board minutes show that Rex Carr "proposed that the tables be arranged so that he and the salary committee could sit across from the board and discuss mutual differences and agreements, and this was done." In a single stroke Carr had negotiated the board physically, and one has to believe psychologically as well, off of its self-constructed pedestal.

I have often wondered if Carr had been influenced by or was somehow party to the armistice talks of 1951 at Kaesong, Korea where and when the North Koreans tied up talks literally for months seeking agreement on who sat where at the table, on what chairs and at what height the chairs might be, across from whom, and who would speak first, to whom, and who should follow, in what order, and about what.

The thorough, nearly verbatim board minutes provided by board secretary Grovesteen offer a fascinating view of the unfolding drama. The minutes state that

> Mr. Carr then said that he had assumed that this meeting was for the purpose of negotiating and resolving differences. Instead, Mr. Lutz read a typed speech and Mr. Stumph came prepared with notes on index cards. Mr. Carr said he did not come prepared to make speeches, but to negotiate. He charged the administration with either deliberately or if not deliberately, with inadvertently misleading the Board and the public as to the actual financial condition of the junior college so that it could have a free hand with the money. He charged the administration with not wanting the Board Members to examine the budget for fear that they would be mesmerized by him into giving raises. He charged the administration with being duplicitous. He charged the administration with trying to get between

the faculty and the Board and attempting to break down the relationship that heretofore existed. He said that he knows there is money in the budget for all of the programs proposed and for a decent raise for the faculty. President Haberaecker asked if this could be done and still have a balanced budget. Mr. Carr said that it could be done without deficit financing.

As if gazing into a dimension somewhat beyond their vision, Carr assured board members that the budget contained enough money to meet faculty demands and still operate the school in the black.
The minutes continue:

> Mr. Tedesco said that Mr. Carr had charged the administration with misleading the Board, with duplicity, with coming between the Board and the faculty, and with having $250,000 available for salary raises. He said that as a Board Member he has an obligation to know about these charges and has a right to ask for information concerning them. 'If you have this information, please give it to me,' he said. Mr. Carr said again, "If I show it to you, will you use a portion of it for teachers' raises?"
>
> Mr. Tedesco replied that he would exercise his mandate to make a judgment on that question. Mr. Carr said that he appreciated Mr. Tedesco's statements, but they didn't help his clients. All he was asking, he said, was for the Board to state publicly that if he gave them the information, they would grant the raises.
>
> Mr. Tedesco said again that he wanted to see the figures. After all, he said, if the administration had pulled the wool over his eyes for two and a half years, he had a right to know. Mr. Carr then said that the administration hadn't lied—the figures were right there all the time. The Board was used to accepting the administration's statements on this, and that they just didn't look closely enough. All they need to do is to analyze it from a different viewpoint. He said he did not mean to imply that the Board members were incompetent—they just didn't have the same interest in the matter that the faculty had. Also, most of the Board Members had closed minds on the subject.

Somewhat combatively,

> Mr. Haberaecker said that Mr. Carr seems to have lost sight of the total picture. For example, he asked, how are occupational programs going to be financed? Where is the money coming from to operate the school?

Mr. Haberaecker insisted that the money must go for salaries <u>and</u> program development. The College must continue to develop programs to stay in business, he said. Program development, said Mr. Carr, is not to be subsidized with teachers' salaries. The money should be gotten from some other source—not from the pocketbooks of teachers.

From the beginning Rex Carr attempted to cut into the practice of privileged compensation. He had analyzed the budget and arrived at a bottom-line at odds with what Dean of Business Services Wayne Stumph had told the board, and that the board had taken as gospel. Carr reiterated, "All teachers should be paid alike, on the same scale, regardless of what they teach."

Suffice it to say the details on either side of the confrontation are not that important. The negotiating session was not unusual in discussing working conditions and salaries. Far more important, Carr's arguments during negotiations that summer separated the AAUP Salary Committee from the board and defined the BAC faculty for the first time as an educational work-group, distinct from the administration and the board in a way that had not been done before, and laid the groundwork for the unionization of the faculty, and eventually the unionization of the entire school.

* * * * *

Traditionally, the faculty and administration in high schools and small colleges are intertwined in an amorphous blend of tasks and privileges of teaching and power. In some colleges the positions of deans and provosts are filled by older professors. Until boards began employing nonteaching managers, "educrats"—people who know nothing about classroom operations and certainly nothing about the difficulties of instruction—in many colleges, beyond the titles of individual positions, little distinction seems to have been made between administration and faculty.

With Carr's leadership the BAC faculty separated itself for the first time from the board and its administration as a distinct entity with which the board would have to bargain and otherwise come to terms. Rex Carr had literally pried loose a duly appointed board committee and re-designated it as an independent faculty bargaining unit.

Of course, Carr's strategy was not missed by the board. At one point "Mr. Lutz stated that until someone else is elected, this board has the responsibility of running the school, and it is the board's responsibility to figure out how the money will be spent, and the board will have the final 'say-so,' based on guidelines established by the Illinois Junior College Board." Still, though the board had the "say-so," there was not yet any way to determine what that "say-so" might be, so it was back to square one.

Lutz talked about running the college as if it were a small town grade school over which a board, maybe the local pharmacist, a farmer or two, and the owner of the hardware store, had absolute authority, dictating to a handful of docile and dependent teachers, rather than addressing the problem in terms of oversight or guidance, which would have been more appropriate for a college board.

Even so, though the college operation was larger and more complex than the novices on the board, business managers though they claimed to be, had yet to comprehend, the first board members seemed, for the most, approachable and reasonably amenable to compromise and working things out. But even well-meaning people sometimes get caught in conditions, small as the historical drift may be, when the sands shift, the footing becomes unreliable, and it is very nearly impossible to maintain one's balance.

Regardless of the hassle of the 1969 negotiations, and regardless of what the board minutes show, "Pep" Lutz and the other board members were not mean people. During the '80s' troubles we had with the Eckert Board (when there was a great deal of malevolence), once in a moment of reverie, Don Libby (Counseling) remarked that "This wouldn't have happened if Pep Lutz was still here."

June 11, 1969 fireworks erupted again. The board met ". . . for the purpose of continuing to negotiate the Faculty Personnel Procedures for 1969-70," and Chairman Lutz asked the secretary to read the letter calling for the Special Meeting. Carr ". . . immediately said that he did not consider this an official board meeting, but an informal negotiating session. If the board wanted to hold a meeting, it should do so, but he did not consider himself to be part of the meeting. When the board got through, he said, then they could all sit down together and negotiate as equals." Lutz ". . . reminded Mr. Carr that it had been agreed to hold a public meeting," and Carr ". . . repeated that he was not a part of the 'board meeting.' He could not agree, he said, to meet according to board rules—there should be (for negotiations) joint rules with all having an equal voice. Again, he said that when the board got through with its meeting, they could begin the negotiating session, with the public invited and present."

At the beginning of the session Lutz read a prepared statement. He returned to the board's axiom that ". . . we do not intend for any outsider to tell us how this institution should be run and operated." Carr replied that, as a taxpayer and district resident, he was not an outsider, at which point the exchange turned decidedly antagonistic.

> Mr. Carr objected to the comparison made in the newspaper be-tween the Dean of Instruction's salary and that of a faculty member. The faculty member in mind, he said, got $17,500 only

because he was willing to work fifteen additional credit hours over and above his regular load. The impression was given that this was his salary. The Dean of Instruction [Henry Milander], the newspaper article stated, received only a thousand dollars more. It must also be remembered, he [Carr] said, that the Dean of Instruction has two years' experience, whereas the faculty member has twenty-one-years' experience with this College. In addition, the faculty member has a Ph. D. degree and the Dean of Instruction has a Doctor of Education degree, which, Mr. Carr said, is an inferior degree. Mr. Tedesco said, "I disagree," to which Mr. Carr replied, "You may—I say it's an inferior degree."

Mrs. Schroeder asked if it wasn't just Mr. Carr's opinion that the Ph. D. degree is superior to the Doctor of Education degree. He (Carr) agreed that it was his opinion, just as Board Members are entitled to have their opinion.

Mr. Haberaecker asked again if the faculty agreed on the matter of doctor's degrees and Mr. Carr answered, "I have the opinion that the Ph. D. is better than a Doctor of Education degree."

An opinion which may help explain why education school degrees in administration are now titled PhD and twenty-first century administrators, in a shoddy and shabby break with academic tradition, include the PhD insignia whenever they sign or wherever they hang their names. As if the saying makes it so.

In my novel *The Final Days* Professor John Carter reflects on the phenomenon of degree-flaunting.

The black letters on the glass of the office wall and doors had been removed and replaced with even larger, bolder inscriptions for the Academic Corporate Vice Chancellor for Instruction, Marvin Crowly, B.S., M.S., PhD, Ed. and Administrative Dean of Humanities, Lamar Landeau, B.R.E., M.A., Ed.D., M.B.A., Ph.D.

Academic tradition had it that scholars seldom referred to degree titles. Degrees were for resumes, to get jobs. Your value after that had to do with job performance—research, publication, and teaching. Self-advertisement by degree title or designation was viewed as inconsistent with good academics and something only the most desperate and inadequate would do.

The problem resided in the quality of the granting institution. Advanced degrees, MA or PhD, where too easily obtained from inferior institutions requiring little scholarship, and often even less diligence. A degree title did not have any more meaning than the title of gentleman or lady.

The pretense and hype of PR, Carter thought. There were faculty at Barker who confided that they had sent off some few dollars to a fly-by-night mail-order Seminary and received a Divinity degree. Of course, most would not put this on their office door, or include the designation whenever they signed their name. But then some do.

They collect administration and education degrees like kids collect baseball cards, he thought. The easier and cheaper, the better. Then given the high-corn of playground authority and power gleaned from the bogus degree titles they set straight away to provide themselves with position and pay.

At any rate, this had already become practice in 1969. Later Secretary Grovesteen tells that:

> Mr. Carr then said that he does not mean to demean the administrator in question, but Dr. Milander replied that he had already done it. Mr. Carr also said it was not fair to pick out the faculty member in question and use his salary for comparison purposes.
>
> President Haberaecker asked if Mr. Carr was accusing him of giving this information to the press. Mr. Carr answere d by saying, "All I know is what I read in the paper." He said he assumed that a spokesman for the administration gave the information to the paper. Mr. Haberaecker reminded him that this was public information. Mr. Carr said that the newspaper article stated, "the News Democrat learned." How did it learn, he asked, except from someone connected with the administration? Mr. Haberaecker asked him to prove that he was the one. Mr. Carr said that he really had no opinion as to whether or not Mr. Haberaecker put it in the paper, but that he was part of the administration. It had to come from somewhere, he said. Mr. Haberaecker called Mr. Carr's attention to the fact that at the last meeting when he (Mr. Haberaecker) referred to teacher's salaries he made it very clear that the amount he gave was the "total salary for the year."
>
> President Haberaecker pointed out that the responsibilities of the faculty member in question and the Dean of Instruction are different. In that case, Mr. Carr said he felt the faculty member should be getting twice as much.
>
> Mr. Keck then stated that he had been here an hour and ten minutes, and unless Mr. Carr showed more respect to the Board, the President, and the administrative staff, he was going to leave. Mr. Carr replied that it was his privilege to leave, but his duty to stay.

> Mr. Hilgard told Mr. Carr that he thought he was alienating the
> Board and hurting his cause by his approach, but Mr. Carr replied
> that people have to be shocked before they are willing to change.

Carr's observation-opinion about Milander's degree so rattled Milander that the following August (two months later) he resigned, giving, among other reasons, that he could no longer work in an environment where he was so little appreciated. It was as if Carr's remarks had outed Milander, as if he had been exposed as a fraud. On the other hand, anyone who has taken a required education course, to prepare for a teaching or an educational administrative position, knows what Rex Carr was talking about.

Carr's arguments that summer were succinct and viable. He pointed out that the board had only a part-time interest in the school and seemed initially not to have an interest in the cultural significance of their positions as members of a college board of trustees. Carr maintained, on the other hand, that the school was at the heart of the faculty's primary enterprise. In the years to come, board members' financial interest in the school would become an important tenet of this position. If board members did not have a personal interest (financial or other) in the decisions they were making in running the school, beyond not spending tax dollars, it would be important to give them one. Possibly they would be a bit more judicious if their edicts as board members, beyond grandstanding public relations, carried some degree of financial weight in their individual businesses and/or personal lives.

Carr's arguments further set the administration aside as hired-hands meant to do the board's bidding, generally with little knowledge of education or of the mission the college faculty had undertaken.

Additionally, Rex Carr's arguments that summer politicized the BAC faculty, dragging it for the first time into the political arena. And this was no small or easy task. Traditionally, professors have not wanted to deal with the commercial and/or political. The majority simply want to concentrate on their profession, not just a job, but their profession and teaching, which means becoming knowledgeable in their discipline and then sharing or presenting what they have found and how they found it. Like most other humans who do things well, professors prefer to be paid a decent wage, and left alone to do what they do best. Of course, there were faculty members, even in the AAUP, who refused to recognize the new arrangement and continued to see themselves as part of the board-administrative structure.

Moreover, the decent-wage conundrum is always present. Too often salaries of professors, especially those at community colleges, who have postponed earnings and suffered extensive financial hardships to get legitimate advanced degrees, are compared with the salaries of drugstore clerks and gas station attendants. There is always the complaint from John Q.

Public that teachers are overpaid and that you can't solve a problem (such as getting better teachers) by throwing money at it. But no one has ever thrown money at American public education. In fact, Americans have never come within shouting distance of providing 50-percent of the funds public education needs to be viable.

I would assume a decent wage to be what other professionals with comparable education receive. On two occasions, in the early '80s, when I was in the 30,000-dollar salary range, I had friends ask how much I was paid. One was a Belleville attorney who spent fewer years in school than I had, and therefore had spent less on his education and fewer years without a fulltime salary than I had. When I told him what I was paid, he shook his head and said, "That's ridiculous." When I told the other friend, an executive in a major corporation, what I was paid, after he asked me if I wanted to work for him, he said, "You'll make twice that the first year and three times that in two years." He was several years younger than me and making more than six times what I was. Still, I declined the offer.

The 1969 Recess

During the 1969 negotiations Carr pointed out repeatedly that East St. Louis, Collinsville and Granite City, Illinois high school faculties were paid more than college professors at BAC, to which board member Orsin Seibert, in a *Blackboard Jungle* outburst, suggested that high school teachers were being compensated for hazardous duty rather than for teaching.

"Our teachers don't have to sit at a desk with a gun or knife at their side," Seibert said.

Still, the jockeying continued with Carr poking at the budget for the coming year behind which the board had attempted to hide. During the next several months of meetings the board still refused to negotiate. Then, in September, for five days during the first week of school, some of the AAUP faculty did not show up for class. It was called a "boycott," an activity that would be, again, the method of resistance in late October of 1976, when seventy faculty called in sick to protest stalled negotiations.

Although a good number of the faculty were absent that first week of scheduled classes in the fall of 1969, it is difficult to know how many. The administration gave one number (25), the newspaper (*BND*) gave another (36) and the AAUP gave still another (57). The faculty referred to the absence as a boycott, and not a strike, for although strikes by educational employees in Illinois in 1969 were not necessarily illegal, they were without due process protection.

But regardless what the faculty thought about its absence that week and its effect on board-faculty relations, Haberaecker left no doubt as to his and the board's view. Faculty Senate minutes show that on November 4, 1969, Haberaecker spoke to the senate and stated that there would be a ". .

. lack of recrimination, so far as he was concerned, with reference to the September *recess* [emphasis added] and his desire for harmony in the interest of the whole college." It seems the missing faculty members, in Haberaecker's opinion, were merely errant children who had inadvertently wandered off the playground, in an unfortunate, but harmless diversion, one to be forgiven by a paternal board.

After five days of faculty *recess,* probably because it knew Carr had caught the administration cooking the books, the board caved in. Not only had the budget overestimated the cost of new occupational programs, but it had seriously underestimated revenues. In his claim that the board had "... $250,000 available for salary raises," Carr had not negotiated for monies the board did not have, but for funds the board anticipated and attempted to conceal. The new contract, when finally signed, gave the board the benefit of the doubt. The settlement called for the faculty to receive 60-percent of all revenues beyond what was accounted for in the budget. And as a result, in July of 1970, each faculty member received a check for $1,488.78, and both the board and the faculty came to believe, with or without justification, that the budget's author, director of financial services Wayne Stumph, in what would became known as the "Stumph Budget," intended to hide monies the school had or would have, monies meant for instructional purposes. But if there was subterfuge, you have to believe Haberaecker was in on it.

The Corporatization of the College

Until 1969 the BAC board exercised a general and somewhat regal power, removed from the more mundane workings of the school, leaving the dusting and cleaning and planning to the administration–although on occasion a board member served as a negotiator. Even after the 1969 confrontation the board continued to be somewhat benevolent, amenable and in touch with the faculty. Professor Jim Massey (Chemistry) tells of 1972, his first years at BAC, when he was already chief negotiator for the bargaining unit, of one evening at a party, sitting on the steps of the house of another faculty member, Bill Keel (Chemistry), talking to Ted Gundlach, the chairman of the BAC board. As Massey said, "Before the evening ended we had worked out 80-percent of the general provisions of the contract for the following year." However, in the next few years, BAC boards would shift to a more hands-on (neither amenable nor benevolent), dictatorial approach of immediate or micro-management of the school, something for which, despite their constant claims, they were neither elected nor qualified.

* * * * *

As late as 1980, in the Yeshiva Decision, the U.S. Supreme Court held that faculty in private institutions of postsecondary education are administrators, or at least serve an administrative function. There was still the idea that college and university professors were the school and should have a substantial place in directing its affairs. There is a story, possibly apocryphal, but maybe not, about President Eisenhower speaking at Columbia University (as president of the university?) honoring physics Professor Isidore Rabi. Rabi had worked on the development of the atomic bomb and won a Nobel Prize for his discovery of nuclear magnetic reasonance. At a faculty ceremony honoring Rabi, Eisenhower made a brief speech and remarked that it is was always nice to have an employee of the university recognized. Before he could say more, Professor Rabi interrupted him and said, "Excuse me, sir, but the faculty are not employees of the university. The faculty are the university!" (*Academic Anchor*, August 9, 2012).

In contradistinction to Professor Rabi's correction, by the late '60s more and more American colleges and universities were being fitted to a corporate model, turning them into administrative-consumer institutions that regulated faculty to the second rank as mere workers while elevating administrators to executive positions. No place was this more apparent than in the salaries that college and university presidents, as CEOs, were commanding. In a trend begun forty-years ago, with no sign of peaking soon, university presidents' compensation packages took a substantial leap upward. Today it is not uncommon for a university president's salary to exceed a million dollars annually. *The New York Times* reports "John W. Curtis, director of research and public policy at the AAUP, said rising pay to presidents was consistent with a 'corporate mindset' at colleges, reflecting 'the idea that you have a single person who essentially is running the place.'"

In the same article, *The Times* quotes President Patrick M. Callan of the National Center for Public Policy and Higher Education, as saying "The public has kind of lost confidence in the altruistic mission of higher education. They see higher education as just another institution that's in it for its own bottom-line."

As part of the "corporate mindset," by 1972, with the BAC board and administrations pushing to make a buck, grade inflation and consumerism invaded the BAC classrooms. Students were quick to pick up on the idea that under the new arrangement they were no longer just students, but customers or clients the school wanted to "retain." Shortly after I arrived at BAC in 1972, someone, another professor I think, asked me how I liked teaching at a college. My answer was unequivocal. I was enjoying the experience, except that what my students wanted mostly was for me to reinforce their prejudices and fantasies and then give them an A for their troubles. What I didn't realize at the time, since I had not encountered anything like it in my short teaching experiences at Evanston High School or the University of Iowa, was that there would be as much pressure from the BAC administration, as from students, to undermine the faculty as the university and to cleanse the classroom of academics. In keeping with the administrative adage, I should say promulgation, that "every student should succeed," at one point, although 50-percent of incoming freshmen at BAC tested into the bottom 25-percent of college freshmen nationally, 40-percent of BAC's graduates were graduated with honors—a laundering and sprucing up of the student mind in only two years of consumer-retention schooling that seems mostly implausible.

Of course, the growing board-faculty estrangement at BAC during the late '60s and early '70s did not take place in a vacuum. In K-12 schools and the newly formed community colleges throughout the State of Illinois, although mostly upstate, faculty unions were going to court to enforce their constitutional rights and demand that boards of education better exercise their mandate to *provide quality education* for the people of the state.

Following the 1969 faculty recess the board and the Haberaecker administration persisted in pretending that nothing had changed. On September 22, 1970, Faculty Senate minutes indicate that "Mr. Keel [Administrative Assistant to the President] wrote requesting the Senate to appoint a committee to aid him in preparing a Board-Policy Manual (which will be approved by the Board)." Minutes of the Board-Senate Dinner Meeting, March 10, 1971, report that "In the discussion which followed, the members of the school board [Mr. Lutz, Mr. Gundlach, Mrs. Schroeder, Mr. Keck, and Mr. Seibert] freely participated.

"At this time the school board members that were present indicated their pleasure in being asked to the Board-Senate Dinner Meeting and informed the faculty that they were pleased to get to know teachers better socially."

While social gatherings and verbal amenities may indicate the board and faculty had a pleasant enough working relationship, it had the added effect of providing the faculty with a seriously misplaced sense of its own power and a belief that the board was somehow fearful of the faculty.

Unfortunately, the Illinois General Assembly gave community college boards nearly absolute power over their institutions. Before 1980 there was no tenure or collective bargaining laws for community college faculties in Illinois. And yet, among the AAUP teachers at BAC, there remained an arrogance and bravado fueling the belief that they were in charge and that the board would not mess with them. The question paramount at the time that only a few of the BAC faculty were willing to ask, and fewer willing to attempt to answer, was, with the absolute power the board had over the college, "Why wouldn't the board simply disregard the faculty and do as it pleased?"

A Minor Rebellion of Have-nots

Although the BAC faculty-board standoff appeared to have taken on a wary disquiet, during the early 70s within the faculty ranks matters were not quiet or well. As noted earlier, new faculty tended to feel alienated from and controlled by the ruling older-faculty oligarchy, and many refused to join the AAUP, which served further to exacerbate the have and have-not division. Still, regardless of the discontent, no one had mounted much opposition to the AAUP.

Then, in early May of 1972 a minor rebellion of have-nots surfaced, and a handful of the disgruntled petitioned the Faculty Senate for a referendum to determine an agent for collective bargaining, possibly to replace the AAUP.

Faculty Senate minutes of May 5, 1972 show that:

The secretary read a letter from several unnamed members of the faculty as follows:

Distinguished Senators:
During the past months we have become increasingly aware of the fact that the Belleville Chapter of the AAUP is no longer representative of the entire fulltime faculty body of BAC.

We strongly believe that the Faculty Senate of BAC, being a democratically elected representative body of the entire faculty, is more capable of representing the best interests of all faculty members.

We therefore respectfully request that each fulltime faculty member be polled by either ballot or petition to ascertain whether or not the Faculty Senate of BAC shall be delegated sole responsibility for faculty contract negotiations during the 1972-73 academic year and for each year thereafter. We also request that all interested parties be notified of the results of this referendum.

The request for the referendum degenerated into a political squabble both within the senate and the faculty generally. However, a few months later, the senate dismissed the issue, leaving the discontent that led to the letter to fester. This, however, was only the beginning of the rebellion. There would be attempts again in 1977 and in 1981 to dislodge the AAUP as faculty bargaining agent.

The April 1974 Election

> Never forget that the purpose for which a man lives is the improvement of the man himself, so he may go out of this world having, in his great sphere or his small one, done some little good for his fellow creatures and labored a little to diminish the sin and sorrow that are in the world.
>
> —William E. Gladstone

Financial Exigency and Secrecy

In a rambling three-page letter to the board dated March 20, 1974, Haberaecker announced his retirement, effective August thirty-first of that same year. What is notable about the letter is not so much what it says, but what it does not say. In the first part Haberaecker lauds himself for his accomplishments, both in the high school and college positions he has held, then turns to praising the community for its support in establishing the college. The following pages are dedicated to thanking the current board, five of whom were original members, praising the administrators he has worked with, and again extolling his concern for students and his pleasure at having seen so many graduate. But he doesn't say anything about the faculty. The faculty is mentioned only in passing. Once, in a short phrase, he admits the school needs "good teaching," but not much more is said.

To Haberaecker, and to the board and the administration, the BAC baccalaureate faculty was by now a rather vague entity, maybe like a pack of distant relatives that really do not mean much to anyone but need necessarily to be dealt with from time to time.

Within the next days the board set out to find someone to replace Haberaecker. Faculty Senate minutes include a letter from board secretary Lavette Grovesteen, dated March 25, 1974, to Mr. Wayne Shaw (Art), chairman, informing Mr. Shaw of ". . . the formation of a committee composed of two members appointed by the Faculty Senate, two members by the Student Senate, two by the Administrative Council, and two by the Board of Trustees (with the Chairman of the Board of Trustees to serve as chairman of the committee)—said committee to screen applicants for the position of College President, with the final decision to be made by the Board of Trustees." Once again, we had a committee composed of five members from the board and administration, and four others.

William Saunders and Gene Brandt (Political Science) were taken from the Faculty Senate Major Administrations Appointment Committee and added to the screening committee, to serve with trustees Lutz and Gundlach and Edward O'Malley, who had come on to the board in 1972. The committee eventually recommended the appointment of William Keel,

Haberaecker's administrative assistant, for the college presidency.

* * * * *

The subsequent April 1974 board election proved to be as feeble as it was disastrous for the college. Two of the original board members, Richard W. Hilgard and Joseph P. Keck, chose not to run, but more than that, the ballot did not include anyone who could have been considered an educationally positive candidate. Unlike the scramble for seats that highlighted the original board election in 1967 and attracted forty-three candidates. Although the college had grown to include twenty high school districts (it had begun with seven—and would have thirty-eight by 2009), the 1974 election offered only four candidates: William H. Snare, a cartographer for the federal government; Curt E. Eckert, a real estate agent-secretary-treasurer for Eckert Orchards, Inc.; Martha Sauer, a housewife; and George Uhl, Jr., a construction contractor—all from Belleville.

When, at the March 1974 board meeting, a little over three weeks before the April thirteenth election, Haberaecker announced his retirement, the board candidates immediately added to their campaign pledges the qualifications they would look for in selecting a new president for the college.

At the time local newspapers were occupied with the news of Belleville Grade School District 118's near financial failure and the district's attempt to balance its budget by firing 114 teachers. On April 3, 1974 the Belleville Trades and Labor Assembly executive secretary and a former District 118 board member, Harold Wright, directed by a unanimous vote of the assembly, called for the resignation of the District 118 board. The *BND*, April 3, 1974, quoted Wright from a Trades and Labor Assembly press release as saying:

> The recent firing of 114 teachers and others without the dismissal of one administrative official was partly the basis of the decision reached at the Tuesday meeting. However, the fact that the school board allowed the district to get $2 million in debt and their lack of ability to be aware of all funds of the district also contributed to this harsh decision.
>
> If the board were responsible to the real need to economize by dismissing personnel, they should have first looked at the high salaries paid the school administrators and tried to cut costs in that area. But instead they chose to fire teachers—and other personnel that are vital to the education of the district.

Taking instruction from the District 118 situation, the BAC board candidates quickly added a chant for fiscal responsibility to their opinions about replacing Haberaecker, focused on what they might do or at least have in mind when looking for a new president.

"Three of the candidates, Eckert, Uhl and Mrs. Sauer, said they would like to see Haberaecker replaced by another man who is strongest in business and money management. They said such a man could leave many of the decisions on educational quality to experts who serve under him, just like Haberaecker often does now" (*BND*, April 10, 1974).

By experts, I suspect they meant the BAC administration.

According to the *BND* candidate Snare applauded Haberaecker, saying "Mr. Haberaecker has done a tremendous job managing BAC and putting it on a sound basis. Since he has done such a good job we may now be able to afford to hire someone whose interests lean more to education." The *BND* added, "Snare is also the only candidate to say he is not definitely opposed to deficit financing."

In the end Snare's "deficit" comment may have condemned his candidacy.

The question of fiscal responsibility in poorly funded educational institutions always leads to the question of "If public postsecondary education is not self-supporting, where does the money come from?" That, of course, is the old American commercial dodge that steps over the understanding that some institutions in a culture, other than Wall Street and its failing corporations, must be subsidized. The question is always part of the money-grubbing doctrine of citizens not paying for their privileges, of greed-creed corporations siphoning off benefits from the society without paying for them. The question ignores the reality that the quality of human life depends on the texture and tenor of the culture. To be certain that what is necessary to sustain the best of the culture they live in, and claim otherwise, as their right-to-life, citizens can ill-afford to privatize the profits a culture might provide while ignoring the expenses necessary to keep things such as educational institutions viable and running.

Oftentimes I have heard people oppose school bond issues because "I don't have children in school. Why should I pay to educate other people's kids?" Why, indeed? How about the doctor who treats your heart problems or the lawyer you consult when you run over the neighbor's kid? How about the engineers who design the highways you drive on or the television set you use to watch sit-coms? The majority of college graduates in the United States who provide these services are educated with public monies. The question is how far personal and corporate greed and community nonfeasance might reduce or impair educational institutions without seriously savaging the culture which takes its viability and quality from those institutions.

Illinois community colleges are financed by daily student headcounts reimbursed by the state, personal property taxes, and student tuition, supported by loans and grants (mostly federal), student financial aid (again mostly federal), and propped up by inadequate faculty salaries, both fulltime and part-time.

This is a lethal amalgamation. The Illinois community college head-count reimbursement practice requires keeping teachers in line with the corporate scheme of students as customers—which means pressuring teachers to keep incompetent and unruly students in class to enhance the school's on-the-dole state reimbursement.

Allowing private lending institutions to provide student loans, satis-fies community mandates for lower taxes, but also encourages admin-istrative demands that teachers keep students in class to assure a steady flow of dollars into the school. After all, you don't want to lose a customer —for something as mundane as giving a failing or poor grade, even if the customer does not show up or will not do the work required to pass the course.

The third part of the financing trinity, allowing property owners to dictate property tax funding for K-12 and community colleges, is probably the very worst that could be imagined. Property owners are forced to choose between paying for better schools which most see as giving money away and having enough cash on hand at the end of the month to pay for their new automobile. These are not choices an educational institution wants to put to a vote among the populace, but choices that nonetheless infect every educational school board election—thus, the constant call for fiscal responsibility (do not spend money, for whatever reason) from can-didates running in school board elections.

* * * * *

Unfortunately, beyond their opposition to increasing taxes for edu-cation, Americans are not much interested in school board elections. Most voters do not really care who runs the schools, so those who are interested and who vote, if they do not have children in school, usually support fiscally conservative candidates. Too many times this leaves school board seats to candidates that can best be described as "fringe" and downright anti-educational.

Some years ago, I had a woman in an ethics class, one of the fringe evangelicals who a year earlier had been elected to the Belleville High School District 201 board. Not only was she creating havoc on the 201 board, objecting to the school spending money on "secular instruction," but came into my class as a student ostensibly to dictate what I could and could not teach. Class after class she sat with a rigid straight-spine, the tip of her right index finger pointing and placed on some specific line of whatever text we were examining, to be sure she could return to the proper chapter and verse. She complained continually that the presence of Plato, Thomas Aquinas, and David Hume in the classroom violated her religious freedom, a bit of nonsense, I might add, she insisted upon attempting to impose on the class. She further demanded that I not say anything about morals or religion (this was an ethics class), unless it fit her truncated belief system. Finally, I threatened to drop her from the class (as another teacher had) if she did not adhere to class rules and decorum and desist from violating the rights of other students to be free of her idiot-ology. She intended, both on the District 201 board and in my class, to obstruct normal procedures and disrupt, in whatever way she could, legitimate educational activities.

Usually it is the paucity of voters in school board contests that makes it possible for fringe groups, and some not so fringe but still small, to elect candidates who oppose publicly funded education, and in many ways, education generally. By 1974, the BAC district had nearly doubled, but only 9,671 voters showed up for the board election.

* * * * *

Snare's deficit-funding remarks may have cost him a board seat in the 1974 BAC election. It's hard to tell. Eckert ran on his name and Sauer ran on the sex issue of "providing a woman's viewpoint" for the board, a viewpoint that did not, in Sauer's tenure on the board encourage her to vote even one time in opposition to the board's male majority. Likewise, the press claimed Sauer had the endorsement of the League of Women Voters, an organization I had thought to be nonpartisan—and, yes, school board elections are supposed to be non-partisan. The League's mission statement assures that "League of Women Voters is strictly nonpartisan; it neither supports nor opposes candidates for office at any level of government"—unless, as in this case, the candidate happens to be female.

Eckert collected 6,656 votes, Sauer polled 4,982, Uhl got 3,243, and Snare received 2,283. The same day Vernon Eckert, Curt Eckert's brother was elected to the Belleville High School District 201 board.

In April of 1974, voters handed two board seats to Curt Eckert and Martha Sauer. Snare and Uhl, if elected, may have been as bad for the college as Eckert and Sauer. But they could not have been worse.

Haberaecker Abandons the Faculty

During the summer of 1974, a month or so before he left the school Haberaecker got into another scrape with the faculty. In the process of selecting a Dean of Student Services, the Faculty Senate's Major Administration Appointments Committee (MAAC), a good mixture of haves and have-nots, reached an impasse with Haberaecker. In a letter to Kenneth Pinzke (Earth Science), Faculty Senate Secretary, dated March 19, 1974, MAAC members Vito Benivegna, Chairman, and Gene Brandt, Jack Haskell, Wayne Shaw, and Martha Giordano (Adult Education) resigned from the committee. The letter, to wit:

Dear Mr. Pinzke:
This letter is to inform the Faculty Senate that the Major Administration Appointments Committee has reached an impasse with President Haberaecker over the role of this committee in the selection of a Dean of Student Services.

In essence, we are of the opinion that the rules have been changed in the "middle of the game." The procedures as we first understood them now seem to no longer apply. We feel the President's recent appointments of two additional committees —a student committee and an administrative committee—has in effect so watered down the function of the Major Administrative Appointments Committee that it has become almost meaningless.

We feel that to continue to serve in an important capacity would compromise the committee's integrity and be a disservice to the Senate and the faculty we represent.

The letter caused a considerable flap in the senate, but after all was said, there was nothing it could do about Haberaecker's intransigence.

More than likely Haberaecker meant to reduce the MAAC and faculty influence in the coming selection process for the new college president. William Keel had been Haberaecker's administrative assistant and seems to have been led into the position by Haberaecker's behind-the-scenes manipulations. There is also reason to believe that Bruce Wissore, who appeared at the college in 1973, brought in by Keel, had more than a passing interest in seeing Keel become president. At any rate, in August of 1974, Haberaecker's retirement took effect and the board appointed Keel as Haberaecker's replacement. How exactly Keel got the appointment has always been a source of skepticism and mystery.

Keel had been a chemistry teacher, a Faculty Senate member, and the 1969-70 President of the AAUP chapter before becoming Haberaecker's administrative assistant. Despite the misgivings of some members of the selection committee, certain of the AAUP faculty believed that Keel, because of his senate and AAUP activities, would represent them well as president. I ran into the AAUP fantasy about Keel one day when I observed quite incidentally that the combination of Eckert as a board member and Keel as president did not bode well for the college. The old-guard AAUP in attendance took noisy and, I thought, much too personal exception to my statement. I had walked into the hornet's nest of the original haves who considered Keel a friend, a friend-now-president, who would continue to provide them with privileges and perks.

Otherwise, there was some disagreement about Keel's qualifications for the presidency. Although Keel had taught chemistry, he did not have a master's degree in chemistry. He had a degree in the education of chemistry, which brings to mind Rex Carr's observation about education degrees.

When the selection committee voted on the candidates, no one on the committee remembers having seen the ballots that were cast or having bothered to ask for a recount or question the veracity of the announced results. Later, after an unofficial canvas, several members of the committee voiced surprise that Keel would have had enough votes to secure the nomination. It was noted, however, that Wissore, who would continue as Keel's administrative assistant, conducted the election and handled the ballots. This may have had something to do with Keel's later hesitance to censor Wissore, even after Wissore began hassling faculty and staff. It is possible that Keel could not reprimand Wissore without calling his (Keel's) ascendancy into question.

In many ways Keel's presidency was a mixed bag. On one hand he appeared loyal to his Faculty Senate-AAUP past. Shortly after he became president of the college, senate minutes under President's Report notes, "The Legislative Committee of AAUP has been working with President Keel to alleviate cash flow problems that exist for this college. For example, as of this date, state funds for summer registration have not been received. The President also would like to meet with the President of the BAC Chapter of AAUP, the Chairman of the Faculty Senate, and College Cabinet to discuss financial exigency. President Keel mentioned that the faculty will have an opportunity to discuss the problem of community college financing with key area State Representatives at the AAUP Legislative Cocktail Party to be held at Fischer's Restaurant on Friday, October 24th at 7 p.m."

The key item here is "financial exigency." Shortly after Curt Eckert appeared on the board, the school budget, which Eckert and Keel had inherited from the "fiscally responsible Haberaecker," dropped into a declared state of financial exigency. Indeed, within a very few months, as I had earlier come to believe, Eckert's presence on the BAC Board, combined with the Keel presidency, did not bode well for the college.

* * * * *

From 1968 until 1974 board operations were pretty much what one might expect, given the personages that comprised the board. While some board members' statements were on occasion arrogant and mindless, and the members themselves in some cases seriously misinformed, there seems not to have been anything unusual or underhanded in what the board tried to do. Board policies and practices, if at times misguided in accepting the 1969 Stumph Budget as gospel and not addressing faculty needs, were pretty straight forward.

In 1974, however, that changed. Beginning in April, with Curt Eckert

newly elected to the board, just before Haberaecker retired, and then continuing into the Keel administration with Bruce Wissore as Keel's administrative assistant, the board stepped off into a decidedly different direction.

* * * * *

Curt Eckert was born in Belleville, Illinois, the second son (the other
two were Cornell and Vernon) of the farm family of Alvin O. and Ella
(Heinrich) Eckert. Sometime in the late nineteenth century Alvin inherited
a farm from his father southwest of Belleville, Illinois and in 1910 opened a
roadside stand which became the Eckert market.

Curt Eckert attended the University of Illinois, majored in agriculture,
and after graduation in 1930, returned home to the family business—and
sometime shortly after began dabbling in politics and real estate with the
Realtor Land Institute and his own real estate agency.

* * * * *

I have often thought that national, well publicized events, especially
questionable activities by state or federal government officials, provide
encouragement for similar attitudes or actions by persons at local venues.
In other words, national political figures generate copy-cat attitudes in the
people they have been chosen to instruct and lead. Possibly, the national
miscreants are simply representing the attitudes and practices of their
constituents—or vice versa, or maybe both. Often, sad behavior condones
bad behavior.

In Washington, by the spring of 1974, Spiro Agnew had already been
ousted as Vice President on tax charges dating to his tenure as Governor of
Maryland; and the Senate Watergate Committee investigation of the misdeeds of the Nixon White House were well underway. In August of 1974, as
the Watergate hearings progressed with their inevitable conclusions, and
the scope of Nixon's felonious behavior came to light, he resigned the presidency.

However, far from discouraging others from similar actions, Nixon's
part in aiding and abetting the cover-up of the Watergate break-in, many of
his followers thought of it as politics-as-usual. Anthropologists have noted
that in all human societies, no matter how bad things are, 25-percent of the
people think everything is okay. Anthropologists call this urdummheit or
primal stupidity. The day before Richard Nixon resigned, 24-percent of the
people answering a national poll thought he had done nothing wrong, and
that he was doing a good job as president. Even after his resignation, others
of Nixon's public defended him as having failed only in getting caught, while
pointing out that his activities were politically commonplace.

These are the attitudes that promoted continued unethical and illegal political-administrative activities, both on a national and local level, leading Professor Sam Dash, Chief Council of the Senate Watergate Committee, when asked about the persistence of corruption in politics, to comment that "You keep stepping on them, but the goddamned cockroaches keep coming out of the woodwork."

In 1980, with the Reagan election, when the faculty alluded to the disservice of the board and administration to the school, it was told by the BAC administration that, "The Republicans are in power now. Nobody cares about you people."

* * * * *

In the spring of 1974 shortly after the board election, when little had been said about it before, financial exigency became the BAC board's catch-phrase. This most certainly had to with Curt Eckert's presence on the board. Eckert was a close friend and cardplaying buddy of Belleville City Treasurer Homer Liebig, a fiscal conservative. Liebig was a founding mem- ber of the Illinois Municipal Treasurers Association the year before, 1973, and would serve as its president in 1978. The conservative philosophy of the time held that public bodies should strive to conserve (stockpile) tax revenues, regardless of the harm it does to the community, even if it curtails and truncates services the institution has been created to provide. In 1983, probably at Eckert's encouragement, Liebig ran for the BAC board, though, I am glad to say, his candidacy failed.

Later, in the summer of 1974, by way of a budget put together by the financially responsible Haberaecker, the staff received an 8-percent raise, Haberaecker took a 9-percent raise shortly before retiring, and the board secretary and assistant secretary received 8-percent raises that were, a month later, increased to 9.2-percent. All of this came from a school budget the board claimed to be seriously short of money.

Immediately after taking office, Keel, who called himself "a board president," probably following an Eckert suggestion, set out to limit board and faculty communication by proposing a board policy that would have prohibited individual faculty from talking to board members. This sug-gestion no doubt came through Wissore who had already ingratiated him-self with Eckert and from the Seyfarth Shaw Fairweather and Gerald son law firm the board had just retained as an educational consultant. Lawyers at Seyfarth Shaw had already authored a publication detailing what educa-tional administrators needed and did not need to tell their governing boards.

The proposal to keep the faculty incommunicado was blatant enough that when it came up at a board meeting trustee Edward O'Malley remarked, "This looks like censorship to me." And while the faculty was upset with the proposal, what was not apparent at the time was that this marked the beginning of a board program to isolate the faculty into a quasi-ghetto and ultimately to cleanse the school of fulltime faculty.

Stirring the cauldron, a bit more, at the January 1975 board meeting, citizen and self-appointed board watchdog Leo Seitz, another local politician who appeared with devoted regularity at every board meeting, complained that the board was now violating the Open Meetings Act by not meeting in public. With the tendency and appetite certain board members had for backroom political double-dealing, Seitz might have been onto something. More than likely, any number of times on conference calls or during impromptu meetings in out-of-the-way restaurants, a board quorum had been present. A few years later, when the board wanted to meet officially by way of electronic connections, the Illinois Attorney General issued an opinion that, indeed, a quorum could be legally constituted by means of electronic connections or conference calls.

The secrecy would continue until the end of the Eckert reign, during which most of what the board did was done behind closed doors, at times other than board meetings, and often in places other than the BAC boardroom—and nothing recorded. Giving credence to Seitz' claim, simultaneously with Eckert's appearance on the board, minutes kept of board meetings dwindled to a handful of notes, merely outlining what the board had considered, with little or no record of discussions or presentations.

In February of 1975, attempting to control the coming election, the board proposed cutting polling places for the April board election from fifty-one to twenty-five. Board attorney Nold rationalized the reduction as an attempt to save 7,500 dollars—out of a college budget already in the millions. However, at the next meeting Edward O'Malley objected. Slated to run for re-election, O'Malley complained that the cut had been made in an attempt to gerrymander the district and as a candidate he would rather lose than win that way. That was March 19, 1975. The next day, at a special meeting, the board passed a resolution authorizing 120 polling places for the fall election. Gundlach, O'Malley, Sauer, Milton Smith, who had been elected to the board in 1973, and Seibert voted for the resolution. At the time Eckert and Lutz were the other two board members.

Seyfarth, Shaw, Fairweather and Geraldson

In a hardly noticed, more ominous move at the same meeting, the board designated attorney, Michael Rybicki–from a Chicago law firm, Seyfarth, Shaw, Fairweather and Geraldson, as its chief contract negotiator. He would be paid fifty-dollars an hour plus expenses to negotiate the 1975-76 faculty contract.

Today Seyfarth Shaw (SS) advertises over 650 lawyers in twelve offices around the world. The following is taken from a recent Seyfarth Shaw website, www.Seyfarth.com:

Seyfarth Shaw was established over sixty years ago because our founding attorneys wished to concentrate on labor relations counseling and litigation. This commitment to labor relations remains a cornerstone of our labor and employment practice. Our veteran practitioners handle the full range of traditional labor law issues, including: union organizing campaigns; collective bargaining; grievance arbitration (including rights and interest arbitration); labor contract administration; union avoidance through positive employee relations; union corporate campaigns; and preparing for and dealing with picketing, strikes, lockouts and other economic tactics.

Clients confronted with union organizing attempts, important labor negotiations, union corporate campaigns, unfair labor practice charges or threats of work stoppages turn to us for sophisticated representation by seasoned professionals who routinely have handled hundreds of such cases. A thorough knowledge of the applicable law is only our starting point. Added value comes from our insight into appropriate proactive management.

It doesn't take much imagination to envision the havoc these kinds of people can cause in an educational institution, especially when a board of trustees claiming financial exigency is willing to allocate hundreds of thousands of dollars to fund their activities. By 1980 SS attorneys were paid 150-dollars an hour, portal-to-portal, by BAC. A twenty-four-hour stint was worth 3,600 dollars. Sometimes SS sent two attorneys to Belleville from Chicago for five or six days. Sometimes the bi-monthly payoff ran in excess of 100,000 dollars.

Needless to say, in spite of the largess, they received, SS attorneys did not heal wounds. Rybicki, representing the BAC board, described his approach to negotiations as "Bomb them into the stone-age." Simply enough, the SS presence on campus presaged a prolonged and intense attempt to break the faculty bargaining unit and create lawsuits for SS to handle.

Hiring SS, however, did cause a community backlash. A local school district dumping public funds into the coffers of an up-state law firm did not play well with the St. Clair County legal establishment. Once, when I mentioned SS to Belleville lawyer Bruce Cook, he laughed and said, "Yeah. And they haven't won a case here. We kick their ass every time."

Seyfarth Shaw's failures in St. Clair County had as much to do with the lack of quality of the litigation they encouraged as with the animosity they provoked in the BAC district generally. Later, after the 1980 strike, the SS presence at BAC would add substantially to the willingness of the district's legal, business, and union communities to support the BAC faculty union.

On two occasions, when the Wissore administration tried to fire me for my union activities, while I was being grilled by R. Wayne Clark, Frank Gornick, and Robert Eskridge, an SS lawyer was on a phone in an adjoining office dispensing advice and instructions about how they should proceed and what kinds of questions to ask. One time the grilling went on for several hours, all with SS attorney Ted Clark on the phone soaking up substantial taxpayer dollars that should have been spent on improving classroom instruction rather than on maintaining the dictatorship of the fiefdom.

Jim Massey, who served as chief faculty negotiator during Rybicki's first year (1974) as board negotiator, tells of showing up at the table with attorney Rex Carr. Several months earlier Carr had won the Hooks' personal injury lawsuit in Washington, D.C. for 7.5 million dollars, at the time the largest award ever granted in the United States to a plaintiff for personal injuries. Carr's notoriety for winning the case was not missed by Rybicki. At the first meeting he congratulated Carr on his success.

"What success?" Carr said.

"For your recent win in court," Rybicki replied.

"Win in court? Which one?" Carr said.

By now Rybicki wasn't sure he had the right man.

"The multi-million dollars you won in D.C."

"Oh," Carr said, "that decision. That was several months ago. I thought you were talking about something recent."

Later in the meeting Carr informed Rybicki that "If you think I'm going to sit here and tell you what I want and then listen while you tell me what you want, and then try to work out a compromise, you're wrong. I want what I want, and I'm going to get it, otherwise there's no point in us even talking."

With that Carr picked up his briefcase and headed for the door, leaving Rybicki to protest.

"Wait a minute. Wait. You haven't even heard what I have to say."

That was in April. The contract wasn't completed until October twenty-third.

* * * * *

In April of 1975 Edward O'Malley, Merle Justus (later Sheriff of St. Clair County), and John "Jack" Becker, a banker from Sparta, won three-year terms to the BAC board. The board was then comprised of Becker, Eckert, Gundlach, Justus, O'Malley, Sauer, and Milton Smith. And while O'Malley had already shown he would not always go along with the growing Eckert contingent, and Justus would occasionally stand to one side, Becker quickly fell into the queue with Eckert, Gundlach, Sauer, and Smith. I don't know of one issue during the following year on which Becker, Eckert, Sauer, and Smith did not vote in a block.

Board-faculty contract negotiations, with Rybicki representing the board, became prolonged, drawn out affairs. Rybicki's idea seems to have been that faced with board intransigence the faculty, whose primary duty was teaching, not negotiating contracts, would eventually lose interest or, exhausted with the process and its diminished hope, would capitulate. Then, too, the board was running the school, was not required to negotiate with the faculty and, in the board's estimation, didn't need the faculty anyway. And after all he was collecting one-hundred fifty dollars an hour.

As usual, negotiations began in the spring of 1975, though the contract would not be ratified until October twenty-third, and then for a 2-percent raise, which the board offered at the first meeting of the negotiating teams in the spring. By the fall of 1975 college enrollment had grown to 9,671 (60,800 credit hours—5,066 fulltime equivalent) more than double what it had been two years earlier. And while a cadre of new administrators was hired and half a dozen new voc-ed programs opened, only one or two new fulltime faculty members were appointed.

* * * * *

In the April 1976 board election eight people ran for two seats. Board president Theodore Gundlach's seat and that of Milton Smith had expired. Gundlach chose not to run, though Smith was a candidate. The other candidates were, Leonard Cuoco, Robert H. Dintelmann, Sam Gillespie, Elizabeth Jenner, Eric Lehr, Edward Roof, and Terrance G. Scandretti. Dintelmann and Smith won the seats. Smith was elected by just a handful of votes.

The vote count showed: Dintelmann 5,773; Smith 5,244; Jenner 5,237; Gillespie 3,246; Lehr 3,032; Roof 2,567; Cuoco 1,153; Scandretti 982.

It was Smith's second term. During the first he had, for the most part, gone along with the Eckert party-line, as immediately did Dintelmann. And for all practical purposes, this was the beginning of what came to be known as The Eckert Board.

As I said, Martha Sauer did not ever vote against the board's male majority, most often led by Eckert. At the time Dintelmann was heavily in debt to the First National Bank of Belleville, as well as a stockholder in the bank, and Eckert was a member of that bank's board. And though there appears not to have been any overt conflict of interest with Dintelmann's and Eckert's board positions, the possibility of a conflict of influence was there. On the other hand, Milton Smith, who was also the uncompensated BAC baseball team coach, did not, to my knowledge, ever vote against the majority. I should add, however, that Smith appeared to be a somewhat reluctant performer, and at the end of his term in 1978, probably because he had enough of the double-dealing, did not run again. With Robert Dintelmann on the board Smith was no longer necessary to the Eckert scheme. The addition of Robert Dintelmann to the board gave Eckert, with or without Smith, an intractable majority for whatever issue he chose to promote or endorse.

* * * * *

By the middle of 1976 the Keel administration had distanced itself significantly from the Faculty Senate and the faculty, and faculty-board conflicts took on new proportions. The board continued to add vocational programs, at substantial expense, but was unwilling to raise tuition or repopulate vacated baccalaureate-faculty position. The refusal to raise tuition, it seemed, came more by way of pandering to the public than anything real. Possibly the board didn't need the money or wanted to force a financial crisis to reduce the school to an educational shell with only token programs. More than likely the board had plenty of money and intended or at least hoped, as Rex Carr had accused it of doing seven years before, to take money from faculty salaries to feed even more voc-ed programs.

By the summer of 1975 board restrictions on the academic segment of the college, the essence of the college, had taken a destructive turn. At the May board meeting, Senate President James Massey complained that vacated fulltime faculty positions were not being filled. At the same meeting Otis Miller (History) asked why sabbaticals were being cut.

It is also possible that the attack on faculty came out of a personal animosity Eckert had for some of the teachers who owned farm land around the Eckert family's orchard business. Tribal memories of hostilities and/or imagined perfidies are sometimes long lasting.

1976–Prelude to a Strike

In 1976, for the first time, I joined the faculty negotiating committee headed by Marvin Braasch (Biology). Again, the negotiations committee labored through the summer, meeting on a regular basis with the board committee, without anything one could consider reasonable results. At the first meeting in May the board (Rybicki) offered the faculty a 1-percent pay increase with no increase in benefits and/or changes in working conditions. Four months later the board's offer was for a 1-percent faculty pay increase with no additional benefits and/or changes in working conditions.

In response to the stalemate, early in September, back in the classroom without a contract, Roger Christeck (English) and I—and several others—set up informational pickets at the entrance to the school—the first-time pickets were used at BAC. It was certainly the first time a pictures of the college faculty picketing the school appeared in a local newspapers.

Still, by the middle of September of 1976, there was no contract and conditions had deteriorated sufficiently for the Faculty Senate to send a note to President Keel that it

> . . . very strongly urges that President Keel, as the Chief Administrative Officer of Belleville Area College, exercise any and all influence and authority which he may have, toward a

quick, amiable and equitable settlement of the long with-
standing contract dispute between the faculty and the Board of
Trustees.

We the members of the Senate as duly elected represent-
tatives of the faculty feel that prolonging the situation that now
exists can and will only contribute toward a most uncomfortable, if not destructive relationship between the faculty, the
administration and the board.

At the October board meeting, AAUP attorney Mark Glass requested
arbitration. The board refused. At the same meeting the Faculty Senate,
hoping to re-connect with the board, proposed adding a non-voting member
to the board, to be chosen from the Faculty Senate. As expected, Keel
objected, as he no doubt had to, and the board refused the request.

Teaching: Advocacy and Politics

> What greater or better gift can we offer the republic than to teach and instruct our youth?
>
> —Cicero

The First Line of Defense

I arrived at BAC with the greatest of expectations. Colleges and universities were places I had entered the deep but comforting waters of intellectual and spiritual life, waters that gave sustenance and strength to living, and without which I believed truly one could not live well. Additionally, I wanted to write, and I loved teaching. BAC in the early '70s appeared to be the perfect place for me. I had hoped community college teaching might be free of travail and the internecine conflicts that infect university research and teaching enclaves. But it quickly became apparent that this was a misplaced hope, especially at BAC. Even at BAC, as small and new as it was, conflicts both among the faculty and with the administration were quite bitter.

Within the first few years I decided that since the *Memorandum of Understanding* was becoming the first line of defense, the one instrument that covered the faculty, and could be used to prop up the school, I would involve myself in the contract bargaining process. Robert Frost wrote, "Good fences make good neighbors." Well, good faculty contracts make good schools.

Then, too, sometimes the need for advocacy is self-evident. I had always believed that if someone (in this case the BAC fulltime faculty and the students they serve) needed support, and if I could help, the person or persons in need had a claim on me for whatever I could reasonably provide—my reasons for teaching in the first place. Still, my interest, as well as my sense of advocacy that led to my participation in college politics, had not developed accidentally or without trepidation.

Advocacy

Prior to teaching at BAC I lived in Chicago from 1964-68, and before teaching at Evanston High School in the fall of 1967 I worked in a residential therapy program for the Jewish Children's Bureau (JCB) at one of its Chicago's Northside clinics or residential treatment centers.

The JCB treatment unit, Eisenberg, was a three-story renovated office building at 6400 N California Avenue. The building had a lounge, dining room and kitchen, a couple of offices on the first floor, and six bedrooms and a lounge on both the second and third floors. It housed eighteen adolescent boys with affective disorders and was residential.

The boys usually arrived when they were twelve or so and stayed until they were twenty-one.

At Eisenberg my difficulties of advocacy were not limited to a house-full of estranged and troubled adolescent males—of my attempts to drive them sane before they drove me insane. As with the middle-parts of some human enterprises, it is not just an individual but a sizable chunk of the whole that is sometimes out of whack.

Those years my duties at Eisenberg included scheduling summer activities to keep the boys busy, and from maiming one another. Chicago summers can be brutally hot and dirty. For a cool-down, I tried to schedule as many swimming afternoons as I could. Whenever we could, we used the Lake Michigan Montrose and Oak Street beaches. But the lake was some miles away, and it wasn't always possible to get the boys there for swimming. Transportation was a problem, but so was lake pollution which often contaminated and/or closed the beaches. In fact, the last time I used the Oak Street beach an oil-slick blew in, and I ended with six raging adolescents covered from nose to toes with oil and no reasonable way to get them back to the unit without ruining the interior of my car—which the return trip did.

A Simple Story

However, in the spring of 1965 the director of the unit, Ord Matek (later Assistant Professor Emeritus, Jane Addams College of Social Work, University of Illinois at Chicago), advised me that several blocks from the unit down Peterson Avenue was a private Jewish social club with an Olympic-scaled swimming pool. He had spoken to the manager who said that from 10 a.m. to 2 p.m. on weekdays there was seldom anyone at the pool, and he would be amenable to the boys using it. And so, we did. For the next two summers, four or five times a week, from early June until late August, sometimes as many as nine or ten boys at a time, with a couple of counselors, frequented the pool. That would have been the summers of 1965 and 1966.

The following spring, one morning, I was chatting with Tom Brennan, another counselor, a defrocked priest from Covington, Kentucky I had dubbed the Bishop of Covington. He too was working on his summer schedule and asked what I had planned. I informed him that it was pretty much the same as the previous two summers.

"What about the pool?" he asked.

"I'd assume we could use it again," I said. "No one has said anything to the contrary."

"What about Marsha?"

It was a question that stopped me cold.

The previous fall, two counselors had been added to the staff. One was a young black woman named Marsha Simpson. The plan at the unit was to employ people of differing age, sex, and race to provide as complementary and integrated an environment for the boys as possible. And while some counselors were given specific tasks, assignments were always based on skills and talents, not on age, sex, or race—thus the question of what would happen if Marsha showed up at the club pool with a group of the boys. The possibility of objections to a black woman on our staff swimming in the pool at an upper-middle-class Jewish private club in Chicago had not crossed my mind.

The Bishop suggested I talk to the club manager about the possibility of a conflict, and I did. The next morning, I showed up at the club and asked the manager if the pool would again be open for our use. He said, "Yes." Then I asked what he might say if the black woman counselor we had added to the staff were to bring the boys to the pool. He said, "I'd say the invitation is rescinded."

I replied that I knew why he was doing what he did—for his fifty thousand a year—(a comfortable sum for any job in 1967), but under the circumstances I didn't have to deal with him on those grounds, and so we would not be using the pool that summer.

More than that, the "unit" was located on the cusp of Rogers Park, a "gilded ghetto," as its residents referred to it, a quite wealthy Jewish enclave, maybe 95-percent Jewish, but definitely gilded. A Lawrence Avenue community, on the other hand, slightly to the south of Rogers Park, was also heavily Jewish, but considerably less affluent.

Lawrence Avenue in the 60s featured the open shops and small markets that still grace many European cities. It wasn't uncommon in the middle '60s, watching people moving in and out of the shops, to find more than a few with numbers tattooed on their arms. This was only twenty years after the liberation of the German extermination camps.

At a staff meeting in late May of 1967, I reported on the summer programs for the boys, and specifically the pool situation. I related the story to the staff, as well as my reasons for scratching the pool use from the activities-agenda. It is notable that of the nine people at that meeting, five had close relatives, fathers, mothers, brothers or sisters who had died in German extermination camps. Three others had family living in Israel, family that had come out of Germany and that they (those in attendance that day) were in large part supporting financially. The reaction to my decision was not at all what I expected.

First, I was told Marsha did not have to take the boys swimming–there were others who could do that. Then I was told the boys shouldn't have to suffer just because the pool manager was recalcitrant. Then, I was told it was a private club, and the manager had the right to do what he did. Then I was told I was being overly sensitive to the race issue. Then I was told . . . .

No one said anything about the club members being racist, as recent history had told us the Nazis were racist. No one said anything about standing aside and watching as German citizens stood aside and watched the trains of cattle-cars loaded with prisoners, rumble by on their way to Buchenwald-Dora, Ravensbruck, or Sachsenhausen.

Several of the Jewish counselors volunteered to take the boys to the pool, as they said, "To protect Marsha." Maybe they hoped to protect the boys from a racist assault by the manager and any members of the club that might have been in attendance. But no one said anything about the damage the boys were sure to suffer by being exposed to the racists at the pool or by the racism of the counselors who had agreed to encourage the disease.

Although I did not anticipate the staff's reaction, I did understand there wasn't much I could say to reason with them. So, not at all rashly, I informed the group that if they persisted in overriding my decision, as soon as the meeting ended I was prepared to go into the adjoining office and type up a letter of resignation, leaving the date open until the first one of them took even one of the boys to the pool, at which time I would affix the date to the letter and submit it.

As it turned out there was a great deal of fretting and fussing about my decision, but no one from the unit, to my knowledge, used the pool after that. Several weeks later, the director Ord Matek, a man I hold in high esteem, even today these long years afterward, who had agreed with the others at that meeting, came to me quoting Martin Niemoller's 1946 poem about Nazi Germany.

> First, they came for the Communists,
> and I didn't speak up,
> because I wasn't a Communist.
>
> Then they came for the sick,
> the so-called incurables,
> and I didn't speak up,
> because I wasn't mentally ill.
>
> Then they came for the Jews,
> and I didn't speak up,
> because I wasn't a Jew.
>
> Then they came for me,
> and by that time there was no one left
> to speak up for me.

On two occasions in August of 1966, during the Chicago Freedom Movement's open housing initiative, I joined the Martin Luther King demonstrations and was hauled in. I do not remember being fingerprinted or posing for mug shots, so it is possible only the leaders were printed and booked. There was just too much confusion and too little significance in it to make any real difference.

Of course, the source of the difficulties had to do with us minding our own business, those days, carrying signs accusing Chicago's esteemed aldermen and their constituents of being racists, while crowding up the streets and sidewalks in all-white aldermanic neighborhoods. The residents, good patriotic Americans, recently migrated from the ethnic cleansing mania of central Europe, came out of their houses and apartments to scream and throw rocks at us.

When the police showed up we were forced, that is beaten and prodded with night sticks, into vans and carted off and detained, one time for seven hours, before the wisdom of the times set in, whatever that might have been, and all sixty or seventy of us, black, white, brown, yellow, and beige were turned loose. What became of this, I do not know—maybe some kind of mass pardon or amnesty, if that kind of thing was necessary—or maybe bureaucratic amnesia. The whole thing may have been forgiven in the deal Dr. King made with Mayor Daley and the city that fall. I left Chicago in June of 1968 and was not called back to face charges. But you have to wonder what of the activities ended up in FBI files. Studs Terkel and his wife were active dissidents during the Chicago '60s, and she was always quite proud that her FBI file was thicker than his. But they were well known and so much more visible than others of us. And then, too, when dealing with Chicago's finest, you never know what screwy thing might get going.

* * * * *

More recently I had been in King's March 25, 1967 anti-war demonstration, the assemblage of several tens-of-thousands that gathered on the near-Northside and traced a path down Michigan Avenue to the Coliseum. It was a march the newspapers characteristically reported as "The Reverend King and a small band of followers." But follow him the many of us did, as a symbol, as a spokesman, hoping to touch the deeper moral reaches of a divided and tortured America.

I was still in Chicago the following spring when King was assassinated, and the Westside of the city exploded. In an ominous and prophetic display of "Double, double toil and trouble; Fire burn and cauldron bubble," the April evening after an assassin's bullet killed Martin Luther King, Jr. in Memphis, the weather across the country was bad. The South erupted in tornadoes. A blizzard raked and ravaged Iowa and the Dakotas, and freezing rains pummeled the Upper Great Lakes.

Just before nine that evening I was driving on South Ashland Avenue when the news came over the car radio. I was traveling east on the avenue King had crossed four-years earlier, stepping through the color-barrier carrying a large segment of the city and of the country, black and white, with him.

That day the rain began shortly before noon. After the long Chicago winter, the large trees lining the old south side street had recently taken on foliage. But now Martin King lay dead, shot to death on the balcony of the Lorraine Hotel. The shock and sorrow of that, of that spring night, hung from the newly leaved trees in a mist as mystifying and chilling as the rain. And driving into the shadowed valley of that night, the street glistening beneath the street lights, listening to the heartbeat pulse of the wipers, I was struck again with the terrible dissonance of the cycles of death and rebirth.

* * * * *

I was teaching at Evanston High School at the time, and Monday morning we received a bulletin from the principal's office that the black students (Evanston was about 20-percent black) would be excused from class on Tuesday, April ninth, the day of King's funeral, to attend services. More in passing than with a plan, I mentioned to a colleague and friend, chemistry teacher Elizabeth Brenton, that as usual the school administration had responded to the black community with an insensitive and condescending agenda. That while the black students were excused from school the day of King's funeral, the administration seemed not to think King's death was important enough or worthy of a respect sufficient to close the school. It was little more than the administration saying "Okay, okay, nigger, go bury your dead, but don't bother me with it."

What, I asked Breton, if white students wanted to attend services with their black friends? What if teachers, most of whom were white, wanted to attend services with their black students? And what if, I surmised, within a few months when Chicago is blistering in the summer heat (Evanston is an immediate northern suburb of Chicago) and the memory of how King's death and burial had been minimized and disdained by the school administration still lingered in the minds of the black community, what if someone, or some group, decided to even the score and export a bit of the rage King's killing generated to burn this fine new school house to the ground? What if?

Breton was a member of the Superintendent's Faculty Advisory Council and asked if I would present my thinking to the council that day at an already scheduled noon meeting. So, I did. The faculty members on the council agreed with me, though there was some reluctance among the administrators. At two o'clock a second bulletin was issued, this time announcing that the school would be closed on Tuesday, April ninth, as a day of mourning.

The closing of Evanston High School that Tuesday in April was, however, not without educational significance. I contacted several of my students' (freshmen) parents and we arranged a series (five in all) of two-hour seminars in their homes beginning at nine o'clock in the morning and running until nine that night to discuss what Dr. King's death might mean to the country and how it might affect their (the students') lives. In other words, we set about trying to understand what a "day of mourning" really meant. There were from seven to twelve students at each seminar. I might add, the discussions were wonderfully rational and understanding.

The morning after King's death, Friday, April 5th, a large chunk of the Westside of Chicago was in flames. Fifty blocks away colonnades of smoke could be seen rising over West Madison Street, a giant roiling black monument to bitterness and anger. When you do not have money or power, which are the same thing, this is the only monument you can erect—black columns of smoke from the fires you set. People took to the streets looting and killing and burning. Whole blocks of apartments and stores were burned. Firefighters were greeted by snipers who had furtively secreted themselves in the ruins.

In an attempt to quell the rioting and protect the firefighters, the Lieutenant Governor dispatched five thousand National Guard troops to the area. Within the next week 10,500 police, 6,500 Illinois National Guard, and 4,000 paratroopers would be ordered into the area. But still the burning and looting and killing continued. Somewhere around 125 fires were reported, 11 people killed, most of them black, more than 500 injured, nearly 3,000 people arrested, and several hundred buildings destroyed.

* * * * *

At the time I was living on Juneway Terrace in the far north of the city, the last street in the city, in a totally mixed neighborhood. My barber was Mexican; the couple in the next-door apartment was from India. The kids downstairs were Chinese, and the incense and tie-dye crowd running the headshop around the corner were from the Lake Forest suburb. We were all just a few blocks from the Students for Democratic Society (SDS) headquarters on Howard Avenue.

Of course, the arson and looting of the first few days on the Westside left thousands of people homeless and hungry. Hundreds of families were burned out—black men and women and their children, sometimes families with small children and babies. Throughout the city religious and social organizations set up stations to collect food, blankets, and clothing. The Howard Avenue SDS volunteered its offices as a collection station.

That weekend the two large rooms at SDS filled with canned food, baby food, blankets, and clothing. Volunteers showed up Monday morning to help drivers load cars and small trucks for trips to a Catholic Charities halfway house at the edge of the ghetto.

I joined the supply train. We'd fill the trunk, the back and passenger-side seats of my old, white 1960 Chevrolet, leaving only enough room at the windows to see out. It was a good twenty-minute drive in traffic to the halfway house where we'd unload the cargo for workers who'd come in from community centers and churches in the burned-out neighborhoods to collect the goods.

On the afternoon of Friday, April twelfth, more to pass time than with any intention of making another cargo run, I stopped at the SDS station. I thought by then the supply lines would be well established and running and there would be little left to do. I was surprised to find the truck SDS had commandeered from a local trucking agency parked in the alley. When I arrived at the office a single volunteer, a scruffy white male, twenty-five or so, with a bushy afro and a blue work-shirt, was seated at the desk reading a magazine and drinking coffee. A cigarette burned in the ashtray. The two rooms behind him were piled from floor to ceiling with boxes of canned food and blankets that had accumulated during the day.

"You need help?" I said.

Scruff looked at me and shrugged. "I guess you could help, if you want."

"Is there something wrong with the truck?"

"No. It's okay."

"Then why don't we load it up and move some of this?"

"Well, you can, if you want. But I don't have the keys. Anyway, it's too late." He looked at his watch. It was about three-thirty. "We'd get caught in rush-hour traffic. I have to be out of here by six."

I didn't have plans before eight o'clock, and roughly calculated, considering rush-hour, I figured I could make it to the halfway house and back by seven.

"Will you help me load my car?"

Scruff shrugged. "Sure."

He stuffed out his cigarette and finished his coffee.

When we had the last box piled on the front seat, he held up his hand. "Just a minute. Before you go," he said, and returned inside.

Not only had we utilized every available inch of space in the car, but the weight of the boxes of food set the old Chevy down on its haunches, tailpipe and bumper only a few inches off the brick street.

"The Joad family," I thought, "headed for the Promised Land."

Scruff came back with a piece of paper. "We're delivering to a different address," he said. "The halfway house is closed today."

I didn't recognize the address. "Where is this?"

"About ten blocks down, west on Roosevelt Road."

By four-fifteen I had made it to Clark and Western, in surprisingly light traffic, moving along Western Avenue to the south. I thought it strange that a halfway house operating on the edge of mayhem and catastrophe should close just when people needed help the most. The Corporeal Works of Mercy on a nine-to-five schedule? Nine-to-twelve on Saturdays?

Then I understood. I had already turned west onto Roosevelt Road. Light traffic. This was Good Friday afternoon. There was no rush-hour traffic. Among other things, Chicago's a Catholic town. Many businesses close at noon on Good Friday. The same reason the halfway house was closed. Now I was headed directly into the combat zone. The whole thing about traffic and truck keys was bullshit. Scruff had known it all along—Scruff, just another chickenshit white man who wasn't about to get caught in the crossfire.

For a moment I wasn't sure what to do. Should I go back to Howard and unload the goods? We could wait until Monday. Maybe the halfway house would be open Saturday. Why not wait until Monday? Well, hell, the kids have to eat on Saturday and Sunday too.

Maybe it wouldn't be that bad. Surely there had to be other whites working in there some place. Not even the ghetto is pure ghetto. But you never know.

By then traffic had slowed. The sidewalks were crowded. The smoldering ruins of buildings on both sides of the street left little to the imagination. A block on, people spilled off the sidewalks into the street. Now the faces painted a sea of black, and I spent the next several minutes looking for a white face, somewhere, anywhere, in the street, in a car, just one white face. Speakers attached to light poles blasted soul music. Surely, there had to be one, someone Caucasian walking or riding, making safe passage through all of this. But it wasn't encouraging.

The walls of buildings that had not been totally destroyed were painted with black power slogans—the syllogisms of anger and hate.

KILL HONKIES
KILL THE PEOPLE WHO KILLED THE KING
DEAD HONKIES MAKE GOOD NEIGHBORS

During the week newspapers had carried stories of white motorists dragged from their autos and beaten, their vehicles destroyed. What if? What could I say? Well, I'd say what the two-thousand black people who had been lynched in this country between 1865 and 1900 had said in their last moments with the rope around their necks. I'd say, "You got the wrong man." I'd say, "I marched with King. He was as much to me as to you." I'd say, "I'm bringing in clothes and food for children. Do I look like an enemy?"

I'd say....

For the first time I got a feeling of what it was like to be black in America. What it is like to look around and not see any one your color and to know that many of those of the other color that you do see are hostile, some homicidally so—what it is like to plead your case and know you are not going to be heard.

Like I said, it wasn't encouraging. A white man creeping, not driving, in bumper-to-bumper traffic in a white Cinderella coach, down the darkest street he had ever been on, now wanting to be done with it, to make an escape. I tried to read the numbers on the paper Scruff had given me. Scruff, that gutless, nameless bastard, the Judas goat, had led me into this with full knowledge of what he was doing, leading me into doing what he wouldn't do himself.

People moved freely in the streets among the cars, reminiscent of Mardi Gras or a street carnival. Restaurants and bars with SOUL spray painted on their windows were doing business in spite of Mayor Daley's closing order, and his infamous "shoot-to-kill" directive to the police, whereby a two-by-three foot plastic box of wires and transistors and tubes, albeit admirably arranged, was equated with a human life and individual police officers were anointed judge, jury, and executioner.

Teenagers and young adults carried ghetto blasters on their shoulders, milling about, waiting for another round of five-alarms and shootouts with the National Guard. From what I could tell, the crowds appeared mostly festive, although I couldn't put much stock in that. A crowd's mood is a poor barometer, especially in the wake of the assassination of a beloved, national hero. Levity en mass could easily take a nasty turn.

Then I found the sign: *Food-Clothing, Here,* and eased out of traffic to the curb and onto the sidewalk where a temporary loading dock had been set up. Even before I shut off the engine, the passenger-side door opened, and a young black man stuck his head in.

"Where you from, man?"

"Howard Avenue," I told him. "The North Side."

"Glad you made it," he said. "We need this bad. Not much stuff coming here. An' we got more hungry babies than we can count."

I got out and unlocked the trunk. The man I had been talking to came around the car. He was a lean, muscular man, his chest and arms made larger by a tight white T-shirt with a St. Cecilia logo printed on it. "My name is Willis," he said.

"I've got several cases of baby food," I told him. "I think there are four in all."

When we had emptied the trunk, Willis looked inside the car and added, "We don't take blankets." He straightened up. "See that alley? That store?" He pointed to an alley on the other side of the street.

The stench of burned garbage hung on the air peppered with soft-soot flakes of paper and wood. In the time it took to make the several trips to the dock and back, my arms were covered with black spots.

Across the street on the second floor of a fire-damaged building a black woman worked on a charred windowsill with a dirty white towel, trying to clean the wood. The face of a small child hung behind her. Below the window five or six men were standing around smoking cigarettes.

"Blankets go there," Willis said, his voice dropping off. He turned deliberately and looked at me for a moment. "I tell you, man, you pile that stuff on the dock, and I'll get it to the other side."

I thanked Willis. "Now, how do I get out of here? The shortest, fastest way out."

"That way," Willis said, pointing west to Cicero.

I got back into traffic and headed west–and minutes later, a few surprisingly short blocks later, I was in Cicero where the previous September, with four thousand National Guard troops watching inactively, the people living along the march-route crawled into the trees at the street's edge and bombarded the two hundred Student Non-violent Coordinating Committee (SNCC) and Congress Of Racial Equality (CORE) marchers with beer bottles and bricks, driving them back into Lawndale, the ghetto King had crossed out of.

Research, Teaching and Service

The AAUP has long defined the professor's role as research, teaching and service. I take service by AAUP standards to mean service to the profession, service to the academic institution, and service to the community in which the institution is located geographically. Moreover, I have always believed that profession and avocation are deeply rooted in advocacy. Sartre thought that what we choose for ourselves we choose for the world. And for some of us at BAC, those who saw teaching was an avocation, it was also a trust, a good bit beyond simply having a job or making a living. I always thought I should go around getting into the mix. Go into the town square in ancient Athens, find a shady spot, when the time is proper, as a citizen, offer my opinion and cast my vote to improve the culture upon which we all depend.

In addition to teaching courses at BAC in writing, philosophy, folklore, and directing students in field research, I also sponsored annual traditional music and bluegrass concerts during the BAC Spring Fine Arts Festival. Some of the musicians I brought to the college were/are internationally and nationally renowned. There was George and Ethel McCoy, the niece and nephew of Memphis Minnie, as well as Clarence Johnson, and Henry Townsend, all nationally known blues musicians from East St. Louis. In fact, Clarence Johnson, who died at age eighty-three in 2006, is legendary for his contributions and innovations as a blues guitarist. At one concert we had state fiddle champs from Iowa, Missouri, and Illinois on the stage at the same time. Bringing these people to the school, exposing students to these musicians and their talents was also, advocacy, cultural advocacy.

Those years I was often asked to speak at the college and to local organizations about the labor history and folklore of Southern Illinois. The demand for guest speaking became so frequent that I had to limit it to once a month. Today I am still listed with SWIC Speakers Bureau for "Poetry from the Midwest" and give several seminars a year. But that too is advocacy.

Sometimes advocacy is embodied in recording or keeping an historical perspective. In 1976 I received a National Endowment for the Arts grant to record the religious music of the Scots-Presbyterian Covenanters.

The Covenanters came to the United States from Scotland in the seventeenth century to avoid religious persecution. After a series of religious battles, some Covenanters were brought to the United States and sold as slaves. Others, and those that escaped, settled on the East Coast, in South Carolina, and later migrated to the Midwest and the South. There are two groups of Covenanters in Southern Illinois—one in Red Bud and another in Oakdale. In 1976 there were too few to hold two Sunday services, so the congregations travel on alternate weeks to and from Red Bud and Oakdale. There is also a congregation of black Covenanters in Selma, Alabama.

The Covenanters were of interest to ethnomusicologists because their services include singing psalms unaccompanied or a-cappella, and because the sect is fading from the American landscape. Knowing groups such as the Covenanters sometimes disappear, ethnomusicologists at the Library of Congress and National Folk Archives, in this case Archie Green and Alan Jabor, wanted examples of the music recorder and preserved.

When the award was recognized at the BAC board meeting in January 1976, I was asked to give a short presentation, which I did, explaining why the National Folk Achieves was interested in the Covenanters, an explanation that elicited a side-of-the-mouth remark from board member Curt Eckert that "We already have too many folk around here, and don't need any more."

I also organized and conducted English 101 classes at the college for gifted eighth-graders, without additional remuneration for the time and effort spent preparing these classes. From 1972-79 Roger Christeck and I, by choice and as a matter of service, taught classes at least two nights a week to be certain there would always be a fulltime professor from the English-Philosophy Department on hand between three o'clock in the afternoon and seven o'clock when most evening classes are scheduled, as well as to provide fulltime faculty instruction to night students. We counseled students, took phone calls, and generally provided for the educational non-classroom culture of our small section of the college. We were fulltime faculty, and that was, in part by way of our positions what we provided for the college in extra-contractual services.

I might add that many other fulltime faculty at the college did the same thing. In fact, those days so many of the BAC fulltime faculty provided extra-curricular services for the school that led Don Libby to observe that, "If the fulltime faculty were to reduce their activities just to teaching, the place would cease to function as a college." That is why we came to teaching in the first place, to provide for students, the community and thus, little by little, for the larger society.

Academic Cleansing

Remember that our first great leaders
were also our first great scholars.
—John Fitzgerald Kennedy

Bargaining Agent Election

Once the battle for academic survival and, in many ways, for our spiritual-professional survival, and that of our students and the school itself, had been joined, even in face of the grim realities, the machinations were occasionally humorous. One afternoon in September of 1976, to advance the picketing Christeck and I had started several days before at the main campus, Jim Massey, Jim Lang (Mathematics), Barb Kordenbrock (Speech) and I showed up with picket signs at Curt Eckert's realty office on First Street next to the Turners Hall and the old YMCA in downtown Belleville. Within a few minutes of our arrival, probably summoned by Eckert, Wissore appeared with a camera to take our pictures—for what reason I am not sure. Certainly, people with picket signs out in the bright light of day are not likely to deny having been there. The idea is, among other things, to be seen. As it turned out, Wissore could not get the camera to work, and in a moment of generosity and compassion I suggested that if he would hold the sign for me, I would take the pictures for him. Of course, he turned down my offer. But the opportunity was not lost since Kordenbrock had already walked to the public phone on the corner and called the *BND*, who sent a photographer. The next day our picture appeared in the paper, no doubt satisfying Mr. Eckert's desire for a photo-record of the event.

As threatening as the board now appeared to be to faculty and school interests, and as divided as the faculty was politically, there was still a general bravado circulating among certain precincts of the BAC-AAUP. Jan Milligan was fond of saying that "they" (the board and administration) would not again (after the 1969 recess) cross the faculty. But as late as October 21, 1976, the faculty was still without a contract and the board had not authorized payment of the increment due the faculty by the continuing contract under which it was working. Then, during the last week of October a faculty sickout was called, and one day seventy-six out of one-hundred twenty-two of the BAC faculty did not show up in their classrooms. The boycott, however, failed to elicit a response from the board and we labored on into November without a contract.

* * * * *

Beyond the frustrations of stalled negotiations that fall, internal intrigues continued to plague the faculty. The November third senate minutes report that,

The Senate has received a petition signed by forty-eight fulltime faculty, which reads as follows: 'We the undersigned, petition the Faculty Senate to invite representatives from the AFT and from the Teamsters to appear on campus within the next three weeks to explain the relevance of their organization to next year's faculty-staff negotiations.' After discussion of the petition the senate decided to hold an all-faculty meeting at which time the AFT and Teamsters will be invited to address the meeting. Mr. Ptasnik (Faculty Senate President) will make arrangements to invite the speakers and personnel will be informed as to the date and time when arrangements are finalized.

To add to the rumbles of the revolt, Wayne Ault (Political Science) showed up at the December board meeting with Teamster organizer Vincent Speranza and asked the board to recognize the Teamsters as the faculty collective bargaining agent.

It is hard to imagine that out-of-the-clear-blue, without any preparation whatsoever, anyone would have thought the board might recognize the Teamsters as a bargaining agent for the BAC faculty. In 1976 the board was not yet required to recognize anyone as a bargaining agent for the faculty. The board could have declined to recognize the AAUP, and had already done just that. Despite Rex Carr's early attempts to separate the faculty from the board and give it political standing, as late as 1976 the AAUP Salary Committee was little more than a renegade board committee. The AAUP had returned to fantasying itself as board related, though it still had no power, and very little community support. In other words, the board had matters well under control.

Likewise, several board members were businessmen who had had dealings in one form or another with the Teamsters and clearly, if it could be avoided, did not want further dealings with them. Additionally, the nationally reported and unsolved disappearance of ex-Teamster boss and ex-con Jimmy Hoffa on July 30, 1975, was still fresh in everyone's mind. And it wasn't just the Teamsters. Board members did not want to deal with *any* union, if they could avoid it.

Board minutes from the December 1976 board meeting show that,

President Keel read the request from Vincent Speranza, organizer for the Illinois Conference of Teamsters, dated December 7, 1976, requesting placement on the agenda for the purpose of requesting recognition of Teamsters Union Local 525 for collective bargaining.

Mr. Speranza asked that the Board consider two requests–one, the request for recognition of Teamsters Union Local 525 for collective bargaining, and two, for an appointment with the fiscal officer for the purpose of requesting payroll deductions.

Mr. Speranza said that over 50-percent of faculty who had signed authorization cards represented a majority of the faculty; that the Teamsters were in the College to stay until they have the right for collective bargaining. He went on to say that contrary to newspapers, the Teamsters were interested in education, with optimum environment achieved by the best working conditions, with people satisfied with their jobs. He noted his resentment of slurs cast upon the Teamsters, citing the size of the organization, with recognized powers as a bargaining authority, and as lobbying experts. He stated that negotiations with Teamsters would be good for both sides.

He requested again that the Teamsters be recognized as the new bargaining authority or as an alternative, having an election to determine the recognition of a new authority for collective bargaining for the faculty.

The Board recognized the representative from AFT (Ed Geppert, Jr.), who said that the request of the Teamsters was unparalleled in history, and that if an election were to be held, AFT wished to be included.

Mr. Justus said that in fairness to all persons involved, he wished to move that the decision for recognition or election be made at the next meeting of the Board, after consultation with Mr. Rybicki. Mr. Becker seconded, and the motion carried by acclamation.

The meeting then turned to current negotiations, and after a reading of the faculty proposal, "Chairman Eckert said that the faculty counteroffer had been referred to the negotiations committee, who had advised its rejection. Mrs. Sauer moved, seconded by Mr. Smith, to reject the counteroffer of the college faculty. Motion carried by ..." a unanimous roll call vote.

Board minutes further relate that,

President Keel recommended that the Board issue the general contract by the Board of Trustees for the faculty of Belleville Area College, with individual contracts for faculty members, excluding AAUP, with the option of the faculty to sign or not sign.

Mr. Smith moved, seconded by Mrs. Sauer, that individual general contracts of the Board of Trustees be issued to faculty members. Motion carried unanimously.

At this point there was an exodus of many of the faculty members from the room.

Mr. Jim Massey, faculty member, informed the Board that

although 51% of the faculty had signed Teamster cards, the action of the Board would drive the remaining 49% into the same action.

Mr. Tom Cochran, faculty member, said that he had already been issued a contract signed by the President, and the revised contract would be placed in file 13.

Cochran's remark suggests that Keel had anticipated the board's intentions or had been directed by individual board members behind the scenes and had already issued individual contracts to the faculty. There is, however, nothing in the board minutes to substantiate this.

Mr. Joe Evans, faculty member, and president of AAUP at Belleville Area College, asked if this action meant that negotiations were at an end. Chairman Eckert said that the Board had not taken away the negotiating process, but the negotiations for 1976-77 were now at an end, settling the issue once and for all.

Mr. Marvin Braasch, faculty member, and head of their negotiating team, told the Board that their actions would not result in a good atmosphere in January, but rather would destroy the educational process. He spoke of his efforts to meet privately with the Board's negotiating team and the Board to reach what he termed could have been a quick solution to the problems.

Chairman Eckert made the following statement: Although this action may not bring the financial settlement which some faculty may have hoped for, we believe it is a fair one. It is one which will allow us to use our financial resources to support our educational program as we should. Hopefully, it will allow us to restore badly needed funds to department budgets. And finally, we believe that it will allow us to avoid leaving fulltime staff positions vacant as attrition affects our staffing levels.

Going into the 1976 Christmas break, the faculty again appears to have been wearied by the negotiating process, aware that it wasn't going to get anything more, and having maintained something of the status quo, decided to move on. And although the faculty finally ratified the new contract in early January, the faculty bargaining-agent issue was neither resolved nor abandoned. A few years down the road it would become clear that Ault and his people had given SS, who always had a special interest in exploiting faculty division, a good bit of insight as to how to proceed.

Again, in January Ault showed up at the board meeting, this time referring to himself as "Shop Steward for the Teamsters."

The January 1977 board minutes indicate that,

Mr. Smith moved, seconded by Mr. Dintelmann, to reject

recognition or election for collective bargaining for faculty of Belleville Area College. Motion carried by a unanimous roll-call vote.

Chairman Eckert recognized Wayne Ault, faculty member. Mr. Ault asked if this was the opinion of the Board and the negotiating attorney, and requested that the Board reconsider, stating that an election might prove that a majority of the faculty do not support the AAUP.

Don Anderson, of the firm of Seyfarth, Shaw, Fairweather & Geraldson, the Board's negotiating firm, said that this was not an appropriate question at this time, that the ratification by the faculty of the *Memorandum* concludes the matter.

Mr. Ault said that an election on representation was part of the democratic process.

The Chairman noted that the Board, in the *Memorandum of Understanding*, recognizes the AAUP as the duly authorized representative for collective negotiations.

In response to Mr. Ault's question with regard to represent-ation for the next year's negotiations, Mr. Anderson stated that at the current time the faculty were represented by AAUP, and the matter was closed.

Miss Padden asked for clarification of motive with regard to recognition of the faculty's authorized representative for collec-tive negotiations. Mr. Ault said that an election would clarify the representation, ending the division within the faculty.

Mr. Nold, the college attorney, stated that the matter was decided and closed, and certainly such action as recommended by Mr. Ault could not follow on the heels of ratification of the contract just approved.

Ed Wren, Student Senate member, stated that he had been involved in the conflict since its beginning, and requested that the Board consider an election to determine faculty representation for collective negotiations.

Mr. Becker moved, seconded by Mr. Dintelmann, to approve the *Memorandum of Understanding* for 1976-77 between the Board of Trustees and Faculty of BAC. Motion carried by a unanimous roll-call vote.

Chairman Eckert read the following statement:

Please be advised that on Wednesday, January 12, 1977, a majority of the Belleville Area College faculty members ratified a new collective bargaining agreement between the Board and AAUP. From this voluntary action by the faculty, it is clear that a majority of bargaining unit employees wish to continue their representation by the AAUP. Since this is clearly the case, there is no question concerning representation at the College. Therefore, your demand for recognition of the Teamsters (or an election) is rejected and the Board considers the subject closed.

That Ault thought he needed permission from the board to hold an election to determine faculty representation indicates that he still thought of the bargaining agent as a board committee. More than that, Ault's begging demonstrated again just how subservient the faculty had become to board authority.

Don Anderson's presence at the meeting seemed especially pro-phetic. Rybicki was the negotiating attorney, and the contract had been ratified and signed by the faculty, with nothing left but a board vote, so Rybicki need not have been there. But neither did Anderson have to be there, unless SS anticipated more questions on the representation issue. Likewise, it would have been a time for Anderson, who was Rybicki's superior to assess the situation, and to advise the board in preparation for the next assault on the faculty. Certainly, preparations for that assault were given new impetus by the Teamster charade, not the least of which was a verification of the percentage of faculty who might defect from whatever faculty bargaining collective still operated at the college.

And although the next contract negotiations (1977-80) did not involve any major altercations, it did give Keel time to run a series of tests on the board, no doubt with Wissore's advice and encouragement. Wissore-Keel initiated activities to which they knew the bargaining unit would object, to test, in barnyard terms, which board members would "stand hitch" for the fight to come that they were planning.

* * * * *

By 1977 the BAC Faculty Senate was without power, real or persuasive. Usually with Wissore as his counsel, Keel sidestepped senate inquiries and advice more and more. As Keel and/or Wissore avoided senate questions, and then senate contact, the governance gap between the board and the faculty grew into a chasm. At the same time the board was becoming even more secretive and remote, and then downright hostile to the faculty and academic concerns. Because of the tensions, faculty-board relations became increasingly adversarial and could only be addressed through the *Memorandum of Understanding*, through the bargaining unit, or not add-ressed at all. This shift in faculty-board relations reduced the senate, still controlled by the AAUP old guard, to sending flowers to funerals, admin-istering inter-faculty squabbles, and little else.

Then, at the February 2, 1977 Faculty Senate meeting, Lynn Bradley (Earth Science) made the motion:

Whereas, the BAC teamsters have petitioned for a collective bargaining election by filing with the Faculty Senate President, signed authorization cards representing 30-percent or more of the fulltime faculty. I, therefore, move that an election by secret ballot for determination of a collective bargaining agent preferred by a majority of the faculty of BAC be called for Tuesday, March 22, 1977, and notice of subject be announced to all BAC faculty members by campus mail by the secretary of the Faculty Senate no later than Friday, March 4, 1977.

The motion passed by a roll call vote, 8-1. D. C. Edwards cast the lone dissenting vote.

After that, things got strange, very strange indeed. The Faculty Senate received a ". . . petition signed by fourteen fulltime faculty, requesting placement of the AAUP on the ballot for the preferential bargaining agent election."

The same day the Faculty Senate received a ". . . memo from AAUP requesting their organization *not* (emphasis added) be placed on the ballot for preferential bargaining agent election sponsored by Faculty Senate."

I do not know who from the AAUP sent the request. But if it came from the AAUP, why did the AAUP not want to be on the ballot? Possibly the AAUP leaders still thought of the Salary Committee as a board and administrative handmaiden and did not want to be put in an adversarial position with the board by becoming a faculty union.

At the March 1977 board meeting the AAUP and Faculty Senate asked the board to "sanction an election" to determine a bargaining agent. It was becoming increasingly clear by then that maintaining the AAUP Salary Committee with its subservience to the board, as a board committee appointed and sanctioned by the board, would be disastrous for faculty governance. Only an established union local, through collective bargaining, could hold the board responsible and promote quality education by protecting the faculty and the faculty obligation to academic excellence. But again, the AAUP and the Faculty Senate, without duress, but with an excess of servile obeisance, bowed to the board.

Even before the bargaining-agent election it was clear that the Teamster proposal was just another pie-in-the-sky fantasy of Superman stepping out of the phone booth to beat up on the bad guys. In fact, when the faculty who spawned the Teamster alliance met with Teamster officials, they were told that affiliation did not mean salvation and that the local union would still have to provide for itself.

In spite of its claims, the Teamsters of the '70s were not set up to represent academics. The Teamster experience had been with problems and objectives different from those that confront a college faculty. An enormous number of higher education teaching endeavors, the academic activities that make teaching both possible and viable, occur in a variety of places and at times other than the classroom or faculty offices. The college teaching locus et tempus is significantly different from that of textile and food workers and truck drivers.

No matter what occupation they represented, the Teamsters traditionally bargained for money, and sometimes for working conditions, but little else. The deeper part of the BAC fulltime faculty and board conflict had to do not so much with working conditions, but the obstructive priorities the BAC administration was attempting to impose on the faculty, as well as the blighting of educational programs in which the BAC professors were individually and collectively involved. Since the Teamsters had little experience with negotiating for anything other than money, the problems of office assignment, release time, sabbaticals, funds for research, as well as academic freedom, were not likely to have been addressed or remedied by the Teamsters. Even Wissore understood that negotiations with the Teamsters would be mostly about money, though in dealing with the faculty it wasn't a demand for money that gave Wissore his biggest headache. The problem he found with professors is that they (some of them) want to talk about principle, about right and wrong, about doing what they are doing well, and then doing it even better—Wissore found this mystifying.

From the faculty side of the equation, a hook up with a union representing truck drivers, day-laborers and textile and food-service employees, was unlikely. Despite Ault's representations there would always be the "blue collar," "white collar" and "professional" perceptions and ident-ifications to deal with. American college professors have seldom seen themselves as "workers" or proletariat. Unlike their European counterparts, American professors have not willingly or easily identified with the labor movement. So, the teamsters would have been of little help or significance for the BAC faculty.

On April 6, 1977, the Faculty Senate called a full-faculty meeting to determine if a collective-bargaining agent election would be held. The faculty voted sixty-five to thirty-six in favor of the election. And on April 25, 1977, in an election overseen by an Illinois Department of Labor representative (although teachers did not yet have collective bargaining rights), the AFT-IFT received twenty-seven votes (23-percent), the AAUP received seventy votes (57-percent), and the Teamsters Local 525 received twenty-four votes (20-percent). If the election results did not change the BAC faculty's collective bargaining agent, the vote did cast a good bit of doubt on Ault's claim that 51-percent of the faculty would support the Teamsters. On the other hand, not only had the AAUP preference among the faculty slipped, but it appeared that a meaningful number of the faculty might be looking for an alternative to what the AAUP Salary Committee could provide.

Tenured-Faculty Evaluation

From 1977-80 (with a one-year opener for salary in 1979-80) matters lumbered on with the board pontificating impending financial calamity while at the same time lauding the wisdom of its sound fiscal management. What the Eckert block wanted but did not quite know how to go about doing, was to cut salaries, which to them meant academic cleansing or ridding the school of fulltime faculty, the one high-priced variable in the college budget. The board claimed that it needed to reduce the number of fulltime faculty to save the school money and keep it financially solvent— though leaks from board executive sessions added stories of vicious and vindictive personal vendettas to the scheme.

The board clung to the corporate party-line that 82-percent of college expenditures for salaries was unacceptable. And though at this time BAC was seriously overloaded with high paid administrators, and fulltime faculty salaries at BAC accounted for only 41-percent of total personnel expenses (which was 82-percent of the total BAC budget), the plan was still to dispose of as many fulltime faculty as possible.

This was, of course, corporate-think at its worst. Public schools are not factories providing a product but are non-profit organizations that offer a people-community service. Taxpayers pay for the services teachers offer. Beyond teachers and those who provide immediate close-order support, such as librarians and counselors, everyone else in a school is simply an expendable addon. In spite of the claims of the Information Technology people, and other industries trying to corner the college and university expenditure markets, the closer the expenses of a college, or of any school for that matter, come to 100-percent for research and teaching, the better the institution.

One of the more striking ironies of the Eckert Board fiasco was that the board relied on outside, non-academic agencies—public relations, accounting, and law firms to provide guidance and to instruct the board about what to do and how to do it. If the per-student cost of a college education is high, it's nothing compared to the per-board-member cost of hiring high-priced corporations to tell an incompetent board how to run a college.

The Eckert Board set out to cut the number of fulltime faculty to reduce the burden with which it believed the college saddled taxpayers, especially large land-owner-taxpayers in the BAC district like Eckert Orchards. Since board members had very little experience with or awareness of education, especially postsecondary education, it seemed not to occur to them or they did not care, that what they were doing would damage the academic veracity of the college, and therefore the community the college represents and serves.

* * * * *

The attacks leveled against American public education in the last century have focused almost entirely on teachers. The myth has been forwarded that American public education is failing and can only be improved by cleansing the system of bad teachers. What has yet to be addressed is whether the system is indeed, failing—and it may not be. But if it is, and the teachers are at fault, then how did so many bad teachers come into the system? Who appointed them?

At least on the K-12 level, education mandated by all the states of the union requires that every citizen by law at one time or another (five years to seventeen) participate as a student in the school system. This means that education is the largest of all socially mandated programs of the several states. Yet no one, no state has yet been willing to provide the money necessary to properly support this massive enterprise.

Of course, at the center of the underfunding is the cold hard reality that teachers have never been paid wages commensurate with their education. This means that schools of education cannot attract better students, and schools of education populated with something less than the better students, as training grounds for teachers, cannot set and/or enforce rigorous standards, lest by the end of day the rolls will have been significantly reduced, if not depleted.

Likewise, even when school administrators have an opportunity to select better students from better colleges and universities for teaching jobs, they seldom do. The understanding is that bright, highly motivated teachers are an administrative nightmare. While they are most often right about teaching and learning, they can also be noisy, irreverent, and down-right obstreperous—most often difficult to control or manage. They seldom adhere to the status quo, political correctness, or the other dull-mindedness that school systems hold as a sacred trust. As I noted earlier, school administrators in selecting teachers prefer the obeisant and servile.

All of that said, I would still submit that under the circumstances of too many classes to teach of rooms overloaded with culturally indifferent or deprived students and burdened by oppressive boards and administrations, most K-12 and community college teachers are doing a remarkable job.

* * * * *

In the spring of 1977, in a further invasion of BAC faculty autonomy and to gather information that could be used to remove individual faculty members, the board resurrected the tenured-teacher evaluation (TTE) ruse. Probably at the suggestion or insistence of Eckert and/or Rybicki, at the April board meeting Keel proposed that the board establish an evaluation process for tenured teachers. I suspect this came from Eckert, an officer at

Eckert Orchards and Farms, an organization that had for years profited from the use of migrant farm workers. Along with other board members at the time, Curt Eckert viewed faculty as day-laborers, no better than migrant workers. Certainly he treated them that way. Once, when Jim Massey as faculty chief-negotiator, opposed one of Eckert's edicts, Eckert told Massey, "I always thought of you as a bright young man. But I've changed my opinion about you." Massey replied, "Well, your opinions are your business. But I haven't changed my mind about you."

The TTE scam as it appeared in 1977 was also supported by the politically conservative, and in many ways anti-educational, Illinois Community College Trustees Association (ICCTA) which had formed in the late '60s and attached itself to the burgeoning Illinois junior (community) college system. The BAC board became an ICCTA member in 1972.

Illinois Community College Tenured Teacher Act

As early as 1940 the Illinois General Assembly enacted a teacher tenure law for primary and secondary schools. The first BAC board, possibly with the K-12 law in mind, incorporated the AAUP document on academic freedom and tenure into the first BAC faculty contract. Even if only stated in the BAC Board Policy, tenure assured that fulltime faculty could not be removed for anything less than "just cause." Moreover, granting BAC faculty tenure was a safeguard against the board election process going haywire. Once established, tenure made it difficult for future maverick or runaway boards and their administrations to interfere in the long-term academic planning and instructional viability of a school by removing fulltime faculty at will or whim.

The tenure safeguard for teachers is informed by the same philosophy that puts federal justices on the bench for life and underlies the federal governmental structure of checks and balances. It also informs the State Department's practice of keeping career diplomats and undersecretaries in place, sometimes for decades, regardless of the political machinations and leanings of Congress or the White House. It is the career diplomats' expertise-held-in-place that is meant to keep elected officials from making fools of themselves and otherwise to ensure that government programs, domestic and foreign, have the continuity to run smoothly.

Most tenured-teacher evaluations schemes ignore the fact that by the time a teacher is granted tenure he/she has already been evaluated numerous times over a three or four-year period and suggests that teachers somehow become faulty with more experience.

In May of 1977 the BAC board formed the Faculty Evaluation Study Committee (FESC) comprised of the vice president for instruction, three faculty members, two students, two administrators, two deans, one department head, and two board members–in other words, two board members, five administrators, four faculty, and two students. You don't need a calculator for that one.

Tenured teacher evaluation at BAC was a proposed contract take-back, an attempt to undo or redo what had been agreed to and established at an earlier time. Simply put, the Eckert Board wanted to remove fulltime faculty from the school and hatched the FESC plot as part of that plan. By then, because of the board's practice of filling vacated fulltime faculty positions with multiple part-timers (after 1972 very few new fulltime faculty was appointed), well onto 95-percent of the fulltime faculty were tenured. More importantly to the board's thinking, nearly 100-percent of the AAUP membership was protected by the tenure shield.

Otherwise, I do not know what complaints there might have been about tenured BAC faculty or that the faculty was in any way derelict or incompetent in its duties. It is difficult to know what problems tenured faculty might have presented beyond having to teach too many classes, with too many students in each class, with little or no moral or material support, and all of it for substandard pay.

December 5, 1978, Keel dismissed the Faculty Evaluation and Study Committee. The committee had been meeting for over a year and had produced a draft of what appeared to be an equitable procedure (as equitable as something like tenured teacher evaluation might be) and was preparing to present the document to the board when Keel dismissed the committee. Keel's stated reasons, and I might add the board's reasons, since Keel could not have dismissed the committee without board approval, were that the committee's proposals gave the faculty too much power in evaluating tenured faculty—as they already had in evaluating non-tenured faculty.

The committee's dissolution elicited a Faculty Senate letter to Keel stating that "The Faculty Senate is extremely upset, shocked, and dismayed with the dissolution of the Faculty Evaluation Study Committee and requests the opportunity to discuss with the Board of Trustees Curriculum Committee and the Board as a committee of the whole, the President's reasoning behind such dissolution."

As far as I know, the board ignored the senate request. A few months later in the spring of 1979, the administration unilaterally prepared a new TTE document. Several administrators were assigned the task and within a few hours fashioned an innocuous document as weak minded as it was spurious, which was passed by the board at its May meeting. D. C. Edwards attended the meeting and reminded the board that "No faculty has seen the document," and that the board and administration had circumvented the faculty in creating the evaluation program.

To her credit, when it came up for a vote, Elizabeth Jenner, who arrived on the board in April of 1977, and had been on the Faculty Evaluation Study Committee, voted "Naye." Jenner's service on the committee and her vote against the board's rigged evaluation document would later lead board member Robert Dintelmann to claim Jenner had ". . . in the past subverted the interests of the board, entertained hidden agendas and sometimes supported special interests instead of the district as a whole."

The evaluation document the administration unilaterally prepared and the board approved was little more than a rating system based on student opinion. It was a questionnaire of some twenty-five or so items to determine how popular a professor was with his/her classes. In most cases it asked students to make judgments they had neither the education nor the skill to make.

The BAC evaluation asked students to approve or disapprove statements such as "Overall my instructor is an effective teacher," and whether or not "The teacher knows his subject."

To enquire of a professor if a colleague he/she has evaluated is or is not well-schooled in his discipline might have some relevance. But asking a nineteen or twenty-year-old student if a professor, who has put in a minimum of six years of college or university study, and many times has been teaching for fifteen or twenty years, knows his/her subject, is ludicrous.

Reams of research have shown that student evaluations of professors are tied to a host of items, almost none of which have to do with a professor's classroom skills or expertise, but always with students liking the professor (receiving a good grade), claiming the professor is fair (receiving a good grade), and having fun in the classroom (receiving a good grade).

Once, after instructing a class on the use of APA documentation for research papers, a student informed me that both he and his mother thought I was crazy, and that there was neither need nor reason to have a reference page on a written document. At least according to that student, I didn't "know my subject."

One evaluation entry asked students to rate whether or not the teacher provided a comfortable environment for learning. This comes in large part from the "high-esteem" babble that schools of education have foisted on the American school system, whereby it is predicated that students must feel good to learn. It's a damaging encouragement that sends students into the college classroom with the inflated-ego belief that they are not only the authority on whatever the topic at hand might be, but that they need not put forth any effort beyond being their not-too-pleasant, wonderfully authoritarian selves. In fact, under the feel-good mantel, one student described his academic pursuits as ". . . sit and watch, complain once in a while, then change the channel."

The high-esteem comfort agenda does not encourage learning and scholarship. I would suggest that any number of my students frequent bars on weekends—and spend a good bit of time feeling good, but do not learn much. Jesuit William Wade, a long-time chair of the Philosophy Department at Saint Louis University and considered by many as one of the great teachers in St. Louis University history, often, quite sardonically, compared students to rats. "A rat won't fight unless it's cornered," Wade was fond of reminding us, "and a student won't think unless he's cornered." He was equally scathing about the entire education process as a matter of "information going from my notes to your notes without passing through either of our heads."

Of course, we were more than pleased with Pere Wade's rat analogy and perfectly willing to gnaw on whatever scholarly fodder he produced, to see if, in fact, we could digest it and get from it what intellectual stimulation or nourishment there might have been. It is also possible, and more than a little likely, that the tension the digestion of the intellectual challenge caused, might be construed as a not too "comfortable environment."

For many years I taught an introductory ethics course, something the British call "a questioning course." Predictably, I had any number of students in the class who were more than a little upset with the questioning environment I provided.

As of habit, the first day of class each semester I would give a series of propositions or questions I wanted the class to think about over the course of our discussions and, hopefully, by the end of the semester, to formulate something in the way of a reasonable response. In one of the assigned questions I asked them to assume that they had just brought home a week-old infant from the hospital and that they were to be the child's caregiver for the next twenty years. I asked them to determine what they wanted that child to know and what skills they wanted the child to have by the time he was twenty. Moreover, I wanted them to consider how much of their time, energy, and resources they were willing to commit to the child's education, both intellectually and physically.

It seems to me there is no more ethical question than this. Immanuel Kant thought that culture was the only absolute in the human condition, and the kind of life each human lives, the character of each of us directly affects and drives the culture, sometimes for hundreds of years beyond our own lives. History is filled with the details of cultures that have gone wrong, where the quality of life has been seriously damaged and/or destroyed by the failure of the culture to properly educate its young.

One semester, three nearing-middle-aged women showed up in the class, probably mothers that time and good luck had recently liberated somewhat from their maternal chores. They occupied the front row center-right of the classroom, from my point of view, sitting in a block each class, reminiscent of the see-no-evil, hear-no-evil, and speak-no-evil vintage. Not only did they form a block each day in class, but on other occasions I'd see them in the library or cafeteria always traveling in tandem or bunched up at a table in the corner nodding over their studies, comparing notes. But always they seemed to be together.

The next class the three noes paraded into the classroom, as I say, in tandem and a bit early, and arranged themselves in their chosen row. As it turned out I too had arrived early that day and was going over my notes when one of them, probably Hear-no, referring to the inquiry I had posed said, "You should have given this assignment to the males in the class."

When I reminded her that there were men in the class, and I expected them to respond every bit as much as I did the women, See-no chimed in with "I guess you spent as much time with your children as your wife did."

I told her, "When my sons were still quite small, and my wife was working on her master's degree, and later when she was teaching, I spent most afternoons and evenings caring for them. When they were a little older, all through grade school and high school, I met them after school every day and either went to the gym with them or took them with me wherever I went. That was my job as a parent, as a teacher."

Not wanting to be left out, Speak-no said, "Thank god there's a man some place who takes care of his children."

"Yes," I told them, "raising children is much too important to be left to women."

That blew the roof off. There was a great wailing and howling, though after they settled down, they did a credible job in the class, determining what it might take to guide a human being into the adulthood of good character. I'm not certain that what we did in class that semester, the discomfort my probing caused them, dissuaded them of their stereotypes and prejudices. But then you never know. Possibly they even discovered that they had done a worthy job with their own children—and maybe the fathers of their children had contributed more to the raising and education of the children than they (the three noes) were at first willing to admit.

In another class, I had a student I will call Student L. Student L was a very boisterous and outspoken young man who showed up intent upon indoctrinating me (and the class) with his Ku Klux Klan theology, and took red-faced and very nearly violent exception when I required that he negotiate a few rational hurdles on his way down the track (tract) to hating and killing people. For him hate, maim, and kill were not four-letter words. Occasionally, the debate spilled over into the hall after class and resumed whenever he could find me in the cafeteria. While his progress was slow, he had overindulged at the poisoned trough of right-wing talk-radio and was therefore certain he had all the answers, he eventually settled down, though not comfortably so, and by the end of the semester thanked me for pointing out to him, "What I otherwise would not have seen." How far his vision had been extended by the uncomfortable environment (for him) of our contests and deliberations, I'm not sure.

Again, countless studies have shown that rather than self-esteem, anxiety and concern are basic ingredients in learning. You can substitute the word "challenge" for anxiety and concern and get the same results. In fact, self-esteem is a re-wording of the ancient Greek idea that the purpose of life is to be happy. Something like, life, liberty, and the pursuit of happiness. But self-esteem and happiness come only at the end of and from other endeavors. While they may be ends we seek, they must necessarily be the result of other activities. The world does not move with Homo sapiens merely sitting around feeling good—and learning from comfort.

Of course, it is obvious that discomfort in and of itself does not necessarily promote learning. And there are those among us who are unwilling to take on discomfiture even for the sake of learning. In the ethics class I devised a graphic hands-on interactive lesson of John Rawl's idea, from *A Theory of Justice* (1970), that human decisions about how a society is to be established and run should be made from behind a "veil of ignorance," as if not knowing where we will fit in the future society. I reminded students that, among many other things, they had not chosen their parents, their skin color, or the geography in which they lived. In fact, they had done very little in their lives that could be attributed to having brought them to where they were at that moment. So, how should we decide if we do not know where we will fit in the financial, sexual, racial, educational, health, and/or social spectrum of the future? Then what kinds of rules and programs would we want to support?

Additionally, I devised a Veil of Ignorance Chart whereby, after they had formulated rules for a future society, they were assigned an at random identity from which to consider their previous choices. Not surprisingly, some students found the lesson alarming. Not wanting to consider the possibility that they could have been not quite as fortunate and well placed as they believed they were, while others were not, they refused to participate in the exercise, saying the lesson was a preposterous game I had devised simply to embarrass them.

Discomfort? Certainly. But a discomfort many students took to heart, and as they noted, a lesson that seriously rearranged their priorities and their thinking, and the opinions they held about themselves, and about why other people behave as they do.

On a more humorous note, some of the BAC classrooms did not have windows, and so occupants were always at the mercy of the erratic climate control system that plagued the school for years. When we were incarcerated in those rooms, even if I had wanted to follow the mundane education-school drivel-directive to teachers that when a room is too hot or cold, to "open or close the window," I couldn't have. Below the entry on the evaluation form, "Teacher provided a comfortable environment for learning," one of my students, quite extemporaneously, wrote, "No. The goddam room was always too hot or too cold." It is understandable why the administration didn't show the faculty the TTE document before taking it to the board.

For years, just to level the field, I gave my students a counterbalance evaluation questionnaire the day before the secretary-in-charge showed up in my classes with the administration's evaluation form. My questionnaire was identical to the one the students would be asked to fill out the following day. Usually, in the "Other comments" section, beyond "I don't like English," or "I don't like to come to class this early in the morning," students did not have much to add to their disapproval. But however they answered a question, I asked them to give a written, detailed explanation for their opinion. When they filled out the same questionnaire the following day, I expected they would have in mind (or at least they should have had in mind) what they had time to think over about the questions they answered the day before. The idea for requiring a response, beyond "Yes" or "No," was to put something of consideration-of-opinion into the system, but also to show the unreliability of student opinions on matters of educational theory and practice that not even the so-called experts understand or agree upon.

* * * * *

For fifteen years, between 1965 and 1980, Illinois community college faculties suffered the abuse and outrages of locally elected boards, and, for nearly as long, from the handmaid of the boards, the Illinois Community College Trustee Association. By browbeating professors, as well as by refusing to bargain reasonably with faculties, locally elected politicians under the tutelage and influences of the ICCTA seriously obstructed and damaged the community college educational fabric throughout Illinois. From its beginning in 1967, the ICCTA supported TTE intervention, a dangerous nonsense that encouraged boards that had bargained or otherwise granted teachers tenure to remove or reduce tenure. By 1976 these ideas had also gained credence with the BAC board. However, before a TTE assault could be mounted at BAC, the 1979 Illinois General Assembly passed community college tenured-teacher legislation.

In October of 1979, by a 122-40 vote, the Illinois House of Representatives overrode Republican Governor James Thompson's veto of Senate Bill 147, which the IFT had sponsored to provide a tenure law for community college professors. Senate Bill 147 was supported by the state AFL-CIO, other major labor organizations, and especially by the United Auto Workers.

The list of must-do's set out in Senate Bill 147 clearly states what community college boards were not doing and includes:

A three-year probationary period, with possible extension to four-years for specific reasons.

If a probationary teacher is not to receive tenure, he or she must be notified at least 60 days before the end of the school year or term. The probationary teacher, at his or her request, must be given specific reasons if tenure is denied.

Tenured teachers may be dismissed only for "just cause."

Dismissal actions are subject to review in a hearing conducted by an impartial hearing officer chosen from a list provided by a nationally recognized arbitration association.

Dismissals because of a reduction of staff or the elimination of programs, must be by seniority; that is, last hired, first dismissed. A teacher dismissed because of a reduction of staff has a preferred right for two years to any position which he or she is competent to fill before the appointments of any new faculty member.

Unexpectedly, the support in the House for the act came from the Republican leadership of George Ryan, who would later as governor put a moratorium on capital punishment in Illinois and then end up in prison on a federal corruption conviction. It also appears that the Illinois General Assembly was, in large part, inspired by and acted in opposition to the ICCTA. Later, however, other types of TTE would surface, sometimes disguised in the claptrap of such things as outcomes assessment and student retention.

In 1980 Illinois did not yet have an Educational Employees' Collective Bargaining Law. That would have to wait until 1984, so "faculty job actions" or "strikes" were still without due process protection. However, Senate Bill 147, enacted into law as of January 1, 1980, provided that tenured faculty could not be fired without a hearing, which, by granting a limited form of legal due process, put a dent in the employee-at-will status under which Illinois community college professors without contract protection had labored until then. Again, a tenure law for Illinois grade school and high school teachers had been enacted in 1940.

* * * * *

The need to limit power-once-granted is as old as government, and among other places is encased in the Magna Carta, as well as in seventeenth century European syndicalist belief that once given power, anyone or any one group will misuse it. And, though it is necessary to have someone in power, it is even more necessary to have methods and means to curb and limit the exercise, and the too often abuse, of power. Few if any of those elected to boards of education understand that the office, they occupy by way of votes they collect from a severely limited voting public to oversee the functioning of a postsecondary educational institution, does not give them sole, private-property dictatorial-authority over the institution—nor should it. Public community colleges are state sanctioned institutions. They belong to the people, not to politicians. In passing the Illinois Community College Tenured Teacher Act in 1980 and the Educational Employee's Collective Bargaining Law in 1984, the General Assembly set out to correct or to add a bit of balance to the community college power ledger.

At the February 1980 BAC board meeting three Seyfarth Shaw (SS) lawyers showed up to counsel the board and to explain the board's options under the new tenure law or how the board might best go about circumventing or minimizing the effects of the law. At the same meeting the board endorsed the law as board policy—but only because it was required by law to do so.

* * * * *

In September of '79 the salary clause for the '79-80 section of the '77-80 *Memorandum of Understanding* was negotiated, giving the faculty a 7-percent salary increase. That the salary opener was quickly completed early in the year suggests a Seyfarth Shaw (SS) ploy to solidify administrative support from the board, on one hand, as well as from faculty who would become Wissore groupies the following year. The 7-percent also gave the board an appearance of generosity in its offering, implying that any faculty objection that might arise to board contract proposals the following year would only come from ingrates and troublemakers.

A Vote of No-confidence

By the fall of 1979 the Eckert Board had decided to divest itself of William Keel. Probably on Wissore's advice (by now Wissore had become an Eckert confidant), the board maneuvered Keel into a conflict with the faculty which resulted in a faculty resolution of no-confidence for Keel.

The faculty's November 19, 1979 resolution stated:

There are several actions taken by President Keel which have prompted this college community to express no-confidence in his leadership. Among such actions are the following:

President Keel's intervention in the grading process in violation of the Board established student grievance procedure in that he, personally, stated that a part-time teacher would not be rehired because the teacher refused a direct order to change the grade of a student demonstrates either a lack of understanding of the principle of faculty academic rights or a cavalier attitude toward them. Either condition is unacceptable in an academic environment.

President Keel's approval and/or recommendation that Dr. Wissore be allowed to enroll as a fulltime student in law school, while receiving full pay and compensation for tuition, by using sick leave and accumulated vacation time. Such compensation comes at a time when faculty sabbaticals have been denied due to an alleged financial crisis.

President Keel's dissolution of the Faculty Evaluation Committee which had been charged by President Keel himself with the development of an evaluation procedure for Tenured Faculty. This committee, consisting of students, faculty, administrators, and Board members, was dissolved before the completion of its charge even though President Keel felt that the evaluation procedure recommended by the committee, while not totally acceptable, would serve as a good starting point for further consideration. Subsequently, an evaluation procedure was developed unilaterally by the administration.

More than likely Keel had been instructed, or at least thought he had better follow whatever was suggested as an instruction, to talk to the teacher about a student grade someone on the board wanted changed. This practice had a habit of popping up not infrequently. More than that, Keel would have had to take a suggestion by Eckert (which probably came through Wissore) as a directive to disband the Tenured Faculty Evaluation Committee. By then Eckert had four board votes he could count on. It also appears that by then Eckert and Wissore had drawn up plans for a full-scale assault on the faculty.

To my knowledge the 1979 vote was the first no-confidence vote the faculty had cast against any BAC administrator. In her account of the history of no-confidence votes, Mae Kuykendall of Michigan State University law school writes in *The Chronicle of Higher Education* (June 12, 2009),

> A vote of no-confidence undermines a leader's claim to legitimacy, a feature made evident by contrast with common, but illegitimate, means of trying to remove a leader, such as mutiny, rebellion, work stoppage, mob action, and assassination. The essence of a vote of no-confidence is that the group need not give reasons or a set of charges. It is simultaneously unauthorized and legitimate.

> In authoritarian groups, regular members cannot demand a change. At the other end of the spectrum, democratic structures have clear, weighty procedures, impeachment and recall, for ousting their leaders. Universities and other non-profit institutions sit in the middle of this spectrum. There is consultation to select leaders and to make decisions.

Or at least there should be.

Whatever Keel did or did not do, more than anything else, the no-confidence vote gave the board a reason to do publicly what it already had in mind—to scupper Keel's presidential dinghy. More than likely, behind the scenes, Wissore was promising Eckert that given the chance, he (Wissore) would get the job done, that is, he would cleanse the school of fulltime faculty. At the February meeting, reading the writing on the wall, possibly hoping to ingratiate himself with the board and delay the obvious, Keel proposed that the board institute productivity measures in the next faculty contract.

A month later the board formed a Blue Ribbon Advisory Committee (BRAC) of citizens, administrators, and a few hand-picked teachers. The committee was formed, purportedly, to give the board advice on how to approach its manufactured financial crises. But there's reason to believe it was also an attempt to cover up and/or legitimize board plans for the 1980 assault on the bargaining unit. The Eckert Board regularly empaneled committees or hired public relations firms as an authenticating or community voice to give credence to its backroom plots.

While the BRAC ruminated, in April of 1980, eight candidates showed up on the BAC Board of Trustees' ballot. Norman Sheble, Avery Schermer, Everett Sakosko, Sr., and Curt Eckert ran for two three-year seats, while Ronald Krause, Michael Hildebrand, Elizabeth Jenner, and Ronald Hageman vied for a one-year position. Eckert and Schermer, a Granite City grocer, won the three-year slots, and Elizabeth Jenner captured the single one-year seat.

What would become a favorite Eckert Board election-engineering tactic had surfaced the previous fall. Board members who did not plan to run for re-election were encouraged to resign six or seven months before the next election, so the board could appoint someone of its choice to the position. The previous September Robert Harris had resigned from the board, and Schermer had been appointed to fill Harris' seat. In the 1980 election, Schermer, by nature of the publicity of his appointment, along with Eckert and Jenner as incumbents, were more familiar to voters and therefore had a substantial advantage over other candidates.

Voter turnout for the April 1980 election was abysmal. The vote count for the two three-year positions showed Eckert 7,858; Schermer 7,745; Sheble 3,616; Sakosko 1,973. For the one-year position Jenner collected 4,236, Hildebrand 3,759, Krause 2,359, and Hageman 1,018.

Still, the election of Eckert and Schermer provided the Eckert plot at hand a new life.

Quickly, the BRAC came back on May 28, 1980 with three so-far-so-obvious recommendations for the board. First, in an echo of the catchword of the times circulating through American business com munities, and proposed by Keel at the February board meeting, the committee advised more "productivity." Second, the committee advised the board to cut profitless programs, and third, it advised the board to lobby Springfield for more money. The board jumped on the first two and ignored the third.

Considering the makeup of the BRAC and the omnipresence of SS in the boardroom, there's every reason to believe that the BRAC had been told by SS and the board what the board needed or wanted to hear, and therefore what to put in the report.

* * * * *

At the May 15, 1980, board meeting Don Libby, the BAC AAUP's chief negotiator, asked the board to begin negotiations for a new contract. Other members of the negotiating committee that year included BAC AAUP President Tom Cochran (Mathematics), Don Chapman (Tech-Ed), Joe Huffman (Psychology), Jim Massey, Bill Sheehy (English), and Leo Welch (Biology).

At that same May meeting Keel was reassigned, and a few weeks later during a special meeting, the board did what everyone knew it would do. It made Bruce Wissore Interim President of Belleville Area College. Apparently, even before Keel was shuffled to the side, Eckert had introduced Wissore to other board members as "BAC's next president." Then, on July 16, 1980, the board gave Wissore a two-year contract as interim president.

When the Wissore appointment came up for a vote, Elizabeth Jenner cast the only dissenting vote and questioned statements made by several board members that giving the position to Wissore "made good sense." Why, Jenner asked, if the appointment was so logical and apparently necessary, was there so much "backroom maneuvering" to set it in place. Of course, the appointment created an uproar among the out-group faculty. In BAC administrative jargon at the time, the original AAUP "haves" were for the most part the "out-group," those who opposed Wissore, and the "have-nots," those who did not want to support the AAUP, roughly coincided with the "in-group," or Wissore's supporters.

* * * * *

Bruce Wissore showed up at BAC in 1973 as a temporary administrative assistant to fill in for six months while Bill Keel, Haberaecker's then administrative assistant, was on sabbatical. Within the next year Wissore extended the six-month appointment into a fulltime position. By 1980 he had collected a batch of degrees. He had a bachelor's and a master's in physical Education, a master's in student personnel, and a doctorate in education—in essence nothing in any way to qualify him for the presidency of a college. To further complicate the web of Wissore's collection of, as Rex Carr had typified them "inferior degrees," R. Wayne Clark, the then vice president for instruction, a Wissore subordinate with a Doctorate in Education, had served on Wissore's doctoral board.

* * * * *

The first schools of education, such as those that supplied Wissore's degrees, "normal" schools, modeled on the French école normale were founded in the U.S. in the late nineteenth century. They were established on the belief that aspiring primary and secondary teachers needed training, though the movement to teach-teachers-to-teach did not gain full credence in the U.S. until the early to mid-twentieth century.

In the early 1900s there was an abundance of poor, uneducated women who could be brought into the classroom for a few dollars and exploited as teachers. In *The One Best System: A History of American Urban Education* (1974), David Tyack tells that "As early as 1841, women classroom teachers were characterized as "unambitious, frugal and filial." Paula O'Conner writes in "Grade School Teachers Become Labor Leaders: Margaret Haley, Florence Rood and Mary Barker" (*Labor's Heritage*. Vol. 7, No. 2, Fall 1995) that "In addition to teaching in physically demanding environments classroom teachers faced a hierarchical and bureaucratic educational structure aimed more at economic efficiency than quality education." Thus, it was the "unambitious, frugal, and filial" were brought into the classroom.

Since compensation for K-12 teaching was ridiculously low, only those (men or women) seeking a second income, or those unable to find other employment, could afford to teach. The task, therefore, was not to weed out the not-too-bright and unsuited, since that would have reduced the obeisant-teacher pool, but to make the frugal-and-filial at hand minimally passable and competent as babysitters. As late as 1940 most grade school and high school teachers were required to have no more than twenty-five or thirty hours of college course work, and in some places even less than that.

As early as 1900 organizations such as the AFT set out to improve teachers' working conditions to further the education of K-12 teachers, and, thus, to improve the quality of instruction. On the other hand, schools of education did little more than encourage the babysitting agenda of the K-12 teachers, the majority (85-percent) of which, even today, are women.

From 1974 to 1988, the Eckert-Wissore alliance promoted the education school K-12 model at BAC, the model the AAUP-AFT faculty at BAC rejected—the model that continues to plague community colleges today, using education degrees as a ticket to postsecondary school administrations and faculties, while encouraging schools called colleges to move farther and farther into the community-center, entertainment, recreation, babysitting morass. On July 1, 1980, Bruce Wissore, with little more than an education-school degree in school administration, was hired as president of BAC.

A Regime of Punishment and Rewards

> The function of education is to teach one to think intensively and to think critically. Intelligence plus character–that is the goal of true education.
> —Martin Luther King, Jr.

Productivity

Lurking in the wings of the Keel administration it appears that Wissore pledged (at least to Curt Eckert) to do what Keel had not done—to marginalize and ultimately to break the faculty bargaining unit. As events later revealed, in an avantgarde scheme (a program that presaged what colleges and university boards and administrations around the country would turn to in the '90s), the BAC board set out to disband the AAUP chapter and to cleanse the college of as many fulltime professors as possible, as quickly as possible. In fact, several BAC-SWIC administrators, at one time or another, told me that a college needed nothing more than a board of trustees, an administration to implement the board's plans, and a few fulltime faculty members to do the paperwork. This is, of course, a long way from a college as a community of scholar-teachers where students come to be instructed, to study, and to learn.

On July 2, 1980, the day after Wissore ascended to the presidency of the college, Vice President for Instruction R. Wayne Clark held a staff meeting as an introduction to the new administration. The draft for that meeting reads like something fashioned in the Nixon Oval Office.

Under "General Comments" Clark informed his administrators that "July 1, 1980, begins a new administration at BAC. With this new administration both major and minor changes will occur. During this staff meeting I want to communicate a number of those changes and will be updating you as the year progresses." Additionally, he puffed, "We are proud of being administrators and make no apologies for our positions. We will confront those people who make derogative remarks or who attempt to take advantage of our position."

Later, Clark directed administrators, in what reads like a rubric for organizing an adolescent gang, to "use reward and punishment as much as possible," and to "use in-group/out-group philosophy."

The prospective claims that as far as the administration is concerned the Faculty Senate is definitely defunctus, and states that:

> 3. Faculty Involvement
> Various (projects) will be assigned.
> Need to seek out faculty input whenever appropriate for projects.

These faculty will not follow the faculty committee structure of the past (re: faculty senate).
Seek out those faculty you have confidence in and you can work with.
Will not vote.
Their services will be terminated by you at any time.

* * * * *

The faculty response to Wissore's appointment was immediate, though as expected, divided. The in-group saw Wissore's ascendancy as an opportunity to even the score with those who controlled the AAUP. The faculty haves, the newly ordained out-group, still believed that the board would not oppose the AAUP (after the 1969 recess) and that faculty complaints alone would be enough to remedy the situation.

* * * * *

There was in 1980 a big push by the business culture across the country to squeeze more work and therefore more dollars out of workers. All problems of business and politics across the Americana countryside were explained as a need for increased productivity. And in the summer of 1980, with Wissore securely at the helm, in a distant echo of the January 1977 board meeting, the board issued the faculty individual contracts with productivity measures (increased work load) for 48-percent, while retaining the status quo for 52-percent. The demand for increased productivity in education, which became the BAC board and administration's rallying cry, originated on the federal level in President Richard Nixon's "Special Message to the Congress on Education Reform" (March 3, 1970). Chester Finn, in *Trouble- maker: A Personal History of School Reform since Sputnik* (2008) notes that "He (Nixon) even demanded that the National Institute of Education (NIE) devise 'new measures of educational output' by which 'accountability' could be assured." Nixon, according to Finn, added further that "We have, as a nation, too long avoided thinking about the productivity of schools."

And this was only the beginning. Sadly enough, the corporate productivity measures of the 1980 BAC faculty fight with the Eckert Board took root across the country and has continued to plague American colleges and universities ever since. As a case in point, in the spring of 2008 the Texas Tech University chancellor, Kent R. Hance, announced university plans to expand the student body from twenty-eight thousand to forty thousand. The idea was to reduce student costs to make the university more attractive. To do this Hance called on faculty to readjust their teaching-release loads and take up the slack. In other words, Hance wanted to increase university revenues by loading the faculty with extra teaching, research, grant writing, student advising, and committee work, which the faculty pointed out would seriously reduce the quality of education at Texas Tech. Hance believed his plan would gain 100,000 student credit-hours and add 16 million dollars a year to Texas Tech's bottom-line.

Just as it did at BAC in 1980, the Texas Tech productivity scheme led a handful of high-ranking administrators to resign. *The Chronicle of Higher Education* (April 17, 2008), in "Texas Tech Faculty Members Challenge Report's View of Their Teaching Time," by Katherine Mangan tells that "The University's president, Jon S. Whitmore, announced in February that he would resign by January 2009 or when the new president takes office. He indicated at the time that he wasn't the right president to lead Chancellor Hance's ambitious growth agenda." Texas Tech University, however, did (does) not have a faculty union. The opposition to Hance's plan, what there was, came from the Texas Tech Faculty Senate. What actual effect the opposition had on Hance's plan is anyone's guess.

* * * * *

As noted earlier, in February of 1980 BAC President William Keel advised the board to initiate productivity measures. What Keel meant by productivity is not entirely clear. He probably meant assigning fulltime faculty more classes and/or reducing lab equations in the sciences, as well as cutting salaries. The productivity scam was probably advanced by the board, and Keel, (to keep his job) had to go along with it.

By 1969 the BAC board and administration were aware of the proliferation in American postsecondary education of people with bachelor's and master's degrees, when anybody with a dime and a bit of time could get one or both. People with degrees, legitimate and otherwise, flooded the market—as they do today. In the early '70s, if minimum instructor requirements were given a liberal interpretation or were non-existent, the supply of cheap teaching labor, especially for community colleges, was seemingly unlimited. Part-timers were non-contract employees. They were (are) paid by the hour and had (have) no benefits. They became an essential ingredient in instructional-cost analysis of the productivity scheme.

I should add here that about this time administrators began euphemizing part-timers as "adjuncts" to sugar-coat the practice of out-sourcing college instruction. Contingent or ephemeral or convenient or expedient or abused could just as easily have been used.

Managerial Control

There is, however, more to the part-timer scam than saving money. There is also convenience and control. Most part-timers have other jobs, teach only one or two classes, and therefore are low maintenance. Since they are usually assigned to night or weekend classes, they have little or no connection with fulltime faculty, are out of the loop, individualized, and easily managed. Moreover, they are not required to do committee work or hold office-hours, and therefore do not need offices.

Part-timers provide a pool that could (can) be dipped into or ignored, as the need requires, quickly located and assigned or dismissed with nothing more than a phone call. The contractual conditions of part-timers, aids and abets administrative control of the workforce since part-timers are employees-at-will and can be easily terminated. The practical reality of part-time teaching is hinged on doing as you are told—not causing trouble (not complaining or otherwise rocking the boat) and assigning students good grades. Student complaints, small or otherwise, legitimate or not, about a part-time teacher most often leads to the teacher not being re-employed.

Under the guise of increased productivity Eckert-Wissore planned eventually to reduce each of the academic departments to three or four fulltime faculty members who would do the committee work, etc., and for all remaining classes to be taught by part-timers. This scheme would, of course, turn the college away from education and even more into a corporate-administrative institution. It is of note that throughout the '70s and '80s the proliferation of part-time faculty (as the school grew and the board refused to appoint additional fulltime faculty) and the proliferation of administrators at BAC went hand-in-hand.

Interesting enough, administrators are also employees-at-will, who can be required in whatever situation to bow to the boss' whim. As an indication of the attitudes of the times, in one instance a newly hired BAC administrator was required (told) or strongly advised, to buy a house from a board member at a price some 20,000 dollars in excess of what the newly hired wanted to pay. I often wondered what would have happened if she had refused. More than likely she would have been an employee no more. This is the kind of thing (dictates and whims–financial and otherwise) local politicians often use on those whose employment they control, and certainly would have used on the faculty at BAC had there not been a collectively bargained contract to protect faculty employment and working conditions.

* * * * *

Of course, the drive for more managerial control (governance) was always at the heart of board-faculty relations. During a negotiating session I once reminded school president and chief board-negotiator, Joe Cipfl, that faculty negotiating committees do not usually negotiate items unless the items have not been addressed or have been addressed in an unsatisfactory manner by the administration. In other words, negotiating is mostly problem solving, at least from a faculty point of view. No problem—nothing to talk about. I reminded Cipfl that the *Memorandum of Understanding* could easily be a detailed record of administrative injustices and failures—about poor management. Then too, board injustices and failures do not affect the faculty alone. Students are also harmed. The history of education in the State of Illinois is replete with this lesson. The K-12 system requires teacher certification, even in individual subjects (although they are most often watered down by colleges of education), because administrators made a habit of plugging a body into a classroom, regardless of qualifications, a practice that substantially damaged K-12 education in Illinois—a practice that surfaced at BAC early on during the 1980 strike, and then became the board's MO for keeping the school open. To curtail the practice in K-12, or at least to slow it down, the General Assembly passed minimum instructor qualifications for K-12 teachers. In 1940 it enacted the Illinois K-12 Tenure Teacher Act for the same reasons. But, unlike the K-12 system in Illinois, there are still no state-mandated instructional requirements for community colleges. And administrators, following the earlier K-12 practice, have been more than willing to exploit the vacuum.

One afternoon in 1981, while serving as department chairman, I was speaking to the vice president for instruction, Frank Gornick, a Wissore acolyte who had started at the school as a counselor. He asked me how my part-time recruitment for the semester was going. I told him I had everything covered except for a logic class in Granite City. Gornick responded with "I'm sure you can find someone. If he can count to ten, give him the job."

As it turned out, I found what I judged to be a qualified instructor, a doctoral grad-student from Washington University in St. Louis. But on the first night of class, before I could get to Granite City to meet him, the night supervisor, an administrator at Granite City High School moonlighting for the college, ran him off because the supervisor didn't like "the way he looked." I later discovered that "the way he looked" was administrative geek-speak for gay.

As a hedge against retrenchment, certain of the faculty were more than willing to aid the administration in keeping as many courses as possible in the hands of part-timers, whether they were qualified or not. In the early '80s the Department of English and Philosophy was asked to develop minimum instructor requirements for department offerings. The need to clarify instructor requirements came about as the college grew and the English department collected people who did not fit elsewhere in the school, and who had varying, and sometimes questionable degrees. Often, to get out of teaching writing, instructors took over courses for which they were, to put it bluntly, not qualified to teach or for which they were not, as stated in the Illinois Community College Teacher Tenure Act, "competent to render service"—except that they could probably count to ten. To cover or hide this practice, when asked by the administration to satisfy a North Central Association accreditation request, the department (led by Jan

Milligan) established minimum instructor requirements (MIR) so general
and vague that ninety of the BAC fulltime faculty of 113 were qualified to
teach any English or philosophy course. This was done ostensibly as a hedge
against retrenchment, but also to provide an avenue of escape for teachers
who did not want to teach writing. In fact, several years later I had a nasty
confrontation with Milligan when she abandoned her English classes and
signed up to teach philosophy. She had no academic preparation for
philosophy. She had never taken a philosophy course. She did not even have
the wherewithal to choose a proper text for the courses she was to teach
and showed up in my office, first asking, then demanding that I select a
proper text for her classes. Needless to say, I refused.

Of course, watered down MIR were perfectly okay with the
administration. It could then cover classes with adjuncts proffering degrees
in anything from basket weaving to comic-book collecting, many of them
obtained from correspondence university or colleges that offered degrees
for a few dollars and a label off a soup can.

The Corporate Mantra

By 1980 the elect-tech-education blitz was whizzing across the
country. Community college boards and administrators were looking for
ways to increase revenue at minimum expense, and distance learning
—mostly television courses—appeared to be just what the corporate
bottom-line ordered.

To circumvent the faculty contract and make the school more
profitable, the Wissore administration instituted telecourses. These were
not television-broadcast courses, but VCR courses. Students would check
out videotapes to view, but, as it turned out in most cases, were required to
do little else. The tapes came from a variety of sources, depending upon the
instructor's choice, which was usually some nationally marketed big-name
giving a lecture. It was a variation on the theme of taping another
instructor's lecture and showing it as your own, except the school bought
the tapes, and the instructor handling the course did not have to show up
for class. Otherwise, students were required to appear on campus for
quizzes or examinations only two or three times a semester. Only
infrequently were they required to turn in a paper.

Wissore brought telecourses (TC) into the school under an agreement
with then union President Ken Pinske. The courses were labeled "experimental" and were to be listed and offered for two years, after which they
were to be evaluated, and a decision made on whether to continue offering
them. However, once they were instituted and proliferated the BAC elec-
tronic-tech scene, as they had in postsecondary education nationwide, and
the board had gotten its teeth into the soft flesh of easy money, while
whetting the public's appetite for something for nothing, there was simply

no way to shed them. The courses were listed as experimental, and though they were in keeping with the ICCB's rules for new courses, they were continued long after they ceased to be experimental, in direct violation of ICCB rules. Telecourses were an electronic version of the voc-ed mentality started at BAC in 1967, presented with a good bit of PR, and promoted as high-tech modernization.

Since telecourses did not require a classroom (they were stay-at-home courses), there were no physical limitations on class size. Enrollment was routinely limited only by the number of videotapes on hand. Sometimes as many as 250 students were registered in one class. Instructors received nine dollars per student, per credit hour, plus two dollars for each student who completed the course satisfactorily or twenty-nine dollars per student who received a passing grade for the course. This was all beyond the *Memorandum of Understanding*, that is, extra-contractual.

As designed, the pay formula for telecourses rewarded instructors for keeping students in class and giving them passing grades–to be certain the student received a good experience (translated as an A)–so the school could collect monies from the state for the student's presence (progressing in the class?), and to insure as far as possible that the student would be retained and return for another course. Good grades were easy enough to get. Telecourses were akin to a TV sales-pitch promise of "buy and enjoy"—just another picket in the fence of "assuring student success" and "promoting student self-esteem." By 1986 BAC had the largest telecourse offering in the state.

After a short time the belief was so prevalent that everyone enrolled in a telecourse class would receive an A that Lloyd Gentry, the director of Learning Resources, who, besides holding Christmas prayer meetings in the library, proposed sending out grades on a card inspired by the Budweiser beer commercial at the time, cards inscribed with "For all you do, this grade's for you." What if the grade was a D or F? What would the King of Good Grades say then?

Since telecourse classes did not meet on a regular basis, it was impossible to know if the enrolled student was actually doing the work, if work was assigned. The student identity problem was not limited to tele-courses or merely to BAC. It came as part of the territory with distance-learning programs, so much so that the United States Congress in 2007 (HR 4137) provided that it is in the public's interest that the accrediting agency or association require "An institution that offers distance-education to have processes through which the institution establishes that the student who registers in a distance-education course or program is the same student who participates in and completes the program and receives the academic credit."

It was not surprising that the Wissore administration would herald telecourses. At the time administrators were assigned one class a semester as an overload, and on at least one occasion an administrator received a less than positive teaching evaluation for taping another instructor's lectures and showing them to her class (in the same subject) as her instruction for that day.

It would be a mistake, however, to think the BAC administration was in the telecourse scam alone. In 1979, because of the twin specters of falling enrollment and financial exigency that the administration constantly raised, the BAC Faculty Senate considered a proposal to add telecourses to the catalogue. Senate notes feature a memo dated March 26, 1979 from earth science teacher Ken Pinzke to BAC Vice President for Instruction R. Wayne Clark, noting among other things, that "Dr. Starnes of the ICCB (Paul M. Starnes, Associate Director for Educational Programs and Services with the Illinois Community College Board and at one time an administrator at St. John's River Community College, Florida) has acknowledged telecourses and has indicated that one half-hour of TV time be equated to 1.5 hours of class time." What didn't get said in the Pinzke memo was that in the further corporatizing of Illinois community colleges, Starnes also advocated allowing businesses to use community colleges to train their workers—a practice board member Ted Farmer would decry in 1987. For years colleges and universities have offered correspondence courses. Many saw telecourses as a mere extension of correspondence courses.

* * * * *

At the time telecourses were instituted I was teaching three philosophy courses, one of which was ethics, a required course for many of the college's academic programs. Fred Friendly, a former Columbia Broadcasting System (CBS) executive, and Lisa Newton, a pop-culture philosopher, had developed and marketed a TV course on ethics—and a not very good one at that. When the Friendly-Newton package showed up on the elec-tech market, Lloyd Gentry came to me with the suggestion that we offer the course. After examining the material, I told him I didn't want anything to do with it. This was junk-bond education, maybe okay for leisurely enrichment (and not much of that), but certainly not worthy of college credit.

However, after thinking it over, knowing the Wissore administration's avarice and penchant for sidestepping the contract, I suspected that if I did not teach the course, Gentry-Wissore would simply plug in someone else who could count to ten. There were any number of local preachers who fancied themselves philosophy teachers (early on, several had been brought into the part-timer ranks by English Department Chair Milligan and had to be removed), and I'm sure they would have been more than willing to administer a philosophy telecourse.

Additionally, it wasn't beyond the administration to turn all philosophy offerings into telecourses. By teaching the Friendly-Newton course I hoped to maintain a bit of control, a holding-action of sorts or at least a voice in whatever other philosophy courses the administration might assign to the telecourse catalogue. So, I agreed to set up the ethics telecourse.

When word got out that the ethics course requirement could be satisfied with a telecourse, the enrollment soared. For students who are in school simply to get a grade and get out, telecourses were ideal. Students enrolled in the course were already out of the classroom, and the grade was usually easy enough. A student who had taken a slate of telecourses described them to me as, "A real piece of cake."

The irony of offering a seriously inferior ethics course and selling it as the real thing, a truly educationally unethical activity, seemed not to bother the school's administrative authorities. Then, when I tried to put teeth into the course to make it reasonably rigorous, I ended up in the office of the vice president for instruction, defending myself against student complaints. I was literally told by two students that if they did not get an A for the course, they would file a complaint—which they did.

When I required telecourse students to meet with me on campus at least twice a semester, I was told that it was a distance-learning course, and students had every right to remain off campus, and if I caused any more trouble someone else would be given the assignment. As a result of all this, because ethics was one of the few required courses offered as a telecourse, despite my attempts to legitimize the course and give it something of academic rigor, enrollment burgeoned, and I became the highest paid telecourse instructor in the school.

Shortly after telecourses were installed a fight erupted on another front between the administration and the out-group faculty about marking or designating telecourses on student transcripts to indicate that they differed from usual classroom instruction. To protect an unethical and inferior method of instruction, and not to have to re-articulate the classes with other institutions, the administration refused to include a telecourse notation on transcripts.

As would be expected, Wissore's in-group faculty went along with the scam. In a Curriculum Committee meeting one day I pointed out that the telecourses offered only about one-hundredth the instruction of a normal classroom class. In response, an in-group teacher said, "Well, my telecourse students do every bit as much work as my classroom students." Did I believe her? Yes, I did. Her telecourse classes weren't any different from her other classes. But I also reminded her that her remark was the most damning indictment of classroom teaching I'd yet heard. This was the same teacher who frequently allowed female students to retake the same exam five or six times or until they finally, as she was fond of saying, "got the grade they deserved."

In another anti-education scheme, in 1980 the BAC board hoped further to reduce the fulltime faculty by adopting a Dallas Community College system that was gaining popularity at the time of replacing teachers with television sets (as they have now replaced many of them with computers). The scheme provided a proctor of some status or other to meet a class, take role, turn on the TV set and then move on to the next class. It was an innovation on the education college dictum of the time, to eliminate teachers as lecturer, to change them from the "sage on the stage" to a "guide on the side." Since the TV programs were usually nothing more than a celebrity (albeit an academic celebrity) giving a lecture, the scheme amounted to little more than replacing a teacher with a TV-sage.

During the first weeks of the fall semester of the 1980 eleven members of the board and administration had scheduled a junket to Dallas, osten- sibly to see just how TV classes worked. That would have been board members, Bartsokas, Dintelmann, Eckert, and Schermer, as well as administrators Wissore, Clark, Eskridge, Gornick, Hines, and the deans Stone and Washburn.

Cohen and Brawer report in their fourth edition of *The American Community College* (2003) that The Dallas Telecollege begun by Dallas Community College in 1972 had, in 1978, over 10,000 students, and over 15,000 by 2002.

The contract conflict in 1980 nixed the administration's planned junket, but the Dallas plan foreshadowed the telecourses the Wissore administration would install at BAC the following year. Faculty participation in the Dallas plan, as intended, was not unlike what the scab faculty did during the 1980 BAC strike, going from room to room taking roll and turning on the TV set for students to watch before going to the next room, while collecting full pay for teaching. One scab instructor told me later she made, ". . . enough to pay for a very nice trip to the Bahamas." This idea was also a precursor of a later Wissore plan to replace fulltime faculty with a handful of education facilitators or ombudsmen who would be on call twenty-four hours a day, to come in wherever, to conduct crisis classes when television instruction went awry.

* * * * *

As early as 1976, though possibly earlier than that, the Eckert-Wissore alliance set out to restructure the school on a corporate model, as the AFT calls it, "operating under a business mantra."

In *Gangs of America: The Rise of Corporate Power and the Disabling of Democracy* (2003), Ted Nace writes:

> . . . the corporation seems on an exorable course toward permeating every aspect of life, not just the traditional economic sphere but increasingly such public spheres as schools and

prisons, and such personal spheres as preparing meals and entertaining children. In many ways the corporation is coming to know us better than we know it. It involves itself with us intimately. It participates in our birthing, our education, even our sexuality; it tracks our personal habits, entertains us, imprisons us; it helps fight off dread diseases, manufactures the food and products that we eat, barters and trades with us in a common economic system, jostles us in the political arena, talks to us in a human voice, sues us if we threaten it.

Since the corporate mantra is to make money, to exploit the environment to make money, corporations must necessarily create desires for what is not needed or better, ignore the less profitable that may also be needed, and go to the lowest common denominator (the largest number of people) to bleed an environment of its resources. The corporate exploitation of education and healthcare, as with the physical environment, too often leaves a scorched-earth wasteland of human suffering in its wake.

We (Americans) refer to our pubic K-12 schools as common schools provided by the community for the common good, of which education is primary. Public schools, including community colleges, in direct opposition to corporations, belong to the people, and so are by design socialist entities. In both structure and operation public institutions exist by mandate of the laws of the state. By law they must be there and will not disappear if they lose a few dollars. In certain cases, they may have to be restructured or refinanced, but until the General Assembly, or whatever governing body that creates them, takes them out of commission, they belong to the people they serve, the people of the state, and by their presence invest those who work in or for them with a unique set of obligations.

During a pre-negotiating meeting in 1992 I reminded SWIC President Joe Cipfl, who got high marks as an administrator simply because he was sane and honest, of our public-servants' mutual obligation, and asked him to remember it during negotiations.

If I were negotiating for the UMWA, I told him, I would go after what I needed and get it or shut you down. But in negotiating contracts for a public institution we are dealing with a legal, public entity, a closed system, and are, therefore, required to work harder to come to an equitable and just settlement without damaging the institution.

In other words, I reminded him, both sides are negotiating for the same constituency, the people of the state. Schools are democratic institutions with mandates from the people, paid for by the people, for the education of the people. Schools exist so teachers may teach students. They are not the private property of boards of trustees or their administrations, and most certainly should not be run as private for-profit corporations. Whether he agreed with me or not, I don't know.

Don Libby, Chief Negotiator, 1980

By the time the Eckert Board made Wissore president it was apparent that to survive, the faculty bargaining unit would have to be politicized and activated. Generally speaking, teachers prefer to be left to their solitary academic pursuits and would rather not soil their hands with the mundane and seamy world of politics. I can sympathize with that. Professor Stanley Fish, and others believe teachers should restrict instruction to non-political subject matter, unless the subject itself is political.

The Fish concept of classroom activity is built around a limited and truncated view of education (more indoctrination than education). It assumes that once an idea or concept is offered to a student it will remain forever in the student's mind or personality and dictate how the student will behave for the remainder of his/her life. Extensive research shows otherwise. Professors just don't have that kind of sway with their students.

More than that, Professor Fish fails to acknowledge that the primary purpose of public education is to educate citizens and that of necessity requires teachers to include or represent the various and variegated aspects of the political. Like it or not, politics is inherent in every teaching assign-ment. Teachers, instructors, professors in public institutions are servants of a public trust, a trust they are obligated to protect and nurture. And as unfortunate and distasteful as it may be, they need involve themselves and their teaching in the political processes that embody that trust. They must be involved in politics at an institutional, local, state, and national level, both in an out of the classroom.

Teachers in a democratic society are political as the populace they serve is political, and despite the deadhead, anti-educational conservative view that anyone who tells the truth, who has a bit of a grip on reality is radical, teachers are obligated to tell the truth as best they know it. As philosopher Thomas Langan observed, you cannot believe anything you want to believe; you are obligated to believe the truth.

The person foremost in politicizing the BAC faculty in 1980 was Don Libby, the chief negotiator for the AAUP. In the troubles with the Eckert Board it was Libby who very nearly single-handedly converted the BAC faculty from a scattering of bickering academics into a truly hardnosed collective determined to protect the trust to which they had been appointed. It was as if the faculty had been waiting for someone like Libby to appear. During the summer and fall of 1980, BAC teachers who probably would not have or could not have done anything overtly political on their own, responded quickly and were immediately supportive of Libby's presence and leadership.

* * * * *

Donald Libby was born in West Des Moines, Iowa in 1929, attended high school in West Des Moines, and graduated from Drake University in West Des Moines. After a three-year stint in the Navy he spent several years in Cleveland and New York working for Massachusetts Mutual (Mass-Mutual) as an investment and pension broker. Sometime around 1960 he returned to West Des Moines, Iowa, still with MassMutual, though home again in Iowa, and became involved with the Democratic Party.

He laughingly told me one time that he had thought of himself as a good speaker, maybe even a first-class orator—as he said, "... until I got in a debate with Hubert Humphrey. I ran out of words and he was just warming up. He buried me"

In 1965, while still working for MassMutual, Libby suffered a massive heart attack. For the next several years he did not work but convalesced and completed a degree in counseling at from the University of Missouri at Columbia, Missouri. After receiving the counseling degree, he worked for a year at West Des Moines High School. He was appointed to the BAC faculty in 1973.

Libby's working experience with pension funds, and later his training as a counselor, and his not inconsiderable natural instincts and talents as a politician, gave him an unusual expertise for negotiating contracts—and for rallying the faculty to defend itself.

I was always amazed by Libby's insights into, and his understandings of, the difficult issues we faced. Usually, before the rest of us got there, he had charted the minefield we were about to stumble into–and just as often had a well-worked-out map in hand fashioned for a reasonable, if not entirely safe, and successful passage.

By the middle of May 1980, when Libby and the negotiating committee petitioned the board for negotiations, the Eckert Board had already prepared for its assault on the faculty. At the time we did not have any way of knowing what the board planned. Information about the operation of the school coming from the administration and/or entered in the board minutes had dried up. Board meetings had, for all practical purposes, turned into secret, almost clan-like gatherings.

The Illinois Open Meetings Act (5 ILCS 120/2.06) (from Ch. 102, par. 42.06) states:

Sec. 2.06. Minutes.
All public bodies shall keep written minutes of all their meetings, whether open or closed, and a verbatim record of all their closed meetings in the form of an audio or video recording. Minutes shall include, but need not be limited to: the date, time and place of the meeting; the members of the public body recoded as either present of absent and whether the members were physically present or present by means of video or audio

conference; and a summary of discussion on all matters proposed, deliberated or decided, and a record of any votes taken.

Yet, in the board minutes from 1980, actually from 1974 until 1988, there is very little about how board decisions were made. With Wissore newly appointed interim president, and Seyfarth Shaw in the backroom advising the board not to negotiate, board minutes for June, July, and August of 1980 look like something out of a Dick and Jane reader. Throughout the confrontation that ran from May of 1980 into the November strike, and culminating with a contract in December of 1980, there is not one entry to indicate how the matters the board considered and eventually voted on were "proposed, deliberated, or decided."

Today it is clear that sometime before May of that year the Eckert Board had determined to break the faculty bargaining unit, so there was nothing much for the board to do that summer but wait for August seventeenth, when the *Memorandum of Understanding* expired. The plan seems to have been that after the contract expired the board would make an offer to show good faith, and then wait until a majority of faculty caved in and signed the individual contracts.

In January of 1977 Wayne Ault's attempt to certify the Teamsters as a faculty bargaining agent had given the Wissore administration and SS all but the design for the 1980 attack on the faculty. The numbers the board used to engineer a faculty divide are discouragingly close to those Ault and Teamster representative Speranza quoted at the January 1977 board meeting, with Don Anderson and Michael Rybicki from SS in attendance. To requote the board minutes from that January 1977 meeting, "Mr. Speranza said that over 50% of faculty who had signed authorization cards represented a majority of the faculty . . ."

A majority of signed individual contracts in 1980 would have invalidated the board's dealings with the fulltime faculty bargaining unit. Since the bargaining unit (the AAUP and the Salary Committee) had been certified by board approval, with a majority of fulltime faculty under individual contracts the board could have claimed that there was no longer a need for a bargaining unit.

The catch at the center of the board's attempt to break the bargaining unit, as it appeared in the individual contracts issued in 1980, was an increased workload for 48-percent of the faculty—increased productivity, i.e., more work, by way of an extra class for English teachers, more hours for librarians and counselors, and a further reduction in the already paltry equations for remuneration for science labs and nursing. Incidentally, librarians, counselors and the English, math, sciences, and nursing departments were the strongholds of the AAUP.

The workload in the individual contracts offered to the social science and business departments (52-percent of the faculty), where most of the in-group taught, remained unchanged. The scheme (more than likely devised by SS) provided all faculty members with a raise of 10-percent a year for each of the following two years.

The board's proposals list:

> . . . the administration . . . seeking a pay cut for teaching laboratory hours, along with more work from instructors, librarians and counselors, with no increase in pay.
>
> As part of cost-cutting measures by the administration, 64 courses were modified earlier this year to reduce the number of laboratory or lecture hours or replace eliminated lecture hours with laboratory hours.
>
> Instructors are paid less money for teaching laboratory hours than lecture hours, and the administration reportedly wants to reduce pay for teaching laboratory hours by 30-percent (*BND*).

Of the faculty's response the *BND* tells that "The resolution, submitted Wednesday afternoon to BAC interim president Bruce Wissore, said the faculty is 'not willing to barter the education futures of our students for purported fiscal gains facetiously referred to as gains in productivity.'" And further, "The faculty also asked for a return to the negotiating table 'in the spirit of cooperation and mutual respect.'"

Although BAC board minutes of August 1980 do not reflect the deliberations that led to the board's decision, board minutes do provide a carefully calculated answer to the faculty's request.

> A Special Meeting of the Board of Trustees of Community College District No. 522 was held on Monday, August 25, 1980, in the Conference Room, Main Campus, 2500 Carlyle Road, Belleville Illinois. Chairman Dintelmann called the meeting to order at 5 p.m.
>
> Members present: Bartsokas, Becker, Dintelmann, Eckert, Jenner, O'Malley, and Student Board Member Potter. Members absent: Schermer."
>
> After an Executive Session that lasted until 5:25 p. m, the Minutes state, "Mr. Becker moved, seconded by Mrs. Bartsokas:
>
> In consideration of the fact that the *Memorandum of Understanding* expired August 17, 1980, and since orientation began on August 18, 1980, we must establish a rate of pay for *our faculty* [emphasis mine]. I move that the faculty be paid rates which will be read following this motion, and that we direct the administration to issue individual contracts for all faculty members containing the provisions of our offer to the

faculty of August 18, 1980.

Any faculty returning the signed contract by 4 p.m., August 29, 1980, should be paid in accordance with the terms of the agreement. Others should continue to be paid at the rate established at this meeting until they sign the individual contracts.

Any salaries paid from the new *Memorandum* will be retroactive to the beginning of the school year if signed prior to 4 p.m. on the twenty-ninth.

If the contracts are signed and returned after 4 p.m. on the twenty-ninth, the new rates of pay should be effective on the day the contract is returned.

Note that this decision, with all of its intricacies and possibilities for success or failure, was "proposed, deliberated, or decided" among seven board members in a matter of twenty-five minutes. At least, looking at the board minutes, that is what we are asked to believe.

The wording of the proposal using the personal pronouns "we" and "our" instead of referring to the board by name is a strong indication of the attitude of that particular board of trustees. Simply put, the board members saw the faculty as serfs, owned and paid by them as the lords owned and rewarded the serfs in the Middle Ages.

Traditionally, when school contracts expire, and the faculty continues to work, it works or instructs under the old contract, within a continuing contract or successor contract. Usually, in a new contract, most of the old contract is brought along as a basis for what is to be added or altered. It was, however, the SS contention that when a contract expired, if the contracting parties wanted a new contract they would, if one of them so chose, have to go back to square one, and that every item in the contract would have to be negotiated anew.

That same day, August 25, 1980, Libby again confronted the board's intransigence. He told the press that "It looks like they're going to go to the mat with it, and nobody is going to win—and somebody sure as hell is going to lose."

As early as or as late as September fourth, depending on one's point of view, with negotiations still at an impasse the faculty team requested binding arbitration on the productivity issue.

The board did not respond to the request for nearly a week. Then, on September tenth, it rejected the proposal. A news release from the BAC Public Information Office dated September eleventh states that "Arbitration is a unilateral approach to the settlement of these issues, and the board does not want a unilateral approach to replace the dialogue of bargaining, but if it did, the unilateral voice would be that of the citizens of the district as expressed through their elected representatives."

Addressing the productivity issue, the news release claims "The update (a letter the board sent to the faculty) denied that the board's position is that the faculty is 'unproductive.'

"The Board team has stated repeatedly," to quote the release, "that it does not believe that the faculty is unproductive, merely that a certain segment of the faculty, in fact a minority of the faculty, could be *more* productive."

On September 24th the *Belleville Journal* reports that "Libby attended the board's monthly meeting last week to read a prepared statement in which he asked the board if its failure to negotiate signaled an attempt to 'break the union.'

"'The strength and resiliency of this faculty is not so brittle and certainly not as divided as perhaps you have been led to believe,' Libby told the board.

"'You are moving toward a confrontation that is of a greater magnitude than your personal whim,' he continued."

With negotiations stalled, in another attempt to circumvent the board's obstinacy and intractability, the faculty negotiating team proposed public negotiations. This time the board's
response was immediate. The following day the *BND* notes "A faculty proposal for public negotiations was greeted with a chilly response by a BAC spokesman Wednesday night.

"Speaking for the board, Wissore said, 'As we've said in the past, the negotiations are a private thing and we want to keep this between the (faculty) negotiating committee and ourselves.'"

* * * * *

By now the college was rife with rumors of administrators brow-beating faculty who had not signed the individual contracts. As it turned out, most of the faculty had disregarded the contracts. A week or so after they were issued Libby collected several dozen and in the best of Gandhi tradition of defying the Black Act and General Smuts by burning registration certificates, Libby had an official contract burning in a trash barrel on the east side of the campus.

In the following days, despite long negotiating sessions and dozens of faculty counter proposals, there was still no settlement in sight. Through October of 1980 the board's idea seems to have been to stall negotiations as long as possible to give the administration time to intimidate and coerce faculty with threats, real and imagined, into signing the individual contracts. Especially vulnerable were the non-tenured faculty. In fact, one non-tenured faculty member was reminded that if he wanted to continue at BAC he had best sign the contract. And although he signed the contract and did not participate in the November strike, in appreciation for his timidity and obeisance, the following semester he was summarily dismissed.

October 17, 1980, Gordon Stone, who had been Dean of the Baccalaureate Division since 1970, and Clyde Washburn, Dean of the Career Division since 1971, filed a petition with the board detailing the administration's Gestapo-like tactics in attempting to coerce faculty members to sign individual contracts, as well as outlining their objections to the Wissore administration's plans for the college. On November fourth, Stone and Washburn were told to "stay home," and were placed on administrative leave (referred to as college business). Eventually they would be replaced by Wissore hires Frank Gornick and Robert Eskridge, whose inept-comic antics led administrative practices to be characterized by the faculty as administrative underthink. No matter what ridiculous and/or insipid, belligerent activity one might imagine, the administration came up with something even beneath what had been anticipated. The administrators' moves were usually accompanied by faculty disbelief and a "They wouldn't do that. I mean . . . ." But they always did.

The Stone and Washburn petition claimed the Wissore program violated faculty members' civil rights. Stone and Washburn wrote, "Our instructors cannot be 'shaped' through the techniques of reward and punishment and stifled in their constructive dissent, and to the extent it is attempted, educational productivity will be sorely diminished at BAC." The board ignored the petition, and in December of 1980 Stone and Washburn took early retirement.

As it turned out, Stone and Washburn were not the only administrators and/or staff to defect. As Wissore cronies were brought into the administration, more and more of the staff departed. Board Secretary Ruth Kombrink resigned. Registrar Vincent Margerum retired. After a hassle of several months, Dean of Special Services, Warren Nieburg, resigned. R. Wayne Clark, who became Wissore's righthand man and the top administrator, was the only administrator who remained at the college.

By 1980, Wayne Ault, still looking for a foothold in the faculty power structure, had become chairman of the Faculty Senate. In many ways Ault reminded me of Richard Nixon. He wanted always and desperately to be president of something, anything that was available, and was never very good at it, no matter what.

As one of his more revealing moves, in the middle of the negotiating hassle, on October 23, 1980, Ault sent a memo "To: ALL FULLTIME FACULTY," canceling an all faculty meeting that had been scheduled by the senate to discuss negotiations. The letter was a not-too-subtle attempt to keep the Faculty Senate, which began as a board committee, as an instrument of administrative compliance. The Faculty Senate (and Ault) could just as easily have supported the board by sponsoring a faculty meeting to discuss negotiations and, as a board committee composed of faculty, attempt to improve faculty and board relations.

Then, in late October of 1980 one-hundred faculty voted for a resolution that the board of trustees replace Wissore. According to the *Belleville Journal,* "The faculty's resolution, which was presented to board members attending a finance committee meeting last Wednesday [October twenty-second], lists several instances in which it claims Wissore initiated changes, thus overstepping his temporary authority.

"Wissore's establishment of the College Counsel, the faculty believes, is an attempt to usurp the traditional functions of the Faculty Senate.

"'A College Counsel, consisting of administrators and hand-picked [not democratically elected] teachers, now undertakes matters formerly given over to the Faculty Senate,' the resolution states."

A few days later the faculty issued a vote of no-confidence in Wissore, a vote most college and university presidents do not survive. After all, it had worked with Keel. Although the Keel no-confidence vote seemed at the time to have had nothing to do with Keel's presidential demise, other than to give the board an excuse to do what it had already intended to do; eight months later Keel was gone.

As it did in Keel's case, the board appeared to ignore the faculty resolution and further demonstrate that traditional methods of faculty influence on the board were no longer available. When Wissore became president, Eckert publicly announced that God had told him to hire Wissore. Regardless of what else it may have been meant to accomplish, a statement like that is not intended to encourage rational discourse.

* * * * *

In March of 1978 BAC board member Curt Eckert voted on a sewer project in which BAC was involved with the Weatherstone housing development across Greenmount Road from the BAC Main Campus, a development in which Eckert had a 10-percent financial interest. Both the board and the faculty were aware that Eckert's vote involved a conflict of interest, but the State's Attorney's Office said it would not file charges unless someone complained. So, we complained, and complained, and then complained again. When conducted, the ensuing investigation showed that in addition to voting on the Weatherstone sewer project, in 1977 and 1978 Eckert had apparently failed to file a Conflict of Interest Statement, as required by Illinois law of public officials.

The November 3, 1980 issue of *The St. Louis Globe Democrat* reports, "The company's development is across Greenmount Road from the campus. At the time of the vote on the contract, Eckert was chairman of the BAC Board of Trustees. He cast a vote for the contract."

Periodically, Eckert blamed the faculty for his misfortune. He blamed the BAC faculty for objecting to a public official possibly breaking the law. "But he told the *Globe* in addition, 'I guess I don't understand what conflict of interest means.'"

The day the *Globe* carried the Eckert article, November third, the BAC faculty took a strike vote, although the vote, technically, was not for a strike, but for a job-action. The vote had been precipitated the week before when, after the negotiating teams reached a verbal agreement on a variety of contract items, the administration reneged on the agreement. The administration insisted that it was an administrative prerogative to reduce the verbal agreements to writing. However, when the teams met again, faculty negotiators discovered the transcribed items were substantially different from those to which they had agreed.

Transcribing verbal agreements, as they had been agreed to, was always a problem with Wissore, a practice he probably picked up from the SS lawyers. Additionally, even after an item had been negotiated and placed in the contract, often times Wissore would reinterpret the intent and, therefore, the contract item itself, claiming it meant something different from what had been agreed to. It was akin to the country boy whose girlfriend catches him with another girl. He asks her, almost factiously, "Who are you going to believe, your lying eyes or me?" The habit was so pervasive with the administration and SS that we finally demanded that a secretary be present at negotiating sessions to provide detailed minutes of discussions leading to agreements that were to be embedded in the *Memorandum of Understanding.*

Contract discussion or negotiation are rife language disagreements. The problem is as old as language. One time, Joe Cipfl and the board's team got onto the idea that in a certain contract clause the word "or" meant that the items in the series did not apply equally, but were mutually exclusive, and one "or" the other applied, but not both. When they finished elaborating their interpretation, I asked Cipfl if he had notified his wife that the phrase in his wedding vows of "in sickness or in health," only applied to one "or" the other, and she could have her choice, but under no circumstances was he to be obligated to both.

In addition to the vote of no-confidence in Wissore, the faculty demanded direct negotiations with the board. The November 3, 1980, *BND* reports "The faculty of BAC will no longer treat with Bruce Wissore or members of an in-group. It is their (the board's) first order of business to find redress for this situation.

"We, therefore, demand negotiations be reconvened with representatives of the board that are inclined toward reason, logic, and are individuals of professional and ethical integrity or with the board itself."

Strike!

> As long as justice and injustice have not terminated their ever renewing fight for ascendancy in the affairs of mankind, human beings must be willing, when need is, to do battle for the one against the other.
> —John Stuart Mill

Roll of Honor

Moving into November of 1980 the board made no attempt to address the faculty's grievance with Wissore or to advance negotiations. Then, the morning of November 4, 1980, eighty-three BAC faculty members went out on strike.

By the fall of 1980, only six of the original fifteen AAUP (1966) members that came from Belleville High School District 201 to the college in 1967, along with nine others who had taught at 201 but did not belong to the original AAUP chapter, were still at the college. Of the six original AAUP members, Jan Milligan, Genevieve Snider, William Saunders, and Jack Stokes joined the strike. Of the nine non-AAUP-former-District 201 teachers, Gertrude Brainerd, Grace Brashier, D.C. Edwards, Neale Fadden, Richard Mills, Charles Pruitt, and Farrell Wilson joined the walkout. William Keel was the other original non-AAUP teacher from District 201 who remained at BAC, but he was still loosely attached to the BAC administration and so, obviously, did not join the strike.

No matter the cause, there will always be those who find excuses for not striking. I suspect there are as many excuses as there are scabs. Original AAUP members Otis Miller and Elizabeth Oelrich, and non-AAUP former District 201 teacher Byron Hargis, did not join the strike.

Without checking the roles, I would guess most of the 1980 strikers were current AAUP members, although I'm somewhat certain any number (many) of the scabs were also AAUP members.

We were never sure how many of the faculty signed individual contracts. Our guess at the time was that as few as twenty or twenty-five, but not more than thirty. Though forty-eight of the faculty did not join the strike, if only twenty or so signed the individual contracts, there were numerous fence-sitters, watching to see just which way the wind would blow. Alinisky's observation about liberals leaving the room when the argument turns into a fistfight, also applies to some teachers—maybe most teachers. Of course, their cowardice shines a bright light on the courage of those who stick around to see the troubles through and get bloodied-up in the process.

The Honor Roll of 1980 Strikers:

Robert Arndt; Albert Becker; Raynold Bertrand; Jerald Bolen; Dorothy Bowers; Marvin Braasch; Lynn Bradley; Gertrude Brainerd; Gene Brandt; Grace Brashier; Judy Bravin; Don Chapman; Roger Christeck; Thomas Cochran; David Cordes; Byron Davidson; D. C. Edwards; Joseph Evans; Neale Fadden; Shirley Fitzgerald; Allen Friedman; Bea Ann Fries; Charles Giedeman; Martha Giordano; Sharon Graville; Clarence Hall; Rose Marie Hall; Lucille Hammond; Joseph Huffman; John Jacobs; Josephine Jones; Richard Kamm; Darrell Kohlmiller; Jan Kramer; Wayne Lanter; Donald Libby; Eugene Masek; James Massey; Helen McIlvan; Janet Milligan; Richard Mills; Barbara Monken; Eldred Mueller; Christopher Nieman; Roberta Peduzzi; Kenneth Pinzke; Charles Pruitt; Walter Ptasnik; William Saunders; Michael Schneider; Elizabeth Schoeberle; John David Shannahan; Wayne Shaw; William Sheehy; Bruce Sisko; Genevieve Snider; A. Dennis Sparger; John Sprengeler; Lyleen Stewart; Jack Stokes; Barbara Taylor; Gerald Taylor; Lynn Threlkeld; Margaret Ubben; Leo Welch; John West; Leslie Wiemerslage; Farrell Wilson; Margaret Wottowa; and Celeste Zalecki.

The 1980 fulltime faculty who did not join the strike were: Rao Ahmad; Wayne Ault; Clay Baitman; Vito Benevegna; Richard Boyer; Edward Brady; William Burns; Donald Koleson; James Corcoran; James Cox; Thomas Cress; Victor Darnell; Donald Distler; Ronald Eads; James Feverston; Mary Frew; Alice Geary; Paul Greenwood; Charles Gulash; Byron Hargis; Jack Haskell; Rita Heberer; Norma Irwin; Robert Jannotta; Don Kassing; Garner Kimbrell; Barbara Kordenbrock; Bernadine Limper; Charles Linberg; Kenneth Luke; P. T. Mak; Richard Melinder; Otis Miller; Harold Oakley; Elizabeth Oelrich; Tony O'Truk; Arthur Parrish; Wayne Pfingsten; Bobby Poe; Harlan Raymond; Dennis Shannon; Thomas Sloan; James Splitstone; Judy Thomas; Bernice Vallino; Larry Wakefield; William Wilson; and John Zanotti.

* * * * *

During the early days of the strike Wissore made repeated attempts to contact strikers and convert them to the in-group—encouraging them to give up the strike and sign the individual contracts. That only twenty-some-odd signed the SS contracts is a strong indication that the board and Wissore had made a serious miscalculation.

Later, in 1986 toward the end of negotiations, as chief-negotiator I put an offer on the table that Wissore claimed I could never get the faculty to agree to. I told him that out of the possible 113 faculty votes, I could get 89 or 90 for the proposal. When we put the contract to a vote, with the item included, the contract was ratified with 88 votes. But then Wissore was, as traditionally presidents at BAC have been, never in very close contact with the faculty.

Major among Wissore's miscalculations was that a majority of the faculty would respond positively to the pay increases in the individual contracts the board offered. But the 1980 conflict was not about money, at least not on the faculty side of the ledger. The individual two-year contracts Wissore and SS offered the faculty contained a 20-percent salary increase. When in the history of education has a college faculty been offered a 20-percent raise in a two-year contract and gone on strike for more money? That was more money than the BAC faculty had ever been offered at any one time. Suffice it to say the issues at the college in 1980 were academic and struck at the heart of what the faculty had taken upon itself to do. The problem was that the contract came with the 52-percent to 48-percent productivity catch, as well as a pile of other anti-educational items the faculty would have had to accept to get the money. Additionally, twenty faculty members or 15-percent of the striking faculty could have signed the individual contracts for a 20-percent salary increase without any additional workload, but did not.

* * * * *

Still, negotiations continued. Then on November sixth in what appeared to be a break-through negotiators agreed to federal mediation. I don't know if at the time many of the striking faculty thought mediation might succeed. I know I didn't have much hope for it.

One doesn't have to be at the table very long to understand that the center of negotiations is always goodwill. An attempt to solve problems and, hard-nosed as it may be, a willingness to get the thing done are essential. In the months leading up to the strike I had not seen anything of goodwill from Eckert, Wissore or SS. Most of what we got from Eckert was wisecracks and a megalomania that precluded any attempt at reconciliation. What we got from Wissore was grinning compliance with Eckert and off-the-wall, facetious statements to the press about how much the board appreciated the BAC faculty.

The following day, November seventh, mediation began and after a prolonged session Libby returned to strike headquarters disgruntled and not very hopeful. "No matter what we offer, the sons-of-bitches are not going to move," he said. "Even the mediator doesn't have much hope for this. That little fart-in-the-skillet (Libby always referred to the SS lawyer Rybicki as a fart-in-the-skillet) hasn't any intention of negotiating." The agreement for mediation turned out to be a charade, merely another of SS's stalling tactics. Two days later, November 9, 1980, the mediator called off mediation, packed his briefcase and left.

BAC-FAC-In-Exile

So, what now? Well, we walked picket lines and hoped. Sometimes we were entertained or at least amused by antics the strike generated or encouraged. Early on the first morning of the strike, Von Berger, Super-intendent of Buildings and Grounds, along with a contingent of his workers, chugged up with a truck and a tractor to the school's south entrance where pickets were already working. Apparently, Berger had spotted a duplicitous ten- or twelve-inch Sycamore near the road that looked healthy enough but was a serious threat to passersby. Not wanting it to fall and harm someone, quite authoritatively he declared it anathema and apostate and ordered its execution. He fired up his chainsaw and quickly felled the heretic arboreal misanthrope, which dropped across the entrance road. This was surprising, that a tree would fall in that direction and the workers were so dismayed with the incident they went off to do other chores—to recover their composure—leaving the entrance blocked for several hours before return-ing under demands from the administration that they chop up the renegade and remove it.

Not to be outdone by the workers' dismay, Don Koleson, an original striker who would later capitulate to Wissore's threats and his own fears, was picketing at the entrance road to the college. When he realized what Berger and his soon-to-be-dismayed workers were doing, Koleson began shouting, "You can't do that! You can't do that! It's illegal! It's illegal!" Unable to make himself heard over the rattle and clatter of the chainsaws, and thoroughly distressed by the operation, he threw down his picket sign and ran off across the school grounds. I don't know if he ever returned to picketing—but then the dismay and distress that come with striking can be unnerving.

Otherwise, we walked picket-lines, tried to keep everyone up-to-date on negotiations, when there were negotiations, walked picket-lines and advised the media as best we could about what we were doing, and walked picket-lines and talked to each other.

Since it was middle-to-late November and the weather was cold, we set up large metal barrels to use for fires at the picketing sites at the two entrances leading to the school. I had a pretty good supply of firewood at home and kept the picket areas supplied with wood and stoked the fires as best I could.

One morning I showed up at six o'clock with my youngest son, Joshua, who was eight at the time, to get the fires going so we'd have a base of hot coals by seven-thirty when the picketers arrived. On occasion Josh walked the picket-lines with me, as an essential part of his social-awareness train-ing. That morning we were unloading firewood when two cars from the sheriff's office descended on us with four deputies wanting to know what

119

we were doing. I explained that we were building fires in the barrels to keep the good people warm, and if they wanted to hang around, since I considered them good people, they too could use the barrels. We wouldn't mind.

Once we were on strike, after we counted noses to see who was there, we tagged ourselves the BAC-FAC-In-Exile, and immediately set up strike-committees. We had a Rally Committee of Jan Kramer, Mike Schneider, Wayne Lanter, Helen McIllvain, Walt Ptasnik, Tom Cochran (and someone who signed in red ink, "Superman's Girl Friend"— probably Lois Riedenour, a part-time librarian but loyal striker). No doubt Lois was playing off the Lois Lane comic-strip character and the rallying cry among the strikers at the time that "Superman won't save you. You have to do that for yourself."

Once a week we held gatherings at the St. Clair Village Recreational Center announced by fliers with short but thorough instructions:

RALLY! RALLY! RALLY! RALLY! RALLY!
    Everyone who supports the AAUP Belleville Chapter's
    current action is invited to a rally.
TIME: Sunday, November 9, 1980. 7 p.m.-10 p.m.
PLACE: St. Clair Village Recreational Center.
PRICE: $2 per person to pay for mixes, snacks and ice.
    Please bring your own beer, wine or booze.
DÉCOR: Strike Signs.

We also set up a public relations committee to ". . . coordinate and disseminate all written information to the public. This includes letters, advertisements, and news releases."

The Picketing Committee scheduled and assigned picketers' times, both at the Belleville and Granite City campuses.

Then we waited. We walked the lines and waited and took hope as sporadic mailgrams floated in from a handful of local unions and several AAUP units to the east and northeast.

Bill Gushleff, President of IFT Local 434, District 201 (Belleville High School) sent a letter informing us that:

> The administration of BAC is making an attempt to fill the classrooms of striking teachers with part-time people. Several members of our local have been contacted to participate in this strike breaking tactic.
>
> We feel that it is not in the best interest of the union or the teachers to participate in this type of dispute.
>
> Furthermore, we urge all union members to refuse any aid to the administration of BAC and support the striking teachers.

The Dupo (Illinois) Federation of Teachers sent a note of support, and Dee Ann Philpott, President of IFT, Local 4131, Harmony-Emge District 175, sent an encouraging mailgram, adding that a District 175 board member, Susan Teuteur, a BAC English part-timer, was crossing the picket-lines.

Mailgrams arrived from the following AAUP chapters: Temple University in Middletown, Virginia; Connecticut State College in New Britain, Connecticut; Wayne State University in Detroit, Michigan; Western Michigan University in Kalamazoo, Michigan; Delaware State College in Newark, Delaware; Pennsylvania State College in Harrisburg, Pennsylvania; and Eastern Michigan University in Ypsilanti, Michigan.

Graciously, John West and his family made their house in the Weatherstone subdivision, across Greenmount Road from the college, available for our use during the strike. West's house served as strike head-quarters and each morning curious strikers, looking for news, crowded up the kitchen and living room.

There was always hot coffee and chili for returning cold, hungry picketers, and for those waiting to return to the lines. What else might have been on the menu, I do not remember, though the steamings and boilings in the kitchen produced a respectable *Recipes for Strikers: and other Outcasts, Radicals, Rebels ... and Hungry People* cookbook, assembled and printed by librarian Jan Kramer. Other than that, we tried to remain optimistic.

＊ ＊ ＊ ＊ ＊

Of course, not everyone in the BAC community supported the strikers. On principal alone, or prejudice, many people in the district were anti-labor and did not especially like teachers. Strikers reported being verbally assaulted and maligned by district residents. Sometimes the assaults came from family members—in my case a somewhat removed family member.

I'm not certain how long the Lanter surname has been around. Depending on whom you want to believe and on what findings you accept, some claim it has Roman origins. The name appears in Central Europe, Switzerland, and France in the early sixteenth century. There is a Lanterville in Switzerland.

The influx of Lanters into the United States began on the East Coast in the seventeenth century. By 1800 small colonies of French were established in Southern Illinois and the American Bottom along the east bank of the Mississippi river by the voyagers who traveled with Joliet and Marquette. Then in 1850 a hand full of immigrants from Herange, France settled in French Village and Belleville. Later individuals followed, and after 1850 the sire-name Lanter was substantial in Southwestern Illinois. By 1980 there were no fewer than three, and possibly four, Wayne Lanters living in the BAC district.

Sometime before 1980, after receiving a dozen-or-so phone calls and some mail meant for another Wayne Lanter, to simplify life and to avoid further confusion, I requested an unlisted phone number. My number remained in the faculty directory, and as a habit I included it in my syllabi for my students.

The two other Wayne Lanters, with whom I was familiar, were both cousins somewhat removed. One was in his late twenties, from Belleville, and a student at BAC in the middle '70s. His great-grandfather and my grandfather were brothers. The other was from Mascoutah and four-years older than I was. He had inherited a trucking delivery service, which he was in the process of expanding into a larger commercial enterprise called Lanter, Inc., during which time he had gained a strong anti-union reputation.

I did not have much contact with the commercial Wayne Lanter, though one day during the strike I received a phone call from an attorney who claimed to represent the CEO of Lanter, Inc. He informed me that my students and their parents were calling his client to air their grievances about my striking misdeeds, and that his client demanded that I put a stop to this.

The matter was not without irony—anti-union-daddy-big-bucks adding his two cents to the attack on the BAC faculty, an attack that had caused the strike in the first place. At any rate I informed the (his?) attorney that since I was on strike, I no longer had access to my students, and anyway, I wasn't certain I wanted to talk to their parents.

Moreover, I reminded him that his and his client's belief that my command might in some way influence my students' behavior was totally unrealistic. I had never known my students to do what I said, and even if I could reach them, I wouldn't expect they might follow my directives now.

But to be kind and helpful, I suggested that his client had several alternatives at his disposal. If the phone calls continued, and if so inclined, his client could get an unlisted phone number, as I had done to avoid receiving Lanter, Inc.'s calls. Otherwise his client could change his name. If that was asking too much, he could always leave town. I'm sure any of these would have worked.

* * * * *

Beyond escalating the conflict and bringing the malignancy of the Eckert Board and the Wissore administration to public attention, the strike served to acquaint faculty members with one another, in some cases bringing together total strangers. And though I'm not sure how much camaraderie developed, going three weeks without knowing whether they had a job caused some strikers a good bit of consternation. They needed consoling.

Keeping teachers on strike in the middle of a semester, people who want to be in their classrooms with their students, and who have adjusted to and built their lives around the responsibilities of teaching, is no easy task. There were financial problems. Granted, some of the faculty had spouses with second incomes, but some did not. Financial help was available in limited measure by way of strike loans, but in most cases this was not enough to satisfy the creditors quickly turned to predators of already seriously underpaid people.

Faculty financial hardship and uncertainty about jobs were central to the SS-Wissore plan to wait out the strikers' psychological breakdown. Even before the strike, the idea appears to have been that by prolonging negotiations faculty resistance could be weakened. The Friday (October 31st) before the strike, when a recess in negotiations resulting from board intractability was called, the *Globe-Democrat* quotes Wissore as saying, "... let's not jeopardize what we think we have done in the interest of speed."

In other words, let's wait while the faculty sweats it out.

Return to Class or be Dismissed

Then on November fourteenth the board issued an ultimatum to the faculty to return to their classes or be fired. The order was not to take effect until November nineteenth. This gave the strikers plenty of time to think about the consequences and, within the board's scheme (set by SS and Wissore), for faculty members to fold.

And think the faculty did, but worry, too. Since Libby was the chief negotiator, the strike leader, and a counselor by training, when strikers' trepidations and doubts got the best of them, they usually wanted to talk to Libby. On at least three occasions I sat in on sessions Libby conducted with individuals in from the thin outer layer of the striking amalgam who were about to flake off. Always straightforward and tough, though understanding, Libby had a good grip on what we were into and what the possibilities were. Unfortunately, some of the strikers wanted childlike assurances that, regardless, all would be well. It usually came up in the form of, "Can you promise me ..."

Even before the sentence was completed, Libby would be shaking his head. "I can't promise you anything. It isn't my job to promise you. You have to stand up for yourself. You have to promise yourself that you'll do what's right." To Libby's credit, two of the three stuck it out.

There were others of the more-determined who tried to shore-up the resolve of those who were wavering. I know I did. One day Libby asked me to retrieve a briefcase he had left at Roger Christeck's house. I was without a vehicle that day and striker Betty Thompson, the Director of Nursing, volunteered to chauffeur me across town.

I didn't know much about Thompson, except that she was African-American, intelligent, and by whatever accounts had done a splendid job in the few years she had been with the nursing program at BAC. In the short conversation we had that morning I had the feeling that she was not as certain about continuing the strike as I would have hoped she would be. I got the impression that she was, after two weeks on strike, what might be categorized as a reluctant striker in that she saw the whole thing as a white man's affair and, in the lexicon of middle-range and more immediate history of black America, the fight at BAC had little to do with her.

Simply put, she was caught in the crossfire and could not see her way clear to improving her profession and/or her life by joining either side. She wasn't particularly enamored of her white overseers, but did not, on the other hand, feel drawn to support white colleagues, many of whom were openly racist.

I spoke to her at length about her position as one of the three African-Americans on the BAC faculty at the time, the only African-American woman on the faculty, and tried to assure her that she would be the last person the board or administration would want to end up in court for firing. Unfortunately, whatever encouragement she found in my words that day, it was not sufficient to see her through to the end of the strike.

Barnacles Attached to the Scholarship

Ads soliciting teachers to replace strikers appeared in the *St. Louis Globe Democrat* and in the *St. Louis Post Dispatch* adding further to the faculty's psychological disquiet. As a bit of strike guerilla-warfare, on November 12, 1980, the faculty ran a horse-and-rider ad in the *St. Louis Post Dispatch* advertising for, and advising persons looking for a teaching position to contact the AAUP at 522 Windrift, Belleville (John West's house). Regardless of what the Wissore administration was planning, the bargaining unit was always amenable to appointing a few good professors—if the faculty did the selecting.

The board's interviewing and hiring process for scabs was assigned to an H. J. Tyrell agency in St. Louis County, so we set up pickets, or at least warning signs, across the street from their offices at 121 Creve Coeur Ave. in Creve Coeur, Missouri, reminding the potential scabs as they departed their easy money interviews that:

THERE ARE NO
TEACHING JOBS AT
BELLEVILLE AREA COLLEGE

Still, scabs were hired, at least temporarily. In the comedy of it all, possibly out of shame or fear, none of them gave their correct names or addresses. Although I'm sure their correct personal data was on file somewhere, to us they were phantom imports, without identification (and one must suspect, more than likely without qualification or proper credentials since they were selected by the Wissore administration). They appeared anonymously out of the morning mist and, at the end of the day, clutching a fist of seriously tainted dollars, disappeared just as anonymously into the gathering dusk.

* * * * *

By the end of the first week of the strike the board's negotiating action-reaction became significantly truncated. The board seemed to believe it no longer needed to deliberate and could, regardless of what the faculty offered, respond both immediately and out-of-hand. On November 11 the faculty requested binding arbitration and on the same day without an official meeting the board refused binding arbitration.

November fourteenth a four-hour afternoon session with a federal mediator failed to provide anything of an agreement. Even as the negotiating teams met in the mediation session, the administration busied itself preparing letters of termination for the striking faculty. At its meeting that evening the board voted to fire striking faculty who did not return to work by 7:30 a.m., November 19th.

* * * * *

Not only did the SS people sell themselves as union-busters, several of them, notably Clark, Anderson, and Rybicki had authored articles and manuals or guides about how to degrade public employees and discourage or break unionizing efforts. The *Belleville Journal* reports that shortly after the mediation session on November fourteenth, before the board went into closed session to finalize its resolution,

> Libby . . . held up two thick documents which, he told the board, constituted a "secret" administrative-oriented strike manual. The manual, he added, includes actions to be taken by public service agencies during negotiations and strikes. One section of the manual, Libby said, advised that board members should not be told about certain actions by administrators during negotiations.
>
> The manual was authored, Libby claimed, by some of the same attorneys that the board has hired as its labor relations consultants.
>
> While the board was in closed session, Libby allowed reporters to examine his copy of the document which was entitled "Maintaining Public Services: Strike Planning Manual." According to information in the document, it was prepared for the National Public Employers Labor Relations Association

(NPELRA). Its authors were listed as James Baird, R. Theodore Clark, Jr. and Michael Rybicki.

Rybicki and Clark are two members of the law firm hired by the board for labor relations consultation."

Six years later, at a board meeting in April of 1986, another of SS's publications, Don Anderson's *The Role of the Elected Official during Negotiations* would be passed out to BAC board members. The publication was devised to encourage boards of education to employ Seyfarth Shaw to direct negotiations and keep college faculties "in check or under control."

I am not sure there are any more insidious and parasitical human beings than those who dip into public coffers to profit by destroying the very thing for which tax monies have been collected to support.

* * * * *

It would have been one thing, albeit a major disgrace for the board, if the soiling of the academic-educational fabric of the college had alienated only the faculty and a couple of top administrators. But it did not. The Eckert-Wissore attack on the school violated the moral-ethical sensibilities of a good number of BAC administration and staff, and drove off any number of decent, intelligent and otherwise dedicated people.

November 12, 1980 the *St. Louis Globe Democrat* reports, "BAC sends home dissident deans." Following Stone's and Washburn's petition former registrar Vincent Margerum, who had retired on June 30, 1980, and called the Stone-Washburn reassignment "fictitious college business," wrote an open letter that appeared first in the *BND* on November sixteenth as an AAUP ad, then again two-days later as a "Guest Viewpoint" on the editorial page of the *BND*. Warren Nieburg, Dean of General Studies and Continuing Services, had already been reassigned/demoted at the September board meeting to the Programs and Services for Older People (PSOP) at the uptown (Belleville) campus.

Two months later the BAC Veterans Office was under audit for a possible illegal transfer of funds within the college, and Lois Filla, who had been temporarily running the program, left the college. Filla had notified The Veterans Affairs Administration in Washington that the unusual transfer had been made, and after being passed over when Wissore appointed a new director for the BAC Veterans' Office, Filla resigned, taking her staff with her.

A month later, long-time board secretary, Ruthe Kombrink resigned. The March 23, 1981 issue of the student newspaper, *BAC Talk,* quotes Kombrink as saying "I hold high respect for the rights and privileges of our students and staff, and of great importance to me is that my work can be done with integrity and in the best interests of this institution. I am not willing to sacrifice my own personal code of ethics, and will leave with this code intact." Even Keel got into the act, although it came only after the board advised him to resign or they would not permit him to retire. By February 1981 Keel had found a job as president of a Lutheran College in Missouri and filed suit against the board for breach of contract.

Sit-down

> Agitators are a set of interfering, med-
> dling people, who come down to some
> perfectly contented class of the commun-
> ity and sow the seeds of discontent
> amongst them. That is the reason why
> agitators are absolutely necessary. With-
> out them, in our incomplete state, there
> would be no advance towards civilization.
> —Oscar Wilde

We're All Going to Jail

The morning of November 19, 1980, the day the give-up-the-strike-
or-be-fired edict the BAC board issued on Friday November fourteenth was
to take effect, at 7 a.m. the striking faculty gathered at the two roadway
entrances leading onto the college grounds and sat down in the inter-
sections blocking commuter access to the campus. The press quoted Libby
as saying the sit-down was partially planned and partially spontaneous, but
I had the feeling that most of the strikers knew about it as a plan. The
morning of the sit-down Libby told me he expected forty or so people to be
arrested. I am also certain that some of the strikers turned-coat and
informed the administration of the plan. The administration requested that
the Sheriff's Office have deputies on the scene at 6 that morning. And once
the sit-down was under way, the Belleville police arrived within ten or
fifteen minutes. Fifty-nine people were arrested and carted off to the St.
Clair County jail.

* * * * *

Shortly before the strike, on October twenty-second, the evening after
ninety-six of the faculty cast a Wissore no-confidence vote, eighty faculty
members took over the school cafeteria and as a rehearsal for things to
come, staged a sit-in. At some point in the evening Libby gave me the task of
securing the back door of the cafeteria.

"I don't want anyone to come in or go out that door," he said.

"What if they insist? What do you want me to do?"

"It's a command decision," he said.

That night in the cafeteria, I laughed and mentioned to Libby the good
old days of getting beaten by the police in Chicago, of the locals hiding in the
trees and throwing bricks and beer bottles at the demonstrators,
reminiscing that it would be good to get back to an activist agenda, while
wondering what kind of record I might still have in Chicago. But nothing
more was said.

The morning of the sit-down at the school roadway entrance, Libby came to me and as a complete surprise said, "We're all going to jail. I need someone to handle the bail money to get us out. No sense taking a chance on them digging up your Chicago record. You stay out of it."

As it turned out, regardless of Libby's concern, I wasn't all that willing to stay out of it and joined Libby and Christeck and Welch in the sit-down in the middle of the road in the main entrance leading to the college. Who else was there? I remember Martha Giordano, Lynn Bradley, Lucille Hammond, and Tom Cochran, and his wife, Barbara.

I was still there when the sheriff's deputies decided to haul us away. Then I felt a pretty good kick in the rump and looked up at Libby scowling at me.

"Get out of here," he said.

"You sure?"

"Goddammit, get out of here. I need you to handle the money."

There was a road grader parked nearby, so I slipped behind it, while Christeck ran a diversionary tactic. Sitting in the middle of the road accommodated Christeck so well he seemed to have grown roots or was somehow otherwise attached to the pavement. Three deputies were trying to get all of him off the ground and into a car, and they weren't having much luck. Finally, Gentleman Christeck, not wanting the deputies to strain themselves, proffered that if they would ". . . just stand back for a moment," he would right himself and walk to the patrol car. While he had the troops occupied, I slipped away from the squatters and made it down the road to strike headquarters at John West's house.

A Brief History of Sitting-down

The first industrial sit-down strike in the U.S. was by the United Rubber Workers in Akron, Ohio in February and March of 1935 against Goodyear Tire Co. It was an outgrowth of an earlier tactic used in 1934 against the General Tire and Rubber Company, when the rank-and-file showed up "At work but not working." By 1936 the sit-down had become a tactic of choice for unions representing unskilled workers. It is difficult to replace skilled or trained workers who might be on strike. Conversely, unskilled workers, upon leaving a work site, can most often be replaced quickly by other unskilled workers.

My dad told me that during the depression of the '30s he worked ten hours, and sometimes twelve hours a day at a foundry—an unskilled laborer with only a third-grade education, mostly shoveling sand into molds and doing other menial but backbreaking tasks. One day the foreman warned my dad and the two men working with him that they were taking too long to fill the molds. "When you stick your shovel in the sand make sure it comes out full," the foreman barked. When one of the men replied that he was ". . .

already getting a full shovel," the foreman reminded him that "For every one of you in here, there are twenty-five outside the door who would like this job. Make sure you get a shovel full every time."

To prevent being replaced and to insure the production site could not be used by scabs, unskilled strikers employed by the Ohio tire companies decided to sit-down to occupy the premises—the factory, foundry, assembly-line, etc.

Sitting down in the road that morning the BAC strikers had taken a page out of Illinois and Southern Illinois labor history, an historical page from an area of the country heavily populated in the nineteenth century by central Europeans who brought with them socialist political theories and beliefs that not only led to unionizing, but to a specific brand of unionism.

In 1875 Belleville was the largest coal producing area in the world. By 1900 the United Mine Workers of America (UMWA) was deeply embedded in Illinois, so much so that Mother Jones, the labor organizer, thought Illinois was the best union-organized state in the country. The problem may have been that the coalfields were overly organized, if that's possible. In his oral memoir on file at the University of Illinois at Springfield, miner Jack Battuello from Wilsonville claimed "Illinois was probably the most articulate, knowledgeable section of the United Mine Workers in affairs of unionism, of economics and politics." That would have been before 1932.

Then in 1932, maybe because of their dedication as the ". . . most articulate, knowledgeable section of the United Mine Workers in affairs of unionism," the miners of Central Illinois got into a hassle with UMWA President John L. Lewis. Because of the depression, and to accommodate his political aspirations, that year Lewis gave in to the coal owners, and the Illinois UMWA District 12 ended taking a pay cut from $6.10 to $5 a day. The miners in Central Illinois (the State of Illinois was District 12 of the UMWA) saw the cut as a concession to provide John L. a better national political image and a closer hook-up with the federal government. In the ensuing ratification (only Illinois had the right of contract ratification—Lewis had removed it from the rest of the UMWA) District 12 voted down the new contract 2-1 and John L. called for another vote. However, before the ballots could be counted, they were hijacked from the Farmers and Mechanics Bank in Springfield, Illinois. The tallies were not taken from the bank but lifted at gunpoint from two miners who had picked them up at the bank and were to deliver them to district union headquarters for counting. The two miners carrying the ballots, John Fee and George Dahm, were from Belleville. George Dahm was a close friend of my uncle Henry Schaefer and though I saw him many times at my uncle's house when I was a boy, I did not know until years later his bit in the history of the Illinois miners' rebellion of 1932.

With the ballots gone missing, UMWA President John L. Lewis issued an executive order commanding the miners to return to work under the new contract. A later informal tally of the second vote had the contract on track to being rejected by Illinois miners by a 3-1 count.

The District 12 constitution provided that at any time, 5-percent of the membership, in any local, could call a Conference of the Rank and File. And that is what happened in Benld, Illinois in 1932. A Conference of the Rank and File was convened that eventually led to the miners of Central Illinois separating from the UMWA and forming the Progressive Mine Workers of America (PMWA). That meeting of the rank and file that led to the PMWA was chaired by Joe Pusich from Wilsonville, Illinois and supported by large numbers of miners who were in Pusich's words, "syndicalists"—the French word for union.

Most of the Illinois syndicalists were first- and second-generation immigrants from England and Europe infused with a nineteenth century political-philosophical belief that human anomalies make it nearly impossible to find incorruptible people for positions of power or, if for some strange reason you can find honest people, it is impossible to keep them uncorrupted. The syndicalist believes, therefore, that when people are given power, they cannot be left unattended. Once the elected take office, the electorate must immediately set out to remove them. In other words, if it is impossible to keep the humans in public office uncorrupted, at least have a means for removing the bad ones. The philosophy is grounded in the Hegelian dialectic, whereby a thesis is set up, i.e., a government or governing body, and immediately an antithesis develops to contest it, the contest producing a synthesis which becomes the new thesis-government—on and on, making governing a living, progressive enterprise. The better parts of the practice attempt to provide a remedy for democracy's failure as it failed in pre-Socratic Athens.

In spirit, syndicalism's intent to control an elected individual's power is not unlike Amendment XXII to the United States Constitution limiting the U.S. presidency to two terms. The U.S. Constitution also provides separate branches of government in a system of checks and balances to keep any one person from gaining or exercising too much power, at least theoretically. The English system of parliamentary no-confidence votes and the Prime Minister's power to dismiss parliament is even more ingenious. The underlying idea is to keep politicians from ruining the society they are elected to govern—a propensity politicians have that led H.L. Mencken to observe that "The finest creative act of God is a dead politician." The syndicalist prayer is that politicians will all die peaceful deaths—of old age, out of office, and without having done too much harm.

* * * * *

In the early 1932 hassle with John L. the miners of Central Illinois split from the UMWA to form the Progressive Miner Workers of America (PMWA). The same year PMWA attempts to invade and convert UMWA strongholds in the southern parts of the state turned the split nasty. A mine war erupted, this time between the two miners' unions rather than with the coal owners. Men and women were killed and property destroyed, leaving grievances and animosities that remained for years.

At one point the Illinois District miners got an injunction against John L. Lewis prohibiting him and/or his representatives from coming into Illinois. A second cousin of mine, Jerome Munie, Sheriff of St. Clair County at the time (1930-34), espoused a decided sympathy for the PMWA which accounted for only 40-percent of the miners in Illinois, but over 95-percent in St. Clair County. The grapevine had it that Munie warned John L. that if he (Munie) caught John L. or any of his men in St. Clair County, he would kill them.

During the '30s Pusich and Battuello belonged to the same UMWA Local but did not much like one another. They both worked for Superior Coal Company in four mines of the complex beneath most of Egarville, Sawyerville, Mt. Clare and Wilsonville, in Macoupin County.

John Battuello came from a rather typical early twentieth century coal mining family. He started in the mines when he was thirteen. That would have been 1913. His father and a brother, Camille, were killed in the mines. Another brother, Colombo, worked for Superior for years and survived, although he twice suffered severe injuries. When I asked Jack Battuello if conditions in the coal mines were as bad as the old miners claimed they were, he said, "Son, some days we carried out more dead and injured men than we did coal." Battuello would later serve as PMWA Local 1 president as well as on the Executive Board of the PMWA. In 1937 the 2,500 miners from the four Superior Coal Company mines in Wilsonville, comprising Local No. 1 of the PMWA, were the largest union local in the United States.

In the spring of 1937 Superior closed one of the mines for repairs, and a conflict broke out with the union. As Battuello said, "There had always been an unwritten law—it was not stipulated in the contract— that if one of the mines of the Superior Coal Company closed down, then the company automatically divided the work of the membership mine that was closed down, with the three remaining mines that continued to operate."

This is still the practice in Great Britain. When times are hard, and work scarce, the British government and businesses, rather than lay off workers, often drop everyone to a three- or four-day week, thus sharing the income any one job might provide.

When Superior refused the miners' demand for work-sharing, and negotiations deadlocked, the Wilsonville miners went on strike. Well, it was a little more than a strike. Again Battuello (who led the strike) tells that "We decided to sit down and we sat down in the Number Four (Wilsonville) Mine. There was [sic] 544 miners at the Number Four mine. To my knowledge this was the first sit-down in a mine in the history of the United States." The miners were 385 feet beneath the ground and remained there for nine days before their work-share demand was met.

The UMWA had been founded in 1895 as an extension of the old Knights of Labor. From the beginning strikes were a part of the UMWA bargaining process. It also had a history of never working without a contract. Teachers, on the other hand, were latecomers to unionization and job actions and picket-lines, and to sitting-down. Still, the similarities of the Wilsonville 1937 sit-down strike and the BAC November 1980 sit-down were very real.

During the '60s and '70s civil rights activists employed the sit-in to occupy lunch counters in the South and organizer-activist Saul Alinsky once promoted a shop-in, an off-shoot of the sit-in, at a large grocery store. For several days, whenever the store was open, four thousand women went "Shopping but not buying," in a particularly overpriced white owned-and-managed noncompetitive store with a captive ghetto-customer base. Additionally, sit-ins were used in student protests at colleges and universities. The student sit-ins, however, often did not generally affect school efficacy since they usually occupied the president's office. But I am not aware of any college faculty strike before 1980 that used sit-down tactics.

Education Strikes in Illinois

Student protests and strikes, even in high schools, have been around a lot longer than one might suspect. Almost as a prelude to the BAC 1980 strike, forty-five years earlier, in 1935, at Belleville Township High School (BTHS) in Belleville, students led by senior class President Homer Wiedmann conducted a three-day strike to protest the dismissal of six teachers. The Belleville teachers had been summarily "not re-employed" or not offered new contracts by a quorum of the District 201 board, which consisted of the board president and three members of the board's Teachers' Committee. The action violated the board's procedural rules and was opposed by at least two other board members. As student protests go, at the time of the Belleville strike, students in Madison and Peoria, Illinois were also out on strike protesting the dismissal of a principal, in one case, and an assistant principal and a coach in another.

Reputedly, a Belleville District 201 board member promised his daughter one of the positions to be made vacant by the Belleville dismissals, a practice that had been, if not condoned, at least tolerated by previous boards. Additionally, it was claimed certain board members had decided to not re-employ teachers who had not worked on the board members' election campaigns. The teachers targeted had been at the school from four to nine years and there seems not to have been any concerns about their competence or previous questions about their re-employment.

In its coverage of the strike, the *Belleville Daily Advocate* reports that one of the dissenting board members, Arthur Buesch, claimed, "I am informed that Dr. Rauth told one of the teachers, 'I'm boss now of the hiring and firing of teachers and I've a good notion to have you fired.'"

To protest the board's actions the students organized and staged a three-day strike with parades, led by the school's band, and bonfire rallies to burn board members in effigy. They even rallied and convinced the eighth-graders from the local junior high, the next year's freshman class, to join the strike. It is interesting that in Wilsonville, during the thirties when the mines Pusich and Battuello worked went on strike, the Wilsonville high school and grade school students joined the walkouts.

Not only did the 1935 Belleville student strike succeed in retaining the six teachers, it also dragged a particularly corrupt board of education out into the clearing of public scrutiny and gave impetus to the teachers protecting themselves. Seven months later, the *Belleville Daily Advocate* (December 23, 1935), reports that the "Belleville township high school's faculty of 52 teachers Saturday afternoon organized a chapter of the American Federation of Teachers and thus affiliated themselves with the American Federation of Labor.

"The teachers elected Harold Glover, biology instructor, as president, and Miss Ruth Miller, English teacher, secretary of the new chapter."

The *Belleville Daily Advocate* reports further that at the next board meeting, January 23, 1936, "Regulations governing the American Federation of Teachers, Local 434, comprising the faculty of Belleville Township High School were received by the high school board of education at its regular session last night."

Of special interest in the regulations were items "(6) to protect the school from all forms of exploitation (7) to insure absolute freedom of the school from any political entanglement (8) to secure adequate school revenues for educational facilities, and (9) to employ the greatest integrity in the expenditure of school funds." These were given to a school board already under investigation by the federal government for suspected irregularities in granting building contracts—the same board, that seven months earlier with its unethical treatment of BTHS teachers, had generated the student strike.

Although teachers' unions were organized in the early twentieth century, the first recorded teachers' strike in the United States didn't appear until November 25, 1946 at Van Buren School in St. Paul, Minnesota, sponsored by the St. Paul Federation of Teachers, Local 28, "the women's union." Reportedly teachers and administrators, even the principal, were members of Local 28.

The first community college faculty strike in Illinois was the CCCTU strike in November of 1966. Following the enactment of the Illinois Junior College Act in 1965—in January 1966—the Cook County College faculty, from fifteen Chicago city and suburban community colleges, which had been part of the Chicago Teachers Union, Local 1, formed the AFT-IFT CCCTU, Local

1600. That same year, November 30th, to secure recognition and the right to serve as a bargaining agent, CCCTU called its first strike. As a strike by a postsecondary education faculty, it was only preceded by the UFCT-AFT walkout, led by Israel Kugler, at St. John's University in New York City in January of 1966.

The 1935 Belleville student strike not only led to the faculty organizing Local 434 of the AFT, but the following year Local 434 was instrumental in the formation of the IFT and bringing the AAUP to BJC.

* * * * *

Though teachers are by no means unskilled workers, classroom instruction can easily be rescheduled to other sites, so it didn't make sense for striking BAC faculty to sit-down in their classrooms—usually there are too many classrooms and too few union teachers anyway. However, once outside school property, access by scabs at commuter schools, students, and whoever else might want to cross picket-lines, can be stopped by taking over the roadways leading into the school. One way to do this is to sit-down in the road. But while it can be an effective tactic, it can also be dangerous. You never know when a hostile driver might intentionally or accidentally drive into the strikers.

The 1937 Wilsonville strike was the first sit-down mine strike in the United States, and the 1980 BAC faculty sit-down was, as far as I know, the first strike in education-labor history in the United States to employ sit-down tactics, certainly the first in higher-education-labor history in the United States to employ a sit-down.

Looking at the BAC strikers sitting in the road that day was like looking at a photo taken forty years before of the Wilsonville miners with dirt and pride on their faces. That day their faces became ours.

Fifty-nine Militant Academics

By 1980 several AAUP chapters had led brief strikes at Northern Michigan University (1977) and at the University of Rhode Island and Boston University (1979). But otherwise the national office seemed not to have had much experience with these kinds of labor struggles. This became apparent when several representatives from the AAUP Washington office showed up at strike headquarters. You need to remember that the first faculty strike in postsecondary education was at St. John's University, 1966-67, led by Israel Kugler. Both the AAUP and the UFCT had chapters at St. John's University and were involved in the dispute with the administration when the university fired 31 teachers without due process hearings. However, the AAUP at St. John's did not support Kugler and the UFCT. When Kugler called a strike the AAUP refused to honor the walkout and withdrew from the conflict.

Anyway, the day of the sit-down, while I was waiting for a call from Libby to liberate the strikers from jail, I spent some time talking to Sally McCracken, one of the AAUP representatives visiting strike headquarters. When I inquired what she thought about what we were doing, she replied, "I don't know. This is the first time I've been in a strike." So, I asked what she and her colleagues were doing at strike headquarters. "Like everybody else," she said, "we're learning."

Well, I'm not sure. Some people had already learned. Tom Cochran, the BAC-AAUP chapter president at the time, had been fired some years before for participating in a school strike. And he was leading the current insurrection. I always had the feeling that Libby and many other strikers knew well what the stakes were and what we were doing out there sitting down on the cold asphalt. So, it might be fair to say some people had already learned.

Eventually, McCracken did send a telegram to Illinois Governor James Thompson (who had vetoed the Community College Tenured Teacher Act the year before, forcing a General Assembly veto-override vote) asking him to stop the board from firing us. But from the tone of her voice in our conversation, and from that of several others from the national AAUP with her the day the fifty-nine strikers were arrested, I got the distinct impression that she did not approve of what we were doing. Though McCracken was a tough lady and had a reputation in academic circles as a liberal, the condescension in her voice implied that faculty should be above this kind of behavior. Saul Alinsky defined a liberal as someone who leaves the room when the argument turns into a fistfight. But then, as she said, she was learning to bob and weave—and maybe to sharpen her left jab.

What was she really learning? Well, on November 19, 1980, the argument the BAC faculty had with the Eckert-Wissore people turned into a little more than a fistfight. The striking faculty sat down in the two roadway entrances of the college and sixty demonstrators were carted off (fifty-nine to jail and one to the hospital—Leo Welch had been injured picketing in the roadway when a scab ran him down). The BAC faculty occupied the roadways to the school that morning because they believed that the quality of education they had been appointed by the citizens of Illinois to provide for the BAC district was being seriously obstructed and impaired by the Eckert-Wissore cartel's attempt to demean and marginalize the BAC faculty, and to redefine the faculty and their relationship to the community they served.

* * * * *

As early as 1837, Jasper Adams, chaplain and professor of geography, history, and ethics at West Point, wrote, "The relation of the faculty member to the trustees . . . is not that of a workman to his employer; it is rather like that of a lawyer to his client or the minister to his congregation—a relation in which the person retained has special skills, experiences and qualities that put him in a position to advise and in a sense direct the man who retains him."

Following the Adams' assertion, the AAUP "1915 Declaration of Principles on Academic Freedom and Academic Tenure" affirms that college and university professors ". . . are the appointees, but not in any proper sense the employees of the trustees." He states further, that "Once appointed the scholar has professional functions to perform in which the appointing authorities have neither competency nor the moral right to intervene. The responsibility of the university [college] teacher is primarily to the public itself and to the judgment of his own profession; . . . his duty is to the wider public to which the institution itself is morally amenable."

Implicitly the AAUP document burdens teachers with a responsibility, to the public and to their professions, to provide the very best, accurate, and thorough instruction possible to the students entrusted to their guidance. This is exactly the confluence at which the Eckert-Wissore hucksters, with their attempt to water down instruction and reduce professors to drugstore clerks, had attacked the BAC faculty. Wissore was fond of referring to students as clients or customers and babbling the inanity that "We don't teach subjects, we teach students." However, in the equivocation lexicon dealing with administrators, too often, comes down to "Teaching the un-teachable."

I noted earlier that local politicians often imitate or otherwise take permission and guidance from ideas and practices that infuse the current national political scene. In 1980 the Reagan administration had set out to scrap government regulations on corporations in favor of the economic lawless-market. It seems to me that the Eckert Board and Wissore were attempting to de-regulate the traditional educational structure of the college which the professors provided and open it to the American corporate pragmatic of "whatever makes money is right." Also, if the noncompliant professors were removed, the administration could operate the college with "corporate flexibility," which would provide corporate invisibility—the two essential characteristics of a modern corporation. Since there would be no one to oppose whatever scheme the administration wished to implement, whatever was done could be done out of public view.

* * * * *

Granted, some of the faculty arrested that November day had other and attenuating motives for putting themselves in jeopardy. There were some among us, I discovered later, who did not object so much to what Wissore and the Eckert Board were doing—as they did to the fact that

Wissore and Eckert were doing it. You have to remember that many of the AAUP faculty saw themselves, in the first instance, as an appendage of the governing administration—they viewed themselves as quasi-administrators, even more than they thought of themselves as teachers. In other words, certain of the faculty objected not so much to sacking programs or diluting the quality of the college's academics, as they did to having their personal power diminished and/or stripped.

Still they stood their ground. And for many of them it was a painful experience. These were not activists at heart. Not Bernadette Devlin or Saul Alinsky or William Kunstler. As teachers, and as morally responsible people, breaking the law and giving themselves up to apprehension and incarceration was repugnant. But from what would have otherwise been a scar on their character, with the courage to attempt to remedy a wrong, a wrong that could not be ignored, they fashioned a badge of honor.

In any case, for many of the BAC teachers and students, adjusting their academic robes and defying the authorities that day in November of 1980 was not easy. To them, for their courage as citizens, scholars, students, and teachers—for their character, I offer my admiration and gratitude. I am exceptionally proud to have been their colleague.

* * * * *

Arresting fifty-seven faculty members and two students and hauling them off to jail was one thing but arraigning them was another. On the way to the jail, Leo Welch had to be dropped off at the hospital. During the sit-down Welch had been injured—though not seriously. Welch was the only casualty of the day, but with the vehemence the Wissore administration generated in its attack on the faculty, there easily could have been more.

I'm not sure the people at the St. Clair County jail had ever handled fifty-nine militant academics before. Once the roadway squatters were patted-down and carted off en masse by the Sheriff's deputies and the Belleville police, they were deposited at the county jail and fingerprinted. Circuit Court Judge Joseph Cunningham held an arraignment at the jail and scheduled a bail hearing. Then, what appeared from the point of view of the attendant authorities to be a se ious matter, turned decidedly comic.

English professor Darrell Kohlmiller entertained the jail workers and deputies and rallied the strikers by reciting Kipling's "Gunga Din."

> So I'll meet 'im later on
> In the place where 'e is gone—
> Where it's always double drill and no canteen;
> 'E'll be squattin' on the coals
> Givin' drink to pore damned souls,
> An' I'll get a swig in Hell from Gunga Din!

All the strikers, men and women, were herded into a single, large holding cell without private restroom facilities. And because it was mid-morning and many of the incarcerated had already consumed numerous cups of coffee, several needed to avail themselves of the one not-so-private facility in the cell. To provide privacy for these relieving-activities, in a demonstration of solidarity, a group with large coats (this was winter, after all) with their backs to the relievee and their arms outspread formed a semi-circle curtain around the facility.

When the initial arraignment finally got underway, St. Clair County Associate Circuit Judge Dennis Jacobson ordered that the arrested remain in St. Clair County until the charges against them had been adjudicated. This brought a rousing of protests.

"But Your Honor, I live in St. Louis and have small children."

"Well, okay, you can travel to your home, but nowhere else."

"Your Honor, I have a paper to give at a nursing conference in Denver next week."

"Well, you can go, but only to Denver."

"Your Honor, I'm teaching a night class at Webster University in St. Louis."

"Your Honor, I'm on the state board for English teachers and have a meeting in Springfield this weekend."

"Your Honor, I have to conduct a seminar on 'Ethics in Community Colleges' in Chicago."

Exasperated, His Honor capitulated. "Okay, okay. Those that live in St. Louis will have to post a 35-dollar bond. The rest of you can make arrangements with your parole officer," he conceded, possibly aware by then that the rules under which the striking faculty had been brought before him were, if not suspect, then mostly inapplicable. Clearly these were not run-of-the-mill trespassers and disturbers-of-the-peace, and the one-size-fits-all bail restrictions used for perpetrators that usually came before his court were hardly relevant.

Music professor Jerry Bolen showed up at the sit-down with a base-drum—but had also made a run on the bank to withdraw his entire savings, much to the consternation of his wife, Sue, who was pregnant at the time with their first child and was horrified that not only was it possible, but more than likely, that her husband no longer had a job, and more than that, that they no longer had any money at all. Bolen posted bond for the strikers saving Libby from having to call me to get everybody out. I had been sitting dutifully by the phone waiting for Libby's call and must admit I was surprised at not having heard from him, as I was when he walked into strike headquarters.

I discovered later, from Libby, that he intended to call and instruct me to go to his bank. He had arranged with the bank for me to sign for a basket of dollars (or whatever he determined the sum would be) in cash to pay the bail for the sitters-down. As it turned out no one was fined or served any jail time. I would hope Jerry Bolen got his money back—I know he kept his job.

Several years later the arrest records of the demonstrators were expunged, although, for what they did that day their names should be inscribed and enshrined at the front door of the school as a commemorative to its current status as a college. Maybe an historical marker could be placed at the north Greenmount Road entrance. "Here sat down fifty-nine teachers and students to be arrested and jailed on November 19, 1980 so this educational institution might endure."

The day of the sit-down, the *St. Louis Globe-Democrat* reports that "An investigation into a possible conflict of interest on the part of BAC trustee Curt Eckert will be turned over to a St. Clair County Grand Jury, State's Attorney Clyde L. Kuehn said Tuesday.

"The *Globe-Democrat* also learned Tuesday of possible violation of the Illinois Governmental Ethics Act by Eckert."

Further on, the *Globe* article notes that "As chairman of the BAC Board of Trustees, Eckert voted for a contract requiring the college to share the cost of a sewer pump station ($70,000) with Weatherstone, a development company in which he owned 10-percent interest."

Additionally, the *Globe* reports "Public records indicate Eckert apparently violated the state's Governmental Ethics Act in 1978 and 1979 by not filing a required economic interest statement, which he was required to do by virtue of his position on the BAC board.

"Failure to file within the time prescribed shall result in ineligibility for or forfeiture of, office or position of employment.

"Filing a false or incomplete statement is a Class A misdemeanor subject to a maximum penalty of $1000 fine and one year in jail."

The investigation probably cost Eckert a good bit more than a thousand dollars. Rumor had it he paid a well-connected Belleville attorney 25,000 dollars to have the charges dropped. True or not, Eckert never went to trial, and appears not to have paid a fine or served time.

Figure # 1

Belleville Junior College AAUP 1967
First row: James Bowman, Herbert Sieg, Frank Scott, Otis Miller, Roger Crane, Jack Stokes, William Saunders. Standing: Robert Saforza, Marjorie Murray, Genevieve Snider, Jean Aldog, Betty Oelrich, Madge Ream, Thelma Phillips and Jan Milligan

Figure # 2

BJC Faculty Senate 1967
Jack Stokes, William Saunders, Jan Milligan, Evelyn Best, Madge Ream, Barbara Dooling, Ferrel Wilson and Robert Maybry

Figure # 3

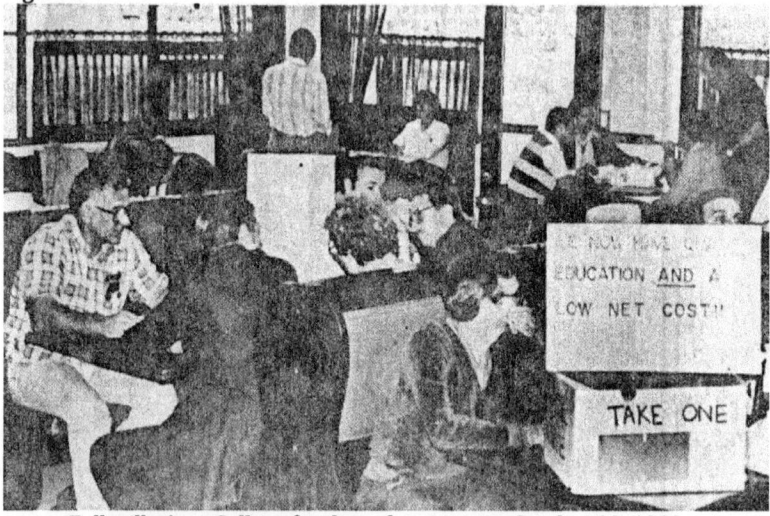

Belleville Area College faculty cafeteria sit-in, October 22, 1980

Figure # 4

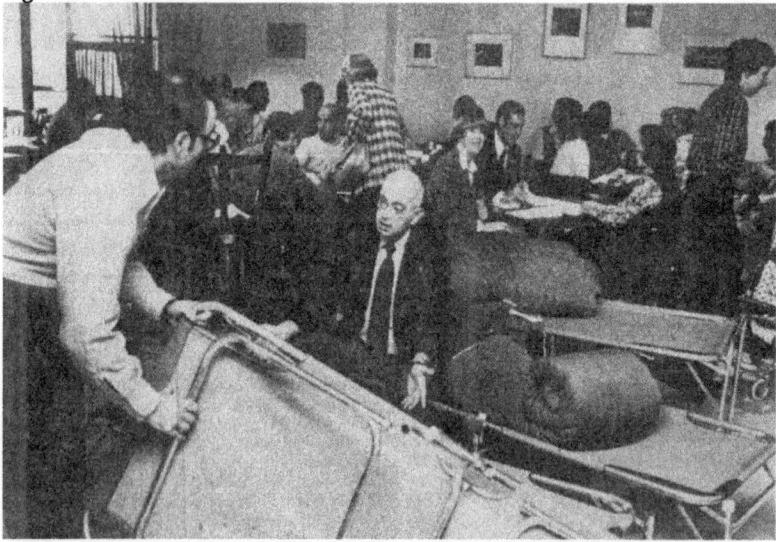

William Sheehy and Donald Libby at the October 22, 1980 faculty cafeteria
sit-in

Figure # 5

Kenneth Pinzke–the Lone Striker

Figure # 6

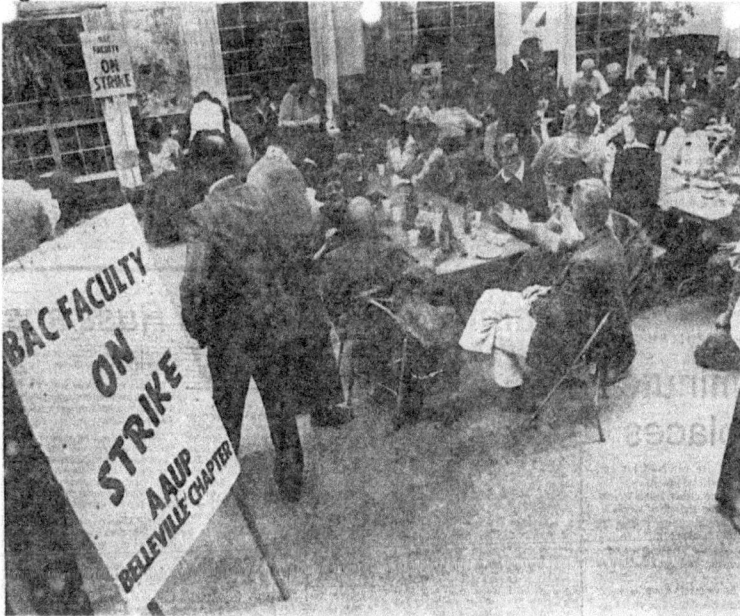

Faculty strike rally November 1980

Figure #7

8B St. Louis Globe-Democrat Tues. Nov. 11, 1980

TEACHERS
PROFESSORS
33K PER ANNUM

* Chemical
* Math
* Biology
* Physics/Engineering
* ACHR/Instrumentation
* English
* Agriculture
* Horticulture
* Drafting
* Law Enforcement
* Security Administration

Masters Degree required, experience desirable, 40 hrs. per week. Indefinite duration and need approximately 30 people to provide instruction in classrooms. for further information write to or contact in person: A.A.U.P., 552 Windrift, Belleville, Ill. 62221, 1-618-277-5617

TEACHERS
PROFESSORS
33K PER ANNUM

CHEMICAL
MATH
BIOLOGY
PHYSICS/ENGINEERING
ACHR/INSTRUMENTATION
ENGLISH
AGRICULTURE
HORTICULTURE
DRAFTING
ART/MUSIC
GEOLOGY

Master's degree required, experience desirable, 40 hours per week, indefinite duration and need approx. 30 people to provide instruction in classrooms. Apply in person with resume to:

H. J. TYRRELL CO. INC.
121 Creve Coeur Ave.
Manchester, MO 63011
1 blk. West of Hwy 141 off Manchester Rd.
391-8482

Ad for teachers to replace strikers

Figure # 8

Josephine Jones, Genevieve Snider, Barbara Stehle and Sally McCracken,
waiting for news

Figure#9

Sit-down

Figure #10

Belleville Area College sit-down, Donald Libby, Chief Negotiator, the
first of the Belleville strikers to be arrested, November 19, 1980

Figure # 11

Strikers on their way to jail

Figure # 12

Belleville Area College Board meeting (November 19, 1980)

Figure # 13

Belleville Area College Board meeting (November 19, 1980)

Figure # 14

Chief Negotiator Donald Libby and AAUP President Thomas Cochran

Figure # 15

Donald Libby (1929-1988)

Be it Resolved . . .

> What does labor want? We want more
> schoolhouses and less jails; more books
> and less arsenals; more learning and less
> vice; more leisure and less greed; more
> justice and less revenge; in fact more of the
> opportunities to cultivate our better
> natures.
>
> —Samuel Gompers

Resolution for Termination

Several days prior to November 19, 1980, the board consented to an AAUP negotiating team request for a meeting with the board in closed session without any administrators present to discuss Wissore's mistreatment of the faculty. The board agreed to the meeting, though when the faculty team arrived it found the board surrounded by Wissore and his entire administrative staff. Needless to say there was for the faculty no balm in Gilead that night.

The public part of the board meeting that evening was held in the BAC Intramural Gym, which was set up with a crescent of tables draped with white cloths on the far side opposite the main entrance (See Figures #13 and #14). The board and administration were seated with their backs to the wall facing across the gym floor into a bank of flood lights behind which a capacity crowd would be seated (and sometimes standing and shouting) in the gym bleachers. At the center of the gym floor was a flat console to control the microphones on the tables with black cords leading from the console to the mikes.

Why this peculiar arrangement for a board meeting? Well, early on Eckert-Wissore adopted a corporate-siege mentality. No matter the issue, Wissore always saw himself and the board as under attack from the faculty, other schools, the district, the voters, etc. He was always certain there were spies within their ranks. Or at least he wanted the board to believe that there were.

Wissore often staged confrontations or set-ups for imagined confrontations. For example, one evening before the strike a group of concerned faculty gathered in the hall outside a board meeting. When the meeting adjourned, Wissore assigned an administrator-bodyguard to walk each board member to his car. The theatrics were to indulge administrators' fantasies that they were in some way St. George, and to further convince board members of the hostile and dangerous nature of the fire-breathing, deceptive faculty. The evening of the November 19, 1980 meeting a squad of State Police cars gathered ominously in the lot outside the gym. It looked like something out of a German Expressionist movie.

I have often thought the high theatrics and spectacle of the setting the meeting provided fit well with Wissore's vision of himself and the board as ordained saviors bravely facing the maddened crowd. I did not think this alone. A number of people referring to the set-up in the Intermural Gym that night commented, "My god, it reminded me of the pictures you see of Nazi Germany." A month later a Vincent Margerum letter in the *BND's* "Readers Forum" noted that faculty members had been arrested that day as a ". . . protest against despotism, the kind that spawned the very wars our country has fought and for which our forefathers and relatives have died."

For its concern and trust all the AAUP negotiating team received from the board that night was another "resolution for termination" and a public reading of the list of strikers who would be dismissed if they did not return to work by 7:30 a.m. November 20, 1980.

Under the pressure of the termination edict, it was very difficult to hold the striking unit together. A couple days after the first return-or-be-fired order was issued, but before it went into effect, sometime around three in the afternoon on my way to strike headquarters, I walked up to a group of pickets and students gathered at the south driveway entrance to the school. One of the people there, though I do not think he was picketing at the time, was faculty member William Allen, the coordinator of the police academy and a close friend of Libby's. Allen was one of only three African-Americans on the BAC faculty at the time. The other two were Betty Thompson, head of the nursing, and William Meekins of allied health. As I said, Allen was a close friend of Libby's.

That afternoon he was talking to a student, and I do not think he saw me or otherwise realized I was standing a few feet behind him. The conversation of the moment concerned the duration of the strike, to which Allen suggested "We'll be back in by Monday or a day or two after that."

I wasn't on the negotiating committee that year, or on the AAUP Executive Committee, and so was not privy to any more information than any of the other strikers. I simply assumed that Allen had general information that I did not have. Possibly he had been talking to Libby and had been informed that a settlement was in the works. On the other hand, knowing Libby, I expected that had there been an agreement afoot, he would not have accepted it unilaterally, and would have passed it on to the striking faculty. Of course, these were crazy times, and anything was possible. Well, almost.

I didn't stay to speak to Allen but crossed the street to strike headquarters and decided I'd quiz Libby about Allen's remarks. As it turned out, Libby had not yet returned from a mediation-negotiating session, and I had to get home to meet my sons after school.

Saturday morning, after thinking about it, I imagined that Allen's remarks were either innocuous or merely a guess, and so I did not make an attempt to contact Libby until Monday morning. I couched what I said as merely speculative. I told Libby, "Bill Allen thinks we will be back inside in a couple days." Libby was involved with another matter at the moment and did not answer. And as far as I know nothing more was made of it.

Tuesday night in the gym, after the board issued its edict that the faculty had to return to class or be terminated, a reading of the rolls of the condemned proceeded alphabetically. The calling of names was surprising only in that several names that should have been sounded were not. The second name on the list should have been that of William Allen. But it was, to say the least, conspicuously absent. When it became apparent that Allen's name had not been overlooked, but that it was not included with those of other strikers because Allen had already crossed over, Libby was livid. I don't know if Libby ever talked about the betrayal to anyone—but on several occasions when Bill Allen's name came up Libby told me "Things can never be the same." And they never were.

The Horrid Deed

The board meeting ended about 10:30. The next morning Libby referred to the decree quoting *Macbeth*.

"Well," he said, "they did the 'horrid deed.'"

The Shakespeare passage is a good bit more revealing than just the horrid deed.

In Act I, Scene IV, Macbeth laments his rash act. Besides this Duncan (the faculty?):

> Hath borne his faculties so meek, hath been
> So clear in his great office, that his virtue
> Will plead like angels, trumpet tongu'd, against
> The deep damnation of his taking-off;
> And pity, like a naked new-born babe
> Striding the blast or heaven's cherubim hors'd
> Upon the sightless couriers of the air,
> Shall blow the horrid deed in every eye,
> That tears shall drown the wind. I have no spur
> To prick the sides of my intent, but only
> Vaulting ambition, which ov'erleaps itself
> And falls on th' other—

Following the board edict, along with Allen, several of those on the fragile outer layer of the striking assemblage peeled off. Some had capitulated a few days earlier, but we did not know it at the time. The following day the *BND* reports, "Under the cover of darkness, a dozen teachers reported in at the college between 11 p.m. Tuesday and 3:30 a.m. Wednesday, quietly complying with an earlier board directive to return by 7:30 a.m. Wednesday or face possible firing."

There were thirteen, several before 11 p.m. on Tuesday, and two who did not even show up at the college campus but capitulated by phone. Strikers' signatures that do not appear on the sign-in sheet when striking fulltime faculty re-entered the school, beginning at 8:59 a.m. November 20, 1980, but whose names are referenced as "see attached" were: Paula Allen; William Allen; Fred Barber; Marvin Cox; Harold Johnson; Robert Klube; Donald Koleson; William Meekins; Shirley Saverson; Wallace Strittmatter; Richard Swift; Betty Thompson; and Doris Walk.

* * * * *

For the remaining seventy people the strike held until the morning of November 20, 1980 when we had to decide how to respond to the board's ultimatum. The meeting started about 7:00 or 7:15 and ended about 8:30.

Shortly before the meeting Libby asked me what I was going to do. I said, "I'll tell you two things. First, I'm going to do what the striking unit decides to do. That's what I'm going to do. Now I'll tell you what I think we should do. I think we should call off the strike and go in." I told him I thought of strikes as tools, as weapons if you will, and knew well enough that a tool may, after extensive use, become dull and ineffective.

I reasoned that if we did not go in and were fired, the Eckert Board would have had its way. I assumed the Eckert-Wissore people fully expected we would not give up the strike. It was obvious to me that if we were fired the quality of the faculty would be reduced substantially. I'm talking about the quality of the educational instruction provided by people who believe in what they are doing enough to oppose those who attempt to disrupt and demean that quality. More than that, the board would leave the strikers who did not return to work to rot at strike headquarters across the road from the campus and after a few days or a week simply appeal to the public that the strike was broken and its remains was old hat, and it (the board) needed to get on with running the college and so would quickly refurbish the faculty ranks with whatever part-timers were available.

Additionally, if we were fired, the heart would have been cut out of the bargaining unit. We would have been replaced with the docile and inept. Another piece of the educational fabric of the school would have been destroyed. What we had worked for would be gone.

I didn't know it at the time, but this is pretty much what Charles Kolker, the AAUP attorney, had told the strikers. This is pretty much what Rex Carr had told the striking East St. Louis teachers, who had been in a similar situation in 1968.

But to be honest, even in face of impending unemployment, there wasn't much sympathy for ending the strike. I remember Judy Bravin (Nursing) and Dottie Bowers (Nursing) sitting on the living room floor of the John West house during that morning meeting. When, after an hour or so of discussion we decided to end the strike, they burst into tears. And they weren't the only ones. Libby sat at the table in the dining room where he had encamped throughout the strike. He too was crying.

Return to Class

That day fifty-seven faculty signed in and returned to classes. Twelve signed in but refused to return to classes. One did not sign in. Within the next two days the reluctant twelve also returned to class, leaving the unsigned-in AAUP Chapter President Tom Cochran as the lone holdout.

It took Cochran nearly a week to get it through his head that the strike was over. He didn't make it to class for four days. It wasn't so much that he was a diehard striker, as that he had made up his mind he would be fired. On numerous occasions those days he told the press he expected to be fired. Ten years before, in Lockport, Illinois, along with 185 other teachers, he had been fired for striking. Now he was trying to make it two in a row. You know how it is. When you set your mind to something, it's hard to give it up. He just couldn't bring himself to settle for less. But that's how mathematicians (and sometimes teachers) are. What is right is right and you have to believe in what you are doing. That's the way of it.

* * * * *

We were never sure why the board didn't fire us—though it certainly wasn't from kindness or consideration for the viability of the school. On one hand, the Illinois Community College Tenured Teacher Act had gone into effect the previous January first. The law had yet to be tested in the courts, but the process for dismissing tenured teachers called for hearings "Before a disinterested hearing officer" from "A list of 5 qualified arbitrators provided by a nationally recognized arbitration organization." Further, "The tenured faculty member has the privilege of being present at the hearing with counsel and of cross-examining witnesses and may offer evidence and witnesses and present defenses to the charges. The hearing officer upon request of either party may issue subpoenas requiring the attendance of witnesses and production of documents."

It is easy to imagine that the Eckert Board and the Wissore administration did not relish the idea of being cross-examined in a public hearing before an arbitrator (which is basically a court hearing) about their activities in and out of the college.

The board may have decided against the firing because of the money it would have had to shell out to SS to handle the hearings and the court battles that would surely have followed. Also, SS lawyers had very little success in St. Clair County courtrooms. This may have been because they sponsored or generated questionable litigation manufactured mostly to make money for SS. But it is also likely the SS lack of success was vitiated by the St. Clair County legal establishment's concern that local tax dollars were being siphoned into the coffers of an anti-union, upstate law firm. At any rate, the prospects of SS and the board prevailing in court against the striking faculty appeared unlikely.

Community Support

Additionally, the strike generated a great deal of union sympathy in the BAC community for the striking faculty, which I think gave the board fanatics a good bit of pause. After the dust cleared a month or so later, Libby and I were talking to a member of an operating engineers local, who quite casually remarked that when we decided to sit down in the road at the entrances to the college there had been a road grader parked nearby. "You do something like that, you should let us know," he said. "Every once in a while, one of them things (the grader) gets across the road and the motor dies and we have one-hell-of-a-time finding the keys. They're always getting lost." That was one of the better ex post facto offers we had.

Several students who were miners, UMWA members, who had worked with my dad and brother-in-law, and who one day when they joined me on the picket line, suggested that what we needed was someone to talk to the board and the administration "by hand." I never took them seriously, but who knows who might have.

The tip of the retaliation iceberg had already surfaced. A *BND*, November 23, 1980, article states, "Vandalism reported in wake of BAC strike."

"Three cars owned by college employees were vandalized Friday when a corrosive substance, probably acid, was sprayed on the hoods and fenders, according to reports from the St. Clair County Sheriff's office.

"A similar act of vandalism was reported Tuesday, the police said. A corrosive liquid was sprayed on a BAC employee's car."

What might the reaction have been had the board attempted to dismiss the striking faculty?

The spectacle of fifty-nine women and men, young, middle-aged, and older, reasonable and peace-loving people taking off their robes and descending from their ivory tower, vacating their classrooms on a cold November day, to sit in the road, ostensibly to get themselves arrested and locked up in order to call attention to the misdeeds and malfeasance of a Board of Trustees and its administration, had to be a sobering experience for the board. This was beyond what the board expected the docile and obeisant to do.

Also, it is possible, though I find it hard to believe, that Eckert and Wissore could not get a fourth vote to implement a mass firing. It's hard to know what went on in executive sessions or elsewhere. Maybe Schermer or

Dintelmann or Bartsokas or Becker or a combination of two, could not bring themselves to fire the faculty.

I often wished, as a teacher, I could have as an immediate effect or influence on the culture, as say, sports figures or entertainers have. On the other hand, I realize that in most cases pop-culture influences are fleeting, and beyond the dollars they generate, otherwise meaningless. As Oscar Wilde observes, "Fashion is so ugly it has to be replaced every six months. Beauty lives forever."

The enduring quality-of-life-values teachers provide for their students, and for the culture, are not only subtle, but also beautiful. The better parts of western culture, 2,500 years of it, are imbued with the names of teachers—Socrates, Plato, Aristotle, Epicurus, and those who followed them into the village square or classroom.

In my years at BAC-SWIC, I instructed more than twelve thousand students which made (makes) it nearly impossible for me to walk into the local grocery store, hospital, courthouse, bank, or any number of other public and/or private places, without running into a former student. Often, the electrician who shows up to wire my furnace, the lawyer I chat with in the drugstore, the nurse in the operating room taking my blood pressure, are former students. I'm sure the guidance and instruction the BAC faculty provided during the years preceding the strike had a palliative effect on the public's assessment of what the faculty was doing walking picket-lines and sitting in the middle of the road that grey November day. Possibly, in a strange and hazy way, the board members may have recognized this.

So, we came to the end of the strike, and since the bargaining unit had not signed an agreement with the board for services for 1980-81 the faculty worked from the middle of August until early November under the terms of an implied or extended contract. Within the basic rules of contractual non-compliance, courts have held that once the parties have agreed, say in this case for services for monetary compensation, that whatever riff may interfere with the execution of the agreement, the non-compliance of a part does not necessarily negate the whole, and both parties remain bound by the agreement. Thus, the necessity for the board to issue multiple demands that the faculty return to classes, lest the board be considered, if the matter ended in court, as surely it would have, to have engineered and/or manufactured and encouraged the breech. The sign-in sheet of November 20, 1980 served as the compliance document, a bandage binding the wound of the breech.

Aftermath: Retribution and Rededication

> Education makes a people easy to lead, but
> difficult to drive; easy to govern, but im-
> possible to enslave.
>
> —Lord Brougham

A December Contract

When we returned to the classroom the Wissore administration continued to gloat and hassle the outgroup faculty. Accordingly, the notes from the July 2 meeting held by Vice President for Instruction R. Wayne Clark, with Wissore's newly assigned deans of the college, detailed in part the administration's plan for dealing with the faculty.

> C. The procedure of keeping records of rewards and punishment from the period of July 1, 1980, to the end of the 1980 Fall Semester (July 23, 1980– Instructions From Acting President Wissore via Dr. Clark)
> 1. The instructional deans shall keep records of how well they punish the "out-group" faculty and how well they reward the "in-group" faculty. These records shall be used, in part, for the evaluations of the deans for maintaining their positions at BAC.

These instructions encouraged dozens of petty, and some not so petty, attacks on dissident faculty. Christeck tore his pants one day and had to skip a scheduled office hour to return home for a different pair of trousers. The administration found out about it, quite by accident, and docked him an hour's pay.

Political science professor Gene Brandt tells of his return to the classroom, to a class he had been teaching before the strike, where he found a student, a lawyer from Belleville, conducting the class. When he walked in, his students gave him an ovation. As the scab passed on her way out, he chided her for what she had attempted to do.

"You should be ashamed of yourself," he said.

The following day he received a call to meet with Wissore, who reprimanded him for his "unethical behavior." Brandt replied, "If you want to duel with me, with your record, you had better find something other than ethics to talk about."

Libby ended up literally with a broom-closet for an office for a couple of years until we negotiated him out of it with a detailed and comprehensive schema for assigning vacated offices by seniority, before the administration could declare abandoned or vacated faculty offices administrative territory.

Without a public-education-employee collective bargaining law in Illinois, bargaining-unit business within the college was not yet a legally sanctioned activity. This meant, among other things, the bargaining unit needed permission from the administration to use the intercampus mail system, for whatever purposes. Considering the administration's attitude and penchant for double-dealing and treachery, even if we could have used it, we did not trust its privacy or confidentiality. Before and after the strike, philosophy professor Peg Ubben handled all of our in-house mail deliveries and tagged herself the BAC-Ubben's Postal Service (UPS).

Still, Wissore continued to thump his chest and claim that the board had won the strike. As late as August 29, 1986, in a letter to the *BND* he wrote, "Many of you will recall the bitter strike of 1980 where the trustees won the first round of the fight." That was always Wissore's attitude. No matter the disagreement or conflict, he believed someone would win and someone would lose.

The proletariat writer Jack Conroy (*The Disinherited,* 1933) once told me, "I was never in a strike that we won." Then he paused and said, "But then no one ever wins a strike." Winning a strike makes about as much sense as winning a tornado or winning an earthquake.

Strikes are extreme measures taken most often as a last resort. People, institutions, especially educational institutions, survive strikes, but many times not very well. Libby and I often talked about the damage that had been done to the school by the events of 1980—and how long it could take an institution to recover, although it might never. The dilemma was that the only alternative to the strike, not calling the Eckert Board's hand, would have been even more damaging to the school.

After the strike, however, time was on our side. The longer the fight, the more the board and administration lost in public opinion and support. For months Wissore's and the board's antics were reported in the news-papers. Although the board attempted to conceal what it did at the college, it seemed not to have recognized that even the little that leaked out, as well as any number of its more overt actions, would further alienate the BAC community.

On occasions, in passing, people I knew to be apolitical and not much interested in educational politics, said to me, "That Wissore sure is making a mess of things." No doubt they were responding to the folk adage my grandmother often recited. "Fools names and fools faces always appear in public places." There will always be questions about the quality of public institutions, but the people of the state want them run smoothly and quietly and will eventually take exception to those who demand or gather too much publicity managing them—especially too much publicity from or for unsavory activities.

Wissore's remarks reported in the press not only alienated the public, but also indicated his and the board's intention to further corporatize the school. In keeping with education as industry, Wissore's idea was to turn the school into an assembly-line of consumers going in a door at one end of the building and out a door on the other end, while floating the sophistry of sweet-soap PR about the process intended to cover the stench of profit-based instruction. In the Wissorian scheme the quality of those working the assembly-line did not matter, other than that they not interfere with the corporate mandate. Of course, if the results of classroom instruction are pre-determined—always to be the same—regardless of education, training or expertise, teachers are not only interchangeable but also expendable.

The scheme cowered under the general rubric of such things as retention, hidden by the sleight-of-hand, and I should say, of mind, that students buying an education are not different from students purchasing a ticket to a rock concert. It passed over the obvious, that education is participatory beyond buying a ticket and watching the show—that admittance to an educational institution must always be tentative, merely an opportunity to learn—that students must indeed perform academically (learn) to gain the right to return, in other words to be retained.

The concept of student-customers as a returning source of revenue that must be maintained and retained is, of course, at the sales-heart of the corporate-college. The idea is to give students a good experience which means nothing more than giving them As and Bs, regardless, so they will identify with the corporate logo, product-identification it's called, and return to spend more money. In keeping with the college's mission statement, among other corporate goals, to "provide student success," in 2005-2006 SWIC ranked in the top 4-percent of accredited two-year colleges (63 out of 1,706) in the United States as 1,420 associate degrees tumbled off the diploma-mill assembly line.

* * * * *

On December 1, 1980 the *BND* quotes Wissore issuing two of his favorite huckster's platitudes: "Our teachers teach students, not subjects," and "Our teachers' knowledge level is of secondary importance to teaching ability."

Without going too deeply into the epistemology of what goes on in the college classroom, of what people know and how they come to know it, to anyone with a gram of intelligence and integrity it is apparent that the education-babble that "Our teachers teach students not subjects" is just that, babble—an education college dictum promoted by "child-centered edu-cation" advocates that has prompted various faculty blogs to observe that "It makes one wonder why all schools of education haven't been burnt to the ground." The idea of teaching teachers to teach without regard to subject matter or content is hollow at the core. It is interesting that many of the better American universities, say Harvard and Yale, do not have undergraduate schools of education. But Harvard and Yale do not have under-graduate schools of business either.

The schema of what humans know includes a progression of data-to-information-to-knowledge. As astrophysicist Cliff Stoll has pointed out, most of what we collect is data without context. It takes a good mind to give data context and turn it into information, and an even better mind to turn information into knowledge. In *Silicon Snake Oil: Second Thoughts on the Information Highway*, he writes that "... there's a wide gulf between data and information. There's a long distance from information to knowledge."

* * * * *

Once we abandoned the strike during the final month of 1980, it was Libby and the negotiating committee's Herculean efforts that carried the faculty though the final stages to a contract. The negotiation sessions con-tinued, as did SS's and Wissore's refusal to consider faculty demands and to ridicule and belittle the faculty negotiators.

Several times in the weeks before finalizing the contract, negoti-ations came within a hair of breaking down. Again and again, SS and Wissore came to verbal agreements with faculty negotiators, only to return to the table demanding that the faculty accept a written document that included items other than what had been agreed upon.

December 2, 1980 the *BND* reports, "Libby said talks broke down when the board negotiators reneged on verbal agreements that had been made in earlier talks.

"'I'm not going to say anyone lied,' Libby said. 'But it would be difficult to say there is any degree of trust when the only agreements they acknowledge must be in writing. And then there are childish arguments on who is to do the writing.'"

Again, a federal mediator was called in to aid with negotiations.

Finally, December 8, 1980, the faculty ratified a three-year contract, 76-8. And as distasteful as it was to give in to board dictates, over the next three years the faculty received a 29.5-percent increase in pay, which brought the four years' (1979-83) increase in faculty salary to 36.5-percent, all a product of the bargaining unit's tenacity and, while claiming financial exigency, the board's willing expenditures in its ill-advised attempt to break the bargaining unit. Moreover, with the 1980-83 agreement, the contract held, and the bargaining unit had not only been politicized, but was still intact.

The Drive to Unionize the College

"Faculty attorney Charles Kolker told the teachers that the fight will be lost—and that they would be fools—if they do not band together with the 4,000 unionized teachers in the area to form a united political voice. And their first priority should be to replace the BAC Board of Trustees, which Kolker said, sought to destroy the AAUP during the contract dispute, which began in August" (*BND,* December 8,1980).

After the strike, even while negotiations were still underway, Roger Christeck and I were talking to faculty members about expanding the AAUP bargaining base and creating alliances with local unions (teachers and others) to give us more clout next time. And we were certain there would be a next time.

Shortly before Christmas, after the contract was ratified, we secured permission to use the Recreational Hall at St. Clair Village, the same hall we had used for rallies during the strike. We invited the faculty for a gathering and provided a keg of beer and a table of hors d'oeuvres. Twenty or twenty-five faculty showed up to listen to our plans to expand or move the AAUP into the AFL-CIO. In February we held another meeting. The number in attendance was not as important as that we were offering a beleaguered faculty a new approach to solving problems, with something of hope for standing firm while doing it. Certainly, those who showed up would talk to others and the word would spread.

Many on the faculty were not as unconcerned about sacking the AAUP as I was, though in the end it didn't much matter. The idea was to get into the AFT-IFT AFL-CIO and legitimize the bargaining unit, and to garner both financial and political support on a local and state level. In truth, regardless of what we did or how well we handled our current adversity, the majority of the BAC community saw teachers and the AAUP as elitist, mystical, maybe fairy tale creatures of some child's imagination, without much connection to the realities of a unionized bargaining process. There was in 1980, and still today, the belief that those who can, do, and those who can't, teach. As noted in the Introduction, teachers, even college professors, were and are still seen as bumbling, lightweight eggheads. During the strike, when we were picketing, we were often asked, "Is this a real strike? Do you have a union?"

* * * * *

In 1980 as part of its corporatizing-outsourcing strategy, the Eckert Board split off BAC part-timers from the fulltime faculty contract. The original *BAC Faculty Personnel Procedures* of 1967 set up a two-tiered pay-scale, which include employment stipulations and conditions for part-time faculty. Until 1980 part-time instructor compensation at BAC under the *Memorandum of Understanding* was based on the fulltime faculty pay-scale. The inclusion of articles for part-time employment in the original BAC faculty contract more than likely came from the assumption (brought along from secondary schools) that part-time faculty would be used mostly to enhance already existing programs, to fill gaps, when fulltime faculty were not available, or in an emergency, and so, could be compensated as merely extra-occasional performers. This is how substitute teachers or guest speakers are used in the K-12 system.

Even after 1981, as the union moved into a governance role at BAC, it would have been extremely difficult for the fulltime faculty to represent part-timers. By nature of their limited assignments most part-timers remained at the fringe of what the union was doing—out of touch with the basic operations of the school. Moreover, part time rolls shift from semester-to-semester, from year-to-year, depending on the availability of courses and the individual part-timer's needs and personal or family obligations. Even today part-timers do not have a vested or continuing organizational interest in their teaching positions—nor can they have.

As unfortunate as splitting off the part-time faculty was in 1980, if they had remained under the *Memorandum of Understanding* and could have been brought into the union, it is likely their demands and those of the fulltime faculty would have clashed. Even if the voting share of union membership could have been worked out, which was unlikely, increasingly the fulltime faculty had come to view part-timers as interlopers and were not keen on seeing educational dollars eaten up by increasing the salaries and benefits of part-timers. There are only so many dollars in the till. The money the fulltime faculty could bargain out of the pot was already severely limited by the constraints of revenue and the board's self-indulgent whims.

For years Christeck taught most of his classes in the evening, and as a result became acquainted with a good number of the part-time faculty, both in English and in other departments. On several occasions, in 1984 and again in 1988, he spoke with me about organizing the part-timers. And while it was a worthwhile idea, we did not find much sympathy for the project among the fulltime faculty, and probably would have, even with a modicum of success, faced a good bit of resistance. Many of the old guard AAUP, though they remained in the union, still thought of themselves as administrators, above and better than part-timers.

The difficulties of unionizing part-timers were obvious. In the first place, the vast majority worked jobs elsewhere and were simply teaching a course or two for extra money and/or the enjoyment of teaching. They wanted to teach a class or a few classes at the college to supplement their income with whatever loose change it was worth, as well as for the tall-corn prestige of saying they taught at the college. What they did not want was a confrontation with an administration that was doling out the few dollars they were receiving, a confrontation unionizing was likely to bring. This was before state law allowed part-timers to organize. Also, many part-timers were anti-union, and believed the administration had the right to treat the faculty in whatever way it chose.

Anyway, in 1980, the part-timers were removed from the *Memorandum of Understanding,* and as it turned out, though it profited the fulltime faculty, the removal may have been the one most damaging consequence for the school in the 1980 contract hassle. It created a second salary schedule for BAC teachers, and not too subtly exacerbated the board's already anemic interest in appointing fulltime faculty. Further, increasing the number of part-time faculty encouraged certain fulltime faculty to join the administration in managing (keeping in check) the part-time hoard as a means to insure themselves (fulltimers) the lion's share of future educational monies available for instruction. It also provided the ruling faculty with the playground-power of having someone to push around. Part-time faculty are not included on most academic committees, not even those drafting edicts for part-timers. They do not participate in such instructional matters as textbook selection—in spite of the fact that the overwhelming majority of classes at BAC-SWIC were/are handled by part-timers. For instance, in English-philosophy alone the course offerings and release time equivalents by 2010 listed eighteen fulltime faculty positions (90 courses) and thirty-eight Full Time Equivalent (FTE) positions (190 courses).

Of course, it didn't stop there. After 1980 the full-part divide seduced a handful of fulltime faculty into joining the administration in managing the part-timers to better solidify and protect fulltime positions, salaries and individual and/or departmental power. In the complicity, for their temerity, fulltime faculty was required to sign off on the blind and self-destructive anti-educational administrative initiatives of post-tenure-teacher evaluation, expert-teacher designation, and outcomes assessment.

The Dispute over Department Chairs

Until Wissore took over the college in 1980 department chairs were closely aligned with the administration and had a good deal of power—as they do in most universities and colleges—which included the quasi-right of new faculty selection. Because of the power chairs had been granted by past boards, Wissore set out to eliminate them and thus limit future faculty involvement in college governance.

As soon as the ink on the 1980 contract had dried, the various departments, as they were required to do, submitted nominations to the administration for chairs. The contract called for "A Department Chairman to be mutually agreed upon by the department and the administration," but Wissore turned down most of them. So, for several months some departments were without chairs.

The *Belleville Journal* reports on December 28, 1980 that "Wissore does not believe the administration or board are breaking the contract in the selection of department heads. He said that if the faculty has problems with the selections, grievance procedures are available to them.

"An appeal of the selections to the Faculty Senate would be the first step in the grievance procedure.

"Libby said the faculty will seek court action to correct any breach of the contract as it pertains to department head selections rather than seek a Faculty Senate appeal. The Faculty Senate, according to Libby, has been 'emasculated' by administration policies, and the faculty does not believe it would be helpful in resolving the conflict."

Several years earlier I had been a candidate for the English Department Chair, but because I had been critical of the board and the Keel presidency, the AAUP people voted me down. But because I had played ball (literally, basketball), sometimes on weekends with Wissore and Gornick and their cohorts, had served on the selection committee for a Director of Public Relations for the college, and had only nominally objected to the choice of Doris Slocum a friend of Wissore's, I was pretty sure if my name was submitted Wissore would accept it. More than likely Wissore thought my presence in the gym those days was an attempt at ingratiation for some future perk. In fact, all I wanted was exercise. It was difficult to find someone to play basketball with. Still, I was pretty sure Wissore would accept my nomination and suggested my candidacy to the department. I thought that if selected, I might help hold matters in balance and further discourage the growing inclination of the administration to invade department classrooms with further corporate lock-step requirements. I thought I might, in some small way, preserve whatever semblance of academic integrity the baccalaureate faculty had been able to hold on to. Wissore still thought I would join the team and so approved my appointment—though that thinking was as nonsensical as the rest of what he had done and would do. Of course, my appointment gave Wissore another talking point. He could claim that by accepting me for the appointment he was, in fact, forgiving and forgetting faculty opposition to his administration.

> Tom Cochran, president of the AAUP, said that harassment of the members of the bargaining unit is "continuing and intensifying."
>
> Cochran and Libby said the faculty is still upset about appointments of some department heads.
>
> Both Cochran and Libby did admit to being pleasantly surprised with last Wednesday's appointment of Wayne Lanter as English Department Chairman. Lanter is the only teacher who participated in the strike to receive administration approval as a department head.
>
> He (Wissore) pointed to the Lanter appointment as proof that harassment of union faculty members does not exist.
>
> "We just picked a department head," Wissore said, "who not only struck this time, but picketed Eckert's (the business of Board member Curt Eckert of Belleville) in the 1967 (sic) strike." (*Belleville Journal*)

The picketing took place in 1976 and there was no strike that year, so possibly the *Belleville Journal* reporter got it wrong or the *Journal* transposed the 7 and the 6. But then, so did Wissore get it wrong. Shortly after the appointment Wissore called me to his office, along with Frank Gornick, R. Wayne Clark, and Weldon Tallant, to announce that he had taken me "on board" and given me a chance to "join the team" and make something of myself—as if the quality of my character and welfare somehow resided within the purview of his power and eminence.

Other faculty who had gone out on strike were denied appointments or removed from positions they might have had directing or overseeing programs. Director of Adult Basic Education and the Granite City Day Program, Martha Giordano, a striker, was removed. Clay Baitman, who signed an individual contract and who scabbed through the strike was made acting supervisor of the Allied Health Division.

The Biology Department sent in Walter Ptasnik's name and when it was rejected, following each subsequent rejection, sent in another department member's name, including Ptasnik's a second time, using his middle name, John. What biology did not do was to send in the name of Richard Melinder, the only scab in the department, the one name the Wissore administration wanted.

Eventually Wissore appointed his choices to department chairs, violating the contract, though the point became mute the following year with the board funded Ernst-Whinney plan for reorganizing the Instructional Division of the school. In the 1984 negotiating fiasco with Donald Kassing (Business) as the faculty chief negotiator, department chairs were dropped from the *Memorandum of Understanding.* To replace the chairs a battery of six associate deans was installed to oversee the faculty. Melinder was one of the new deans—a man I did not know well. In my dealings with him, on several occasions, I was more than a little amused that he refused to look at me and continued to stare at the wall in front of his desk while answering my queries or suggestions with only a yes or mostly no.

* * * * *

In 1981, as department chairman, the adventure of standing between an educational institution administration run amuck and a very nearly totally alienated faculty provided a few interesting moments. Of the many incidents, several stand out dramatically.

Sometime shortly after Frank Gornick became vice-president for instruction, William Sheehy claimed four-thousand-some dollars in pay for a teaching assignment that by contract he should have had, but that Gornick had denied him. Sheehy had a conference with Gornick to resolve the issue and asked that I attend the meeting. The upshot was that whatever Gornick did or did not understand about education, he clearly did not have idea one about the contract. He did not even know he had violated the contract by denying Sheehy the classes. More than likely he had done it solely on the merits of Sheehy's membership in the out-group.

Finally, Gornick agreed that yes, indeed, from what we said, Sheehy did have the money coming. So far so good—until Wissore got wind of the settlement and called a meeting of his own, ostensibly to deny the claim and the promise. Shortly thereafter, Wissore, Gornick, Sheehy, and I sat down in Gornick's office, and Wissore explained that, yes, the contract appeared to stipulate that Sheehy should have had the teaching assignment, but that was not what the contract meant.

In the end it came down to Gornick denying what he had said and Wissore claiming the contract meant something other than what the words on paper said, leaving it up to me to verify whether Gornick said what Sheehy claimed he had said. Probably, Wissore thought that since I had been newly appointed department chairman and was now a quasi-administrator, I would want to protect my position and side with him and Gornick. He asked me if Gornick did in fact agree to pay Sheehy the money. I said, "Yes he did." And that ended it. Sheehy got the money. No doubt Wissore did not want to test Sheehy's demand, which would have ended in another battle with the union and certainly in court (with my testimony supporting Sheehy's claim) and would have cost a good bit more than it was worth.

The other incident involved Gornick again, but this time with philosophy professor Byron Davidson. Davidson was an outrageous, though engaging character, who was overtly and demonstrably gay. That spring Davidson had a young woman in class who had gotten into her last semester at BAC with a straight A average. With grade inflation, droves of straight A students were infecting the school, becoming the rule rather than the exception. But this one also happened to be the wife of an Air Force captain stationed at nearby Scott Air Force Base. As it turned out Davidson gave her a B in his logic class and she showed up at his office wanting him to change the grade. Davidson talked to her at length but refused to reassign the grade. The following day she showed up again, with the same rap, and again Davidson was polite, but refused to change the grade.

A week later her husband, the Captain, showed up at Davidson's office, demanding Davidson retest his wife and give her a different grade. The man showed up with more than that in mind. He was not only abusive of Davidson's position as a college professor but included in the conversation slurs about Davidson's sexual orientation. I got a good bit of this from Peg Ubben who also taught philosophy and shared an office with Davidson. Again, Davidson refused, though he was truly frightened of the man and came to my office in a panic asking me to help him. I instructed him not to meet with either the captain or his wife again, but to direct them to my office, and I would see what I could do.

I did not have long to wait. The following day the woman came in and whined at me about how unfair Davidson was, that he would not meet with her, and that he didn't like her because she was a woman. In checking, I discovered that six women in the class (it was a class of thirty-two students) received As from Davidson, and that her (the captain's wife's) test papers were decidedly inferior. In truth, Davidson had been quite generous in assigning her a B. I explained all of this to her. But again, to no avail.

Two days later her husband, the Captain, appeared at my door to rail about Davidson and to inform me that he himself had a master's degree in psychology from UCLA. He demanded that I expunge his wife's grade in Davidson's logic class and allow him (the Captain) to test his wife and assign her a grade for the class.

With all due respect to degrees from UCLA, I promised the man that no such thing would happen. He threatened to go to the vice president for instruction (Frank Gornick) to straighten this out. I assured him that if he wished to do so, he should. However, after he had gone, I called Scott Air Force Base, located the captain's superior officer and that night wrote a sufficiently censorious letter to the commanding officer detailing the captain's behavior as something unbecoming an officer and a gentleman.

Directly, the commanding officer called Gornick and wanted to know why underlings like faculty and department chairmen were confronting military officers. Gornick in turn whined at me about it. "I would have handled that," he said. "We don't want trouble with the military." I don't know what he anticipated. Maybe he thought they'd call in an air strike or something.

Anyway, I assured him the matter had been adjudicated with utmost dispatch, and we would not hear more about it. We never did, though I'm sure when the commanding officer got off the phone the good captain heard more than a little about it.

It's quite probable that had I not intervened as quickly as I did, Gornick and Wissore would have used the incident on Davidson, and not for the best of reasons or in the most reasonable way, and certainly not with the idea of improving instruction.

Twenty-seven Designated for Retraining

Once the contract was signed in December of 1980, the Wissore administration pushed ahead with plans to downsize the faculty and tagged twenty-seven faculty members for retraining or for dismissal. The idea of retraining professors, as if somehow, they had become untrained, maybe like an errant circus canine that has forgotten which hoop to jump through or how to jump, always struck me as ludicrous.

Of course, I was listed among the twenty-seven faculty to be retrained. But why did we need retraining? Most of us could count to ten as the Wissore-Gornick qualifications stipulated for part-timers. Well, not if you want to rid the place of fulltime faculty. More than that, I had not been trained at all. Educated, perhaps, by Jesuits and by studying with some of the best novelists and poets in the country, but not trained.

Education is something like the Christian idea of grace. While many of them claim to be "saved," few actually show signs of it. Hoping to trick Joan d'Arc, the English Inquisitor enquired of her if she was in a "state of grace." Knowing the church doctrine that no one could be certain of this (only God could know that) but knowing also that her tormentors would require that she be so endowed to be qualified for sacred warfare, she answered with perfect theological simplicity.

"If I am," she said, "may God keep me there. And if I am not, may God put me there." I would suggest that the question and proof of whether one is educated is much the same. If I am not, may I one day become educated, and if I am, may I remain so.

Certainly, Eckert and Wissore were in no position, ethically or intellectually, to render this kind of judgment to require that faculty be retrained. And all of it came with the board sitting on a several million dollar "emergency fund" or as they called it, a "fund balance," created by the Eckert Board and kept in the First National Bank of Belleville—tax dollars that should have been spent bestowing an educational "state of grace" on the college's students.

* * * * *

The *BND*, on February 11, 1981, carried a peculiar bit of double-talk and illogic with Wissore trying to explain why, as a quality instructor I had been appointed English Department Chairman and then assigned to the list of twenty-seven for retraining or dismissal. The *BND* had already reported that "Wissore said he denied the faculty's nomination for Department Chairmen because he wanted only those most qualified to administer the college," and so accepted my nomination—as a quality instructor?

In Wissore's view faculty were interchangeable. He did not elaborate on what made me more qualified than the other strikers. Of course, within the Wissore administration a department chair was little more than a glorified secretary. Then, in referring to a board decision to dismiss or retrain twenty-seven faculty members, "He (Wissore) said that Lanter and other teachers at the college who are considered high quality were not exempt from potential dismissal." In other words, remaining at the college had nothing to do with quality, but only that it was cheaper to employ part-time faculty.

How the twenty-seven were chosen for retraining was never made clear, though it was readily apparent. All of the twenty-seven were AAUP members, and all but one had been on strike. The twenty-seven targeted faculty constituted about 25-percent of the BAC AAUP membership.

When the retraining announcement was made, my name was listed with the others in the student newspaper *BAC Talk*, which ran the following excerpt:

> Wayne Lanter, head of the English Department, was not surprised by his notification. Low man on the totem pole, he was aware that his job was on the line if the administration ever made a decision to cut faculty. What does surprise him is that they would want to tamper with the success rate BAC students currently enjoy when they transfer to four-year institutions. 'It has been proven in a study with over 8,000 students from SIU-E and SIU-C that BAC students have grade-point averages .5 higher than students who began their studies at the four-year institutions.' He feels the changes will destroy advantages BAC students presently enjoy.
>
> Lanter also stated that the large number of faculty cuts in the English Department (sic) are ridiculous because every semester the department turns away students because there are not enough teachers to man the classes. Lanter went on to say he thought the board was being 'penny wise and dollar foolish' in making the proposed changes to save money because the community would eventually pay for the lack of quality education in terms of decreased productivity in the job market.

Seven or eight of the twenty-seven designated to be retrained headed back to school. One of the re-trainees to be, Sharon Graville, who already had a master's in English, completed a second master's in psychology, and though she was not dismissed, and BAC paid for her second master's, she was not allowed to teach psychology classes at BAC. Those were reserved for Wissore's in-group practitioners.

Most of the others tagged for retraining, to my knowledge, simply went on about their business. I know I did. I was looking for a job when I found the job at BAC, and to tell the truth, there were better places to work. Just then the coal mines didn't look that bad. At least the miners had a union strong enough to keep the company off their backs, something we did not yet have. Not only did many of the other faculty feel as I did, but several of the better faculty took it to heart and left the college for other employment.

* * * * *

Although Wissore had been given a two-year appointment as president pro tempore and had taken over the position attempting to make changes college-wide that only a permanent president should have made, the January 22, 1981, *BND* carried an announcement that Wissore would not apply for permanent presidency of the college. It was an Eckert ploy to keep critics from complaining or initiating an opposition to Wissore until he was made president, when it would be too late. Also, the board could then conclude its search without having found a suitable candidate—one who did not have Wissore's qualifications, whatever that might have meant—and could draft Wissore —which it did.

* * * * *

During the early months of 1981 Libby continued his assaults on board policies. The one crack in the board's stonewall secrecy façade was the *Public Comments* item on board meeting agendas. Meeting after board meeting Libby showed up with a prepared statement, forcing the board to respond and giving reporters on the BAC beat something to write about. Libby's missives, as much as anything, kept public attention focused on the board and subsequently on Wissore—providing a publicity that would, seven years later, play a large part in the dissolution of the Eckert Board and Wissore's ultimate removal from the school's presidency.

At the January 1981 board meeting, the board hired the Fleischman-Hillard public relations firm at a cost of 1,500 dollars a month.

> BAC Interim President Bruce Wissore said the need for the firm became obvious during the recent contract dispute. He said . . . Fleischman-Hillard will undertake . . . a review of past and present communications efforts of the college and recommend-ation of prospects for improved public relations.
>
> In addition, he continued, the firm will be asked to determine the present public perception of the college and suggest a time frame that might be 'right' for seeking a tax referendum (*Belleville Journal*).

Apparently, the board had already determined to hold a tax referendum three or four years down the road. I say apparently, because there is no reference in any of the board minutes to a proposed referendum, though board member Elizabeth Jenner thought putting Fleischman-Hillard on the BAC dole was ". . . a bit premature," and trustee O'Malley complained that "If we hire them for *four years* (emphasis added), we have spent $72,000 plus the cost (Doris Slocum's salary of $27,000) of the (BAC) public information office."

At the same meeting the *Belleville Journal* reports trustee Avery Schermer as saying, "I feel we have had bad public relations with the public and the teachers. We need to do something to correct them."

The Journal continues:

> Schermer referred to frequent statements criticizing board

and administration policies read at board meetings by Don Libby, chairman of the faculty negotiations committee.

He said it was "obvious" that the board had bad relations with the (sic) board if Libby appeared at every board meeting to address the board.

Schermer's comments on faculty relations came on the heels of another public statement, submitted at the board meeting by Libby, accusing the board and administration of continuing harassment of members of the faculty bargaining unit who participated in the contract dispute.

It seems likely that if a board member disagreed with Wissore's practices, which were sanctioned by Eckert, short of publicly criticizing Eckert and Wissore or voting against whatever scam the Eckert contingent might try to run next, he/she had no way of directly confronting the problem. Having established the Wissore administration or better yet, not having blocked its formation, as events unfolded, board members who might have objected were without means to affect change.

Still, there were those of us who could affect change. Sometime in the spring of 1981 a colleague confided in me that a particular vehement anti-faculty board member had confessed that if his board activities ever interfered with his business interests, and let's say, just possibly, that he was a banker, he would have to resign from the board. One has to wonder, if board meetings and practices were on the up-and-up, what it might have or could have been about his involvement that would have cast a shadow on his reputation and therefore on his business. But playing hope against chance, not wanting to deprive the gentleman of an opportunity to exercise his better judgment, I visited the town in which he conducted business and spoke with several local union leaders. These were AFL-CIO people who agreed that something should be said to the man about his anti-union activities, and who agreed to say it to him. From the tenor of the conversations, I got the impression that even before I showed up, those I spoke with had serious misgivings about the gentleman.

I do not know what, if anything, transpired, but that fall the man kept his promise and, as he said, "... for personal reasons," did not run for another term on the BAC Board. One down and four to go. I say four because board member Elizabeth Jenner from Mascoutah was a very fair trustee. She was judicious, understanding, and tough–in other words, honest and sane. Biology professor, and by then union President Leo Welch, once kidded Jenner that she and the BAC board plus Wissore reminded him of Snow White and the Seven Dwarfs.

* * * * *

On March 18, 1981 the BAC board voted to conduct a nation-wide search for a new president. The motion carried 6-1. The vote included the student board member, with Pat Bartsokas, an employee of the First National Bank of Belleville voting "Present" and Curt Eckert voting "Naye." Apparently Eckert's board cronies believed that even if they were going to appoint Wissore president, which eventually they did, they needed at least to spend some taxpayers' money and make a good show of it.

Interesting enough, after the hullabaloo, Wissore still received only four votes for president: Bartsokas, Dintelmann, Eckert, and Schermer. Jenner and O'Malley voted "Naye." John Becker, the banker from Sparta, was absent, and so did not vote. One does wonder why a board member would miss a vote on the selection of a president for the college. I know, Becker was sick that night—his letter to the board claimed so, though it did not disclose the nature of his disease.

Christeck and the AFT

> The strongest bond of human sympathy
> outside the family relation should be one
> uniting working people of all nations and
> tongues and kindreds.
>
> —Abraham Lincoln

Christeck as President of the BAC-AAUP

The general rap among the American political-economic right-wing during the last half of the twentieth century was that teacher unionization led to the loss of professionalism. I would argue exactly the opposite. When higher education institutional leadership is shot through with the corrupt, dishonest, and incompetent, a faculty's only alternative is to unionize to implement or assure faculty self-governance or at least shared-governance. If Illinois community colleges were under a regulatory agency, say such as the Security and Exchange Commission, as lax as it is, in a short time most boards, administrations and, unfortunately, some of the faculty, would be under indictment for fraud. The bargaining unit transformed into a union at BAC-SWIC during the Eckert Board years was the one entity or organization that prevented the board and administration from degrading the institution and destroying whatever there is or ever was of academic veracity in the college.

In fact, the dishonesty and corruption of boards and their administrators was the reason for unions forming in the first place. Daniel H. Pollitt and Jordan E. Kurland, in "Entering the Academic Freedom Arena Running: The AAUP's First Year," (*Academe* July-August 1998) tell of the conditions at the University of Utah, as given in Arthur Lovejoy's ground-breaking investigation by a faculty organization (the AAUP) of a major university in 1915. Lovejoy's report was submitted to AAUP Committee A detailing faculty abuse at the university, to wit:

> Lovejoy spent four days at the university gathering information about the school's tenure policies and procedures and its commitment to academic freedom. The president and the regents cooperated with the inquiry, as did many current and former members of the faculty. The eighty-page report, written by Lovejoy and approved first by an ad hoc investigating committee and then by the full membership of Committee A, described the conditions in Utah as abysmal. All appointments were for the term of one year, "subject to termination at the will of the Board." Grounds for dismissal were not set forth in any document but were determined on an individual basis by the president and board. In this sense, the report stated, "The

government of this university is a government of men and not of laws."

The administration had discharged two professors, refused to reappoint an instructor, and demoted the head of the English Department, all without even a semblance of due process. The faculty was quite rightly alarmed, and at a meeting called on the board to provide hearings and publish the results. When this was ignored, seventeen faculty members resigned in protest. The protesters included the Dean of the Law School and the Dean of the College of Arts and Sciences.

The regents told the AAUP that there had been no need for any sort of hearings because, if the board reinstated the two dismissed professors, "President J. T. Kingsbury . . . would submit his resignation." In such circumstances the board was not concerned with the question [of] "who is right and who is wrong," but only with the question of "whose services it considers the more valuable to the University." One regent explained, "Now the President has been a faithful and valuable servant of the University for twenty years, and it is not advisable to part with his services. It is better to secure mediocre instructors and secure harmony than to get the best and most efficient professors and not secure harmony."

The AAUP report rejected the concept of "harmony" as a legitimate reason for dismissing professors. And it supported the mass resignations on the grounds that the board had "denied the limits of freedom of speech at the University in such a way as to justify any member of the Faculty in resigning forthwith."

Lovejoy's report is not talking about money or salaries. Nor was the faculty at BAC during the '70s and '80s. The BAC faculty's argument with the board was not about money, although in some cases it needed to be. The true conflict hinged on the conditions and principles the administration pursued that interfered with the school's educational mission, a mission the faculty alone honored and protected. But as in a room with a precious vase, if thirty people want to preserve the vase and one or two want to destroy it, the chances of the vase surviving the ensuing melee are very small, very small indeed.

* * * * *

By the spring of 1981 it was clear that if we were going to stand our ground and continue to represent the faculty in the bigger world, the AAUP bargaining unit could not do it alone. The business-politicians, both local and petty, that frequent community college boards of trustees have organized contacts and alliances in the community that the confined and isolated enterprises of teaching simply do not provide for the faculty. And although the AAUP had national and state offices, it could not promote the close-quarter support we needed at BAC. Simply put, we needed stronger ties to the BAC community and the labor (union-political) structure at the local, state and national levels. Remember, the Illinois Community College Tenured Teacher Act was passed with the support of the United Auto Workers. It was imperative that we move the BAC bargaining unit into the AFL–CIO.

In April of 1981 AAUP officers were up for election. Libby, Christeck, and I were pretty sure that if Christeck ran for president, he could win the election. Generally, at that time, there was a great deal of unrest within the faculty. This was the good old political unrest of people looking for a new way to handle pressing problems, as well as people scared out of their wits.

The power structure controlling BAC surrounded it like a series of electrical or magnetic concentric circles. The State Assembly had created the college, the Illinois Community College Board (ICCB) oversaw the general operation of the college, and the BAC Board of Trustees (under the influence of the ICCTA) ran the immediate financial and administrative functions of the school. Within this arrangement the faculty, although vital to the success of the school and set at the core of the configuration, was isolated and basically kept inert by the design. If we were, as faculty, going to honor our obligation of academic governance, it would be necessary to actively involve the faculty in the larger college political community.

The discussions about who might best serve the BAC faculty as AAUP president had begun for real in early February of 1981. During the following two months Libby and I made the faculty rounds campaigning for Christeck. The platform was simple enough. As Charles Kolker, faculty counsel, had suggested after the strike, it was imperative that we align the bargaining unit with sympathetic political and union networks in the BAC district. The upshot of it was that the faculty agreed with the assessment, at least a majority of the faculty did.

On April 10, 1981 Roger Christeck took over the presidency of the BAC-AAUP Chapter, and we set out to revamp the structure and affiliation of the bargaining unit. We intended to turn what began as a BAC board faculty Salary Committee and had morphed into an AAUP bargaining unit, into a full-fledged union local.

Our first choice for affiliation was the AFT. And as the first order of business, even before the election dust settled, Christeck made a pilgrimage to AFT-IFT headquarters to talk to Ed Geppert, the American Federation of Teacher's field representative.

As noted earlier, community colleges are in many ways more closely related to the common schools (K-12) than they are to universities or four-year colleges—private or public. Although the AFT was mostly K-12, joining the AFT made good sense. A few years earlier the AFT-AFL-CIO had formed a Department for Professional Employees (DPE) to represent health care, education, journalism, science, technology, engineering, psychology, public administration, arts and entertainment, and others. Additionally, the IFT was interested in community colleges, and had annually lobbied the legislature for improved funding for community colleges at a time when neither the Illinois Community College Board nor the Illinois Board of Higher Education would.

On Easter Sunday evening, 1981, Christeck, Geppert, and I met in Christeck's kitchen, an Easter rising, so to speak. Though not as dramatic as the one in Dublin described by William Butler Yeats in "Easter 1916," it was a *rising* nevertheless. Several weeks later Geppert, Cochran, Libby, and I met at Fischer's Restaurant in Belleville.

Our first task would be to find a way to bring the two organizations (AAUP and AFT) and the two factions of faculty together. We needed to bridge the faculty schism that had grown into a chasm during the previous decade. That meant representing the new AFT-AAUP to those who had not honored the strike. We thought the AFT would be easier to sell than the NEA. We also thought the AFT had better connections in the BAC district and in the state of Illinois. Of course, it was an onerous task to have to go to those who had sided with the administration to try to bring them into the union. But we had to forget the past, as best we could, and move on.

Essentially Christeck and Libby and I were operating more out of pragmatics than idealism. If we could get the AFT-IFT in without severing ties with the AAUP, so be it. If not, some other arrangement would need to be made.

We did not realize in June of 1981, when the faculty voted overwhelmingly to join the AFT-AFL-CIO, that the AAUP-AFT affiliation would make the new union more attractive to faculty who had been AFL-CIO and/or high school AFT members or even NEA members. Of course, moving away from the AAUP at BAC, even if only by a step or two, had its attractions for a good number of Wissore's in-group. Later, the public employee collective bargaining law of 1984 made the union even more attractive, adding to the rolls people who until then had seen union activity as illegal or were frightened that as union members they might be asked to do something illegal or singled out by the administration for reprisals.

Additionally, the affiliation would open doors to future unionization of other parts of the college. Local 116 Maintenance Personnel and Service Employees had been at the college since 1967. In 1982 Secretaries and Clerical Workers formed a council under faculty Local 4183 and then their own Local 6224 in 1989. Public Safety formed Local 4408 in 1993 and the Part-time Support Staff (1989), and the Part-time Professionals (1995) councils joined Local 4183. In 2003 the Part-time College Professionals (PTCP) formed Local 6270.

* * * * *

Of course, the ultimate unionization of the college was an evolutionary process, and many times in the process what appeared as a loss, was actually a gain. The pre-1981 AAUP-AFT leadership, Tom Cochran, Jim Massey, Genevieve Snider, D.C. Edwards, and so many others, did an admirable job representing the faculty, a job well done that was, on occasion, recognized by people both in and out of the BAC district. Following the 1980 strike Massey and Cochran attended the National AAUP Convention in Washington, D. C. When they were announced to the assembly the delegates, the embattled professorate from around the country, rose to give them a standing ovation. The appreciation of their dedication and leadership at BAC had spread nationwide and was recognized by those who knew how difficult and frustrating, though necessary, collectively representing higher education faculties can be.

* * * * *

Our attempts to reconcile the faculty in 1981 were by no means an enjoyable undertaking. It meant going to people who, when you tried to help them and the school, had turned away out of fear or hatred or petty greed, all at your expense, the expense of the school and students, and for their profit. It meant propping up people and asking them in their weakened, though belligerent stance, to support you and themselves when you were certain that if and when another conflict erupted, they would probably break and run as they had before.

In representing the faculty, the belligerent and incompetent as well as the exceptional, what you get mostly is harassment from the administration and endless hours of evasion at the negotiating table. One year as chief negotiator I had Mike Schneider (Mathematics) and Richard Mills (Chemistry) on the negotiating team. We first met with the board team in March and reached a tentative agreement in May. But lo and behold the board and SS turned it down. So we had to go back to the table and were still meeting and talking during the last week of July when summer school ended. Since the contract didn't expire until August fifteenth, the administration was in no particular hurry to get the thing done.

We finally completed bargaining four days before classes were to begin. That meant Mills and Schneider, and whoever else was on the negotiating team, had no summer vacation that year. Then we caught flak from some of the vacationing faculty that the raise they received was not enough, as Bobby Poe was in the habit of complaining, ". . . to support the lifestyle I'm accustomed to."

This was the same Bobby Poe the student newspaper had referenced in 1982, reporting that "Dr. Bobby Poe, psychology teacher at BAC, is presently the head of the Social Science Department, but will lose that position with restructuring. Dr. Poe did not join the striking teachers in 1980. He didn't feel represented by the union then because, remembers Poe,

> "The group in power seemed to represent particular disciplines . . . When they went on strike, I think most people felt like I did; they didn't represent us." The psychology teacher listed the teachers with lab classes as most represented, because of the administration's reduction in the equation of lab hours to semester hours.
>
> Poe is currently not a member of the union and does not believe he would be represented if he was ". . . since the strike, the union has made it plain that they do not wish to represent me. The people who were running the union then, are still basically doing it." Poe emphasized that he is not against a union or striking, with a legitimate reason. But, continues the depart-ment head, "any item that's negotiated on should affect, if not the whole, then the majority of the faculty."

The irony is that Poe had been a very good instructor, who a few years before had capitulated to administrative censorship and folded his academic tent. For several years after arriving at BAC he taught a psychology of human sexuality course that was, by all standards, a well-designed, presented, and enlightened course, that is, until he was told by the administration to "tone it down" because "people were complaining," and if he did not, well . . . . Poe's course was the kind and type of consideration and instruction that needs to be in a college psychology curriculum. I am not sure Poe was ever told who complained or exactly what the complaints were, but the following semester, rather than resist the incursion, he dropped the course. Once again the administration had invaded the classroom to violate a professor's academic freedom and to dummy down instruction. And unfortunately, once again, a faculty member had refused or failed to stand his ground.

*****

After Christeck was elected in the 1981 faculty election, and we decided on a joint AFT-AAUP affiliation, there were numerous issues to be worked out between the AAUP and the AFT, on both a state and national level.

To begin with, the AAUP did not want the merger. However, when it became clear that if the AAUP did not approve the affiliation BAC would simply go over to the AFT, wisdom prevailed and the AAUP, reluctantly, agreed to a joint chapter-local—the first college or university AAUP-AFT merger in the nation, bringing the AAUP one step closer to the union movement.

Naturally, longstanding AAUP members at BAC did not want to sack the AAUP, reasoning, when it was reason, that the AAUP was, regardless of whatever it was not, more collegiate than the AFT. The merger produced a good bit of resentment and animosity from those who, by friendship with and obeisance to past administrations, had controlled the BAC-AAUP and the Faculty Senate, who had lost their power and privilege to the Eckert Board and Wissore, and who now saw the possibility of regaining their previous clout severely diminished.

After the faculty approved the affiliation, in May of 1981, while President Christeck administered the newly endorsed chapter-local, Libby continued to harangue the board, and I set out to contact and connect with other unions in the BAC district.

I represented Local 4183 to the Belleville Trades and Labor Council and the Tri-City Labor Council in Granite City, and eventually became a member of the Executive Committee for the Tri-City Council. Sometimes I attended three or four meetings a week. Mostly though, the labor councils met only once a month. For the next seven years I regularly attended council meetings. Additionally, we represented Local 4183 in Labor Day parades, sponsored a stand at the Labor Day picnic at Hough Park in Belleville and sent delegates to the Labor Day Awards dinner each year. I might add here that when he was elected president of the local in 1984, Leo Welch joined in the representation, as did Jim Massey, the perennial vice-president of the BAC Local. Though he was a socialist, with tongue in cheek, somewhat, Oscar Wilde remarked that "The problem with socialism is that it takes up too many nights a week." And so it is with union work.

With AFT membership, the BAC faculty had not only stepped into the labor history of Illinois, added its presence and support to future of unionism in Illinois, but had also moved on to the national union scene.

Illinois is scattered with union graves and memorials. In addition to the Mother Jones Monument and the Miners' Cemetery at Mt. Olive, the only cemetery in the United States owned by a union, there is a statue of a coal miner in front of the capital building in Springfield, the Coal Museum in Marissa, and historical buildings such as the Miners' Theater in Collinsville and the Labor Temple in Granite City.

When I joined the Tri-City Labor Council it met in the Labor Temple, which it still does. In those days the Labor Temple was a wonderful old ramshackle building, steeped in the sweat and blood and good sense of the union men and women who over the years met and deliberated there. It was dimly lit and dusty with worn and warped wooden floors and low ceilings with slowly turning fans, the whole place smelling of chewed-down cigars, cheap perfume, and sweeping compound. The tables and chairs of the assembly room were always stacked with papers, grievances that had been or were yet to be filed, as well as strike placards and solidarity posters. It was a good place to meet with other union reps, to hear what they had to say and to solicit their advice and aid. It was a good place to listen to agents from the Steelworkers, Boilermakers, or the Brotherhood of Electrical Workers, people like Bob Means, Burl Hand, Ed Rieski, and many others.

During those years there were only two or three teachers' locals represented on the council, and those came mostly from the predominantly black schools along the Mississippi river in Southwestern Illinois. Madison High School was there, as was Venice, Dupo, and sometimes Lovejoy. The white middle-class and rural school districts, many of them NEA, were not represented. American Midwestern white middle-class teachers do not generally identify with labor or blue-collar organizations. Several times I invited BAC-SWIC teachers to attend labor council meetings with me, ostensibly to acquaint them with and to integrate them into the union process, but always, to no avail.

To fund some of our activities, Christeck, Libby, and I tapped our bank accounts. We could have requested remuneration from Local 4183, but the activities in which we were involved, such as political fundraisers, conferences and conventions, in many cases, were beyond the scope of what the Union Executive Committee, still stacked with AAUP people who were not happy about the AFT affiliation, was inclined to support. I did not keep track of the expenditures, but at one point it was in excess of several thou- sands of dollars each. And I imagine there were others who gave more than their fair share to the task, in time and in money.

In 1986 an accreditation team from North Central Association (NCA) visited BAC. Libby, Christeck, and I suspected that in keeping with other corporate practices already instituted at the school, and because of some of the people the BAC board had hired, we thought it would be worth knowing who on the administrative staff provided what kinds of benefits for certain of the visiting NCA team. We suspected the NCA team would be wined and dined by the board and the Wissore administration. What we did not know, and eventually hired a private-eye to discern, was what might transpire after the dining and wining. The report cost us a couple hundred dollars each, but confirmed our suspicions as possibly another reason that, in spite of the serious damage the Eckert Board and Wissore had done to the school in attacking and harassing the faculty and cutting programs, North Central (which is nothing more than a public relations organization) looked the other way and gave the school a mostly clean bill of health, stating only that there seemed to be some communications problems between the administration and the faculty.

As a result of his continuing surveillance of board activities, in June of 1981 Libby filed a complaint with the State's Attorney's Office that the board, on at least two occasions that spring, had violated the Open Meetings

Act. The State's Attorney's Office was not very enthusiastic about pursuing the matter but did write a couple of letters to the board asking the board's lawyer, Norman Nold, who had not attended the meetings in question, what he thought of the complaint. When Nold replied that nothing improper had taken place, the State's Attorney's Office concurred. But one has to remember, Nold had worked in the St. Clair County State's Attorney's Office a few years earlier.

The 1981 Board Election

By now it was apparent that if we were going to improve faculty governance at the college, we would need board members who, if not faculty-friendly, were at least pro-education. So, on several Saturday mornings during the summer of 1981 interested faculty met with Charlie Kolker at his law offices in West Belleville. I do not recall who all was there. Those I remember included: Martha Giordano; Lyleen Stewart (Nursing); William Sheehy; Lynn Bradley; Lucille Hammond (Nursing); and Roger Christeck. Ostensibly we had gathered to be instructed on political campaigning.

By 1981 the history of BAC board elections had shown pretty clearly that while there was in the beginning some enthusiasm for board seats the glow had worn off rather rapidly. Few wanted the job. That fall three seats, those of Becker, Jenner, and O'Malley, were open. Edward O'Malley and John Becker would not run for re-election. Elizabeth Jenner, an already pro-education board member, was a candidate for re-election.

The problem in finding someone willing to run was compounded by a need for people who, if elected, could represent a point of view different from that of the Eckert Board. They also needed to be educationally sound.

Most of those who attended the Saturday mornings at Kolker's office were faculty, though there were several others, former staff employees of the college or those who labeled themselves "concerned citizens."

The concerned citizens group believed that in the campaign to elect trustees it would be better if the BAC faculty stayed at a distance and was not noticeably involved in the election. For campaign purposes an organization called Citizens for Quality Education (CQE) was formed.

After attempting to solicit any number of people to enter the race, and failing generally, the CQE settled on Kenneth Fish, a former BAC employee, and Wayne Reynolds, a Belleville lawyer. There was nothing exemplary in the Fish and Reynolds as candidates except that no one else answered the CQE's invitation or supplications.

On the other side of the ledger, Eckert solicited several of his friends to run in the same election. The slate included: Homer Liebig, an Eckert card-playing buddy; Donald Jerome, a Belleville physician; and Esther Vasleff of Granite City, most likely recruited by board member Avery Schermer from Granite City who was also an Eckert crony. The three showed up on the Harmony Party slate, which claimed in a *BND* article, ". . . a single platform of quality education, fiscal responsibility and harmony among BAC interest groups." The *BND* article notes that "All three have close friends on the BAC board." I suppose this referenced Eckert and Schermer.

In addition to the CQE ticket of Fish and Reynolds, and the Harmony ticket of Jerome, Liebig, and Vasleff, names on the ballot included: Randall Bastian of Lebanon; Elizabeth Jenner of Mascoutah; and Ralph Kaeser and Everett Sakosko of Belleville. Sakosko was a personal friend of Libby's, and I'm certain Libby had more than a little to do with his presence in the contest.

And while the two slates agreed on the need for quality education and fiscal responsibility, listening to Eckert recruits talk about bringing harmony to the school reminded me of the Hemingway observation that whenever politicians start talking about peace, you had better get ready for war.

Outside of reciting their party-ticket lines, the other candidates offered a small variety of opinions about what they might do as BAC board members. The *BND* notes that ". . . Bastian advocates a tax increase to complete the task.

"Kaeser said he would eliminate three administrative posts through attrition and would advocate the General Assembly change the tenure policy to make it easier to fire teachers."

"Sakosko advocated cutting administrative positions before educational programs."

Otherwise, there was nothing unusual in the campaign to elect Wayne Reynolds and Ken Fish to the BAC board, except maybe that we ran a campaign at all. Again, the faculty union did not openly or officially endorse the Fish-Reynolds ticket or administer the campaign. That was handled by CQE, chaired by Raymond Uphoff, a seventy-year-old retired Illinois Central Railroad employee who had also served as an officer for the National Association of Retired Veteran and Railroad Employees, the Belleville Salvation Army, and AARP Local 2827. The CQE had fifty or so members, some of them former BAC employees, such as Ruthe Kombrink, former board secretary, and others who had left the school under the acid cloud of the Wissore administration. CQE also counted among its members some few BAC teachers, although many of the faculty who were not CQE members worked on the Fish-Reynolds campaign. For her part, Elizabeth Jenner turned down a CQE endorsement.

* * * * *

So how do you run a board-election campaign? Well, there were posters and fliers and forums and yard sales to raise money, and legwork from precinct-to-precinct throughout the 522 District. What else?

Shortly into the campaign we discovered irregularities in the nominating petitions of some of the candidates. Illinois law requires that to become a candidate, to enter the election, one must have a nomination petition signed by at least 200 citizens, and that the prospective candidate must be present when someone signs his or her petition. We knew that several had simply dropped off their petitions at the desk at the country club or the Elks Club, and had someone, a clerk maybe, have people sign as they came in. So, we took them to court.

We filed against three candidates, and the court removed one from the ballot. The night following the court hearing, maybe about ten-thirty or so, I stopped at Christeck's house (we used his house as campaign head-quarters), but he wasn't home. The only person there was Bill Sheehy, and he was about to leave. On his way out, he was lamenting our failure, as he saw it, earlier in the day in the courtroom. He was despondent. "These things never work," he said.

By this time Sheehy had become a true acolyte to the Fish-Reynolds campaign. He had been on the negotiating committee during the strike and had been burned by the board's mendacity the night of the horrid deed. I don't think he ever really got over that, but he became one of the more diligent campaign workers. Sheehy had a PhD in Victorian literature, but beyond being a superb teacher, was as decidedly naive about political campaigns as he had been about board politics.

"Today was a success," I told him. "We won."

He looked at me with a scholarly skepticism.

"The law and courts have been around for thousands of years," I told him, "and are still here for us to use. But things don't always go your way, no matter how righteous your beliefs or causes. In the least, today we moved the court to awaken people to what we are doing. Maybe it'll even encourage some of them to operate more judiciously in the future. Remember, the courts are a last resort. We won in a last resort enterprise. Do you know how far off-base they had to be for that to happen? They broke the law. It's nearly criminal. We won."

I'm not sure it made him feel any better, but he did a knockout job during the campaign that followed, as did many others.

Naturally, the *BND* jumped in with anti-faculty editorials, howling that "There is nothing wrong with teachers seeking representation on the various boards of education, but the taxpayers had best be aware of what is happening."

And later in the same editorial advised that voters should not:

... be deceived into believing the teachers' motivation has anything to do with quality education.

It doesn't have anything to do with the best interests of the students.

It doesn't have anything to do with the best interests of the taxpayers.

It has to do with the best interests of teachers during the next round of contract negotiations.

Remember that when you cast your vote.

Two days later the *BND* ran another editorial: "Teacher-oriented candidates aren't the best candidates."

On November 3, 1981, Wayne Reynolds and Ken Fish were elected to the BAC Board of Trustees. The vote count came back: Jenner 13,296, Reynolds 9,869, Fish 9,611, Jerome 9,102, Kaeser 8,231, Liebig 7,786, Vasileff 7,039, Sakosko 3,883, and Bastian 2,782.

* * * * *

In the fall of 1981 Becker and O'Malley left the board. Edward O'Malley had been one of the two equitable voices on the board, and while his reasons for not running were surely his own, even before he decided not to run for re-election his wife, Martha O'Malley, told me, "I'm not surprised that Ed's leaving the board. The way they [the Eckert Board members] have maligned him is criminal."

At the October board meeting Libby read a prepared statement thanking both Becker and O'Malley for their time, their efforts, and their service to the college. He said, "I know we are not friends, but neither are we enemies." In this Libby reminded me of e. e. cummings' description of his father, a minister and professor at Harvard who he describes in *six nonlectures* as ". . . a servant of the people who fought Boston's biggest & crookedest politician fiercely all day & a few evenings later sat down with him cheerfully at the Rotary Club . . . ." One evening several months before, Libby, as a counselor working with the BAC Police Academy, had been invited to and attended a Rotary Club dinner and was seated across the table from Curt Eckert. The next morning, when I asked him how it had gone, he replied, "Nothing untoward."

* * * * *

Boards of education do not differ in psychology and personality from most other boards, be they corporate or institutional. Both in character and practice boards frequently take on a gang structure, with one or two dominant members browbeating or cajoling other members into submission. Weaker board members seldom oppose what they see as their more powerful or wealthier or more knowledgeable counterparts. And even when they merely abstain or remain silent, tacitly they give consent. *Qui tacet consentire vidétur*—silence gives consent.

Now we had two board members who had run in opposition to the

Eckert cartel, two members we trusted might support Elizabeth Jenner in bringing a bit of sanity to board deliberations. We hoped that they would join Jenner in making noise about what the Eckert Board was doing, but it simply did not work that way. Reynolds immediately fell in with the Wissore schema, and the best Fish could do was chide teachers for whining about their misfortunes.

* * * * *

Following the election, in keeping with its scheme to further corporatize the college, to strip down and centralize the school, the Eckert Board enlisted the national accounting firm Ernst and Whinney to prepare a report for reorganizing the BAC Instructional Division. The reorganization was intended to eliminate academic departments, and as Christopher Newfield observes in *Unmaking the Public University* (2008), to make the college more responsive to market forces and business methods.

College departments aligned by academic discipline have for years been an organizational mainstay in colleges and universities, as well as in some of the better, larger secondary schools in the U.S. But the idea here was to break down the traditional structure and pool what faculty remained into mixed-breed collectives, with faculty ombudsman to be sent out or assigned whenever to whatever facilitating hotspot needed them.

The restructuring design further augmented the assumption that all means of instruction are the same–that one classroom method or practice is no better than another or at least it doesn't make any difference if it is. Besides replacing fulltime professors in the classroom with people who worked at something else most of the time or by replacing instructors with televisions, the move seriously damaged the on-location culture teachers provide for the students. Though BAC-SWIC is a community college serving students who do not live on campus, the faculty had maintained a highly sophisticated non-classroom educational environment, and a large part of this had to do with academic department discipline identification.

The reorganization abolished department chairs and installed six deans. It was implemented not only without faculty input, but in the face of very nearly total faculty opposition. Even Wissore's in-group opposed the restructuring.

The plan, as it unfolded, was in keeping with the education school tenets of the time to turn teachers from mentors to managers, and to create a heavy layer of administrators to blanket whatever means and personnel the few dollars the board was willing to allocate to instruction could provide.

The board issued the restructuring mandate at the August 18, 1982 board meeting, as usual, when the campus was closed, and it was unlikely anyone would be present to object. Reynolds did not attend the board

185

meeting but sent a long letter in support of the move with a bank of reasons that could only have come from someone who knew nothing about the educational process and/or an educational institution.

* * * * *

In its early years the Faculty Senate had the persuasive sway of the board's attention. But by 1982 it had been eviscerated by the board's indifference and Wissore's assaults, relegated to the periphery of school politics, and was no longer involved in school governance.

In February of 1982 I became President of the Faculty Senate. It was not by charm or charisma that I came to the presidency, but simply because no one else wanted the position, and I was naïve enough to think I might breathe a bit of life into the forum.

Leo Welch, my immediate predecessor, had done a remarkable job, as he would do later as union president. He was, as Roger Christeck said, "Just the best president Local 4183 ever had or is likely to have." I concur with that assessment.

I have never had much interest in political office, either in the union or elsewhere. I do not particularly enjoy the limelight—the attention or the supposed power. But because the senate was in such bad shape in 1982, it seemed an almost perfect place to try out a few ideas I had for reinstating it. I thought we might send out press releases to local newspapers to highlight the board's anti-educational agenda for the faculty and the school. I wanted to use the senate as a faculty voice, though still independent of the union. If the union, by merit of contract, controlled the faculty's share of governance, why not have the senate chant a moral, educationally noteworthy chorus? In other words, I wanted to make a lot of noise about the board's continued attack on academics.

Of course, the plan was not without difficulties. The senate had been viewed by the faculty, both from within and without, as an august forum that spoke with reserve and something of dignity, although at times as ambiguous as the oracle at Delphi. Senators would not be easily persuaded to abandon their elitist AAUP beliefs, so the senate might take on a new persona and move into the larger political fray. The board's and administration's attack on senate personnel had seriously depleted the assembly's moral energy and courage.

Traditionally, the college president attended senate meetings to be advised by the faculty and to inform the senate of the state of the institution. But by February 1981 the administration no longer met with the senate. Sometime earlier Wissore informed the senate that "The Senate was there to inform the president, not the president to inform the Senate."

In the spring of 1982, in another assault on faculty governance, the board proposed a policy for the *Evaluation of Non-Tenured Faculty*

Members. The document prepared by the administration for the Board Policy Manual was designed to nullify the traditional faculty role in evaluating non-tenured faculty. The document was meant to reduce tenure committees, which were usually constituted of three tenured faculty members, to observing and reporting to the administration, and little more. Other parts of the document made it possible, and therefore more than likely, that the administration would ignore or sidestep faculty recommendations. Item 3 (b) read, "Deans' final recommendation to the vice president for instruction *will not be based solely* [emphasis added] on the report of the tenure committee but will include his or her consideration of all procedures used to evaluate the non-tenured faculty member's performance."

Not surprisingly the document gave the administration the right to determine what "all procedures" might mean, stripping tenure committees of whatever power they might have had. If, for example, a non-tenured teacher became too friendly with the out-group or did not properly support the in-group, regardless of his classroom competence, even with a strong recommendation from his tenure committee, he could be dismissed without question.

The non-tenured document was only the first shot in the skirmish to remove the faculty as experts on faculty appointments and retention. It was an attempt to return to the grade and high school administrative practice of keeping faculty the administration wanted, to make administrator's lives easier and the classroom more conformist, though, too often, less instructive. It also made it possible for the administration to dismiss faculty before they had tenure and before they could move onto a higher pay-scale bracket.

Since evaluation of non-tenured faculty was not covered in the *Memorandum of Understanding* the task of defending the faculty's rights, as well as the tradition, fell to the Faculty Senate. As Senate President I called a special meeting to address the proposed policy. As instructed by the senate I sent a letter to each board member—and was surprised when I did not receive a reply from anyone. During the 1980 strike Elizabeth Jenner had come to my house several times to discuss ways to settle the dispute. But now, even she did not call—or otherwise respond to the senate letter. But then, neither did Reynolds nor Fish.

The night of the March 1982 board meeting I had class and so asked Libby to address the board and "request that the new evaluation procedure for non-tenured teachers be amended or returned to the administration to receive comments from the Faculty Senate."

It was all for naught, however. The vote proceeded. The new policy was adopted. To his credit, Ken Fish did vote against the measure.

It seems, however, that the board was still operating under the fantasy that unions within the school were board committees. At the same meeting, Ed Geppert, Jr., the IFT field-rep for BAC, showed up to remind the board that "The Secretarial Association decision to join the AFT (faculty Local 4183) is not a board vote." Harold Wright, Secretary of the St. Clair County Trades and Labor Council AFL-CIO, was also there to encourage the board to understand that the secretaries were a part of Local 4183.

At the beginning, in 1967, the secretaries, through a Board Secretarial Committee that included board members Hilgard and Lutz, had asked to be represented by the Brewery Workers Union, Local 21. Whether or not that happened, I do not know. But Geppert's and Wright's presence and statements at that board meeting were what we meant by involving the larger union presence of Southwestern Illinois in BAC union representation.

The night Geppert and Wright spoke, though board members might have looked disinterestedly the other way and pretended not to hear, the echo of voices representing thousands of union teachers and other union workers in the BAC district had to be ringing in their ears.

SS Again

In the spring of 1982, Reynolds, with whom I made a special effort to stay in touch in hope of establishing an open line of communication between the faculty and the board, gave me a flier for a public-employees collective-bargaining seminar in New York and suggested the union send someone.

The seminar was on a Tuesday. I was headed to Boston on Wednesday for the Associated Writers Program convention anyway, so I booked passage and made it to New York on Monday. I had school leave for the AWP convention, though I had to pay my own way. By then Wissore had shut down all faculty travel funds. To cover the additional expenses for the stop in New York, Christeck, Libby, and I again pooled funds.

The seminar was a professional development seminar for people negotiating or overseeing public employee contracts, as well as for those who would later implement the contracts or have to arbitrate them. Most of the day I sat between the Attorney General from the State of New Jersey and the lawyer who served as chief counsel and negotiator for the New York City Transit Workers Union.

To attend the seminar, following the Wissore precedent, I claimed two days of sick leave, and no one seemed bothered until several months later the people running the seminar sent the school a notification that I should be given credit for having successfully completed the seminar. The registration form I had taken with me to New York had Wayne Reynolds' name on it. At the seminar I was going to check in as Wayne Reynolds, but decided not to, not because I wanted credit for being there, but because Reynolds had put me up to it in the first place, and I assumed I should at least be straight up with a board member. It would have been a strange scene, indeed, if I had signed in as Wayne Reynolds, and the school had received confirmation that Reynolds had been in New York and should be given credit for attending a collective bargaining seminar. How would the administration have rewarded Reynolds? And what would Reynolds have said? Would he have said "That wasn't me—that was Wayne Lanter?"

Claiming sick leave for what was seen as not quite school business, though the seminar had been recommended and encouraged by a board member, was conventional practice at BAC among both administration and faculty, and so not all that questionable. More questionable were the numerous occasions when I found notes scrawled on notebook paper attached to classroom doors by in-group faculty canceling class without the absence ever being reported as leave time. On two occasions I saw Gornick taking down class-cancelation notices and discarding them in a waste can. Also, Wissore's use of sick leave to attend law school had a whole lot less to do with school business than my trip to New York and Boston.

When the administration received the certification letter from the seminar sponsors, with a verification that I had been in attendance, they leapt at the opportunity. On Monday, May tenth, Gornick ordered me to appear at his office. When I told him I needed an agenda, he sent me a one paragraph memo that stated, "Dismissal Hearing."

The following day, Gornick, Clark, and Eskridge spent the morning in Gornick's office pounding me about where I had been that Monday and Tuesday. I told them I had been ill. I had hypertension, exacerbated by their nonsense, and so simply was off sick. They had not identified me as a chronic violator of sick-leave policy and so could not really require a note from my doctor. However, later in the scuffle my doctor reported to me that someone from the administration called and threatened him with a lawsuit if he gave me an excuse or reason for my absence. I wasn't surprised. The Eckert-Wissore people were always threatening someone with a lawsuit.

On the other hand, in spite of Eckert and Wissore's blabbering bravado, the union worried them, and I was told that Wissore went to union president Ken Pinzke with the request or a deal of some kind to encourage the union to "cut Lanter loose" and not defend me. To his credit, and the union's credit, Pinzke ignored the request.

During the interrogation session there were periodic lulls or breaks when one of the three interrogators would leave the room. I assumed they were either on the phone consulting an SS attorney or had one secreted in the next room dispensing advice.

When I asked if they were operating with the aid of counsel, R. Wayne Clark said, "Yes," and I said, "Gentlemen, the meeting is over until I can consult my attorney."

Dismissal Proceedings

That afternoon, May eleventh, sometime around two o'clock, Gornick appeared in my office hand-carrying a letter saying that if I did not resign by four o'clock that day, the administration would initiate dismissal proceedings against me at the board meeting the following evening. I had no rabbits to pull out of the proverbial hat and figured that my days at BAC had ended. Well, I was looking for a job when I found that one.

Actually I wasn't that cavalier about it. I had two sons, aged ten and eleven at the time, and losing a position at the college would have seriously disrupted their lives and the plans they were making for high school and college. But other than their welfare I had never put much stock in security or money. Certainly, I had never thought of money as security, and if need be, I was quite prepared to return to the mines.

* * * * *

The evening of the day Gornick handed me the dismissal letter the Belleville Trades and Labor Council met at its monthly meeting, and, as was my habit, I attended the meeting. After the meeting, I was talking to Hugo "Hook" Schewe, the business agent for the Belleville Laborer Local 100, and mentioned my hassle with the Wissore people.

"You don't happen to know anybody who has a little influence with the First National Bank, do you?" I said, "Somebody whose cage you can rattle?"

Eckert had been on the board of the First National Bank (later Magna Bank) for nearly fifty years. BAC board member Bartsokas worked at the bank and had probably been recruited for the BAC board by Eckert. Likewise, Eckert had a reputation for getting elected or appointed to boards of local institutions and then causing trouble. There was any number of bank investors, some with a good bit of money, who were not all that fond of Curt Eckert. I surmised that if someone could show that Eckert's activities were sullying the bank's image, there might be a few who would object.

Hook Schewe was a short, heavy, physically powerful man with a round face and a quick smile. He laughed and nodded. "Yeah," he said, "I got a meeting over there tomorrow morning. We're gonna lend them a couple million to finance one of their projects. Yeah," he said.

Several years before, during a bitter wage dispute with the City of Belleville's elected elite, and after having worked all of a cold winter day in the grime and stench of a broken sewer line they were repairing, Hook led a troupe of unwashed laborers into a city council meeting, tracking up the carpeting of the chamber with fecal matter and otherwise adding to the stench of the place, to illustrate just what his workers were doing that the city didn't want to pay them for. The contract was settled the following day, or at least that's how the story goes.

Again, I don't know what was said at the meeting at the bank the following morning, but knowing Hook, it could have been substantial. What I do know is that no dismissal proceedings were initiated against me at the board meeting on Wednesday May 12th, the second Wednesday of the month. Instead, I got a call that evening shortly after the board meeting instructing me to show up at Reynolds' office at seven the next morning.

When I arrived, Reynolds seemed somewhat cautious. He didn't have much to say but gave me a printed statement I assumed he had prepared. By signing, I would agree to forfeit two days' pay and further, agree to comply in the future with the terms of the contract—which meant, in this case, claiming sick-leave only when I was sick. He told me to sign it and take it to Wissore who would be waiting for me.

When I left Reynolds' office, I thanked him for helping, for making a deal for me, and he looked at me as if he didn't understand what I had said.

"What deal are you talking about?" he said. "There are so many deals being made."

The more I thought about it, the more likely it seems he didn't know much about what was going on.

Wissore, on the other hand, appeared disgruntled. I gave him the signed statement, and he said, as he was wont to say, "This is nothing personal. You're just the first duck across the pond."

At the time I didn't want to encourage that kind of conversation, but I was thinking, "Yeah, and there are a lot more where I came from." I wasn't sure whose pond it was, and who was the duck and who the hunter, though I was surprised he was talking about ducks.

More often he used sports' clichés or quoted Benito Mussolini or some other such illustrious historical personage. One day, after a particularly innocuous Mussolini quote, I asked him (Wissore) why he was so fond of quoting someone who led the destruction of his country and ended hanged by his heels in the town square, rotting in the sun with hundreds of bullets in him and his countrymen spitting on him? I had serious reservations about the Fascist mind. It did occur to me that had Il Duce been familiar with the Wissore administration, he would have been pleased. Wissore didn't respond to my query.

I was glad the matter had ended. Well, it had almost ended. Apparently the scrap had sufficiently poisoned the air at the bank. Pat Bartsokas, sometime later, quite unexpectedly, and very quietly, resigned from the BAC board, and the board appointed Leo Konzen, a Granite City lawyer to fill the vacancy. I was told Bartsokas had become disillusioned with Wissore. Again, what Hook might have said at the meeting he attended that morning at the bank, if anything, I do not know. Later I thanked him for his help and he made some cynical, humorous remark about bankers.

* * * * *

My stint as chairman of the Faculty Senate, as well as that of department chairman the year before, amounted to little more than a holding action, and a not very good one at that. By 1982 the Faculty Senate was practically defunct, though it would hang around for another seven years before going belly-up entirely. After a few months at the helm of the senate it was obvious that I was wasting my time and so, September 17, 1982, I resigned.

My assessment of the senate at the time was echoed in the board minutes from December of 1982 when Dintelmann suggested restructuring the Faculty Senate. Possibly he intended to resurrect it for Wissore's in-group, as a board committee or company-union populated with administrative handpicked faculty to sit opposite the AAUP-AFT Local 4183. Maybe Dintelmann intended this as a pay-off to Ault and other Wissore chauvinists.

Immediately following Dintelmann's comment, Wissore advised the board that ". . . a significant *minority* [emphasis added] of community colleges in Illinois have a Faculty Senate, and a minority bargain with their teachers." If Wissore meant only a minority of community colleges bargain with their teachers at all or that only a minority of community colleges bargain with their teachers through a Faculty Senate, I do not know. However, nothing more was said or at least not reported, though it would seem the board, too, knew the Faculty Senate was no longer of value or interest to the faculty, and so the corpus might otherwise be open to board exploitation.

* * * * *

That summer (1982) the academic cleansing continued. Pat Hunsaker, who had worked closely with Martha Giordano in the Basic Education Department, was terminated for reasons significantly extra-pedagogical. In a "Public Comment" to the board on July 23, 1982, Hunsaker stated that "The reason I am being discarded, as stated by Larry Schmalenberger (another of Wissore's administrative yes-men) is not because I have not more than adequately performed my job, but because 'we all know the side Pat is on.'"

Pat's husband, Richard Hunsaker, a District 201 teacher, would be a BAC faculty sponsored candidate for the BAC board in 1983.

A Union and a New Life

> Life has a certain flavor for those who have
> fought and risked all that the sheltered and
> protected can never experience.
> —John Stuart Mill

A Wage Freeze

Even before the spring semester began in 1983 Libby and the negotiating committee completed the 1983-84 contract with the board. Libby thought the faculty would profit from a one-year respite, even if it included a salary freeze. I agreed, as did many others.

I spoke to Libby the day before he concluded the verbal agreement on the contract, and he noted that the union executive committee had made it clear that it would not be willing to go very far on money matters. Also, the other issues on the table were neither pressing nor significant. Additionally, the contract was only for one year and contained substantial increases in the insurance benefits package—a benefits package that also applied to the administration.

The bargaining units reached an agreement in a record four days (January 10-14), and the IFT-AAUP membership voted to accept it on January seventeenth. The board ratified the contract on January nineteenth.

In 1982, after only a year in office, because of illness, Christeck had handed over the presidency to Ken Pinzke. At that juncture the newly formed AFT-AAUP Local still needed time to solidify its legitimacy and solidarity. More than that, the BAC faculty had not before seen anything like the 36.5-percent salary jump from 1979-83 of 7-percent, 10-percent, 10-percent and 9.5-percent pay raises. Needless to say, there was very little union sentiment in 1983 to stand and fight—for money or otherwise. Of course, the Wissore in-group expected another handout, and Libby and the union executive committee understood that by beating Wissore to the board with a wage freeze we could drive a wedge into the in-group.

The May 1982 board minutes show college revenue for 1981-82 as 522,199 dollars greater than budgeted. I might add, revenues were greater than budgeted throughout most of the '70s. And even with the board's profligate spending for administrative perks and Chicago law firms, while whining about financial exigency, the school operated in the black. Under a practice instituted in 1969 the board continued to stockpile money, even at the expense of allowing the physical structure of the school to deteriorate.

From 1979-83, the board signed off on 36.5-percent in raises for the faculty. I have often thought that possibly SS and Wissore were running a scam on Eckert and the board, designed to give SS more business and to give the administration and its faculty buddies a great deal of money. Board members know only what they are told by the administration. Harold

Wright from the St. Clair County Trades and Labor Council, who had served on grade school District 118's board, told me that after a few months on the District 118 board he suddenly realized that as a board member he was voting for and signing-off on items about which he knew nothing—which meant that he knew only what the District 118 administration told him. This is a not uncommon problem with boards of education.

As predicted, the wage freeze brought a howling response from the in-group. The March fifteenth issue of the student newspaper *BAC Talk* contends that "Twenty to twenty-five percent of BAC's faculty have recently formed an independent teachers' union, according to Don Kassing, the new union committee chairman. The co-chairman was Wayne Ault."

These were the same people who, during the 1980 strike, gathered in Wissore's office for a handclapping, foot-stomping cheering session, with Wissore leading the cheers to rally the troops and fortify their courage to fend off the out-group insurgents preparing to storm the ramparts.

According to *BAC Talk*, "Kassing was a member of the majority union, but Ault never has been, but both believe their membership would not give them a voice in matters because of a certain coalition of faculty that has controlled the union for many years. Ault refused to point fingers, but insisted that, 'they (the controlling group) negotiate special interests among themselves, instead of for the whole faculty.' Kassing pointed out that 'certain teachers are allowed more overload hours (under contract)—the same ones that negotiate the contract.'"

Kassing's complaint was only true in part. In order to align the hourly teaching structure of certain math courses with the college's articulation agreement with four-year state institutions, and to provide minimum and equitable overloads for math faculty, it was possible under certain circumstances that math instructors could pick up an extra .32 hour of overload pay in any one semester. But the math faculty did not negotiate the *Memorandum of Understanding.* Many times there was no one from the mathematics department on the negotiating committee.

Ault and Kassing complained further that the new contract included board recognition for the new AFT-AAUP affiliation. "Ault and Kassing believe the 'wage freeze' contract was just a coverup for the union's major goal in acquiring AFT representation. The AFT would give recognition by the local labor council. AFL-CIO (to which the AFT belongs) affiliated unions won't cross the picket lines. Many part-time teachers are members of AFT,' stated Ault. Ault and Kassing believe affiliation with the powerful AFL-CIO would give the union more 'muscle,' should it decide to strike in the future."

Again, Ault and Kassing were right—but only in part. Whether the board recognized the AFT or not didn't much matter since the AFT-AAUP amalgamation was not a merger but an affiliation. The bargaining unit had not changed intrinsically, but merely added a new look. Now the bargaining agent had the two faces of Janus. We could turn the IFT union face to the local labor structure of the BAC community, to the state AFT-IFT, and to the national AFL-CIO for political support, while keeping the AAUP as the bargaining agent recognized by the board.

As a sign of the times, by March 1983 the Illinois Community College Trustees Association Report had become a mainstay item on the board agenda, and board minutes report an ICCTA seminar entitled "Moving For - ward, While Cutting Back." That this item appeared in the board minutes indicates a good bit about board thinking and the board's attempt to operate the school while curtailing or cutting back future educational spending.

Boo-birds in the Cheap Seats

On several occasions I served on or chaired negotiating teams that settled for multi-year contracts. When we finalized these agreements, the child in me was always pleased to be relieved of the travail of negotiations for whatever the term of years might be, although hassles could arise, as they often did, with the administration re-interpreting what had been agreed upon. On the other hand, the adult in me remained skeptical. Good sense advised that one-year contracts and annual negotiations lend them- selves to problem-solving on a more immediate basis. Short term contracts are usually to the faculty's benefit.

The boo-birds in the cheap seats predictably promulgate the idea that if you negotiate you might not get what you want or might lose what you already have, and so should stay away from the table. I was never much impressed with this attitude. You don't stay in the dugout because you're afraid you'll strikeout or hit into a double-play. No one gets everything he wants, regardless. Of course, sometimes mistakes are made, and occasion- ally contract items don't work the way you thought they would. But too often the status quo of enduring a multi-year contract that cannot be cor- rected or improved is loss, pure and simple. The status quo is always carved up by time.

Boards and administrations claim multi-year contracts give them an advantage of knowing what they're dealing with and therefore enhance institutional planning. In truth, since nothing is ever the same from month- to-month, and certainly not from year-to-year, the comfort of knowing what is coming, even by contract, is often illusory.

Unfortunately, multi-year contracts provide school administrations and their boards time out of the public eye, time to pursue bogus or ques- tionable practices without scrutiny—certainly without negotiating. More than once, to avoid public attention, the Eckert Board waited until school was out, when literally there were no classes meeting and the faculty was off campus, physically and mentally, to implement one of its schemes. Some- times in a stretch of a multi-year contract more problems surface than can be reasonably addressed in one negotiating season. Faculty, too, can become

complacent in the security-illusion of long-term contracts, assuming everything is settled, and what they don't see or don't hear won't hurt them.

* * * * *

By early 1983 Eckert had four intractable votes, and on most
occasions, he could also count on Reynolds and Fish. This majority didn't
mean, however, that because the board had solidified its power and the
administration considered itself the victor, as Wissore did, that the administration would adopt educational sound or even decent management
policies. The Wissore administration was forever on the attack, as it demonstrated in May of 1983 when Byron Davidson requested "unpaid leave" for
medical reasons.

Davidson's open homosexuality had not been overlooked by the
administration. On one occasion, walking in the hall with Davidson, two
administrators Keel and Wissore) passed and made it a point to openly
mock his homosexuality. I was later told by Davidson that this was not an
uncommon occurance. But by May of 1983, dying of AIDS, Davidson requested unpaid leave—for one year—which meant the school could have, in his
absence, farmed out his classes to part-timers at a savings of 24,000 dollars.
Davidson made about 32,000 dollars a year at the time, which he would have
given up for a year, and his ten classes could have been assigned to part-
timers for 800 dollars each or for 8,000 dollars. However, Robert Eskridge
(a retired US Air Force double-dipper—one who collects a government
pension and a government salary), handled the request and demanded, as
part of Davidson's application for leave (unpaid), that Davidson include
details of how he intended to support himself and where he would live.

The Wissore administration was always attempting to embarrass or
belittle certain faculty members. When I requested two days of personal
leave, which was provided by contract, I ended in the office asking Rita
Heberer, another of Wissore's in-groupers, who became vice president for
instruction, why the leave had been denied.

"What are you going to use it for?" she said.

"It's personal, personal leave for a personal matter that I do not have
to discuss with you."

"What are you going to use it for?" she said again, and I left the office.

If I had given her the reason or a reason, no doubt the administration
would have said my reason was not legitimate. She seemed not to have any
concern about violating my right to privacy (requiring me to divulge the
personal nature of my contractual-granted absence), and on the other hand
was no doubt quite willing to hold me responsible for any discrepancy I
might have included in the leave request.

Her inappropriate questioning redirected both the spirit and intent of
the negotiations that had put personal leave into the contract. The original

idea was that the administration should be given the privilege to grant leave in order to facilitate a coherent and responsible operation of the school, not for the sleazy purposes of using granting authority to invade or violate a faculty member's privacy.

In his response to Eskridge, Davidson pointed out succinctly and correctly that where he lived and how, for the duration of an unpaid leave for convalescence had nothing to do with BAC. Nonetheless, Eskridge denied the request, a decision that had to be supported and endorsed by Wissore. This appears to have been vindictiveness, pure and simple, more than likely because of Davidson's homosexuality, and because as a member of the out-group he had been on strike in 1980. There was also the outside chance that because of the seriousness of his illness, without leave for convalescence, Davidson might have to resign or would die before he could resign, and therefore closeout a fulltime faculty position.

A Pissing Contest with a Skunk

In addition to hassling college faculty and staff, Eckert and Wissore carried their vendetta from the college halls to the outside political world. On Saturday, June 22, 1983 the administration staged a Rotary-Chamber of Commerce rally at the college. Selected Belleville city politicians were there, as well as the African-American state senator from the 57th District, Kenneth Hall. Besides being a master politician, Hall was an exemplary human being, a man who truly represented his constituency over a long career in the Illinois General Assembly, and who had, time after time, supported and fought for programs that had profited Illinois education, including BAC. Following the ceremony all the dignitaries and the BAC board members present were shuffled off to a cocktail party. Well, almost all the dignitaries. Notably, Kenny Hall was not invited, and as the others departed en masse, he was left alone sitting in the bleachers. So, what appeared to be quiet times at the college were not ethically or politically quiet at all.

Several months later at a fundraiser I apologized to Hall for his mistreatment by the BAC administration and board. I wondered out loud why he had not commented on the insult. In typical Hall fashion he told me something he knew and that I should have known. Hall was an old warhorse who had been through dozens of years of political battles. To him the BAC board was not only transient, but in the bigger mix of things also insig-nificant. He smiled and said, "My granddaddy always told me, you never get in a pissing contest with a skunk."

* * * * *

In my experience teachers generally prefer to be left to their solitary pursuits and would rather not soil their hands with the mundane and seamy world of politics. I can sympathize with that. But in truth, like it or not, even without getting into pissing contests, politics is inherent in teaching.

Public educational institutions are created by state governments, political bodies, and are administrated by locally elected officials, which form boards of education or boards of trustees, that are also political bodies. And despite our idealistic hopes about education, what we do in the classroom is directly influenced, economically, socially, and psychologically by politics, both locally and nationally.

It is the obligation of professionals and teachers, as human beings, as citizens, and as union members, to involve themselves politically, as well as academically, to provide the very best education possible for students. Occasionally teachers have allies in the political arena, non-academics with political power who come to faculties to say, "How can I help you? What do you need?" But if teachers are not there, if they are not politically available, those asking do not get an answer. If teachers do not hear the questions, there is, there can be, no conversation, and therefore no chance to improve the educational conditions of the school or district.

The 1983 Board Election

All of that said, there is nothing to assure that even well-planned political activity will succeed. The board election campaign we ran in the fall of 1983 was not successful. As usual we had trouble finding candidates, and I suggested Betty Gerfen, who had been a neighbor of my parents for years and who, besides raising ten children, had been involved in all sorts of civic organizations and causes. Betty was an exemplary woman, maybe too good for politics, though when I asked her to run, she agreed. To tell the truth, I was a little sorry to ask her to get into the mix of these grimy affairs, although, unbeknownst to me, sometime earlier as a delegate to a Democratic state convention she had gotten into an interaparty squabble with the St. Clair County Democratic Party powers by not supporting an anointed can - didate.

On the slate with Gerfen was Richard Hunsaker, a teacher from Belleville East High School, a former IFT Local 424 president, whose wife, Pat, had been removed from her position at BAC by the Wissore administration.

Because of the Eckert-Wissore charade, the Democratic Party was just then finding interest in getting into the BAC mix–though not in the way we hoped it might. Before the election, following the advice of a friend of Francis Touchette, the St. Clair County Democratic boss, I sent Touchette a letter attempting to interest him in our activities. The answer came back through the grapevine that, while the party was not against what we were doing, the cost those days for getting an election up and running was somewhere around fifty thousand dollars. Clearly, to Democratic Party thinking, a school board election was not worth that kind of money. This accounts for Democrats in St. Clair, Madison, Monroe, and Randolph counties, at that time, leaving board positions mostly to petty and sometimes unaligned politicians.

When we tried to interest Sandy Korien, one of the more esteemed lawyers in Southern Illinois, a partner in Rex Carr's law firm and a powerful Democratic fundraiser, into running for the board, he said pretty much the same thing. "Those positions should be filled by parents," he said, laughing about his time on the District 118 Board, where he earned the reputation for breaking the district by engineering a raise for the teachers. Of course, in their accusation that Korien had bankrupted the school, District 118 administration had seriously overstated the crisis. The district is still there and still solvent.

Anyway, a college board of trustees is not a high school or grade school board of education. Parents are not involved in the education of post-secondary students in the same way they are in grade and high school. The schools are usually different in size and certainly in nature (or at least should be) and require something more than parenting to oversee their management, although I am sure any number of parents of BAC students could have done better than the people on the Eckert Board.

Another afternoon Christeck, Libby, Giordano, and I spent several hours in the office of lawyer Bruce Cook, a State Democratic Central Committeeman, trying to interest him in leaning on some of the precinct workers to aid our cause. Cook was amenable, polite, and encouraging. He humorously chided us for our invitation. "You know," he said, "you get in bed with us, you don't get out." But I suspect he knew he could not, and would not, after her rebellion or defection, generate much support for Betty Gerfen.

When we approached the Democratic precinct committeemen to solicit their support, the bigger names refused to help us. I remember going with Libby to a St. Clair County Democratic Precinct Committeeman meeting in Caseyville to ask for their help in the Gerfen-Hunsaker campaign. Though most committeemen were enthusiastic about the possibility, John Baricevic, the County Board Chairman and later a St. Clair County Circuit Court judge, responded with a deep scowl and a decided "No." I got the same reaction from Randolph County Democrats. On two occasions I had scheduled meetings with Chester precinct committeemen who failed to keep the appointment—though we did get some small help from the people in Madison County.

I don't know what BAC board member Robert Dintelmann's politics were in 1983. I do know that during the campaign I spoke to Mike King, the then Democratic mayor of Cahokia, about supporting Gerfen and Hunsaker, who were directly opposed to the Bartsokas and Dintelmann ticket. When I asked for his support, King went into a tirade defending Dintelmann as one of the most outstanding people he knew, and literally refused my request. Of course, King was a Democrat and more than likely was giving voice to

Gerfen's hassle with the St. Clair County Democratic Party. Maybe he thought Dintelmann was a Democrat. And maybe he was. Then, too, there's a peculiar syndrome that some St. Clair County Democrats develop—and this has to do with quasi-liberals all over the country. After they get a little money and power, they start sounding like Republicans. Who knows? Maybe it was just a mindless evocation of Cahokia politics, and without party affiliation.

But we were learning. We were also coming to appreciate what Charlie Kolker had told us at that very first meeting in his office in June of 1981. "You may elect board members, but there is no way to be sure they will stay on your side or even help you."

During the Gerfen-Hunsaker campaign, Wayne Reynolds, whom we had run successfully in the previous election along with Ken Fish, served as secretary for the Dintelmann-Bartsokas campaign. Reynolds was a diehard, right-wing Republican and was probably wanted to impress Eckert and Eckert's money with his support. It is a sad commentary on the BAC board that a member we supported—elected to the board—would a few years later be asked to surrender his bar certification and lose his privilege to practice law in Illinois.

As part of the Dintelmann and Bartsokas blather during the 1983 campaign "Board member Wayne Reynolds, an attorney, said Richard Hunsaker failed under one of the provisions of the form (Statement of Economic Interests) to list his affiliation with Belleville High School District 201, which does business with BAC.

"Reynolds also said Hunsaker should have listed his prior position as president of the IFT local that represents District 201 teachers.

"But Beth Bosch of the attorney general's office said Hunsaker's position as teacher and past position as union president are not possible conflicts of interest" (*BND*).

Again, *BND* editorials chimed in supporting the incumbents, Dintelmann and Bartsokas. The irony of the endorsement was that the *BND* claimed the teachers had been well-treated and were now well-paid and so did not need any more help on the board. And in a sense this was true. Because of the refusal of the board to appoint new teachers to positions vacated by retirement and death, the *average salary* of the few teachers remaining had increased. But in another sense there was another truth. In an attempt to break the bargaining unit, Wissore had offered large raises to his in-group, raises which, when the attempt failed, had to be applied to the out-group as well. This move escalated salaries increases to which Dintelmann and Bartsokas had assented. Still, the *BND* endorsed Dintelmann and Bartsokas.

When precincts in an election go 35-29 for or against your candidate one year, and then go 50-14 against you in the next election, you know someone has been messing with you. And that's pretty much what happened with the Gerfen-Hunsaker ticket in 1983. Dintelmann, who may have featured himself a Democrat, received a good bit of help from the Democratic Party in St. Clair, Madison, Randolph, and Monroe counties.

The final vote count for the November 1983 election was: Dintelmann 16,376; Bartsokas 16,021; Hunsaker 11,522; and Gerfen 11,297.

Now the board was fully Eckert-packed with Bartsokas, Dintelmann, Eckert, Fish, Reynolds, and Schermer. Moreover, the failure of Gerfen and Hunsaker to win and provide support for Elizabeth Jenner contributed significantly to the faculty backing away from future board elections. The following year (1984), before the next board election, the Illinois Educational Employees Collective Bargaining Act (IEECB) was passed by the General Assembly, leveling the playing field a bit. This made faculty involvement in future board elections much less necessary, though even with the IEECB in place boards could still seriously impair or damage the educational viability of schools.

*****

By 1984 Libby was having serious health problems and was no longer available to serve on the negotiating committee. Also, four years after the strike, the faculty had wearied of the fight with the Wissore administration and was again becoming increasingly politically passive. People forget quickly or maybe go numb with the struggle and forget to remember. Libby thought maybe if things got really difficult, if the faculty got burned badly, they might again become energized.

Possibly hoping to make the union more attractive to the in-group and to put Don Kassing's and Wayne Ault's feet in the fire, Local 4183 President Ken Pinzke appointed Kassing chief negotiator for the 1984 contract deliberations. Libby had concurred in the suggestion, but whatever Libby thought, Pinzke was union president. It was his choice. He made the appointment. At the time Kassing was an AAUP member. Wayne Ault was not an AAUP member, and if he had been, no doubt he would have been added to the negotiating team.

I served on that negotiating committee with Kassing, Pinzke, and Charlie Giedeman (Horticulture). This was the same Don Kassing, who, during the 1980 strike one morning on his way across the picket lines, when reminded by Leo Welch that twenty-five faculty members were in danger of losing their jobs, responded with, "So what, it happens in business all the time." So does lying and cheating and stealing. As poet Earl Coleman, who ran a publishing company for forty years, told me once, "In business you cheat every day of the year, all day long." Since he was a knowledgeable human being and always aware of the facts, I'm sure Kassing was aware of this, too.

As one might expect, negotiations that late winter were a fiasco. In the first place, negotiations were assigned by the administration to a conference room adjacent the president's office, a location to which I objected, to no avail. Then for the next weeks of deliberation, Kassing spent most of his time away from the table answering phone calls, which weren't phone calls at all, but Wissore in his office instructing Kassing as to what should be in the contract. There's also good reason to think that before negotiations began Wissore briefed Pinzke and Kassing on what would and what would not be acceptable, to him and, therefore, to them.

One of the more objectionable items agreed to that year, to which I dissented, again vehemently, was the two-tiered pay scale, whereby newly appointed fulltime faculty would be paid even less than those at the bottom of the current scale. When I pointed out that the two-tiered pay scale was literally selling out the future faculty, Kassing answered with, "Nobody cares about those people anyway."

To meet Wissore's timeline negotiations were completed almost as quickly as they had been in 1983 and provided nothing of value to the faculty. In fact, I was snowbound one Monday and could not get to school, which was closed anyway, when I received a call from Pinzke telling me he had talked to Wissore and had scheduled a negotiating meeting for ten o'clock that morning. I questioned the wisdom of letting Wissore railroad us into an agreement, especially when the weather prohibited some of the negotiating team from making the meeting. There was no deadline, no urgency. But meet they did, and when I got to school Tuesday morning, I was informed that negotiations had been completed. For agreeing to a second and lower faculty pay scale for new faculty, the resident faculty received a 6-percent pay raise for 1984-85, a 0-percent raise for 1985-86, and in establishing a two-tiered pay scale, sold off a good part of the future educational vitality of the school.

The BAC *Student Outlook* claimed the contract settlement encouraged non-union faculty members to join the union. I don't know who they were or how many. But maybe Libby had been right after all. Maybe the faculty needed another crisis.

The contract was ratified and signed in March, giving Wissore a chance to boast to the board, after two consecutive early contracts, one for a wage freeze and another for little more, that he now had the union under control.

In truth, Wissore did have part of the union under control. He had Kassing. In January of 1985 Don Kassing, as a member of Team Wissore, was appointed Provost of the Granite City Campus. A year later he left the college, no doubt seeking other precincts to contaminate. In April, as a reward for having held the faculty to minimal raises for the next two years, the board put out bids for a new car for the president. However, all of that was about to change. That month Leo Welch took over the presidency of AAUP-AFT Local 4183.

By now the Faculty Senate was defunct. Since everything about governance is a working condition—the collective bargaining law required that because grievances arise out of working conditions, they are the baili-wick of the bargaining unit. To comply with the law, grievance procedures were incorporated into the 1984 contract, moving the grievance process from the Faculty Senate to the Union Executive Committee.

It had been apparent for some time that for faculty governance to be a reality, the union had to be the shadow government, the loyal opposition, if you will, and if not the loyal opposition, at least the vigilant watchdog of the school's academic integrity. One of the more important tenets of democracy, often overlooked by patriots and ideologues, is that while government comes from the will of the majority, if it is to work at all, the majority must consent to hear the voice and respond to the needs of the minority. Otherwise, the democratic process becomes, as Thomas Jefferson warned, a majority of 51-percent beating up on a minority of 49-percent. Unfortunately, the Eckert Board and the Wissore administration's idea of a democratic institution was, "What I say goes, and what you say is irrelevant."

In early April a memo to the faculty from Faculty Senate President Judy Bravin further presaged the senate's demise.

To: All Faculty
From: Judy Bravin, Chairman
Date: April 5, 1984
Subject: Future of the Faculty Senate

The last contract negotiations have had an impact on the functions of the Faculty Senate. We will no longer be directly involved in the grievance procedure. However, we will con-tinue to function in an ombudsman capacity, speaking for the entire faculty. The reasons for our existence remain valid, namely, to provide a unified voice for the faculty, to provide a means of communication between the faculty and administration, to pro-mote faculty participation in the formulation of policy, and to channel faculty contribution to the development and welfare of the college.

Keeping these functions in mind, the Faculty Senate is polling the faculty as to what they would like to see the Senate accomp-lish in the future. Give us your ideas and practical suggestions and we will work to bring them to reality. We believe we have a vital role to play at BAC, but we must all participate to be successful.

* * * * *

By the time Leo Welch took over the presidency of Local 4183 in March of 1984 he had already served in a variety of capacities with the Illinois Community College Faculty Association, the Illinois Board of Higher Education, and the Illinois Community College Board. As union president he immediately stepped into the larger AFT-IFT structure of the state and national union, taking the BAC AAUP-AFT, Local 4183 with him. He would serve the Illinois Federation of Teachers as Vice President, on the IFT Executive Committee, as the Chair of the IFT Community College Council, and as Legislative Officer IFT Community College Council. He kept Local 4183's foot in the door as President of the AAUP Illinois Conference and served as editor for *Illinois Academe*.

Welch was instrumental in forming the BAC Political Action Committee (BAC-PAC). Politically speaking, begging does not get much done. In political activities, board elections, etc., we discovered that we had to back up our hopes and words with money, and the smart way to come up with political money is to set up political action committees.

These were the kind of connections Libby, Christeck, and I had hoped to make possible and encourage when we aligned the faculty with the AFT-IFT. But it necessarily took someone with the interest and skill to do it, and more than anyone else, Leo Welch did it.

* * * * *

Despite his illness Libby continued his presentations at board meetings. By then I had become a member of the Tri-City Labor Council headquartered in Granite City. And as more and more reports of the turmoil created by the Eckert Board showed up in local newspapers, members of the council quizzed me about what was going on at BAC. So, I told them.

Then in August of 1984, the council, alarmed by what was happening with the BAC board and with enough smack and clout to expect that Avery Schermer, the Granite City grocer and BAC board member, could not ignore the invitation, demanded that Schermer appear and explain his anti-union activities.

Unfortunately, I was out of town that night and could not attend the Schermer interview. As reported by council members, however, Schermer showed up with Wissore in tow. Whatever the double talk, council members remained skeptical. They had heard the nonsense a hundred times before, in a hundred different ways. One council member even referred to Wissore as Schermer's "mouthpiece."

* * * * *

A not-too-successful segment of the faculty union's venture into board-election politics ended with the March 1985 board meeting. That night Ken Fish resigned his board seat and the board hired his wife for a BAC job.

Fish's March 1985 resignation gave the Eckert Board time to appoint someone (in this case Dr. James Vest, a Belleville pulmonary physician) who would then be in the public eye for nearly seven months before the November election, and therefore would have an incumbent's leg up on whoever else might run. Before resigning, however, Fish voted to hire his wife as Assistant Registrar at 21,100 dollars a year. In the rollcall vote of Bartsokas, Dintelmann , Eckert, Fish, Jenner, Reynolds, and Schermer, Fish cast the fourth and deciding vote for his wife's employment at the college, just to be certain the motion to hire her did, indeed, pass. After the vote he apologized his abdication as an attempt to avoid a conflict of interest—though definitely after-the-fact.

The courts have long held there to be no conflict of interest in a husband or a wife working for a public institution upon whose board the other sits, as long as they have separate incomes or livelihoods. Otherwise, knowing the employment would create a conflict of interest for a board member, why did the board hire Mrs. Fish? Why did Fish not recuse himself from the vote? Likewise, I am not aware that Mrs. Fish was so eminently qualified to assist the college registrar that it would have been harmful to the school to pass over her or hire someone equally or better qualified. When the question of her employment came to a vote, ethics and common decency required that Fish recuse himself. But he did not. He dealt away his board seat in exchange for a job for his wife.

I was never very sure about Ken Fish or Wayne Reynolds, for that matter. After the 1981 election Fish thanked me effusively for the work I had done on his behalf, but later when I explained to him the problems removing department heads would create for the faculty, he responded with, "You sound like a man who's got his underwear in a knot." It is possible, though somewhat unlikely, that Fish allowed himself to be bought off to get out from under the mindlessness of the board and the notoriety its misadventures were generating. But he was still bought off.

Referendum or Fantasy?

> Education is not the filling of the pail, but
> the lighting of a fire.
> —William Butler Yeats

Wissore in Court

The nadir or zenith, depending on how you look at it, of the Eckert Board and the Wissore administration came in the fall of 1985 when the board placed a BAC tax referendum on the ballot. From the beginning the Eckert Board had been stamping its feet and chanting financial exigency while heralding its attempts to cut faculty costs, as well as to reduce general school expenditures. Meanwhile, the board funneled large sums of money into administrative salaries and perks and paid substantial prices for outside counseling and studies to further claims of a financial crisis. In the fall of 1985, more than likely believing it had made a case for needing more revenue to run the school, the board placed two tax propositions on the ballot. It is also possible that the board had no serious intention of asking taxpayers for more money, but to be certain that another would not be proposed, not even in the distant future, simply ran a referendum so preposterous in its propositions that no one would vote for it.

Early on, even after it was decided to run a referendum, very little was said to the public about it. In fact, nothing at all was said during the summer months of 1985 about the need for more money or even that a referendum was planned. There appears to have been very little preliminary work to prepare voters for what was to be sprung on them in early August. It was almost as if the board, in its obsession with secrecy, wanted to keep the public from knowing that the referendum would be on the ballot. In fact, what publicity the referendum did get came not from the BAC board, but from the *BND's* opposition editorials.

In the late days of the campaign, the notoriety the board and Wissore as its chief executor had gained over the five or six previous years bubbled to the surface. In early August, three months before the vote, the *BND* began its assault on the proposals. As usual, the paper turned immediately to the turmoil and noise generated by the BAC board and the Wissore administration. The *BND* pointed out, illogically though correctly, that the referendum had nothing to do with improving education at BAC. The central intent of the referendum, the *BND* contended, was to create an athletic-sports complex of buildings and fields.

Election day, Tuesday November 5, 1985, the *BND* carried an editorial advising "Voters of the BAC district should not be fooled by Proposition 1 and Proposition 2 when they get to the polls today.

"Both propositions are written in legalese that might confuse some voters. Proposition 1 is a sentence 71 words long. Proposition 2 is a 75 word sentence. By the time the voter gets to the end of either sentence, he might be somewhat perplexed."

The rhetoric of the propositions was the least of the problems. More important, the tax revenues the propositions were to provide for the school were earmarked to build a 3,000-seat civic center (10 million dollars) and a 1,000-seat recreation center (10 million dollars), both on the Belleville campus. Most of the money, however, 75-percent, was to be used to upgrade the college's Granite City and Red Bud campuses. And as the *BND* observed, "We haven't heard a word about education."

The referendum, as stated in the propositions, and as portrayed in the ultimate unveiling of their intent, detailed one of the board's more bizarre fantasies. The preposterousness of even imagining the taxpaying public, especially the still quasi-rural, lower-middle-class taxpaying public of Southwestern Illinois, would okay tax dollars for the construction of a pair of 10 million dollar sports facilities on a community college campus, a school long heralded for its cut-rate, affordable education, could only have come from someone who was not only out of touch with the reality of the situation, but also who had gotten caught up in the sports-mania of the American mind. Maybe you could sell overpriced sports facilities to large, wealthy suburban or urban populations who believe they can make money off the enterprise, but not to the voters of rural, small-town Southwestern Illinois.

Wissore had a couple of degrees in physical education, and as I said earlier, was always mucking around with the sports programs at the college, most often to their detriment. He always saw operations at the school, and the attendant effects they had on education, as a game of who could muster the most points under the time allotted in a win-lose contest.

In sponsoring the propositions the board was simply gravitating toward what Wissore advised or directed, indulging his sports fantasies as he did in the bathos of having the theme from the movie *Rocky* played at graduation one year, as if graduation from a college, even a community college, was little more than a celebration of a B movie pastime of belligerents beating each other bloody or as the board did in the grand pretense of board members showing up at graduation overdressed in doctoral robes.

* * * * *

In July of 1985 the BAC board granted raises to Wissore and four of his top administrators, R. Wayne Clark, Robert Eskridge, James Hines, and Weldon Talent, to cover at least half of their contributions to the State University Retirement System. How these raises were enacted is not clear. BAC board minutes during the middle months of 1985 do not mention anything about administrative contracts being renewed, extended or otherwise affected by the board.

According to the *BND* Wissore collected a full 8-percent reimbursement while the others received only 4-percent. Other administrators and staff did not receive this raise, and it was clear from the beginning the money was to be used for the referendum campaign. Sometime later the four listed above, along with Wissore, contributed 7,000-dollars each to repay a loan for the 35,000-dollars paid to the Committee for Economic Development and Quality Education, a committee created by the administration to oversee the referendum. The Committee then paid a public relations firm, Public Response, Inc., the 35,000-dollars to advertise the referendum.

* * * * *

In late October, a week before the election, the *BND* filed an election engineering complaint in circuit court against Wissore for allowing Public Response, Inc. to use a Granite City campus classroom to run a phone bank to support the referendum.

"To pay the public relations firm, Wissore and four vice-chancellors personally took out a $35,000 loan. In reporting the loan, they did not include their names on the campaign finance disclosure report form, as required by law. Their loan might have remained a secret, but we filed a formal complaint, which brought the names to light" (*BND*).

On Wednesday, October thirtieth, St. Clair County Circuit Court Judge Joseph Cunningham issued a court order prohibiting Wissore and the Committee for Economic Development and Quality Education from using school property and facilities to promote the referendum. The order took effect at noon on Wednesday, October 30, 1985—five days before the election.

To add to the mayhem, the Thursday evening before the election, Wissore participated in a League of Women Voters debate at Belleville East High School with Ted Farmer, a Belleville insurance broker and self-appointed BAC board critic. Earlier in the week Farmer, who several years later would become a disruptive BAC board member, had been patrolling the Granite City Campus, supposedly checking the use of classrooms to ascertain if there was in fact overcrowding as Wissore claimed, when he (Farmer) discovered the phonebank operation.

That Wissore, as a college president sponsoring the referendum, would accept an offer to a public debate on the referendum he had more than likely orchestrated, had more to do with Wissore's win-lose sports mentality than to good political judgment. For an educational matter, an open forum, a panel or round table discussion would have been more appropriate than an ego-centered contest of debate. The results were predictable. The school got nothing out of it, though the debate gave Farmer an opportunity he could not have otherwise had.

Ted Farmer was no more party to the referendum than any other taxpayer and had not been hired or elected as a representative by any public body. Nor was he at that time running for public office. Farmer represented himself and a few friends, and political common-sense alone should have warned Wissore against participating in the debate and giving Farmer and his ideas a legitimacy they would not have otherwise had, and certainly a prestige they didn't deserve.

But debate they did. The exchange, which was more a list of accusations and denials than a debate, accomplished three things. It allowed Farmer to pontificate his superfluous, clichéd, anti-educational prejudices, while exposing Wissore's use of college funds and facilities in campaigning for the referendum, and therefore condemned the referendum. It exposed Wissore's grand non-educational plans for tax monies that the school would receive if the referendum were passed, and therefore condemned the referendum. It further served to elucidate selective anti-referendum issues the *BND* would exploit, which helped condemn the referendum.

The following Sunday, November 3, 1985, the *BND* carried an editorial, "A Tax Hike That Is No Bargain." The editorial enumerated the *BND*'s reasons for opposing the referendum as well as an accusation that the board and Wissore had seriously maligned and mistreated board member Elizabeth Jenner.

* * * * *

As noted earlier, during the 1980 strike Elizabeth Jenner had stopped in several times at my house to talk about the strike. At the time I shared an office with Martha Giordano, a close friend with artist Nancy Webb who worked in the BAC graphics and print shop. As networks go, Webb was a close friend, if not an immediate neighbor of Jenner. One day, during the 1980 strike, Giordano asked me if I would be interested in talking to Elizabeth Jenner about the strike. I said I would first have to clear the contact with Libby, but I thought he might welcome an audience with a board member.

When I queried Libby about the contact and what I might or might not discuss with Jenner, he was most agreeable, and we laid out an informal agenda of what we wanted the board to know about our position, and of our hopes for a solution to the problems we were having with the Eckert Board.

At any rate, the contact led to my meeting with Jenner. We talked about the strike in terms of what might resolve the conflict. She wanted to know what could be done to encourage the faculty to return to classes. Without hesitation I responded, "Get rid of Wissore."

She paused a moment, and referring to the board, said, "I know those are honorable men, but I do not think they will do that. And I don't know why."

At the time I wondered about her use of "honorable men." I wondered if her reference was merely diplomatic or if she truly did not see the dishonesty, deception, and malevolence of the votes that hired Wissore and, at that time, held him in place. By 1985 I imagine she had learned, as we all had learned. However it was, the citizens of District 522 still owe a great debt to Elizabeth Jenner for her honesty, integrity, and courage.

* * * * *

The Monday before the referendum vote, November 4, 1985, Jenner, who was in the first place decidedly skeptical about the referendum, filed a petition in Circuit Court to have Wissore held in contempt for violating the October thirtieth court order to cease and desist from using school facilities and funds to promote the referendum. The following day, election day, Wissore ended up in court.

On November 6, 1985 the *BND* headlines read, "Wissore Found in Contempt of Court." The accompanying article detailed the contempt hearing before Judge Joseph Cunningham.

> "These people created a sham committee to try to enforce their will on the public, and they shouldn't have done it," said Bruce Cook, the attorney who filed the petition for the contempt citation. "Dr. Wissore should be told, if you do these things, you do them at your own peril."
>
> Cook, arguing that Wissore should be punished for violating the order, said; "No one is above the law."
>
> "No one has the right to ignore the orders of the court," Cook said. "Somewhere someone is going to have to get Dr. Wissore's attention, to let him know he cannot do anything he wants to."
>
> Cook said; "This man (Wissore) has deliberately prevented me and Mrs. Jenner, and you (the judge) and Mr. Alvey (Wissore's attorney) from having a free and impartial election."
>
> Cook pointed to Jenner and said; "This lady has stood up and tried to stop them from doing something wrong."
>
> "Only the people who borrowed the money for the committee got the raise?" Cook asked.
>
> "That's the way it is," Wissore responded.
>
> Wissore also said the payments were not raises.
>
> The BAC chancellor characterized the payments instead as "merit fringe benefits."
>
> Cook asked, "Do you understand that when he (Cunningham) writes an order, you must obey it?"
>
> Wissore said, "I did not understand it the way you understand

it."

"Is there any other way for a person with a PhD to understand this statement?" Cook said.

Cunningham found that the phone banks continued to operate until 9 p.m. the day the court order took effect, and additionally that to instruct workers in the campaign on October 30, 1985 at 4 p.m. Wissore had held a meeting in the college theatre.

St. Clair County Circuit Court Judge Joseph Cunningham said he would assess the fine later and it would be payable to the county treasurer or the college.

The Citizens Say, "No"

Voter reaction on November 5, 1985 was overwhelming. The referendum failed in a preposterously one-sided vote. Proposition 1 was voted down 34,960–4,268 (89-percent to 11-percent) and Proposition 2 lost 34,310–4,398 (87-percent to 13-percent). The voters of BAC District 522 had given Wissore and the Eckert Board a resounding vote of no-confidence.

The only question is, how could they (Wissore and Eckert) have missed so badly?

* * * * *

You have to suspect that in sponsoring the referendum Wissore fantasized himself as some kind of budding public-works mogul who would build buildings and create new vistas on the local landscape, and after whom, someday, gyms and highways, maybe even a school would be named. It was a comic-book, empire-building fantasy run amuck. As part of this illusion, shortly after his appointment as BAC president, Wissore had his title changed from President to Chancellor. So he was now the Chancellor of the college domain in the cities and towns of Belleville, Granite City, and Red Bud, in Southwestern Illinois.

At the meeting following the referendum defeat, the board should have stripped Wissore of his title and of his job and gutted his administration. The board members who rubber stamped the fiasco should have resigned their offices. I don't know of another college chancellor or president held in contempt of court that would have kept his position or should have. And though nothing was done at BAC—board and administrative activities continued as before—the voters of District 522 were getting the message.

* * * * *

Despite the political double-dealing, and probably because of it, in the same November 1985 election Francis Braswell defeated Vest for Fish's two-year seat, and Larry Reinneck out-polled both Curt Eckert and Avery Schermer for one of the two six-year seats. Eckert, Schermer, and Vest ran on a slate, as did Braswell and Reinneck.

Reinneck led all candidates with 23,958 votes. Braswell was second with 19,356. Eckert got the remaining six-year seat by default or maybe as the best known of the names on his ticket. Since only three people were running for two six-year seats, the possibility is that had there been another six-year-seat candidate who was not on the Eckert ticket, nobody on the Eckert slate would have been elected.

Because of the referendum, the number of voters going to the polls in the 1985 board election increased dramatically. While Avery Schermer received twice as many votes as he had in his first election campaign, he still lost by a substantial margin, polling ten thousand fewer votes than Reinneck. Over all Larry Reinneck out polled him 62- percent to 38-percent. Schermer's Granite City-Madison numbers also were off substantially. I would guess Schermer's séance with the Tri-City's Labor Council had as much to do with his defeat, as did the tax propositions. It is also apparent that by then the educational voting public of District 522, the people who vote in school-board elections had developed definite opinions about Wissore and the BAC board.

Again, the Eckert Board and the Wissore administration seemed never to understand that the educational process consists of two ingredients: teachers and students. And education is a school's purpose, its mission, its raison d'être. People queried by the *BND* shortly before the election thought that, had the referendum focused on education instead of buildings, they might have voted for it. At any rate, the referendum failed stupendously and along with Braswell's and Reinneck's election opened a crack in the Eckert Board's dike that would ultimately lead to its demise.

* * * * *

Francis Braswell was a patrician dame, a fine woman, though perhaps a bit politically naïve. Reinneck was a savvy and frequently combative, but mostly fair-minded farmer-citizen, who had run unsuccessfully for the BAC board in 1979 and had a good bit of experience on governing boards. The *BND* listed him as a "... former president, secretary and treasurer of the St. Clair County Farm Bureau." He served on "The St. Clair County Building Commission for 10 years. He also served as Chairman for the Commission," was also a member of the Belleville Mental Health Board of Directors, and the advisory board of the East-West Gateway Coordinating Council.

With Reinneck and Braswell on the board, the first salvo of the ensuing battle came during the November meeting, right after the election, when the board selected a chairman. Reynolds nominated Dintelmann, who declined, and in turn nominated Reynolds. In the ensuing vote, Bartsokas, Braswell, Dintelmann, and Reynolds voted for Reynolds. Jenner and Reinneck voted no.

Then, at the December meeting, Reinneck confronted Wissore, and the rest of the board. Wissore had appointed Larry Friederich (Director of Personnel-Human Resources) as chief negotiator for the board's upcoming contract deliberations with the faculty. Reinneck wanted Wissore to handle negotiations, more than likely so Wissore could not evade responsibility for the failure to negotiate by disappearing into the fog and mist that administrators can too easily create between the board and its committees.

In January, board chairman Wayne Reynolds (no doubt at Wissore's instigation) put Braswell, Jenner, and Reinneck on the Personnel Committee, to handle negotiations, which set them in direct conflict with the faculty they were perceived as wanting to protect. As a member of the Personnel Committee, and later as board president, Reinneck often sat in on negotiating sessions. Occasionally, he asked tough questions or offered reasonable suggestions. I suspect he showed up at those sessions looking for information eventually to spin the Eckert-Wissore Trojan Horse on its heels and send it back at them in flames.

1986 Negotiations

In February of 1986 the union again found itself in a hassle with the board in trying to protect BAC faculty assigned to Menard Penitentiary in Chester. Edward Brady (Psychology), Thomas Cress (Welding-tech), Charles Gulash (Welding-tech), Mike Roeder (AC-tech), William Wilson (AC-tech), and John Zanotti (Construction-tech) were about to be dismissed by the Illinois Department of Corrections (IDOC). Another teacher, Richard Boyer (Business), had already been moved to the main campus from Menard in April of 1985.

The problem with IDOC hinged on the fact that though the education programs at the prison had been administered by BAC, the teachers at the prison were paid by grants from the IDOC. The grant provided monies for administration and other services, so the BAC board had been more than willing to supply the teachers. But there was more to teaching at the prison than money. While the prison faculty salaries were paid by a grant from the IDOC, the teachers were still members of the BAC faculty and had gained tenure through the process established for fulltime faculty at the college. The catch came when the IDOC objected to the limitation on the number of classes the teachers could teach, as well as other conditions of employment set by the *Memorandum of Understanding* and notified the college that the faculty at Menard would serve under IDOC regulations or not at all.

When the problem with IDOC surfaced, the board initially did not want to retain the Menard faculty, even though they were tenured. The board's first impulse was to void the *Memorandum* and write a new contract for the Menard faculty to satisfy IDOC. This brought in the union. The board's second impulse was, since a new contract couldn't be written, to simply cut the Menard faculty loose. The union answered by demanding that the Menard faculty be brought to the main campus. After all, they were fulltime college faculty, and there were sufficient classes for which they were qualified that were being taught by part-timers.

In an ironic but not at all surprising twist, the Menard faculty, except for Roeder, who was not yet a faculty member in 1980, had not supported the 1980 strike. They had excused themselves, claiming that as grant employees they would lose their jobs if they went on strike.

Additionally, bringing the Menard faculty to the main campus presented a very real threat of displacement or retrenchment for certain Belleville campus fulltime faculty. Several Menard faculty members were senior to main-campus teachers in departments to which they would be assigned. There was now a collective bargaining law, and under the IEECB, in matters of retrenchment, seniority counts. The 1980 non-striking Menard faculty found that in 1986 their timidity and obeisance during the '80 strike had done nothing to save them from the Eckert Board. For protection they had to rely on the bargaining unit they had spurned. They (the Menard teachers) were asking colleagues they had refused to support in 1980, to help them find positions at the main campus, even at the possible cost of the colleagues' jobs. But too often that is the task of the union—defending and supporting people who will not defend themselves and who refuse to support those who are defending them.

As it turned out, in a strange split vote, the board agreed to bring the "Menard Six" to the main campus. Braswell, Jenner, and Reinneck, members of the Personnel Committee, who found that the Menard faculty should be retained, voted in favor of the report. The committee report to the full board said there were five members to be retained. I am not certain of Mike Roeder's dates, but imagine he might have been un-tenured. Anyway, Bartsokas and Dintelmann voted against it, and Eckert voted "Present." Wayne Reynolds, the absent board member, had probably already stated he would vote for retention if it came to a vote later, and/or the administration's calculations showed that the cost of lawsuits the Menard faculty's dismissal would generate made it cheaper and less troublesome to retain them.

The November 1985 election had removed Avery Schermer from the board, and the referendum defeat, along with the assignment of new board members, seriously impaired Eckert's control of the board. At the May meeting Eckert read a statement commending Schermer and lamenting the loss of the Eckert-Wissore plan.

On two occasions Eckert would publicly lament the Menard decision–though he seems never to have known how much it cost the school. Once he referred to four teachers and 172,000 dollars and at another time to four teachers and 150,000 dollars. There were six faculty members, five who were tenured. At other times Wissore claimed the move cost the school 180,000 dollars.

Without question, during her first few months on the board in 1986, Braswell acquiesced to the Eckert entourage. Then in April Bartsokas resigned and the six remaining board members had the task (defined by statute) of appointing a replacement. It seems reasonable to assume that Eckert wanted someone amenable to his influences, but also one who would at least give the appearance of independence. The Bartsokas resignation left a three (Dintelmann, Eckert, Reynolds)-three (Braswell, Jenner, Reinneck) board, so the negotiations selecting a new board member could have been substantial. However, in a completely unpredictable and mysterious move, Braswell crossed over and voted with Dintelmann, Eckert, and Reynolds to appoint Leo Konzen, a Granite City lawyer. What connection Braswell had with Konzen, what kind of agreement was made or what threats had been made against Braswell, may never be known.

After the Konzen appointment, matters moved on for several months with Braswell leaning towards the Eckert camp, until a vote came up in July of 1986 to extend Wissore's contract. The Personnel Committee (Braswell, Jenner, and Reinneck) advised the board to limit the renewal of admin- istrative contracts which, in Wissore's case, ran for three years, although the board had been renewing it every six months. During what little discussion there was, Braswell asked why the contract was being extended when it still had two-and-a-half-years to run. Whether she didn't really know what was going on or meant to confront the process intending to sidetrack the prac- tice, I do not know. She was told that as a matter of common courtesy around the state and across the country colleges renewed administrative contracts every six months. When she asked for more information she met a stone- wall, and so took it upon herself to talk to colleges in Illinois, especially com- munity colleges, and found that what she had been told was clearly not what other colleges did.

Reading the board minutes, you can almost feel Madame Braswell's disapproving stare and see her scoot her chair a little closer to Jenner and Reinneck, who early on appear to have had a natural political-geopolitical affinity. Dintelmann's and Eckert's association on the board and otherwise was Business Ag-minded, if you can call it that. Dintelmann ran a nursery, but also had substantial farm land. Eckert was an heir to Eckert's Orchards and Farms, with large business properties in Southern Illinois and Missouri. Eckert had a seat on the board of directors of the First National Bank of Belleville, and Dintelmann was a stock holder in the bank.

But Reinneck, too, was a farmer. And Jenner regularly talked about representing the farm community. So there seems to have been more than a little animosity bubbling between the Eckert-Dintelmann banking-business idea of agriculture, and the Reinneck-Jenner view of the farm as a work place, maybe as the old German heimaten (those centers of family farm life) that populate St. Clair, Monroe, and Randolph counties in Southern Illinois. Board minutes show Jenner and Dintelmann, and later Reinneck-Jenner, and Dintelmann were frequently at odds, and openly so, even as Eckert and Wissore attempted to keep board riffs behind closed doors. Eckert pressured the board to vote unanimously in public, especially on items over which the board was split in private. He wanted it to appear that the board agreed. The more ridiculous the issue, the more he pressed for compliance, although it was becoming increasingly difficult for the board to hide its divisions.

Office Moves, Telecourses, and Eight Percent

In educational-labor bargaining circles it is generally understood that good union negotiators try to determine what the other side wants or needs, and then maneuver enough to give something the faculty can live with while securing what they can of what the faculty needs. Good union negotiators also know the negotiators across the table. Libby always said that Wissore was not a negotiator, but a horse trader. Wissore always wanted to trade a worn out nag for your thoroughbred, claiming all the while you could win the Kentucky Derby with the nag, and, anyway, most owners were unhappy with their thoroughbreds.

In 1986 I served as chief negotiator for the first time. By then I had had several years of experience at the table and had attended AFT-IFT training seminars for contract negotiators. And although I have never had much affinity for psychodrama, several of the AFT training sessions were significant in providing instruction in the mental-set required of a negotiator in securing a good contract.

Additionally, to our advantage the collective bargaining law had been in effect for two years and had significantly leveled the playing field—which meant mostly that it discouraged boards and administrations from dictatorial, authoritarian stances. Now it was easy enough to remind the board's negotiation team that regressive bargaining could result in an unfair labor practice being filed with the Illinois Educational Labor Relations Board. Illinois state representative Jim McPike told me that in 1983, the year before the law was enacted, Illinois had over 100 school strikes. The following year, 1985, there were only a dozen or so. But that's what happens when people *have to talk* to one another.

In 1986 Larry Friederich headed the board's negotiating team. It was the Eckert-Wissore practice to put people they did not like into what they saw as fail-fail or at least unlikely-to-succeed situations. For whatever reason, I got the impression Wissore not only did not like Friederich, but didn't trust him either, and so assigned Robert Eskridge to accompany

Friederich to the table for the sole purpose of reporting on Friederich. During the negotiations Eskridge took pages of notes–but did not talk. I think he laughed once—at something.

Eskridge came to BAC as a retired Air Force NCO double-dipper. He had migrated from the Air Force to McKendree College in Lebanon (which had been on the AAUP censured list for years) then to BAC. Eskridge's most notable contribution to the school came one evening when he was the administrator on duty and a General from Scott Air Force Base showed up in the office on some small business or other and had to talk to Eskridge. When he departed, the General inquired of a teacher he knew, "What in the hell is that sergeant doing running a college?"

By then the collective bargaining law was in full effect, and it was damned-near inspiring when Friederich, certainly following Wissore's orders, offered some retrograde proposal, to be able to say, as I did several times, "Larry, the only thing that proposal will get you is a citation for an unfair labor practice."

Negotiations went smoothly enough that year, highlighted by Eskridge's scribbling, and the introduction of "Office Moves" into the *Memorandum*. In spite of a non-recrimination article in the 1980 contract to discourage faculty and administrators from attacking each other after the strike, Weldon Tallant, the Dean of Counseling, following Wissore's orders, assigned Libby to a broom closet—literally to a broom closet—for an office. I determined that at first chance, by god, we would put an end to that juvenile nonsense—and we did. We got a section in the contract delineating the reassignment of vacated offices. Several months into the contract an office opened and as the senior member needing a new office, Libby claimed it. And it was a nice office, too. It even had a window.

Several years later, to make convenient and pleasant room for more administrative space, then President Joe Cipfl decided to move the counselors out of the suite of offices they occupied to a fluvial of cubicles at the far end of the hall. When the counselors (faculty) objected, citing the "Office Moves" section of the *Memorandum of Understanding,* Cipfl was incredulous. "You mean to tell me I can't move the faculty of this institution wherever I want them?"

The union answer was, "That's right. If the counselors don't agree, you would be violating the contract."

That year we also moved telecourses into the contract, at least in part. Total inclusion would have to wait until 1992, ostensibly because the faculty teaching them did not want to give up the extra-contractual money, and we did not want to force the issue. However, in 1986 we did reduce the number of students that could be enrolled in any one telecourse to 75. I say "We," but Leo Welch, who had been union president for two years by then, in a bit of sidebar negotiations, pushed Wissore on it and got an agreement.

As part of the plan to reduce faculty salaries in 1986, the board put the first early retirement proposal on the table. When I inquired about the contents of the plan, the board team quickly reduced the offer, in essence negotiating against itself. Other than asking questions about what they had in mind, I didn't see any reason to attempt to negotiate the content of the proposal. It seemed apparent that if the offer was not good enough, no one would take it, so whatever had been set out would be worthless.

I wasn't interested in losing faculty, especially seasoned union faculty, that I assumed the administration would replace with part-timers. It wasn't my job to bargain people out of the place. We had enough trouble bargaining their security and well-being while they were in the building. If there were faculty who could benefit from an early retirement, it was okay with me. But it was up to the board to put enough sugar into the pudding to make it attractive, and I wasn't going to haggle over that. I told Friederich that whatever he wanted to give away was his business. My only requirement was that the option be the individual faculty member's choice to participate and that it be administered equitably.

When we came to a tentative agreement in May, Friederich told me Wissore said, "Lanter will never get the faculty to accept this." I didn't know it at the time, but Wissore had promised his in-group a wage hike of 8-percent. All that we had on the table was a 3.4-percent pay increase. I passed information on to Wissore that when the tentative agreement came to a vote, we would get 89 to 90 affirmative votes from the faculty. And we did. The faculty ratified the tentative agreement 88 to 31. But as I said, Wissore never did have a good handle on what the faculty thought, or anyone else for that matter. But, of course, he was only talking to his in-group.

About this time Wissore collected several non-union faculty into a group he dubbed the Knights of the Round Table. I do not know who all was involved, though I do know Ault, Poe, and several others of the in-group were there. In violation of the Illinois EECBA, they met numerous times with Wissore and R. Wayne Clark to negotiate a new contract. When word got around, because of the liaison, the board came very nearly having an unfair labor practice filed against it.

In May of 1986 Friederich took the agreement we had hammered out to the board Personnel Committee of Braswell, Jenner, and Reinneck, who took it to the board at its June meeting. The board dismissed it without a vote. Dintelmann railed at the committee for not explaining the tentative agreement to the board. Konzen, a recent arrival on the board, said he did not have time to digest it, so he could not vote for or against it.

Anderson from SS claimed that since nothing becomes law until the board votes (what he didn't say was that even then it is not a law since boards of education do not make laws), nothing more needed to be done. I knew what the board vote would be, that the tentative agreement would not get four votes, but I also knew that I was not going to submit to Anderson's arrogance. I was quite prepared to howl to the newspapers that the board had failed its primary responsibility and was encouraging an impending labor crisis. I also reminded Friederich to remind the committee to remind Wissore to remind the board to remind Anderson that ignoring a tentative agreement (not voting on it) reached by a board negotiator amounted to bargaining in bad faith, also an unfair labor practice. Anderson might have disagreed with me, but no doubt aware that he was in St. Clair County, quickly saw the errors in his thinking. He advised the board to vote on the agreement, which it did, resulting in a 3-3 stalemate with Konzen abstaining. So we headed back to the table.

The upshot of the matter was that the May agreement called for a faculty salary increase of only 3.4-percent but contained a good benefits supplement. That year we instituted the cafeteria plan, which gave teachers receiving benefits a list of options that could be tailored more closely to individual needs—such things as medical care, life insurance, etc. Even with a substantial increase in benefits, I had a noisy though not difficult time getting the agreement ratified by the faculty. As I said, the faculty approved the agreement 88-31. However, the Wissore in-group howled and chaffed and accused me of selling out the faculty, telling me that if the faculty turned down the tentative agreement and returned to the table, we could get an 8-percent salary increase.

The leader of "Why didn't you take the 8-percent they offered?" was Wayne Pfingsten (Business), a Wissore in-grouper who had not joined the union until the EECBA was enacted, and who, a year later in April of 1987, would be nominated for the Illinois Community College Trustees' Association Faculty Member of the Year award, a spurious award at best—a nomination that could only have come from Wissore.

William Faulkner, the 1949 Nobel Laureate for literature, gave the 1950 commencement address at Oxford, Mississippi high school. In the speech he commissioned the graduates to move into their new lives with courage and goodwill. He reminded them that "The only things that will enslave you are greed and fear." Some years after that, merely in passing, I asked a friend of mine, Tanzanian novelist and United Nations Ambassador Peter Palangyo, for his impression of Americans. "What," I asked Peter, "is the one thing that strikes you most about Americans?"

He did not hesitate, as if the answer was ready-made.

"Greed," he said. "Greed, and fear of the outside world."

Faulkner and Palangyo could have been speaking with the BAC-SWIC in-group faculty in mind. Clearly, what the they wanted in 1986, I was told, was not benefits, but money, money, money, so the older members could buck-up their retirement base. I must admit I was mystified at the accusation that I had betrayed them by turning down an offer for an 8-percent raise. At no time during negotiations did we receive an offer of more than 3.4-percent. I talked to Libby about it at length, and we decided that Wissore probably had made the 8-percent promise to his groupies knowing he could get the four Eckert Board votes to approve it to make the Personnel Committee look bad. Years later when the minutes of the board Personnel Committee were released, I discovered that Friederich had been instructed by the Committee to hold the line at somewhere around 3.5-percent. We had ended at 3.4-percent.

Anyway, we went back to the table and sure enough, there it was. Now we were offered 8-percent instead of 3.4-percent, with little if any change to the benefits package. Other items in the renewed negotiations had to be worked out, but by the middle of August we had the thing nearly completed.

I mentioned earlier that in 1968 the board adopted the AAUP statement on tenure and academic freedom as a matter of policy. As long as a board remained honorable and conciliatory, the policy provided something of guidance and protection to professors in the classroom.

However, as English Department Chair in 1981, it became increasingly apparent to me that since board policy on tenure had been rewritten in 1980 to accommodate the Tenured Teacher Act, and the AAUP "1940 Statement of Principles on Academic Freedom and Tenure" had been deleted from the Board Policy Manual, the academic freedom curtain protecting the doorway to the classroom was now gossamer-thin.

Already in several community colleges in Illinois, absent an academic freedom agreement or policy, administrators attempted to use academic performance as a ploy to discourage or dismiss professors they did not like. In one case a college professor was required to provide the administration with a detailed lesson plan for each of his classes, and at specific points during the semester an administrator interrupted a class to check if the professor was in fact on the given page, section, and paragraph assigned by the lesson plan for that moment. In fact, in 1980, Wissore tried to implement this type of faculty micromanagement.

* * * * *

What is academic freedom? In the Introduction to *"Academic Freedom in the 21st-Century College and University: Academic Freedom for All Faculty and Instructional Staff,"* the AFT "Statement on Academic Freedom" relates that "The First Global Colloquium of University Presidents," a 2005 gathering of more than 40 university leaders and professors convened at the request of United Nations Secretary-General Kofi Annan, stated that:

> At its simplest, academic freedom may be defined as the freedom to conduct research, teach, speak, and publish, subject to the norms and standards of scholarly enquiry, without interference or penalty, wherever the search for truth and understanding may lead.

The AFT describes academic freedom as ". . . the hallmark of excellence in education," and further that ". . . the AFT issues this statement out of a deep sense of urgency about the status of academic freedom now and in the future. Increasingly we see a variety of threats to the practices that support academic freedom. These include: the increasingly vocational focus of higher education; loss of financial support for colleges and universities; corporate-style management practices; political attacks on faculty and instructional staff; the erosion of academic staffing through the loss of fulltime tenured positions; and the financial and professional mistreatment of contingent faculty members."

As late as June of 2009, the University of Minnesota, under the direction of Provost Thomas Sullivan, a lawyer and former law school dean, adopted a revised statement that,

> Academic Freedom is the freedom to discuss all relevant matters in the classroom, to explore all avenues of scholarship, research, and creative expression, and to speak or write without institutional discipline or restraint on matters of public concern as well as on matters related to professional duties and the functioning of the university.

Following the 1980 deletion of the academic freedom section from BAC board policy, there was nothing to keep administrators from wedging a foot in the classroom door and dictating subject matter and how it was to be taught, a practice comparable to allowing clerks at the courthouse to prescribe courtroom procedure or dictate what instructtions should be read to the jury. It is similar to what HMOs did by taking upon themselves to determine and delineate by judging the severity of an individual's illness who of their subscribers would receive covered medical care and who could not. The courts subsequently judged that the HMOs were breaking the law (exposure to liability they called it) by practicing medicine without a license.

It doesn't matter if the administration invades the academics of the individual's classroom or if teachers supporting the administration do it. For whatever reasons, a fascination with the petty power and prestige of college politics or because of sheer classroom ineptitude or not wanting to continue to meet the rigors of their profession, teachers often solicit administrative favor with the intention of one day insinuating themselves into the bureaucratic structure. On several occasions a teacher-turned-administrator I had the misfortune of working with, Paula Wilson (Sociology), told me her reasons for becoming an administrator.

"I don't have to keep up with the newest developments in sociology and can spend more time in Cancun. Also, it pays better," she said.

Such people are seldom good teachers, and usually even worse administrators. The individual professor-scholar in the classroom needs the freedom and safeguards from the intrusions these kinds of people generate that only a negotiated legally binding document can provide.

* * * * *

In 1986 I made it a point to get the AAUP "1940 Statement on the Principles of Academic Freedom and Tenure" on the table. In fact, I wrote a preamble to the basic statement that would have put the board in double jeopardy if it even approached the issue. It took Anderson from SS four readings before he realized what I had done. Needless to say, we didn't get it into the contract that year.

Actually, we did get an agreement for the AAUP "1940 Statement" at the table in 1986, though I thought at the time it was too easy. And just so. When the printed copy of the issues we had agreed to came back at the next session, it wasn't included.

* * * * *

As chief negotiator there are numerous pitfalls and hazards to which one is exposed. In 1986, after Wissore's and SS's double-dealing prolonged negotiations, as it is sometimes when you have been at the table too long, I got locked into a mental fix. In trying to hold the line and secure what the faculty needed without giving away what they already had and also needed, with only the academic freedom item left on the table, I hit a stone wall. For three or four sessions I held out on the academic freedom demand, refusing to give in or give it away. Why? I don't know. Maybe exhaustion or as I said, fear of not getting enough of what the faculty needed. In other years I saw this happen to other people on our negotiating teams.

You always hope that at the end of contract the mountains are high enough and valleys not too low. In the back of my mind, at the faculty meeting explaining what the team had done, I could always hear the boo-birds and Brooklyn raspberries in the last row.

As it turned out, Mike Hade, the IFT field rep, finally showed up. I was sitting alone at the table during a caucus when Hade walked in. He had been apprised of the situation and knew where we were and what was left. He asked me what I was doing about the academic freedom issue, the last item on the table, and I said something to the effect that I wasn't going to give in on this.

"You're going to strike over it?" he said.

"No," I said. "I don't think so."

"Then why are you acting like you are?'

"You mean, give it up?"

"Yeah."

"How?"

"Say, 'okay, we're finished.'"

"I can't do that."

"Why not?"

"I just can't. I don't want that part of the apple"

"It's easy."

"Well, hell. Really? No, I can't do that."

Then I thought about it for a moment. Why not? Well, I was still pissed about Wissore and the in-group manipulating the bargaining process and the board turning down the May agreement that sent us back to the table simply so Eckert and Wissore could add money to the package to feed the in-group and to make Braswell, Jenner, and Reinneck (the Personnel Committee) look bad.

Then it was as if the clouds rolled back. Six months of sleepless nights, of anger dropped away. Six months of piles of paper dropped away like leaves on a fall day. Jesus, I could just walk away from this.

"But what about all those people? This isn't just about protecting jobs. This is the guts of the educational process."

"What people?"

"Well. You really think so?"

"You've finished it," Hade said.

We took the contract to the executive committee the next day and that was that. And it was a good contract, too. But Hade's advice was just another service the union provided–telling you when you were about to make a damned fool of yourself. As President Lincoln said, "The taste was still a little bitter in my mouth." But we did get it done and done well, though we had to wait until the Eckert Board disintegrated and Joe Cipfl was at the helm in 1992 to re-establish the AAUP "1940 Statement on the Principles of Academic Freedom and Tenure with 1970 Interpretive Comments" in the *Memorandum of Understanding* and the *Board Policy Manual.*

Wissore's expanded salary offer to the faculty in June of 1986 only added to the conflict on the board. To justify what he had done, Wissore wrote a letter to the editor of the *BND*, dated August 6, 1986, in which he claimed, "The hallmark of my career has been battling faculty salaries at Belleville Area College," and "Yes, our faculty salaries are still too high."

During the Wissore's administration from 1980 to 1986 the faculty raises were: 1980, 10-percent; 1981, 10-percent; 1982, 9.5-percent; 1983, 0-percent; 1984, 6-percent; 1985, 0-percent; and 1986, 8-percent.

The total is 43.5-percent over seven years or an average of 6.2 percent a year. If Wissore was battling salaries, either he was grossly incompetent, the union was enormously capable, or both.

In August, referring to the board's rejection of the May tentative agreement, Wissore was quoted in the *BND* as claiming that, "This fall the BAC trustees saved $330,000 by rejecting the proposed accord ratified by the faculty and endorsed by the Trustees' Personnel Committee.

"The new package, with the 8-percent hike, will cost $312,000. The contract rejected by the trustees last month would have cost $642,000."

I do not know where Wissore got the 642,000-dollar figure. But then I was never sure where he got his numbers. Sometimes the logic was inverse as with the husband who reports to his wife that she is indeed a lucky woman, and especially so today since he has saved them 3,000 dollars by purchasing a 4,000-dollar automobile they neither needed nor could afford for only 1,000 dollars.

I do not know where Wissore got the 330,000 dollars savings or how, but it certainly was not in the differences between the May tentative agreement and the final contract as ratified by both the AAUP-AFT and the board in August of 1986.

The savings were probably a smoke and mirrors project of creative accounting. For example, say the school has ten teachers making 50,000 dollars each for 500,000 dollars a year, and each teaches four classes a semester or eight classes a year for a total of eighty classes. At the same time, let's say there are twenty part-timers teaching one class each at 800 dollars a class, for 16,000 dollars. Together the 100 classes cost 516,000 dollars a year.

Suppose, further, we do a cost per-class breakdown and find that each class taught by the fulltime faculty (50,000 divided by eight) comes to 6,250 dollars a class. Now we institute productivity measures and require the fulltime faculty to teach one more class a semester or ten for the year and have a cost of 5,000 dollars (50,000 dollars divided by ten) per class and have created a savings of 1,250 dollars per class. And since each faculty member is teaching ten classes, and we have a savings of 1,250 dollars per class, times ten classes, times ten faculty members, for a total savings of 125,000 dollars for the year. Correct? Well, not quite. All we've done is put twenty part-timers out of work at a savings of 16,000 dollars to the school. The school is still paying out 500,000 dollars in teachers' salaries for teaching the 100 classes.

Wissore often claimed the austerity measures of his tenure as BAC president and chancellor set the school on a firm financial footing. The claim is, at best, dubious. In the first place there is no reason to believe the school ever had financial problems. Most of the financial exigency was a red herring, created, as was the Stumph Budget of 1969, by underestimating revenues and overestimating expenses. The school met the burgeoning student population of the 70s and 80s with the cheap labor of part-time faculty, so even with the Eckert-Wissore spending binge, by 1982 the college was sitting on 1.2 million dollars in excess funds.

Moreover, the Eckert Board's attack on the faculty did absolutely nothing to reduce fulltime faculty salaries to save the school money. As I noted, the Wissore administration raised fulltime faculty salaries 43.5-percent from 1980 to 1986.

In his August 19, 1986 letter to the *BND* Wissore claimed, "According to the most recent state report we (BAC) ranked tenth among the largest 10 community college districts on dollars spent on salary and fringe benefits per student.

"(In 1984 the average of the top 10 was $1,964 per student. BAC was $1,546—or 27-percent lower than the average and 19-percent below the ninth rank—ranking college figure of $1,842.)"

In truth, those years less money was spent on instruction per student and more money was spent on Chicago law firms, administrative salaries, fruitless referenda, and developing and grooming athletic fields.

The Demise of the Eckert Board

> We must learn to live together as brothers
> or we are going to perish together as fools.
> —Martin Luther King, Jr.

Farmer, Jenner, Reinneck, and Wolford

By 1986 the Eckert Board was coming apart. Braswell had moved to the Jenner-Reinneck end of the table, and while Eckert's four votes still controlled most board decisions, sometimes Konzen appeared indifferent to Eckert's influence. But the writing was on the wall.

By nature, public boards of education are transient bodies–and they should be. Mark Twain remarked, and not entirely with tongue-in-cheek, that "The first thing God did was create an idiot. But that was just for practice. Then he created school boards."

The transient nature of boards of education is one of their more endearing qualities, although there have been, and are, petty politicians who sometimes occupy them for life, as Curt Eckert tried to do. English department stalwart Gertrude Brainerd, who provided the North Central Association that accredits BAC-SWIC with over a ton (though I'm not sure but that someone might have had a foot on the scale) of printed material detailing the Wissore administration's misguided adventures, was fond of saying, "I've been teaching for twenty-five years and I've seen administrators and boards come and go, and when these people are gone, by God I'll still be here."

The final blow to the Eckert Board came in the fall 1987. That November, eleven people, five women and six men stood for election to the BAC Board of Trustees. Eight candidates filed for the three six-year terms, and three for the one two-year term. Those vying for the six-year terms were: Catherine Bennett; Francis Braswell; Susanne Briggs; Robert Eden; Ted Farmer; Elizabeth Jenner; Avery Schermer; and Stephen Trautt. Jenner and Braswell were incumbents and Schermer, a pro-Wissore-Eckert ally, had been on the board previously but lost his seat in the referendum debacle of 1985. Those running for the one two-year term were Shirley Highlander; Wyatt Rawlings III; and Dan Wolford. Wolford, along with Jenner and Farmer, was staunchly anti-Wissore.

Wayne Reynolds, whom the faculty helped elect in 1981, and Leo Konzen, who had been appointed by the board (with the vote of Francis Braswell) to fill the seat vacated by Patricia Bartsokas, did not run. Curt Eckert, Robert Dintelmann and Larry Reinneck were not up for re-election.

Although, beginning in 1974, Curt Eckert had solicited several of his friends and business associates to run for the BAC board, the first candidates to openly identify themselves as a ticket—seeking election to the board—

were Wayne Reynolds and Ken Fish in 1981. In 1982, as an extension into a formal political process, as noted earlier, we glad-handed the Democratic Party gurus in St. Clair and Madison counties, hoping they would become involved. We issued an invitation, I am sorry to say, that was necessary, but when accepted, eventually politicized the school and everything about it—with patronage and many seriously anti- or un-educational practices. So, by 1987 the BAC board elections had become less a contest of interested citizens and more and more a political-ideological battleground, and candidates bunched up on slates became commonplace. In 1987 Catherine Bennett, Robert Eden, Wyatt Rawlings III, and Avery Schermer ran on the "Project Excel: Putting BAC Back on Track" ticket. On the other side of the ledger, Elizabeth Jenner, Ted Farmer, and Dan Wolford formed their own combine. Briggs, Highlander, and Trautt ran as independents.

Except for Bennett, the election results were overwhelming anti-Wissore, in favor of the women candidates. Jenner, Farmer, and Bennett won the three six-year terms. Wolford took the two-year seat.

The vote-count for the six-year seats was Jenner 14,037, Bennett 12,680, Farmer 12,106, Braswell 10,165, Briggs 8,935, Schermer 8,690, Eden 6,246, Trautt 3,395—and for the two-year seats, Wolford 10,308, Highlander 9,100, Rawlings III 5,626.

There seems to be little doubt that the failed referendum of 1985 substantially affected the 1987 BAC board election. The 1985 charade, including Farmer's debate with Wissore, gave Farmer a forum he would not have had otherwise that he finessed into a board seat. More than that, the raw exposure in the press of the Eckert Board's treatment, I dare say, abuse, of Elizabeth Jenner, no doubt hit a nerve with the women voters of the district.

Not only did Jenner receive the most votes, but Bennett, the one woman on the pro-Wissore Project Excel slate, was the only member of the ticket elected. She was second to Jenner in votes received. Of the 101,288 votes cast, the five women candidates collected 54,917 (55-percent) or an average of 10,983 votes per candidate. The six males received 45-percent of the vote or an average of 7,729. More importantly, the clearly anti-Wissore candidates, Jenner, Farmer, Braswell and Wolford, gathered 46,616 votes or 11,654 on average, while Schermer, Eden, Trautt and Rawlings (three pro-Wissore candidates and an independent) collected only 23,957 or an average of 5,791 votes.

With the election of Ted Farmer and Dan Wolford, and the reseating of Elizabeth Jenner, the Eckert Board had lost its majority. Then only Dintelmann and Eckert remained from the 1982 board. Farmer was stridently anti-Wissore, as was Jenner and Wolford, a teacher and administrator at Belleville District 201 who had been an unsuccessful candidate for the original BAC board in November of 1967. When Kay Bennett, the other new board member, jumped in with Eckert and Dintelmann, Larry Reinneck became the deciding or swing vote. And if not anti-Wissore, he was mostly un-Wissorian.

A few days after the election hostilities erupted. Even before the first meeting a war-of-words broke out in the *BND,* speculating about what the board might do with or to Wissore.

> Reinneck: I'm willing to negotiate ourselves out of our contract with Wissore, which means he will have a say in it, too. Contracts are legal documents for both parties. I do believe that Dr. Wissore can be moved into another area, but I want to discuss my views with the other six members and maybe we can achieve it. I'm only one of seven votes. It is very easy to say Wissore should go, but it must be in an amicable manner.

> Farmer: I will certainly do everything in my power to remove the man and to do everything to make the school the pride of the district. And that means a change. I certainly hope, for the sake of the college and students, that we have the majority—four votes.

> Wissore: The ball is in the board's court and each one of those board members will have the opportunity to do what they want. Under no circumstances will I resign. There is a way of getting someone else to sit in this chair, but it won't be through my resignation.

> Wolford: I would vote to accept Wissore's resignation. We ran our whole campaign on lack of leadership and we have to stick by it.

> Jenner: It is not so much that I want him (Wissore) to resign. It is what the voters want. I think they proved that at the polls. In the last two years Wissore has completely polarized the community.

> Dintelmann: I don't see how we could do that. (Ask for Wissore's resignation) I think they are trying to make life miserable—tough for Dr. Wissore. Just changing one man here or there is not going to change policy—the duty of the board. The question those board members should be asking is what policy changes are they going to make that he cannot carry out? If they have some, bring them forward. If they simply want to fire him, it is nothing but a vendetta.

> Eckert: I challenge anyone to show me any administrator who has done a better job in the state. I believe the administration has

run the college well. I don't think they like him personally. They haven't proven he is a bad administrator

Farmer: When we can't change attitudes, we must change people. The main thing is the Chancellor has to go because he has been in complete control of the college—dominating the board which has practically rubber-stamped everything he has requested. I think we must give Wissore credit for everything good at BAC and at the same token everything bad.

Bennett: A lot of good things have happened at BAC, such as two new campuses, during his (Wissore's) time.

Reinneck: I want to clear up one thing—I won't be the fourth vote on the board, I will be the first. I said when I ran two years ago that the best thing for the college would be for Wissore to resign. I believe that Wissore should be worked out of the system, but I would first want to make sure what our options are with him. The board attorney must research his contract. I've had discussions with him before. We've had discussions on what the contract is worth to him.

Wissore: The contract speaks for itself. The board must understand that this is supposed to be Belleville Area College, not Belleville Area Circus. The handling of personnel matters through the newspaper is very unethical.

Jenner: We do want to be part of his recent lawsuits. We want to do whatever is acceptable to the people of the district, but would not do it without serious legal study. The incredible terms this man is working under. I can't believe the abuse we are going through because of his contract.

Farmer: If he refuses (to resign), that tells the world he is not an educator. I cannot imagine an educator staying on. We have plans to reassign him. I would not pay that man one penny for doing nothing. If we're going to have to pay him, we are going to work him.

Wolford: I think we will first ask for a resignation, and if that's not possible, move him to another position. I think we would all like to see him resign, but if not, we will do it as amicable as we can.

Eckert: I would not support it.

Wissore: I am still not going to resign. We are just waiting to see what the board wants to do. This administration will take the actions the Board of Trustees wants, and we are waiting for the board before taking any further action.

Leo Welch (Faculty Union President): There was no resignation submitted. He (Wissore) just said that under the circumstances , he would probably no longer be chancellor.

Farmer: I don't think anything can be drawn from what has been said. I would be the first to shake the man's hand—even take him to dinner—if he would resign and save us the headache of moving him out of office.

Reinneck: I don't believe the man is going to resign. We took an orderly review of the contract. The only thing we were trying to resolve is an orderly change of the captain of the ship.

Eckert: He has to be there until he is out.

At the first meeting (November), in a 4-3 vote, voting for herself, and supported by votes from Farmer, Reinneck, and Wolford, Jenner became board president.
As could be expected, Dintelmann objected to Jenner's candidacy. "Betty, you have in the past subverted the interests of the board, entertained hidden agendas and sometimes supported special interests [by which I assume he meant the BAC faculty] instead of the district as a whole. I cannot support you for these reasons."
Then as the first item of the new board's business Farmer suggested that Wissore resign. Wissore refused, and Dintelmann attacked Farmer for not appreciating what Wissore had done for the school. Later in the meeting Wissore got into a verbal exchange with Farmer over BAC money used to train people for Granite City Steel.
Community college schemes for providing students with voc-ed training in specified fields to enhance their employment possibilities can easily bleed into programs training employees for select businesses. Unfortunately, this turns colleges into a wing of whatever corporate enterprise is involved. In this case it was Granite City Steel. By way of tax-payers' dollars, Granite City Steel was relieved of the expense of training its own employees—just another example of a private corporation using public-education funds under the pretense of training students for employ- ment. Farmer, to his credit, did not want to subsidize businesses with college funds. That was November 18, 1987.
And while this appears to be a not too important matter in a single community college in Southwestern Illinois, the argument prophetically

foreshadowed the millennium drift of American universities and colleges toward becoming employment agencies and providing students with saleable skills for future employment.

At the Special Board Meeting called for December 9, 1987, nothing much transpired, except that Curt Eckert did not appear. Then, on December 12, 1987, at another Special Board Meeting, Reinneck moved, seconded by Farmer, to remove Wissore as chancellor. Farmer, Jenner, Reinneck, and Wolford voted "Aye." Bennett, Dintelmann, and Eckert voted "Naye."

Four days later, December 16, 1987, the board voted to dump Wissore off on to the faculty. Again, Dintelmann and Eckert voted "Naye." Later, R. Wayne Clark, Robert Eskridge, and Weldon Tallant were also assigned to the faculty, a board action taken without consulting either the faculty or a proper faculty selection process. However, none was given tenure, and all three joined the union the next day. But one does wonder, after their part in the Eckert Board and the Wissore administration anti-education debacle, why, under whatever circumstances, they should have been allowed in the classroom at all.

The same night the board voted to remove Wissore, Eckert resigned with a whining, incoherent, lamentation. Dintelmann would keep his seat for another twenty months, it appears, if for little more than to show his disapproval of the changes that were underway, and to provide a dissenting voice in support of an ideologue-strategy that had not only failed, but had also damaged the school, in some ways irrevocably. Then in October of 1989 he, too, resigned.

* * * * *

From 1974 to 1987, the activities of the BAC Board of Trustees and the administration it employed and sanctioned seriously diminished the educational efficacy of Belleville Area College. During those years the fulltime faculty was constantly under fire from the BAC administration. Faculty members were belittled, harassed, and threatened. Faculty service activities and innovations were ridiculed and reduced to a minimum. Faculty travel and research funds and sabbaticals were eliminated, and a disillusioned faculty was forced to expend a great deal of time and energy holding the school together academically while attempting to ameliorate the board's tyrannical mismanagement.

The quality of instruction at the college had been seriously impaired by the falling fulltime faculty-student population ratio and the dependence on part-time teachers, many who were unqualified and ill-prepared for a college classroom—as well as by questionable administrative and faculty personnel selection practices. Student pop-culture, shopping-center attitudes were nurtured by instructional outsourcing, grade inflation, and administrative hostility toward instructors who attempted to hold the academic line, all of which affected classroom decorum and, therefore, the quality of classroom instruction.

Aristotle thought of institutions as living bodies with the same needs and possibilities as biological organisms. Under the Aristotelian rubric, institutions, like people, are what they do, and what has been done to them. During the '80s BAC was seriously ill and the ramifications of that affliction, as with any serious disease, has been long lasting and debilitating.

* * * * *

Attempting to work out the tangled contractual web the Eckert Board had allowed Wissore to weave, the new board voted to give Wissore 54,488 dollars in leave-pay as part of a severance package. Again, since the Eckert Board had never objected to financing Wissore, and Wissore was on his way out, probably to save face and to show their disapproval of the new board majority, when Wissore's severance package came to a vote, Dintelmann and Eckert voted "Naye."

The board then appointed B.J. Davis as interim president to replace Wissore. Again Dintelmann voted "Naye" and the college moved into 1988 trying to right itself and get back to its educational tasks.

The best thing that can be said about B. J. Davis' eight-month tenure as president is that nothing unusual happened, which gave the faculty time to regroup. As Oscar Wilde remarked, "The first thing to do is to take a stance. The second thing is to figure out what to do next."

During the Eckert Board years Wissore often voiced the equivocation that if someone (anyone) was elected or appointed to a position, he then had the expertise by nature of election or appointment to perform whatever task the power of the position allowed or required him to perform. It doesn't take much insight or intelligence to see the flaws and dishonesty in this assertion—a small twist on the old Soviet Communist Party practice of incarcerating the political opposition in mental hospitals, since anyone who objected to the Communist Party was obviously insane. The right to do something does not always mean people will do the right thing or even a competent thing.

On the other hand, college board-faculty conflicts are natural to the existence of the animal. Because of the financial-oversight role boards play in the educational system, there'll always be tension between school administrations and the faculty. This is not only natural, but in most cases, desirable. Humans do not generally agree, regardless of the issue, important or trivial, nor should they. Seldom do people populating boards of education know anything about education, though most assume that the twelve years or so they spent in the classroom as students, as well as what they see as their assorted personal successes and failures, makes them an authority on education. The faculty struggle in educational institutions is to rid boards of trustees of their usually preconceived assumptions and bring them into the educational process before they seriously damage or destroy the institution. Still, the struggle at BAC and the faculty's attempts to educate the Board of Trustees from 1974 to 1987 was wrought with unusual bitterness and unnecessary conflict.

* * * * *

In preparation for its assault on the faculty, in March of 1975 the BAC Board of Trustees retained the law firm of Seyfarth, Shaw, Fairweather and Geraldson, ostensibly as a professional negotiator. Yet, there may have been more to the hiring. It is of note that Curt Eckert and his brother Vernon had been, for years, populating boards of education of local schools. Vernon had been on the District 201 board in 1965 when the college was still being run by the Belleville High School 201 board.

It is possible that their interest in school boards may have been, in the first instance, altruistic, that of citizens in public service. However, it is also reasonable to think these citizen-servants understood that schools cost money, taxpayers' money, and like many other large landowner-business-men it was to their interests to serve on boards that regulated or at least controlled spending by educational institutions ultimately to reduce a demand for more tax dollars.

Because of their presence on local school boards the Eckerts had more than a passing acquaintance with SS, which billed itself as an edu-cational consultant. By 1974 SS had already infected dozens of Illinois school boards with its particularly virulent brand of anti-education consult-ing practices, the ethics of which, one of the founding members of the firm, Owen Fairweather, actually questioned in a lengthy article, noting that the firm was counseling boards into unnecessary but lucrative (for SS) lawsuits, causing educational tax monies to be spent frivolously and misusing the courts to disrupt educational institutions. Along with Wissore's dismissal and Eckert's resignation, in 1987 the new board severed BAC's ties with Seyfarth Shaw.

Until the last, it appears, however, that the Eckert Board had an underlying true-believer's faith in Wissore, as it did in SS. This was one of the stranger psychological quirks of a misguided governing body. The board hired Wissore. The board literally created him, sanctioned the settling of a chancellor's crown on his head, and then fell to worshiping its creation. "The Chancellor has said . . ." or "We will have to consult with the Chancellor on . . ." were common parlance in board-speak. Other than Elizabeth Jenner and Larry Reinneck, and earlier Ed O'Malley, no one on the Eckert Board questioned what Wissore was doing. This obeisance meant Wissore had only to do the board's bidding or, in the least, indulge its bad judgments, and he was free to do whatever else in whatever way he wanted. Of course, history is replete with people, school board members and others, who have been victimized by their Frankenstein creations.

In hindsight the entire operation could be seen as a gigantic scam. In the end, only one or two fulltime faculty jobs were lost through dismissals, though many of the better faculty simply left for other places and other jobs. On the other hand, when fulltime positions became va-cant, many were not filled, so the number of fulltime faculty was reduced.

Still, the school was never close to insolvency or financial exigency, though the board squandered enormous sums of money on a variety of snake-oil schemes. For whatever thin advice the lawyers of SS gave to save the college money, they carted off hundreds of thousands of dollars. From 1979-83, with SS help, Wissore engineered pay increases of 43.5-percent for his in-group friends, which eventually extended to all fulltime faculty. Of course, administrative salaries are always tied to faculty salaries. So Wissore provided more than that for himself and his administrative hirelings. At least five people in the Wissore administration (Clark, Eskridge, Hines, Tallant, and Wissore) had contracts that called for the school to furnish each of them with a new car.

Likewise, during the Wissore administration, certain in-group faculty, late in their careers, collected substantial extra-contractual salary handouts to pump up the base for their retirement earnings. Some of them received large stipends for nothing more than sitting in the library reading a newspaper for several hours a week. It is interesting that Jack Haskell, an in-group mainstay, retired from BAC in December of 1987, the same month the board reassigned Wissore.

And though the faculty out-group shared in the salary increases, it came at the expense and endangerment of the out-group's teaching and academic lives, and only because the Eckert Board failed to break the bargaining unit. Truthfully, we would have rather spent all of our time teaching. But then, maybe we were teaching a different subject, to indifferent, difficult and reluctant students. After all, the best of politics is a teaching-learning experience, even for college boards and administrators.

Don Libby (1929-1988)

On January 25, 1988, after an extended illness, Don Libby, who had been the leader in BAC reconstituting itself as an institution of higher education, died. He had struggled with advanced emphysema and did not return for the 1988 spring semester. I spoke to him on the phone in the hospital on Thursday, January twenty-second, and in typical Libby fashion, he assured me that he would be home by Saturday. I said I'd give him a few days to rest and would then stop in to see him. He did not make it home Saturday. He died Monday.

Libby often talked about the Stoics, and in dying he was not unlike

Socrates, who Bertrand Russell, in *A History of Western Philosophy* (1945), tells, ". . . was the chief saint of the Stoics throughout their history: his attitude at the time of his trial, his refusal to escape, his calmness in the face of death, and his contention that a perpetrator of injustice injures himself more than his victim . . ."

Remembering my last conversation with Libby, I am also reminded of the Stoic lines from Phillip Larkin's poem, "Aubade."

> Courage is no good:
> It means not scaring others. Being brave
> Lets no one off the grave.
> Death is no different whined at than withstood.

Libby understood this as well as anyone. He knew he was dying and was simply indifferent to the inevitability. It was not withstood, it was ignored. Libby also understood that in the larger scheme of things, BAC-SWIC and its intrigues and nuances wasn't and isn't much, either.

One day in his office he was telling me about the massive heart attack he had suffered twenty years earlier. "If you are ever in this office or come into this office and I am having an attack," he said, "or anything you think might be a heart attack, all you do is leave, quietly, and close the door after you."

Bill Allen, who had crossed over in the 1980 strike, claimed to be the director of ceremonies at Libby's funeral or proposed at least that he was planning a service for Libby, and quite arrogantly informed me that I was scheduled to provide an elegy at the funeral. I declined.

Later, Dave Shanahan (Physics) asked me if I had gone to the funeral, and I said that I had not had the heart to attend a ceremony sponsored by Allen. Funerals are for the living, and I did not know any of Libby's living family or friends. So I did not attend.

"Libby wouldn't have either," Shanahan said.

The image of Libbby that comes to mind most often is of him standing in the hall outside the counseling office talking to someone. Often, he spent his break working the hall, talking to people, faculty, staff, administrators, whoever might be passing. He was enormously curious about people, and an inveterate, though not vicious, gossip.

Maybe as good a portrayal of Libby, as an example of who he was, can be drawn from his dealings with students who were sometimes financially unable to continue in school. Often students who were prepared to drop out of school would come to see a counselor, as they were instructed to do, and some would end up in Libby's office. Naturally enough, along with other inquiries about their decision to leave school, he would ask why they were dropping out, and during the discussion, when the answer centered on something like, "I can't pay the rent and pay tuition too," or "I have medical bills and can't afford books," Libby would ask, "How much do you need to stay in school?"

Invariably the reply would be, "I don't know—maybe four or five hundred dollars." Normally he carried with him several hundred dollars in cash, and if he judged the deficiency to be legitimate, he would reach into his pocket and lay whatever dollars on the table. "Pay the bills, but stay in school," he would say, "and come back and see me at the end of the semester. This is not a loan. You don't owe me a thing."

Sometime after the 1980 strike I asked him why he led the strike. Sounding a bit like George Mallory, who, when asked why he wanted to climb Everest, looked up the slopes toward the summit and answered, "Because it's there." Libby replied, "To see if I could still do it."

Unfortunately, Libby did not live to see the improvements he fought so hard to bring to the college. He was fifty-nine when he died.

Forty-three days later, March 8, 1988, Curt Eckert died.

Joseph Cipfl, President

During BAC's first twelve years (1966-78) there was one board resignation, and that came only four months after the first board election in December of 1966. In April of 1967 Fred R. Schroder resigned, and the board appointed Donald Tedesco to fill Schroder's seat. Tedesco then, with the benefit of the publicity of the position and the advantages of an incumbent, ran successfully in the next election for the seat Schroder had vacated and to which he (Tedesco) had been appointed.

Within the next twelve years (1978-90) there were seven board resignations and seven more appointments. In all cases, as allowed by law, in a self-perpetuating process circumventing the democratic elect-oral mandate that the boards claim as their hallmark, the BAC board always chose someone who agreed with the current board majority. Several times the resignation and appointment took place only a few months before the resigning board member's term expired.

In September of 1979 board member Robert Harris resigned, very nearly six months to the day before the next board election, and Avery Schermer, a close friend of Curt Eckert, was appointed. Schermer ran in the April 1980 election and won.

In March of 1985, eight months before the next board election, which I imagine Ken Fish was not interested in entering, Fish resigned. At the same meeting, the board hired Fish's wife and appointed James Vest to fill Fish's seat, which would suggest that there was a good bit of planning about how and when board members not seeking re-election should vacate their board seat. The resignation probably came that early, as in the Harris-Schermer case, to give the appointee time to gain name recognition. Vest ran in the November 1985 election, but in the heavily unfavorable referendum vote, lost to Francis Braswell.

In May of 1986 Patricia Bartsokas resigned from the BAC board and Leo Konzen was appointed to the board in June. The next election wasn't until November of 1987, though Konzen did not run. There is the strong likelihood that Bartsokas resigned under duress. The grapevine had it that she had become seriously disillusioned with Wissore, and with Eckert (and possibly with their mistreatment of Jenner), so her departure not only came earlier than it might otherwise have but was not planned by the Eckert Board. Also, by the end of 1987 the Eckert Board had fallen into disarray, which may have discouraged Konzen, though Konzen, a lawyer, never appeared to fit in very well with the Eckert menagerie. Still, it did not discourage the early resignation-appointment practice as a board habit— though when Eckert resigned from the board in December of 1987, for the first time (since the Schroder resignation), there seems not to have been any board collusion or a board attempt to politically manipulate the resignation. The Jenner-Farmer-Reinneck-Wolford board, to give proper consideration to the new candidate, waited until February to appoint Van Smith to the vacated seat.

It is possible that our contacts with the Democratic Party in St. Clair, Madison, and Randolph Counties, beginning with a meeting with Belleville lawyer Bruce Cook (trustee Elizabeth Jenner's lawyer in the 1985 refer- endum skirmish), as well as the meeting with the St. Clair County Demo- cratic precinct committeemen in Caseyville to solicit help in the Gerfen- Hunsaker campaign, had encouraged the persuasive, invisible hand of the St. Clair and Madison Counties' Democratic Party. Then, too, there was my letter to St. Clair County Democratic boss Francis Touchette, the Eckert Board's mistreatment of longtime Democrat trustee Edward O'Malley, and the preposterous and ill-fated 1985 referendum.

Anyway, in the spring of 1988 scuttlebutt had it that Joe Cipfl (a Democrat) would be the next president of BAC. This news came as a surprise since Cipfl's name had not been on the search committee's list. When AAUP- IFT President Leo Welch questioned the wisdom of hiring a grade school superintendent as president of a college, the phone started ringing with select members of the St. Clair County Democratic Party on the other end suggesting that it was in the union's best interests to have someone like Cipfl run the college. Bruce Cook had told us that day in his office, "When you get in bed with us, you don't get out." But at least, for the moment, we were no longer trying to get out from under what had previously crawled into bed with us.

In July of 1988 the board hired Joe Cipfl as president of the college, and it is accurate to say there was a good bit of faculty trepidation over the announcement. To tell the truth we didn't know what to expect, though optimistically it didn't appear that he could be any worse than Wissore. Any- way, when Cipfl came in most of the administrative silliness subsided—

though not all of it. Immediately the board and administration became more accountable and transparent, and the faculty became more visible. Among other things, the minutes of board meetings suddenly increased from a few pages recording unanimous votes of agenda items to pages of detailed announcements, discussions, and considerations of issues before the board.

By October 1988 Cipfl had found 1,034,000 dollars more for the college: 741,000 dollars via legislative allocation, 23,000 dollars from increaseed enrollment, and 270,000 dollars by cutting administrative salaries. In 1972 BAC had 75 fulltime faculty, 13 administrators, and 4,000 students. In 1989 there were 111 fulltime faculty, 89 administrators, and 16,000 students. Cipfl probably could have made additional administrative cuts without in any way hampering the functioning of the school.

With Cipfl's arrival the political climate within the college shifted dramatically and with it so did faculty access to the board and college management. Not infrequently those left from the Wissore regime complained that Cipfl exercised too much control and would not let them do their jobs. What they might have seen as "their jobs," I do not know. More than likely their complaints had to do with Cipfl's attempts to keep administrators out of faculty business.

However, the folly of Eckert Board hoarding and squandering had seriously impoverished the school. The main campus physical infra- structure had been neglected and was in serious decay. Traditional academic practices such as sabbaticals and travel had been curtailed or eliminated, and faculty morale was perilously low. It would take some time to correct these problems, when and where they were correctable.

Then, when matters seemed to be improving, the September of 1989 board meeting provided a double misfortune for the college. Dan Wolford who had been instrumental in removing Eckert from the board and Wissore from the administration, resigned his board seat, and Lynn Suydam was hired as the new vice president for instruction.

Wolford's resignation was possibly the only legitimate board resignation after Schroder's in 1967. Wolford, who had run for the first BAC board in 1966 and lost, then ran again in 1987, successfully, to join a new board in scrubbing the Eckert-Wissore fiasco, departed the BAC trustees to run for the Belleville High School District 201 board. In parting Wolford said, "I want to commend the faculty for their steadfastness in believing in BAC, [and] always giving it their best. Also for giving of their time and their knowledge in helping the Board of Trustees, [and] bringing about harmony and cooperation for a better learning environment for the students of BAC."

At the same meeting Cipfl announced that a North Central Association (NCA) report showed faculty-administrative communication had improved from 34-percent in 1987 to 75-percent in 1989. A survey conducted by AFT Local 4183 President Welch and Vice President Massey showed faculty satisfaction with the administration had gone from 25-percent in 1987 to

78-percent in 1989. I would imagine the 25-percent faculty approval rating of the Wissore administration in 1987, after thirteen years of the Eckert regime, could again be attributed to urdummheit—though the communications report was positive, losing board member Dan Wolford was unfortunate.

Sam Wolf for Sam Wolf

A month later, in October 1989, Don Theobold was appointed to Wolford's seat, and in November, the only remaining member of the Eckert Board, Robert Dintelmann, resigned, and Janet McReynolds was appointed.

The following February (1990) Van Smith, who had been taken Eckert's board seat in February of 1980, resigned. To its credit the board instituted a random selection procedure which led to the appointment of Robert Maxwell. But by then three board members held seats gained in a process that disenfranchised the citizens of the district. In 1990 the BAC board was comprised of three members who had been appointed rather than elected. And because a quorum requires only a majority of the board to be present and then only a simple majority of those present to affirm matters before the board, it was not only possible, but more than likely, that there could have been a 3-1 or even 4-0 vote with three *appointed* members advancing items that were meant to be weighed and implemented by a plurality of *elected* officials.

I have to believe Cipfl engineered the random selection procedure the board used in 1990. The lesson, however, if there was a lesson in it, was sorely learned. To my knowledge, the practice was not used again. In 1995, Maxwell, who came onto the board as a result of the random selection procedure, resigned and literally chose his successor. True to the best of despotic, autocratic traditions, Maxwell handpicked Sam Wolf, a former state representative from Granite City or maybe Sam Wolf selected himself and got Maxwell to announce it for him. However, it was, Wolf always claimed to be a champion of democracy and equal representation—if it was Sam Wolf being represented. When Maxwell selected Wolf to be his trustee-heir, Wolf accepted.

* * * * *

In 1988 prior to being appointed to the BAC board, under the guise of providing better representation for the constituents of BAC District 522, Wolf engineered an election-restructuring plan for the college. In November of that year a referendum to divide the BAC district into seven sub-districts passed 57,710 to 53,223, mandating that each district elect a board member in the 1991 election. Until then the board had been elected at large, with voters, district-wide, voting for all of the seats up for election any given year.

Following the redistricting referendum, at the first board election in 1991, each of the sub-districts would elect only one person from that district.

Later, Wolf led a campaign to change the Belleville Area College's name to a generic Southwestern Illinois College because, "The name, Belleville Area College did not represent all of the people of the district." Then adding name-change to name-change, Wolf had the SWIC Granite City campus named Sam Wolf Campus—to represent "all the people?" It seems Sam had a way with names and representation, especially if they represented Sam Wolf.

In some ways the school was lucky the board agreed to Wolf's renaming scheme. At the same time Ted Farmer wanted to sell the college's name to bidding corporations, with bidding to start at 1.5 million dollars. So, the school could have just as easily ended up State Farm Insurance College or maybe Regions Bank Certificate of Deposit Institute. As a rather unfortunate remnant of the "name for sale" project, the college does have a room named after Amiel Cueto, a former lawyer and convicted felon who, before his conviction and disbarment secured his name to the room with a donation to the college.

Of course, it is debatable whether redistricting provided better representation. Now the largest city in District 522, Belleville can no longer, to the exclusion of other areas of District 522, elect four or five board members—although I'm not certain that had ever happened. Even the Eckert Board featured members from Mascoutah, Sparta and Granite City.

The restructuring was, however, more political than practical. Under the original organization the District 522 Board represented the far reaches of the district pretty well. The board had expanded the college to campuses in Granite City on the north and in Red Bud on the south, as well as providing dozens of classes at satellite facilities in many of the small towns throughout the district.

In most political senses, however, the redistricting has been regressive. Beyond providing more fragmented and isolated representation, it has encouraged the board to partisan politics. How board members behave has to do with how representation is defined. Instead of all board members focusing primarily on the college which formerly they all represented to all the people of District 522, after redistricting, since they are no longer defined in a general way by the college district but more specifically by their geographical areas within the bigger district, SWIC now has a house of representatives rather than a board—a house of individual representatives more focused on their individual districts than on the overall school district.

As representatives of their domains, board members became interested in promoting programs and expending college funds in their individual districts. Sometimes this is done at the expense of what is best for the college, and therefore at the expense of education. In other words, with the sub-district realignment good representation has come to mean bringing home the "pork." And as long as it looks like you're getting your fair share of the fat, all is well.

An example of the "sub-district-think" model of representation surfaced the night the board was to decide what to do with the aviation program. Board member Mark Levy, a Collinsville lawyer, showed up with three of his PR people and a stack of posters and visual aids to lobby the board for developing the Troy, Illinois airport to house the BAC aviation program. Renovating the airport would have required an extraordinary and unnecessary expenditure of school funds. That it did not come up on the agenda that night and Levy and his people did not have a chance to run their dog-and-pony show did little to apologize Levy's attempt to dip into the pork-barrel and expend education funds in a highly questionable enterprise—to the benefit of his sub-district.

* * * * *

By 1989 the BAC Faculty Senate was little more than an echo in the hall, although Christeck had made a substantial effort to revive it as a debating-advising council. Senate minutes from January 12, 1989 show "Roger Christeck presented a proposal for change and rationale for the Senate's consideration. He wrote a first draft of a proposal (for a) constitution for an organization he calls the 'Faculty Governance Congress.' This constitution and organization would replace the existing faculty governance structure of the Faculty Senate. Copies of Mr. Christeck's written remarks and constitution are available for inspection for any interested faculty member by contacting Ed Brady."

A year earlier Christeck had rewritten and then seen through the fine-tuning and put the finishing touches on the BAC AAUP-AFT Local 4183 constitution. And although there remained a good bit of sentiment among the faculty for the senate, and there were those who believed the senate might regain something of its authority, within a year, by January of 1990, the senate was no more.

The Faculty Senate had been instituted in 1967 with a great deal of hope and energy as the faculty body directly responsible for shared governance at the college. It had been established as a board advisory committee and each year its officers and members were sanctioned by a board vote. But when the board lost interest in the senate's advice and, therefore in its existence, the senate was out of business. The union, on the other hand, was independent of the board and with the 1984 collective bargaining law the board had no choice but to deal with the union. By 1990, not only had the circumstances and laws governing college faculties in Illinois changed significantly, but so had BAC faculty attitudes and capabilities.

The Academic Factory

> All who have meditated on the art of gov-
> erning mankind have been convinced that
> the fate of empires depends on the educa-
> tion of youth.
>
> —Aristotle

Less Than Admirable Attributes

There were problems created by the ongoing corporatization of the college, problems that did not fall under the general rubric of working conditions and so were beyond the scope of collective bargaining and union purview. While some of the difficulties came as a direct result of board and administrative action, others appeared in the wake of administrative nonfeasance turned sometimes to malfeasance.

When I arrived at BAC in 1972, R. Wayne Clark was the vice president of instruction. During the Wissore years, unlike many of the administrators who left the school rather than support Wissore's corporate operations, Clark stayed on as an in-grouper. Several years before the end of the Eckert Board, when Wissore anointed himself chancellor, Clark moved up to president and Frank Gornick became vice president for instruction (VPI). When Gornick bailed out for a job in California, Rita Heberer, another of Wissore's in-group, took over the vice president's office.

When Cipfl became president of the college—he was hired as president and immediately abolished the title of chancellor—we pretty well knew Clark and Heberer were on their way out. However, what we didn't know was who would be the new vice president for instruction and while waiting for Cipfl to hire a new VPI, the faculty was anxious, but also hopeful.

One of Joe Cipfl's failings as president of the college, if it was a failing, was that he spent a good bit of time representing the school and in some ways the faculty, to the outside world, and left the operations at BAC to the underlings in his administration. As far as the faculty was concerned, since the VPI directed academic affairs, the vice-president for instruction office was as important as the office of the president. And though Cipfl did look outside the college for candidates, in September of 1989, in one of his major mistakes, he hired Lynn Suydam as vice president for instruction.

Lynn Suydam came from New York, did not like unions, and was basically an anti-faculty administrator. Shortly after he arrived, he picked up where Wissore had left off and predictably those subject to his abuse were union officers or members of the union negotiating team, as well as women.

In retrospect it seems that in choosing Suydam, Cipfl, who was well connected with the Democratic Party in the BAC district, wanted someone who would not be a serious threat to his own position, as say Wissore had been to Keel's. He wanted someone who really didn't have the capabilities and/or political connections to threaten the throne and who, if it became necessary, could be discarded without consideration. Of course, these were less than admirable attributes to qualify someone for an upper-level postsecondary-education administrative position.

Anyway, Suydam showed up at BAC armed with the belief that collective bargaining had no place in a college or in any other school for that matter, and the best way to ingratiate himself with the board and the president, would be to attack the union. In fact, when he arrived at BAC, the first thing he did, almost as a reflex reaction, was to go after members of the negotiating team, one at a time. His attacks on school personnel and union faculty were so aggressive that on several occasions the confrontation came within a breath of turning into a fistfight—with real fists. Moreover, as Wissore had done, Suydam hired people who would help him with his broadsides on the faculty.

One among many of the sleazier practices of administrators nationwide is to solicit complaints from students about faculty. In many cases students are advised that if they have trouble with a specific teacher, they should report it to the dean. Too often *trouble with a teacher* is nothing more than a teacher prodding an indolent student to do the work assigned.

On several occasions, using this rubric, students attempted to blackmail me for a grade, warning that if I did not acquiesce to their demands, they would go to Suydam, and he would help them. I responded by telling them that if they had Suydam's help, they certainly didn't need anything more from me. Several times these threats were accompanied by phone calls, in each case from a woman claiming to be the student's mother, screaming and calling me filthy names, while citing Suydam's kindness and willingness to support her progeny's demand.

Several times I ended up in Suydam's office in a confrontation with him about a grade I had assigned. I had taught at BAC from the fall of 1972 until the fall of 1989 without any complaints. Then suddenly within a matter of several months there were three student complaints about my teaching. A nineteen-year-old telecourse student sent an older friend or an aunt or possibly her grandmother to take the mid-term for her. When I discovered the deception, I objected, and the student filed a complaint. I ended up in Suydam's office, facing the girl, her father, her mother (but not the aunt or grandmother or friend who took the exam), and Suydam. For two hours I had to listen to Suydam berate me for bad teaching practices and insensitivity to student needs.

A month later, a student who received a C on the first test in one of my logic classes filed a complaint suggesting that I did not know what I was teaching. He told me in class one day that my instructional material was nonsense and that I should rewrite the syllabus. I reminded him that he had the possibility of getting a bachelor's and master's degree, finding a college teaching position and then writing a syllabus according to his liking. He filed a complaint, and I ended up in Suydam's office.

The same month another student I had failed for not doing the assigned work and missing a month of class filed a complaint, and I ended up in Suydam's office.

It is notable that I was not approached by the department head or the liberal arts dean, but in all cases by Suydam personally.

When I refused to change the student's grade in one of the cases, as Suydam demanded, he sent me a memo stating that "Your perspective is narrow and one-sided, almost to the point of ridiculousness . . . (and) this behavior must be corrected, or additional action will be necessary." The only thing to which he could have been referring was my refusal to assign "good grades" to students who did not do the work and/or did not come to class.

As I departed one inquisition, I remarked that these kinds of things (his attacks on faculty) were destroying the educational viability of the college. He replied that it was just one of the problems that go with being a teacher. I responded that "Teaching is not the problem, you're the problem." After another encounter he told Leo Welch, "Lanter is on report, he had better watch himself." I suspect he thought he might be the commandant of an internment camp of some kind or some other such nonsense.

As it was, I never changed the grade, and he never filed an insubordination charge against me. He probably understood that he would not have had much luck with the fight that was sure to follow, although it was rumored that eventually *he* changed the grade.

Still, his attacks were pronounced enough that I thought it prudent to install a voice-activated tape-recorder in my office and no longer meet with students in my office. Whenever individual consultations were necessary, I would meet students in one of the lounge areas in the hall outside the English office complex. Of course, I wasn't the only faculty member being Suydamized. At least once Suydam was taken to the Illinois Educational Labor Relations Board by the union on an unfair labor practice.

Otherwise, he was noisy, evasive, and mostly unintelligible. One day a teacher from a local high school told me that "Your (BAC's) vice president for instruction spoke at our school today." I asked what Suydam had to say, and the teacher smiled and said, "Well, he talked for almost two hours, and honest to God, no one has the slightest idea what he was talking about."

Another night at a board meeting, when questioned by a not-too-friendly board member about why he had summarily shut down the aviation maintenance program, Suydam went into an incoherent, scrambled verbal ramble, making no sense whatsoever, for a good ten minutes before Cipfl finally and literally told him to shut up. The BAC faculty referred to his office as "the black hole." Whatever went in, memos, letters, phone calls, it didn't much matter—nothing came out.

There is little the union can do about an administrator hassling faculty. As one judge said, there is nothing that can be put into writing, in contract, or in law that will make people get along with one another.

Besides hassling faculty and generally making a nuisance of himself, Suydam did little to advance the academic quality of the school, and although he was constantly at odds with the faculty union, he seldom had anything to show for his belligerence.

There's an adage about administrators—that no matter what he/she has done, if he is looking for another job, when asked, be sure to give a good recommendation. Maybe the misanthrope will be hired elsewhere, and you will be relieved of that particular pestilence. Then, of course, you will get another, who is worse than the one that just left. But if asked, when the time comes, also give the new one a good recommendation. Remember, not all administrators are malefactors. It's just the 99-percent that give the others a bad name.

When it came time, given a plethora of good recommendations, Suydam left SWIC and was duly appointed President of Meramec in the St. Louis Community College system, where, I am told, shortly, in a hassle with the faculty over tenured-teacher evaluation, he collected a faculty no-confidence vote. No doubt he moved on from there, with additional and better recommendations, the best of which would always be that he was again prepared to move on. To paraphrase Shakespeare, nothing so promoted the value of his office as his taking leave of it.

The Right People on the Job

Following Cipfl's appointment (1989), in the next round of talks for a new contract, Cipfl led the board team. Reinneck was board president at the time and probably wanted Cipfl to handle negotiations, as earlier he had wanted Wissore to head the board's team. In special board sessions, in contradistinction to the Seyfarth Shaw idea that there could be admin-istration practices about which an administration might not want to inform its board, Cipfl had already provided the board with a series of tenets or principles delineating his administration's transparency and duties, as he saw them–so he probably wanted the job.

Jim Massey chaired the faculty negotiating team that year. Massey and Libby were two of the best negotiators I ever worked with. Massey started negotiating faculty contracts his first year at BAC in 1972, when he was still not tenured. In those days, negotiations could occasionally have the ear-marks of a gentlemen's discussion that might take place in a personal meet-ing between the chairman of the board and the faculty chief negotiator. Reminiscent of old Belleville high school days, Massey remembers one year putting together more than half of the BAC contract for the following year in a single evening at a party at Bill Keel's house, as he said, sitting on the top step of the stairs talking with then board chairman Ted Gundlach.

In addition to his work of several years as chief negotiator, Massey served as IFT Local 4381 Vice President and, as Welch did, represented the union to the community beyond the school. He served as Vice President for Legislative and Governing Board Affairs on the Community College Faculty Association. He was a member of the Coalition for Preservation of the Nurses Practice Act 1986, and Chairman of the Faculty Advisory Committee of the Illinois Board of Higher Education 1979-80. He served as Vice President for the Illinois State Conference of the AAUP and on the national AAUP Committee V on community colleges.

Besides having a very good sense in negotiations of what the other side was thinking, Massey had an offbeat, disarming, and effectively humorous demeanor. In 1989 union President Welch was on the negotiating team, I was there, as was Jenna Johannpeter, a business professor from Granite City, Gene Brandt from Social Sciences, and Mike Schneider. I think Jim McGowen from the business department might have been there, too.

Negotiations were unusual that year in that Cipfl came to the table with a problem the board had given him. It seems that of the thirty-nine community colleges in Illinois, the fulltime faculty at BAC was, if not the best compensated for summer school teaching, then at least making more money than the BAC board thought it should make teaching summer school classes. It is sometimes hard to understand how conventional, conformist, and regressive boards of education are. They refuse to step out of the box—in public at least—insisting, regardless, that no matter what, everything about the school be average—while continuing to claim their particular school is the best in the state, and sometimes in the country.

In this instance the board wanted to limit the fulltime faculty earnings for teaching summer school—not necessarily the teaching, but the earnings. It seemed not to matter to the board that BAC, as one of the larger community colleges in Illinois, had a huge summer school class schedule or that the BAC faculty's regular-school-year compensation had only recently caught up with the local high schools, and was still well below the average for community colleges in Illinois. Instead of utilizing the traditional nine month, two-semester schedule with summers off, because of inferior wages, as a matter of survival many of the BAC fulltime faculty taught summer school. And this provided faculty summer school compensation beyond what the board thought it should be.

Hoping to accommodate his bosses, Cipfl showed up at the table that spring with the conundrum of wanting to reduce summer school compensation (the board's command) without cutting into the salaries (Cipfl's plan) for fulltime faculty, generally. Since not everyone on the fulltime faculty taught summer school, a limit to summer school teaching loads would reduce the income of the hardest working part of the faculty. Unlike most administrators, Cipfl believed in proper compensation for faculty. In his un-Wissorian thinking, he did not find it acceptable to penalize the hardest working members of the faculty—or anyone else for that matter.

Once, when he complained to me about the school's limited financial condition, and that the union could not expect a salary increase, I offered to negotiate a 5-percent reduction in salary for the faculty for the coming year, if he would do the same with the administration. He just looked the other way and didn't bother commenting on my suggestion. I don't think I could have gotten that one past anybody—maybe that's why he ignored me. But then you never know.

For a week or so the negotiating teams kicked around ideas about how to revise summer school compensation, with the administration demanding that it be allowed to devise the formula or the prospectus by which we might proceed. Several times the board team came back with proposals, none of which would bring salaries in line with the board's demands without penalizing the summer school full-time faculty, as that faculty had been constituted generally and was likely to continue to be constituted in the future.

And this wasn't malevolence. The board-team seemed truly interested in making it work. It's just that they kept losing their way among the ticket of variables the problem presented. Finally, after several weeks of discussing the administrative team's proposals, Jenna Johannpeter showed up at the table with a formula she had worked out to move summer school money onto the base salary of the fulltime faculty who regularly taught summer school without penalizing those who did not usually teach summer school. With the Johannpeter formula summer school money was to be moved onto the base salary, so all fulltime faculty members would get raises. However, for those who had worked more during the summer in the past, and who were likely to teach during the summer in the future, if the classes materialized, the raise was a little better. But from that time on, summer school classes would not be as financially attractive as they had been. Voila! To get the job done, you simply have to have the right people.

Ironically the board members got what they wanted, a reduced summer payload, but thought that in the process Cipfl had misrepresented them. Possibly, rather than merely shifting compensation from summer school to the fulltime base teaching salary, they intended for faculty salaries to be reduced across the board and at the same time for summer school to be off limits to fulltime faculty.

I might add here that in most of what he did Cipfl seemed to be operating in the more traditional role of college and university presidents who often see themselves as emissaries or ambassadors for the faculty, both to the institution's trustees and more generally, in state schools, to the funding powers in government.

In some very real ways Joc Cipfl fit the old academic model. When he became president, in the series of quasi-philosophical documents I mentioned before, he characterized himself as go-between or moderator for the board and faculty. Likewise, he invited faculty to participate in board committee decisions and on a regular basis represented the faculty to the board with special announcements and recognitions. This representation, I believe, was sincere.

By 1989, with the advancing corporatization of postsecondary education, the role of college and university presidents in the United States had changed dramatically. Then as today, on a regular basis, defunct and deposed corporate CEOs and castoff military personnel were injected into the office of the president at many colleges and universities. Of course, on occasion, the recycled managers brought with them funds from advertising budgets of corporations to endow academic chairs (faculty positions) tagged with a corporate logo. Chairs in the humanities and sciences were (are) granted to professor so-and-so, making her the Apex Dog Chow Professor of Literature or the Mixed-Mint Mouthwash Professor of Biology.

Quite naturally, as public colleges and universities turned to the corporate world for funding, they fell more and more under the influence of privatization and non-academic control. People like John Templeton of Templeton Mutual Funds offered (and still offers?) professors tens-of-thousands of dollars a semester to include his (Templeton's) formula for success (corporate access and management, and therefore wealth) in all sorts of college and university classes. As one might imagine or expect, many of the business-family funds or grants given to colleges and universities, also have a not-too-subtle religious flavor to them. And then there's always Bill Gates.

At any rate, in 1989 the negotiating teams met in the farm house on the northeast corner of the BAC campus, a small dwelling that had been gutted and renovated by the college to serve for conferences and meetings. The farm house had only a single large room, so when one side called a caucus, the other would step out until the caucus ended. If the weather was inclement, it meant you wanted to call as many caucuses as possible as quickly as possible and keep the other side out in the rain or wind or whatever there was that might afflict them. Of course, you didn't want to keep them out too long, lest they become unreasonable or just plain quit and go home, and you would have wasted a whole day.

The board priorities for negotiations that year, as outlined by the Board Personnel and Negotiations Committee and recorded in Board Executive Session minutes were for: (1) a three-year contract; (2) to restructure the fulltime faculty compensation (get rid of the two tiered pay-scale); (3) provide more equity in the fulltime and part-time faculty compensation; (4) accelerate retirement of older faculty; (5) control medical insurance; (6) phase in medical compensation over three years; and (7) conduct negotiations in a collaborative, problem solving mode, rather than in an adversarial mode.

We did not know any of this at time of negotiations, and had our own priorities, though I think now that while our priorities were more specific, the 1989 board, with Cipfl's guidance, had read the faculty, the school's needs, and the times well.

Naturally, there were long hours of haggling, and on occasion a comic episode or two. One day we were at variance over some rather monumental (I would like to think) point, say Item #7, whatever it might have been, when Cipfl called a caucus. We picked up our notes and headed out to wait in what was a warm, pleasant spring day. For fifteen minutes, and probably longer than that, we milled around (there were no chairs or benches), chatting and waiting, until eventually Cipfl came to the door to announce that the caucus had ended and we could return to the table.

"We can't come in," Massey said.

Cipfl looked a bit puzzled, probably certain we were, as Twain said, "contemplating an outrage."

"Why not?" he said.

"Well," Massey said, "Leo (Welch) is in a tree and won't come down. We can't get him out of the tree. And we can't go on without him."

For a moment Cipfl stared at Massey, as if he had lost his marbles. Then he walked to the end of the building and peered around the corner, and sure enough, there was Welch perched Gandhi-like in a tree.

At this point I'm not sure what Cipfl thought. He had been over at Belleville District 118 with the grammar school innocent-and-unsuspecting, and this was surely different. This was big league negotiating with college professors, something he had not experienced.

One morning, some months earlier, Massey had descended from the chemistry lab draped in his white lab-frock with a flask of liquid nitrogen, and without an appointment or announcing his presence, stalked into the president's suite, past the protests of Cipfl's secretary whining, "You can't go in there." Without so much as a knock Massey pushed open the door to the office and emptied the flask onto Cipfl's desk, turning the surface into a popping, fizzing, steaming display that made a great deal of noise but quickly evaporated into nothing.

By now Cipfl had retreated with his back pressed to the wall, gasping and white-faced. Without more Massey turned and exited, and on his way out reminded Cipfl that he ". . . should not fuck with chemists or union negotiators."

Now Welch was in a tree and refused to come down. Maybe Cipfl thought he had wandered into a zoo of loonies. Maybe these were dangerous men. Maybe this is what happens to good minds having had to deal for too long with people like Eckert and Wissore.

I'm sure Cipfl had heard of Welch's proclivity for sitting in trees, dating to a biological expedition to Columbia when Welch and a couple friends, trouping the rain forest, came onto a pack of wild peccary and decided, just for the hell of it, to spook the animals. However, the peccary did not take kindly to being spooked, and after a short run, turned what was supposed to be a rout into a reverse charge, sending their tormentors scrambling into trees for safety—where they remained for the better part of two days, until the peccary, somewhat avenged and assuaged, but still disgruntled, wandered off to other things.

Now Welch was again in a tree.

"Leo, you can come down," Massey said.

"I'm not coming down," Welch said, "not until we get Item #7."

I'm not sure how we got Welch out of the tree. I'd like to think Cipfl saw the good reasoning in our demand and strategy and simply said, "All right, all right, I'll give you Item #7, if you'll only come down from the tree"—but then, again, maybe he didn't.

Ted Farmer Takes on the Board

Besides aiding in the defeat of the 1985 referendum, the Wissore-Farmer debate sponsored by League of Women Voters, provided insurance agent Ted Farmer a public notoriety he would not have otherwise had. In the November 1987 election he parlayed his newly found celebrity into a seat on the BAC board and immediately set out to change the college administration. As noted, at the first board meeting (December 9, 1987), he advised Wissore to resign and quarreled with Wissore over the Granite City Steel apprenticeship program. Then at a special board meeting, December 12, 1987, he voted with Jenner, Reinneck, and Wolford to remove Wissore, which he had promised to do, and which we certainly hoped he would do.

And although Ted Farmer had been instrumental in removing Wissore from the college administration and replacing him with Joe Cipfl, I'm not sure Farmer was that much in favor of hiring Cipfl or approved of anything else the board did after that.

While Farmer's initial outspoken activities on the board were a positive first step, they were also a portent of his future activities, some thought-out and positive, and some not-so-positive. After bringing a substantial measure of relief to the school by aiding the dissolution of the Eckert Board, as a board member, he became nearly as menacing as those he had helped remove. As it turned out, his complaints weren't just with the Eckert Board and Wissore administration, but with nearly everything the board, the administration, and the faculty did that did not conform to his belief of the moment. Beyond his initial assault on existing policy, enquiries that were well-directed, and his later confrontations with other board members that were well-founded, he was, all in all, a loose cannon.

An insurance agent by trade, Farmer came onto the board flaunting a self-acclaimed expertise about insurance matters and set out independently, and in violation of board policy, to choose the college's insurance carrier. The board sought to sidestep his attempts, but by May of 1988 his demands to run the school from his single board position had advanced so significantly that Larry Reinneck, board president, had to reprimand him "for usurping administrative jobs."

A year later, in March of 1989, when professor Dan Lowery (Art) requested a sabbatical, ignoring protocol entirely, Farmer and R. Wayne Clark, the vice president for instruction (left over from the Wissore administration), called Lowery in for a lengthy and abusive interrogation. Farmer thought study-leaves were a waste of money and hoped to dissuade the faculty from applying for future sabbaticals. He described the inquisition as academic fact-finding. It was, however, a bit of faculty brow-beating oversight for which Farmer was not elected, Clark not hired, and for which neither Farmer nor Clark had any competence.

Board members are not elected to act alone or as policemen or private investigators in the school. The fiat provided by the electorate is that board members operate in concert as a board. So once again, only with Farmer leading the charge this time, we were back to the board and administration treating faculty members as if they were hired-help.

During the spring of 1990 the board appointed a committee to review and update board policy. At the July meeting the committee presented a list of Items for first reading. As a reflexive action Farmer objected to Item #3004–Equal Employment Opportunity and Item #3016–Access to Personnel Files.

In the case of Item #3004-Equal Employment Opportunity, as in so many other cases they were not, Farmer's objections appeared to be justified. Item #3004 failed to distinguish the criterion for employment or placement of personnel in positions that required little or no education or skills with the rules for placement of personnel in positions that require specialized education or training.

Affirmative action, even in law, is not an absolute, and legally cannot be used any more than any other law, say the First Amendment right to freedom of speech, to provide or create dangerous or damaging ends. Clearly, affirmative action should not apply to academic appointments.

But while Farmer's objection to the board's proposed hiring policies was legitimate, his concern about Item #3016 was not nearly as sanguine or well-founded. Item #3016 intended to formalize the board's access to personnel files, making it a board rather than a board-member prerogative. To this Farmer objected. Simply put, he wanted the privliege of inspecting personnel files. He wanted to replace the requirement that the board act as-a-whole with that of individual board members acting privately.

Reinneck, as chairman, quite concisely, pointed out to Farmer that because personnel matters must be addressed in executive session, and then with the board acting one, board members could not individually at other times inspect personnel files.

Faculty Ethics & SCC

Beyond Farmer's complaints, there were other items in the board policy package under review that adversely affected the faculty. One, an article for faculty ethics, had been retrieved from the College of DuPage by Director of Human Resources, Larry Friederich, and was, to say the least, anti-union and anti-faculty. The imported ethics proposal would have given the board (and therefore the administration) the power to set whatever standards it wished or deemed expedient to be called ethical and used on the faculty for further academic cleansing. The plan to impose arbitrary ethical standards on the faculty was more than likely an overkill extension following the federal mandate to oversee research activity or laboratory experiments with human subjects.

In 1974 the federal government passed the National Research Act, a follow-up to the Nuremberg Code (1948), Kefauver Amendments (1962), Declaration of Helsinki (1964), and a precursor of the Belmont Report (1979) to set ethical standards for biomedical and behavioral research. By 1981 the Department of Health and Human Services (DHS) and the Federal Drug Administration (FDA) had issued regulations based on the Belmont Report. In 1991 the DHS regulations were formally adopted by many U.S. federal agencies.

Shortly thereafter, research institutions using federal funds were required to set up Institutional Review Boards (IRB) to oversee research projects and make certain that DHS guidelines were followed. While the regulations related to using human subjects for scientific research with federal funds set aside social-science classroom situations, there are heavy implications that the regulations could be easily modified to include class-room teaching. And although community colleges are not research institu-tions, in typical overkill fashion, often to placate religious community groups, under the pretense of "averting liability," community college admin-istrators across the county set out to establish ethical guidelines for their faculties.

Most of the ethics rules proposed by the board had to do with faculty activities beyond the classroom, so when "Ethics for BAC Teachers" surfaced, the union had to address the threat. In "BAC–AAUP-AFT 1965-96, Thirty Years Dedicated to Improving the Teaching Profession–Board Pol-icies," faculty members Marvin Braasch and Leo Welch write, "One of the more important debates (in 1990) involved the topic of faculty ethics. The board had already had a draft statement on ethics which the faculty representatives rejected. A fundamental concept was in jeopardy. The board held that it had the right to set ethical standards for the faculty. The faculty held that all professionals, such as lawyers and doctors, set their own standards for ethical conduct."

The impetus for the ethics mandate came also from the ICCB. The

ICCB had recently notified the BAC board that its policies were outdated. It appears that the ICCB pressure for a new policy position on teachers' ethics was generated by Gary Davis, the then chairman of the ICCTA. Davis had a degree in religion and was executive director of the ICCTA from 1986 until 2004. Additionally, he provided retreats for college CEOs, a pastoral counseling service, and listed a resume populated with corporate and lobbying connections. The ICCTA has a Gary Davis Ethical Leadership Award which it bestows annually.

Davis had lobbied the ICCB to update its requirements for community colleges, only incidentally setting up a demand for what could be more business for his community college CEO retreats. Whether anyone from the BAC board or administration ever attended a Davis retreat, I do not know.

About the same time several of the more reactionary members of the ICCTA formed a coalition to solicit and employ "ICCTA Community College Teacher of the Year" recipients for espionage activities. This included, among other things, a plan to plant electronic bugs in the offices of teachers throughout the Illinois community college system, teachers who objected to or criticized CC boards and administrations. Of course, most of the teachers refused to go along with the plot, so it died of its own stench. Still, the attempt, the proposal and intention, were there.

As soon as copies of the proposed BAC board policies were available, Christeck and I met with Welch to examine the objectionable items and prepare language for improving, if not correcting, the policy. We spent the better part of an evening picking through the documents and shaping a union response to each item. After the donnybrook with the Wissore administration, without much of an indication otherwise, the new board policy proposals appeared to us to be a renewed direct attack on the faculty.

* * * * *

By 1966 the AAUP had already formulated an extensive statement for professorial ethics, approved by the Association's Committee on Professional Ethics, adopted by the Association's Council in June 1987, and endorsed at the Seventy-Third Annual Meeting. The AAUP "1940 Statement on Academic Freedom" delineates the role of professors' rights and responsibilities, both in and out of the institution. This is the document we (Local 4183) had tried but failed to negotiate into the *Memorandum of Understanding* in 1986.

The BAC Local 4183 met through the summer of 1991 with the Board Policy Committee and Cipfl to negotiate the ethical policy items, though Cipfl refused, to the end, to admit that these meetings were contract negotiating sessions. Cipfl's reluctance to refer to the meetings as negotiations came from the fact that for the first time at BAC, and maybe at any college or university in the United States, a faculty union told a board that it (the faculty union) would set its own professional standards and then demanded that the board agree to the standards. Ultimately, with the help of AFT field rep Jerry Miller, the 1966 AAUP ethics statement was negotiated into board policy—the first time a college faculty union ever negotiated board policy with a Board of Trustees.

It is interesting that at the June 19, 1991 board meeting there appeared on the agenda an item that might have influenced the board's decision later in the summer to talk to the faculty about board policy. At that meeting the board voted to reduce the salary of one Alice Klein by 1,200 dollars. It seems Ms. Klein, a recent hire, had been misplaced on the salary scale and the union in an advisory capacity notified the administration of the misplacement. When Larry Friederich (BAC Director of Human Resources) admitted there had been a mistake, and that the union had pointed it out, Ted Farmer threw a fit.

He accused board members of bowing to the union and insisted that he would not allow the union to interfere with board operations. Friederich warned Farmer that not only did the error have nothing to do with the union, that it had been an administrative mistake, but that if he (Farmer) continued, he could involve the board in an unfair labor practice. Of course, there were other instances of the union as board watchdog, but at least in this case the board was appreciative of union input—even to point out administrative mistakes or wrong doing.

The following year, 1992, the AAUP "1940 Statement" that had been bargained into the board policy manual the previous summer, would be negotiated into the *Memorandum of Understanding.*

* * * * *

In the fall of 1991 Farmer again tried to take over the board's insurance bidding process, and again, at the October board meeting Chairman Larry Reinneck reprimanded him. Beyond Farmer's "insurance fanaticism," other than what he considered required expenditures, he opposed spending at the college on nearly every level. He objected to and voted against all sabbaticals. He voted against all AAUP-AFT contracts. He objected to and voted against all allocations of funds for board and administrative travel. In a letter to the *BND,* March 5, 1992, he wrote, "For example, the board approved $1,000 this month to pay a magician to come to the college for three hours to do tricks for the students. They also approved sending three board members, including one student board member who has little more than three months left on her term, to Washington, D.C. for a convention (approximate cost $2,000). In my six years input of observation, I have yet to see one board member return from a convention with even one constructive idea."

He failed to mention, although he may not have known, that the money expended for the magician was not tax money, but came from the student activity fee, paid by the students, and controlled by students, needing only the board's oversight imprimatur.

Still the hassles continued. Farmer's attacks on other board members became so vitriolic that one evening when he arrived at the old farm house for a board meeting, a very angry Robert Dintelmann confronted him, and the encounter would have turned into a fistfight had not union President Leo Welch refereed the potential combatants to neutral overstuffed chairs.

* * * * *

The November 1991 election provided four new board members for the college. Since they lived in the same sub-district created by redistricting, the election pitted Reinneck and Farmer. Farmer won the seat 2,558 to 2,378, and Larry Reinneck, one of the better board members to serve at District 522, was off the board. And as a result, Farmer, one of the two senior members of the board (Katherine Bennett was the other), no doubt believing he had a mandate from the voters in his running battle with Larry Reinneck, and with Reinneck gone, again set out to take over the board.

At the second meeting of the new board that December Farmer got into a hassle with Mark Levy, who had just been elected, but seems to have had a pretty good sense of who Farmer was and what he had been up to.

The hassle centered on Farmer's attempts to investigate and then dictate hiring practices at the college. His complaint dated at least to the previous summer when he objected to the proposed Board Policy, Item # 3016-Access to Personnel Files. Literally, he wanted to individually examining all applications and personnel folders to determine if, as he said, the best candidate had been or was to be hired.

Farmer claimed that on numerous occasions the board had hired administrators, staff, and faculty who were not the best qualified of those available. And in that he was correct. Hiring procedures at the college were not only loose, but were, in my opinion, as they are in many colleges and universities, most often infected with the hiring committee's personal preferences, rather than graced by its professional judgment. Many times, personal preference and professional judgement are not the same.

However, Farmer's plan to restructure the hiring and appointing mechanism offered little relief from the problem. He proposed replacing the board's hiring practices, whatever they were, with Ted Farmer's choice. He wanted to decide who did or did not get appointed or hired. Fortunately, he was not successful.

* * * * *

What else Farmer had done beyond the Dan Lowery harassment-vendetta, I am not sure. But at the January 1992 board meeting Levy accused him of abusing employees and violating their privacy. It appears he had already gotten into employee files—at least he had demanded that the board make available, for his inspection, eighty files of applicants for the position of assistant director of personnel, as well as those for director of nursing and director of the BAC veterans administration. When he was refused, he ran an ad in the *BND* requesting that persons interested in the payroll manager position send their resumes and applications to Ted Farmer.

At the February board meeting the verbal exchanges continued, with Board President Maxwell reprimanding Farmer, claiming "It was totally improper for a board member to engage in this type of action."

To stop Farmer, Levy advised the board to file a Complaint for Declarative Judgment in circuit court to determine Farmer's rights as a board member. The board endorsed Levy's interdiction and hired William Beatty, an Edwardsville lawyer, as special counsel to oversee the case.

In a letter to the editor of the *BND* Farmer wrote that "Because of concerns, including disturbing phone calls from constituents, I requested to see certain personnel files. I was allowed by the board in executive session to examine one file but was denied access to the others." And later, "I have certainly lost confidence in BAC President Joe Cipfl and board members Robert Maxwell, Kay Bennett, and Mike Bowen."

On January 28, 1992, a letter from board chairman Robert Maxwell in the *BND* responding to Farmer, asserted that, "Recently Farmer demanded access to many personnel files. At first, he refused to state a purpose for his demand. After some argument, he finally gave a reason that he later changed. His final purpose was based on vague complaints he had allegedly received. He refused to relate how many complaints he had received and the nature of those complaints. He gave no explanation for refusing to share this information with the rest of the board."

Four days later the board's contract settlement with Wissore made the front page of the *BND*. The article that followed reiterated Farmer's complaints about the board.

"Farmer said the final settlement was reached by the newly elected board over his objections about two months ago.

"He believes the agreement is a 'disgrace' because the board spent about $50,000 in attorney fees to fight Wissore's complaint but ended up with nothing. The board either should have settled out of court with Wissore three years ago or decided to fight the case all the way, Farmer said."

Farmer's remarks more than likely had to do with the particular odiousness of the Wissore years as well as the dollars involved. The same newspaper article quoted Elizabeth Jenner, who had left the board the previous October, as saying, "The atmosphere and tenor of the group (the January 1992 board) is entirely different than when I was there . . . Had you not gone through the whole process (the Eckert-Wissore years), it's difficult to appreciate what happened. I can understand their feelings not wanting to deal with it."

In April the board received a Stipulation and Consent Judgment against Farmer, an order often used to force compliance between two public officials or public agencies. In this case, the stipulation ordered Farmer to conform to board policies.

Interesting enough, Farmer's war with the board, in which he sought to override board policy, coincided with my complaint to the board about an English Department faculty selection committee, and the administrators who sponsored a committee not following required procedures in order to circumvent an open evaluation of applicants for department teaching positions.

* * * * *

During the summer of 1992, as Ted Farmer writhed under the Stipulation and Consent Judgment, the college and the faculty union were faced with new and pressing problems. One of these was the insolvency and failing of State Community College (SCC), District 601 in East St. Louis.

The Illinois Junior College Act of 1965 requires that all areas of the state be covered by a community college district. The state is divided into thirty-nine districts, with forty-eight colleges, including seven in Chicago and four eastern Illinois colleges (Frontier Community College in Fairfield; Lincoln Trail College in Robinson; Olney Central College in Olney; and Wabash Valley College in Mt. Carmel) with one (Olney) board of trustees. All of the community college districts are financed by local property taxes and elect their own boards. All, that is, except Chicago where the board of trustees is appointed by the mayor of Chicago, and State Community College (SCC) in East St. Louis.

Unlike other community colleges in Illinois, SCC was funded by the Illinois General Assembly and had a board appointed by the governor. This setup was a ruse created by the upstate politicians to keep control of the college out of local hands but agreed to by East St. Louis legislators because East St. Louis, which was 90-percent black, was also 100-percent poor. East St. Louis politicians wanted their own district, and so were willing to bargain or trade away local autonomy if the district remained independent, though financed by the state.

The scheme to set off SCC as a special territory run from the state capital in Springfield had a host of disingenuous and unworkable historic precedents. In the early 1900s the Illinois legislature attempted to control the city government of East St. Louis from Springfield. At the time East St. Louis was a Midwest railroad hub and a vice (gambling and prostitution) playground for St. Louis. For a several decades East St. Louis had two police departments—one appointed by the Illinois General Assembly in Spring-field, the other sponsored by the city of East St. Louis. As might be expected, eventually the arrangement turned adversarial and hostile and ended, literally, in a gunfight or shootout between the opposing agencies.

By 1990, through failed oversight and mismanagement, as it seemed destined to do, SCC fell on hard times. And since the BAC district was set around SCC like a horseshoe, there was a great deal of speculation that BAC would be required to absorb SCC. In March of 1990 the problems at SCC appeared on the BAC board agenda and by 1992 had become a major concern for the BAC faculty union.

The annexation of SCC to BAC, if there was to be an annexation, would have provided some troubling what-ifs. Would the annexation be an acquisition by BAC, a merger of BAC and SCC or a mere dissolution of SCC? Would BAC become responsible for District 601's debts, liabilities, lawsuits, employees, and service contracts? How would the faculties be merged, and who would have what rights?

In 1992 the SCC issue showed up on the negotiating table, agreed to by both sides as an urgent item, and a security agreement was negotiated into the *Memorandum of Understanding* providing the BAC faculty with maximum protection from displacement by incoming SCC faculty or, for that matter, any other "absorbed" personnel from any other school.

As it turned out, BAC did not inherit full responsibility for SCC, though not necessarily because of the *Memorandum of Understanding*. State Community College became a conglomerate serviced by other state schools. However, the section negotiated into the contract covering the SCC merger-threat and protecting the BAC faculty, is still in the contract.

* * * * *

In 1987 the Second District Appellate Court in Sugar Grove, Illinois opened a gap in the Illinois community college tenure and collective bargaining laws by finding that Wabaunsee Community College had not violated the law by removing tenured teachers without due cause and replacing them with part-timers. Two years later, when it became apparent exactly what the decision entailed, hoping to bandage the opening the decision created, the Illinois General Assembly proposed Illinois HB 613 to keep community colleges from further eliminating tenured faculty and replacing them with part-timers.

Of course, the Illinois Community College Trustees Association opposed the bill. Already the habit of running community colleges with part-timers, replacing retiring or otherwise departing fulltime faculty with part-timers, had generated a law in California requiring that certificates or degrees from California community colleges be constituted of at least 70-percent of classes taught by fulltime instructors.

Ultimately Illinois HB 613 failed, and the only choice the BAC AFT-AAUP had was to negotiate a security clause into the *Memorandum of Understanding.* This was done in 1991.

In Article 10–Seniority of the *Memorandum of Understanding* we added Section 10.6–Security:

> No fulltime faculty member shall be dismissed for reason of a reduction in the number of faculty members in the district or as a result of a decision of the Board to discon-tinue a particular type of teaching service or program if course sections for which the fulltime faculty member is qualified are currently being taught by fulltime faculty with less seniority or by part-time instructors and there are sufficient course sections available to complete the affected faculty member's standard load.

1992 Negotiations

> No group and no government can properly
> prescribe precisely what should constitute
> the body of knowledge with which true
> education is concerned.
>
> —Franklin D. Roosevelt

Even If We Disagree, Let's Not Be Disagreeable

In 1992 I again served as chief negotiator. Several months before negotiations began, Jerry Miller, the IFT representative, suggested we do a contract inventory. In union circles there is sometimes a skepticism, even a prejudice against the "let's simplify the contract" suggestion. In my years on negotiating teams this only came up twice: once when Leo Welch suggested it to correct the double-tiered salary scale brought in by Kassing (Wissore) in the 1984-86 negotiations fiasco, and once when IFT rep Jerry Miller brought it up. In both cases it was necessary and in both cases the faculty and the school profited. I should add that several years earlier, Steve Finner, national AAUP counsel, and Mike Hade, AFT field rep, had also suggested that we do a contract inventory.

A contract inventory meant sitting down for three or four hours for three or four days and meticulously going through every item in the contract to evaluate the language for clarity and meaning, and in the process to discover if there were any redundancies or items which no longer applied. I think Rich Boyer, Jim McGowen, Welch, and Massey were in on this. It was a thankless, but necessary, task that aided us in better understanding exactly what we had in our hands and what we might do with it.

* * * * *

In the spring of 1990 I had had major surgery that necessitated several adjustments to my physical activities. As a telecourse instructor I was required to keep three office hours a week in the telecourse office in the basement beneath the gym. The reasons given by the telecourse guru, Lloyd Gentry, and the administration for demanding that instructors hold office hours in the telecourse complex, well away from classrooms and off the main-beat of students, were that students would not be able to find our regular offices and that if we carried student papers out of the telecourse office we might lose them. Gentry also demanded that Granite City campus telecourse teachers drive to the Belleville campus (30 miles) to hold their telecourse office hours.

Anyway, after the surgery I notified Gentry that I would, for medical reasons, serve my weekly office-hour sentence in my upstairs office. For the next two years I heard nothing more about it. Since there were no student complaints—I did not have one telecourse student visit me in two years or even call my office—Gentry really didn't care. Then, two days before the first negotiating session in 1992, I received a memo from Gentry stating that I would be required to be in the telecourse office for office hours the next day or my pay would be docked for the hours missed. The following day I received another memo, this time a bit more strident, threatening me with disciplinary action if I did not follow orders.

I ignored both. I was, even after two years, still tentatively under a physician's care. But I thought I knew who had prodded Gentry into sending the memos. The following day the negotiating teams gathered at the agreed time, with Cipfl magnanimously and cheerfully welcoming everyone to the table, and saying finally, "Well, I guess we're ready to begin."

What Joe Cipfl understood better than any of the administrators at BAC was that whatever conflicts or disagreements we had, they were not the end of the world. No matter what transpired, he was not going to attempt to browbeat anyone. He could respond to his own maxim of "Even if we disagree, let's not be disagreeable."

As chief negotiator, seated directly across from Cipfl that day, it was my turn, so I smiled and took the opportunity to remind him that I considered Gentry's memos, copies of which I slid out onto the table, as an attempt to intimidate the union negotiating team, and if there was anything even vaguely akin to this, at any time during the ensuing negotiations, I was prepared to call off deliberations and file an unfair labor practice against the board.

To say that this got everyone's attention is to say the least. I'm not sure I've ever seen Joe Cipfl that pissed. He was livid. "Bud Gentry wouldn't do something like that," he said. I guess the question is, then, if Gentry said he didn't do it, and his name is on the memos, who did it? As Cipfl spoke he turned and glared at Lynn Suydam, seated to his left, and who, since he did not say two words during the entire negotiations which took several months, no doubt had been told to keep his mouth shut. After that, things proceeded smoothly. I did not again hear anything about telecourse office hours—upstairs or downstairs.

* * * * *

In an ironic aside to the 1992 negotiations Wissore offered to join the faculty negotiating team. He had been wedged onto the faculty roster five years before by a board weary of conflict and unwilling to stand its ground—and to pay for a court battle. The negotiating team's response to Wissore's suggestion was pretty much what one might expect.

Generally, our views of the administration and the board were informed by our experiences, and to tell the truth we were all still smarting over the 1974-87 Eckert-Wissore travesty. For some, Wissore symbolized that travail, as well he should have, and not only did Welch reject Wissore's offer, but there was, throughout the committee, a revulsion at having even to consider it.

While I still did not trust the board or the administration, I had no special animosity for Wissore. But I was not encouraged that he might have a magic elixir, and I did not have much respect or admiration for his abilities as a teacher or administrator. I did not see in what way his presence on the negotiating team might aid the faculty in getting a good contract.

Wissore, as Libby said, was not a problem solver. In fact, he created more problems than he solved—and I knew if Wissore became a member of the negotiating team his penchant for intrigue and double-dealing would cause me, as chief-negotiator, serious problems. Otherwise, he did not have any special insight into the negotiating process or expertise in under-standing the board we were dealing with, or for that matter, what the faculty needed. Wissore's track record suggested he would attempt to manipulate the negotiation-team into attacking the board and admin- istration he saw as having betrayed him. His reputation and claim to power as a former president of the college was embedded in his alliance with one board member, a petty politician with enough money and the influence money pro-vides, to gather a handful of henchmen to his service. Wissore's history did not recommend him as a faculty representative. So, as I said, the offer was declined.

Telecourses

In 1992 the telecourse issue was again on the table. By now most of the faculty was aware that telecourses were truly an affront to the quality instruction the union faculty was trying to provide, as well as a serious threat to the contract which had become our primary instrument of faculty governance. Since it was impossible to get rid of telecourses it appeared that the best way to defuse the threat was to incorporate them into the base contract.

The argument on our side was good. It was a dollars and cents argument, the only thing the administration understood. It was easy to map out. Telecourse instructors were well paid for what they did. I would suspect the average instructor take per telecourse was about 2,000 dollars. Fulltime instructors were required to teach five classes. If a fulltime instructor dropped a regular class to pick up a telecourse, a part-timer would be given the class the fulltime instructor had abandoned. Part-timers were paid about 800 dollars a class. The school would show a profit of 1,200 dollars or more, on average, per telecourse.

As usual the board negotiators dragged their feet, imagining a monster under the bed—something that might reach out and grab them. As late as 1989, in executive session, the board had noted that "Telecourses were an excellent revenue generator and an area that needs careful consideration, but not as a part of collective bargaining." In the end, however, the board could not refuse the savings of including telecourses in the faculty contract.

At the time, ethics was a required course for several SWIC programs, the only required course that was taught as a telecourse, and the only telecourse over which I had any influence. However, I had never been very satisfied with teaching ethics in the telecourse format, and agreed to do it only because I hoped to maintain a bit of control over what other philosophy courses might have ended up in the telecourse catalogue. Once telecourses were firmly in the contract, I went to the department head and suggested we shut down the ethics telecourse. And we did. To Cipfl's credit, when objections to the cancellation came up the line from the administration, he shook them off. But then, once telecourses were part of the *Memorandum of Understanding* and scheduled as part of a normal teaching load, it didn't matter to the administration if they were offered or not. They were of no more interest to the administration than any other course, good or bad. Because I had the ethics telecourse, and because ethics was required for many licensing programs, it was scheduled four times a year and had a large enrollment. My reward for negotiating telecourses into the contract was an 8,000 dollar a year cut in pay.

Intellectual Property Rights (IPR)

In a practice that dated back to the Pinzke AUUP-AFT presidency, several months before the 1992 negotiations were to begin, as chief negotiator I sent a memo to the faculty asking individual members to submit a wish list for table items.

It's an essential part of the bargaining process to identify faculty problems or at least issues the faculty believes to be problematic, and to determine as reasonably as possible if the problems can be resolved by contract. Certainly, some of the difficulties that arise from humans working in immediate proximity to one another cannot be remedied by contract. But if it can be, then it is the job of the negotiating team to get the item on the table and work out a resolution, and ultimately place language to that effect in the contract.

That year a faculty member suggested negotiating IPR (IPR). If memory serves, Les Wiemerslage (Biology) sent in the idea. At least it makes sense that Wiemerslage would have been the one. Sometime later he got into a hassle with the biology department, and other concerned academics in other departments, when he attempted to include crea-tionism in his biology syllabus. Simply enough, it seems, he wanted to make sure someone or at least something, other than the BAC board, got credit for creating everything.

At any rate, IPR made the short list, and one afternoon I trucked out to union-lawyer Charlie Kolker's office to ask him what we should do about it. Prior to this an administrator teaching a psychology course had taped a faculty member's lectures and then showed the tape as instructional material for his class. Christeck and I thought the precedent-practice of the administration copying and/or commandeering intellectual property rights could easily be used to reduce the number of fulltime faculty and install a system of TV classroom instruction. We thought further that it was paramount to protect the faculty and students from this kind of video-game mindlessness. Unbeknownst to us at the time, the video-tape practice had already surfaced at Eastern Illinois University, and probably at any number of other places.

In *Academic Capitalism and the New Economy* (2004), Slaughter and Rhoades in a ". . . study of institutional policies and practices surrounding educational materials (e.g., lecture notes, syllabi), curricula (e.g., classes, programs), and products (e.g., course management software)," note that "These educational materials are new economy products. They are increasingly being copyrighted by colleges and universities and marketed in ways that foreground their commercial rather than educational potential."

It was Christeck's contention that the faculty created presentations, contracted them to the school at a designated time, in an assigned place, and the material could not be copied for use by others in other places at other times without proper reimbursement for its originator. On the other hand, it was likely the administration would claim the school had purchased the presentation and so could copy and use it any time and/or any place it so chose. Our assertion was that whatever a professor put onto the classroom air was always retained by the professor in the notes he returned to his pocket and could be carried away (but not sold or traded) by students who had paid to hear it. Several years prior to this I had discovered that students were taping my classroom presentations and selling them to future students, so I banned recording devices from my classrooms. If students were profiting financially from the IPR of the professorate, it seemed likely the administration would not be far behind. In fact, there had been a flap a short time before between a school administration and the faculty union at an area high school when the administration used a public-access channel to float schoolwork (a teacher's lesson-plan) and other instructional materials to absent students, and thus to whomever else was tuned in.

Our goals were straightforward. Within the IPR section, we intended to clarify what belonged to whom; when, where, and how it could be recorded; how it could or could not be used; and how professors would be compensated if their creations were used beyond the initial classroom presentation.

When I brought the IPR proposal, as I understood it, to Kolker, he sat and stared at me for a moment, then literally came up out of his seat. He had been a teacher in East St. Louis before becoming a lawyer. Also, he had been

handling education law for several decades, so had a very good understanding and appreciation of the probabilities. I have not often seen anyone
as excited as he was that day. When I explained further what Christeck and
I had in mind, he shook me off, saying "No, no, that's not the issue. That's not
what we need to look at."

I disagreed, but not then and there. If this thing was bigger than my
imagining, it wasn't my part to get in the way. That wasn't my job. In the end
he said we would have to meet later, after he had time to research it. And
research it he did. For the next week, whenever I called, his secretary simply
said, "Mr. Kolker's not in." I'd ask when he would be back, and she'd say, "I
don't know, he's at the law library, and you never can tell about these
things."

A week or so later we met again, and he explained what he had found,
and how we had to go about negotiating IPR into the contract. The underlying Common Law premise, he pointed out, was that people own what they
create. The English Common Law that we use in this country is a law of
property ownership. Property is the metaphysics of the law. The English
believed that everything, even persons, had to be owned by someone. This
is traceable at least back to William the Conqueror, though it probably goes
back a lot farther than that.

However, over the years in colleges and universities in the United
States, and in other places, in keeping with the corporate model and practice
that those financing the research should profit from it, researchers and
other creators of IPR were almost always required to sign over future
discoveries and creations.

In this case the task would be to negotiate ownership back to the
creator, to recreate the Common Law tenet. Later in the meeting Kolker
provided the language he had created for that purpose. (Wiemerslage would
be pleased with the number of "creator," "recreate," and "created" his
suggestion for negotiations "created" in the last few sentences). After reading Kolker's language, I realized we still had not covered the classroom-TV
problem. When I asked, he again shrugged me off. The follow ing day, to
cover our concerns, Christeck and I sat down and wrote our bit into Kolker's
entry. We added "video creations" to the definitions list.

Even as Kolker prepared contract language, Welch was in touch with
the Washington, D.C. office of the AFT. Concurrently, Perry Robinson, AFT
legal counsel, conducted a contract survey to see what there was of IPR
agreements in faculty contracts at colleges and universities across the
country. Generally, the AFT left individual contracts to local unions, and
Robinson found that IPR were addressed only in research universities, and
then as a matter of policy rather than contract. Otherwise, university and
college contracts were silent—especially to the benefit of the creators of the
IPR, since the weight of ownership had over the years shifted to the
corporate-robber-baron coffers of universities and colleges.

Here one cannot help but be reminded of the directive to Congress in Article 1 Section 8.2 of the Constitution of the United States: "To promote the Progress of Science and useful Arts, by securing for limited Times to Authors and Inventors the exclusive Right to their respective Writings and Discoveries." Surely Mr. Franklin must have had a hand in writing that—even if it was only standing at the fireplace one night with a glass of wine talking to Mr. Jefferson.

As it turned out, BAC was an ideal place to negotiate IPR into a faculty contract. Since community colleges are teaching institutions, the school (BAC) did not provide funds for research. Also, most faculty members are not research-minded. The demand at places like BAC-SWIC, that whenever a professor does write a book or do something creative, he not profit from his creation, comes from the backwater-fear that someone will complain that "A professor wrote a book and now he's making all the students buy and read it," and so must be double-dipping. There is always the resident assumption that the work was probably done on company time and there-fore belongs to the company.

Here again we come to the public's, board's, and the administration's view of college professors as clerks dispensing a product to customers, clerks who should not profit from the interaction by anything more than what they are paid by the enterprise providing the product to be dispensed. Yet, in fact, the professor is an educational master who brings to the master-student symbiosis all manner of expertise, some of which may be a public-cation or program of his creation containing material germane to the instruction he offers and from which the student can profit educationally. There is an adage among teachers that the only textbook that fits the class you are teaching is the book you have written.

The IPR proposal remained on the table throughout negotiations that year, stepped over three or four times, and to be honest, I didn't think there was much chance of getting it into the contract. It's not that we didn't make good arguments for it, and certainly we understood its importance. Massey made good arguments for it. Welch made good arguments for it. I made arguments for it. But still I did not sense that the administration thought much of the idea. We had no way of knowing why they didn't.

After Kolker's reaction to the proposal and his explanation of the law and the practice of colleges and universities controlling faculty creations, I pretty well understood the magnitude of what we were trying to do. It was possible that the board and the Cipfl administration also understood the implications of the proposal. Maybe they were unwilling to allow anything that important to the faculty into the contract. Because of our past hassles with the Eckert Board and Wissore, we assumed that the current board was not going to give into anything that did not make it look good. The final day, however, maybe in an attempt to move on with life and having nothing to lose by accepting it as the last item on the table, Joe Cipfl, the board's chief negotiator said, "Okay," and we shook hands.

Later, after we had it all in the contract and the dust cleared, I was talking to Kolker about the items Christeck and I had added, and he said, "I didn't see what you were talking about. I don't know how I missed it." As it was, we covered what we both were thinking, and the rest is a nice minor bit of history. There is also the outside chance that Joe Cipfl knew fully well the importance of the item to faculty-creators and knew, too, the BAC board would care little about it, beyond that it would not cost the school money, and therefore signed off on it. Possibly Cipfl understood the importance of IPR to the academic community throughout the United States. Either way he is to be complimented for his part in agreeing to its inclusion for the first time in a higher-education-faculty contract in the United States.

Now, for the first time in a university or college, a professor's creations and presentations were protected by general contract from the ravages of administrations and boards. In a nutshell, the new section of the *Memorandum of Understanding* reinstated the Common Law tenet that inventors, artists, and scientists own what they create.

Perry Robinson later wrote in "Trespasses on intellectual property: Why the union contract is the faculty's best hope for protection" that,

> An early, outstanding example of an agreement on intellectual property emerged in 1996 (1993-96) from a successor contract negotiated by one of the nation's pioneer community college unions—Belleville Area Community College Employees Union in Illinois, now renamed Southwestern Illinois Community College.
>
> A clause within that contract resolves the work-for-hire issue with precision, contains a degree of freedom for the individual to contract, and awards the "shop right" use to the college. It also contains the union leadership's anticipation of the value of instructional materials connected with asynchronous Web-based distance education.

It took six or eight months, maybe a year, after we completed the 1992-93 contract for word of the IPR coup to seep into the collective bargaining consciousness of colleges and university faculties around the country. Clearly it was time for IPR to be included in university faculty-bargained agreements, especially in research universities.

Within the year calls were coming in for union President Welch and attorney Kolker to address interested faculty assemblages across the country about IPR. Welch gave a presentation for the AAUP reception at the Collective Bargaining Congress in Washington, D.C., and a joint presentation with Kolker for the IFT in Chicago.

Honoring one request, Welch traveled to Rutgers University to give a presentation for the New Jersey AAUP, a trip that not only gathered a large enthusiastic audience but also provided an interesting side note.

On his way to Rutgers Welch was met at Liberty Airport in Newark by a fully liveried chauffeur in a limousine who would deliver him to a variety of university meetings. During a lull in the afternoon, the chauffeur asked Welch what he was doing at Rutgers, and Welch told him he had come to talk to the faculty about the need for IPR and how the union had gone about getting it into the contract at BAC-SWIC.

Welch in turn inquired of the driver what he did besides driving the limousine for the university. The man said he was a ceramic engineer and a teacher at Rutgers.

The *California Occupational Guide Number 329* states that ceramic engineers ". . . develop methods for processing nonmetallic inorganic materials into many ceramic products ranging from glassware, fiber optics products, cement, and bricks, to coatings for space vehicles, materials for microelectronics, components of nuclear fuel, and pollution control devices."

Welch asked the driver-engineer if he owned the IPR to what he engineered or created. The man paused a moment, shook his head, "No," he said, "nothing like that at all."

Once, several years later, the IPR section of the SWIC *Memorandum of Understanding* served to reimburse an instructor teaching an electronic distance-learning class with multiple satellite sites. Jean Dibble, coordinator of the paralegal program at SWIC, was conducting a distance-learning class when the receiving-site's receptor broke down. She was told by the administration, by the then Dean Art Parrish, to repeat the instruction —without pay. She refused and demanded additional pay for the repeat class, which was a second presentation, and under the IPR provision of the *Memorandum of Understanding* she received the pay she deserved. She did the second presentation and was paid for it.

Family Leave

In another progressive contract innovation, during the 1992-93 negotiations, a Family Leave proposal for childbirth or adoption was listed among the faculty table items. I do not know who suggested it or maybe demanded that it be included as a table item, but Jenna Johannpeter was responsible for making certain that it stayed on the table and that the committee saw it into the contract.

When the Family Leave item initially came to the table, I was less than enthusiastic about it. I thought of having and raising children as a personal priority that need not be subsidized by taxpayers. However, during negotiations I held my skepticism in abeyance and pretty much stayed out of the discussion. We had already negotiated Personal Leave which quite equitably covered everyone. We could not have added to that instead of negotiating for a select group (male and female) a contract stipulation that would not be available for others who made a different choice.

Also, when negotiating a union contract, one must be alert to "equal representation" and avoid bargaining perks for select groups, lest you end in court. And maternity leave is a select-group item—in this case for those community college faculty most usually between the ages of twenty-four and thirty-five—at best, a perk that will most often be used by no more than 10-percent of the faculty.

Bearing or adopting and rearing children, I have always believed to be a personal choice—which it has become even more since the development of controlled conception. Having a child is not a disease or injury, and I do not think that it should be treated as such. If people want to have or not have children, a choice they clearly have, I see no reason, and didn't in 1992, why they would expect someone else to pay for their choice. Should we have auto-buying or house-purchasing leave? On the other hand, I could see it as the community looking after the welfare of a new citizen. Family Leave, in some small ways, cuts into the industrial anti-human business agenda of the corporate-academic factory schema. And I could always support that.

In 1992 neither the State of Illinois nor the federal government had yet enacted laws addressing childbirth leave. The inclusion in the *Memorandum of Understanding* of leave for the birth of a child pre-dated the federal Family and Medical Leave Act (February 1993) by almost a year.

Today some colleges and universities have advanced family leave clauses in their contracts (six months to a year of paid family leave) although as late as 2004 more than 400 colleges and universities canvassed throughout the United States by the AAUP had nothing in their faculty contracts for or about family leave.

* * * * *

Overall, I was extremely pleased with the 1992 contract. We put together a one-year contract that included: academic freedom; department heads; early retirement; evaluation of tenured faculty; faculty notification of student complaints; fitness center instructor; IPR; length of summer term; merger and acquisition; mileage reimbursement; minimum instructor standards; PAC checkoff; special leaves (maternity); student conduct code; substitute teaching; and telecommunications committee (telecourses).

Some of the sections addressed new items, such as early retirement, merger and acquisition, and PAC checkoff, while others attended to ongoing difficulties of student conduct code and academic freedom. The new contract brought with it an improved faculty-board connection, and the faculty was better able to exercise its role in college governance. This brought a renewed sense of academic purpose among the faculty.

In Closing

> The significant problems we face cannot
> be solved at the same level of thinking we
> were at when we created them.
> —Albert Einstein

The Exodus

If there is a season for each of our cares and concerns, 1994 appeared to be the season for me to move away from the negotiating business. By then I had labored for the union, and ultimately for the faculty at BAC-SWIC ,for eighteen years—eleven of those years under the Eckert-Wissore regime.

Otherwise, the time comes when . . . . By then my sons were out of the house, in college, and I wanted to get back to research and writing. I had come out of the Writer's Workshop at the University of Iowa in 1970. During the '70s, before the Eckert-Wissore alliance became a menace, besides teaching I had worked with numerous commercial writing and editing projects. In the late '70s I began writing for *St. Louis Magazine*, became sports editor of the magazine and later a contributing editor, as well as a contributing editor for the *St Louis Literary Supplement.*

When I started at BAC in 1972, I had hoped to establish a literary magazine at the college but had been unable to secure the financing from the administration or the English Department for the venture. Even as late as 1979 I was still looking for ways to get it started. Then there was the 1980 strike, the ensuing turmoil and union work, and for the next fourteen years I had put most of my literary activities on hold.

By 1993 the Eckert Board and Wissore were gone, and the turmoil at the college had settled down enough that, even with the stress attendant to college political life, I felt I could now get back to writing and editing and teaching.

* * * * *

By 1990 the exodus from SWIC of weathered union-faculty veterans was underway. Those appointed at BAC in the late '60s and early '70s, many who were already veteran teachers, those who later suffered the trial-by-fire of the Eckert-Wissore regime, were approaching retirement. They had grown up in the thirties, forties, and fifties—when the United States was still largely industrial and the unions across the country were moving first- and second-generation immigrant-labor families—and people off the farm who had come to the city and found jobs in factories and on assembly lines—into the middle class. These faculty arrived at the college, if not dedicated to unionization, at least familiar with it and not opposed to it.

From the late '60s to the "90s, the American economy and occupations within the economy shifted radically from industrial to post-industrial service. In 1990 not only was the full corporatization of colleges and universities underway, but the employment of the hard-industries of factories, coal mines, etc. in the U.S. had shrunk in favor of service occupations. Jobs in manufacturing relocated to other countries for cheaper labor. Much of the remaining available employment in the U.S. was in corporate offices keeping count of what was manufactured in other countries or in the service industries, of which education is one.

By then the granddaughters and grandsons of those to whom unions had brought material prosperity and comfort no longer saw themselves as members of the working class and gravitated toward occupations that promised still more upward economic mobility. More and more, the U.S. was becoming the paper-pusher of the world, and the paper pushers' progeny, who no longer had contact with or awareness of unions, were moving into the schools as teachers.

The shift from heavy industry to a service economy also brought with it an adjustment to the United States' educational platform. It is too often forgotten that laws requiring children to attend school until age sixteen (now seventeen in Illinois, as well as in several other states) were enacted under union organizing pressure to get the children out of sweatshop, textile mill, and coal mining jobs, many of them very bad jobs, even for adults. It is too often forgotten, if acknowledged at all, that ten and eleven-year-old "breaker-boys" working in coal mines, sorting coal in coal-patch tipples, after a few months on the job had lost most of their fingers. For girls as young as ten and eleven working in the textile "sweatshops" sexual abuse (literally prostitution) was simply a price to be paid for keeping their employment.

Many state politicians, beholden to industry barons, were not at all enthusiastic about compulsory schooling laws (by 1918 all states had mandatory school attendance laws) that reduced the pool of child workers. In fact, one year, to appease corporate demands for cheaper labor, the state of Alabama suspended the compulsory component of its K-12 program.

Even though the states agreed to get children out of the sweatshops and mines and into schools, and compulsory school attendance also provided students with the rudiments of reading and writing and basic math, no one has been willing to pay for much beyond babysitting—unless it feeds the construction, textbook and/or information technology indus- tries.

What most state governments have failed to understand, or would rather not recognize, is that K-12 or 5-17 compulsory school attendance is the only legally mandated program (mandated by all states) in the country that applies to every citizen. And because of its all-inclusive dictates, to be even reasonably operative and successful, it requires an enormous expenditure of funds. None of the states (or the federal government) has attempted to properly fund teacher salaries or a proper number of teachers for the mandated public schools, and as a result has had to fill teaching positions with whoever shows up. Of course, the results are predictable. And when students do not advance academically as it is (was) assumed they should, government officials who refuse to properly fund the schools attempt to shift the blame for the supposed failure onto the underpaid over scheduled teachers.

In all the squawk and blather about how bad K-12 and higher-ed teachers are, I have yet to hear any critical evaluation of the administrators who select these teachers and who have incessantly attempted to hammer the teachers into a corporate-production mold. The educational-administrative track record in the United States, throughout, is not only questionable, but in educational terms, most often subversive.

Even without proper funding, the compulsory schooling for children that unions fought for prepared the succeeding generations of Americans for the post WWII quasi-literate technological revolution that is heralded today as an American miracle. In 1900 only 6-percent of the U.S. population had completed high school. By 2000, 85-percent of U.S. citizens had a high school diploma. If you can't read or write, technology is what other people do.

Increasingly, however, the middle-class-liberated-literate children-become-adults coming onto community college faculties in the '90s saw themselves as above labor and as part of the business management-entrepreneur scheme. With growing frequency through the last part of the twentieth century the average American was out for big bucks and perceived the moneyed-pot at the end of the rainbow to be in the lobby of the big-business mega-plex.

Across the country unions shrunk, and even where there were unions in the '70s, '80s and '90s, as Staughton and Alice Lynd note in *The New Rank and File* (2000),

> Employers pushed "jointness," the "team concept," "quality circles," and other forms of labor-management cooperation, to co-opt workers and to weaken the union as an exclusive mechanism for problem solving in the workplace. Collective bargaining agreements tended to become 'living agreements,' subject to perpetual modification by small groups of company and union negotiators. Even for companies not in financial difficulty, concession bargaining became the norm. Ten and twelve-hour shifts became commonplace as management sought to operate expensive equipment continuously. So did the two and three-tier wage schemes, whereby the wages and benefits of senior employees were protected in exchange for evisceration of the compensation package of new hires.

Regardless of the small gains in unionization made through the United States after 1970, and some of that came in the service occupations of which public-sector teaching is one, the process that unionized the country in the first place had to begin again and needs to be brought into American colleges and universities.

The AAUP as a Union

The faculty union at SWIC began in 1946 when teachers from AFT-IFT Local 434 at Belleville Township High School assumed teaching positions at BTJC. Shortly after that several of the teachers (fifteen or so) created an AAUP Chapter which they brought to BAC in 1967. In 1981 the BAC-AAUP was joined with AFT Local 4183, bringing the AAUP into the union business, which also encouraged other AAUP chapters to unionize. In 2006 the AFT recognized SWIC Local 4183 as the oldest (sixty years—from 1946 to 2006) faculty union in higher education in the United States.

In 2007, because of the numbers of affiliate AAUP chapters serving as faculty bargaining agents in colleges and universities around the country, the National Labor Relations Board informed the AAUP that it was now required to register as a union. Likewise, the AFT has expanded significantly into American postsecondary education.

The Union Has Never Done Anything for Me

However, even with these successes, organizing faculty unions in colleges and universities in the future will not be easy. Nor will it be easy to maintain existing faculty unions. Even at SWIC with its union history, as more and more senior faculty retired, and new faculty arrived, many of the concepts of "shared governance" that were negotiated into the *Memorandum of Understanding* over the years have been forgotten or ignored by the faculty in favor of agreeing with or placidly accepting administrative edicts, regardless of the pedagogical implications.

Today beginning teachers at SWIC often see themselves as outside the union or contemptuous of the collective initiative. They are unaware of the school's history and/or the union's history at the school. One example that comes to mind involved an incident with a teacher named Patti Pyrite, who after being appointed to a fulltime English department faculty position (a union benefit) and receiving tenure (a union benefit) at a very good salary (a union benefit), took extended maternal leave (a union benefit) for several months each during consecutive years. Then, when a colleague chose early retirement (a union benefit), Pyrite selected his office (a union benefit) and moved in a full week before he vacated (not a union benefit), then stood in the hall announcing to anyone in earshot that, "I don't know why I should support the union. The union has never done anything for me."

Yeah, But They Do Have a Good Contract

When I retired, I mentioned to Charlie Kolker that with so many new faculty, administrators—many of them left from the Wissore days—had again become emboldened and the faculty was back to square one. By then, even the AFT-AAUP at SWIC had fallen into the hands of the remnants of Wissore's in-group. Wayne Ault, who always wanted to be president of something, ended up president of Local 4183, and Clay Baitman, another Wissore in-group non-striker in 1980, became vice president for instruction.

When I mentioned the square-one misfortune, Kolker said, "Yeah, but they do have a good contract?" And I might add, as long as they have the spit and tackle to stand their ground and not give it away. As Thucydides warned, what happened is likely, given the human situation, to reoccur in a similar or comparable form in the future—even, or maybe especially, at places like Southwestern Illinois College.

* 9 7 8 0 9 8 3 8 4 1 2 0 3 *